PRAISE FOR *A LIVING SACRIFICE: LITURGY AND ESCHATOLOGY IN JOSEPH RATZINGER*

"As a work of academic scholarship, it would have been sufficient for Roland Millare to provide a thorough and faithful guide to Ratzinger's unified vision of liturgical eschatology, something which this book certainly accomplishes. But this is also the contribution of a disciple, who joins Ratzinger in prayerfully attending the God who speaks in his Incarnate Son. Ever *cooperatores in veritatis*, Millare and Ratzinger provide the right focus and orientation for the whole of the Church's faith and life."

*Most Rev. Steven J. Lopes*
*Bishop of the Ordinariate of the Chair of Saint Peter*

———————•———————

"Whether *Logos* is prior to *ethos* or whether *praxis* trumps everything is the most important question in Catholic theology at the beginning of the twenty-first century. Joseph Ratzinger was firmly of the view, as was his intellectual hero of his youth, the great Romano Guardini, that *Logos* must be prior to *ethos* if the world, including the Church, is not to sink into a totalitarian nightmare. Roland Millare offers the best account available of why this is so, with reference to the theology of a raft of contemporary authors, above all, the theology of Joseph Ratzinger/Benedict XVI. This work is a great contribution to the fields of fundamental and liturgical theology."

*Tracey Rowland*
*University of Notre Dame, Australia*

———————•———————

"Millare's eminently scholarly study focuses our appreciation of Ratzinger's vast oeuvre on its central, Christocentric concern and thereby raises our faith above facile political categories—to beholding the form of the Risen Christ and apprehending therein the proper source for a robust and confident New Evangelization."

*Fr. Emery de Gaál*
*University of St. Mary of the Lake, Mundelein Seminary*

# RENEWAL WITHIN TRADITION

## SERIES EDITOR: MATTHEW LEVERING

Matthew Levering is the James N. and Mary D. Perry Jr. Chair of Theology at Mundelein Seminary. Levering is the author or editor of over thirty books. He serves as coeditor of the journals *Nova et Vetera* and the *International Journal of Systematic Theology*.

## ABOUT THE SERIES

Catholic theology reflects upon the content of divine revelation as interpreted and handed down in the Church, but today Catholic theologians often find the scriptural and dogmatic past to be alien territory. The Renewal within Tradition Series undertakes to reform and reinvigorate contemporary theology from within the tradition, with St. Thomas Aquinas as a central exemplar. As part of its purpose, the Series reunites the streams of Catholic theology that, prior to the Council, separated into neo-scholastic and *nouvelle theologie* modes. The biblical, historical-critical, patristic, liturgical, and ecumenical emphases of the Ressourcement movement need the dogmatic, philosophical, scientific, and traditioned enquiries of Thomism, and vice versa. Renewal within Tradition challenges the regnant forms of theological liberalism that, by dissolving the cognitive content of the gospel, impede believers from knowing the love of Christ.

## PUBLISHED OR FORTHCOMING

*Reading the Sermons of Thomas Aquinas: A Beginner's Guide*
Randall B. Smith

*The Culture of the Incarnation: Essays in Catholic Theology*
Tracey Rowland

*Self-Gift: Humanae Vitae and the Thought of John Paul II*
Janet E. Smith

*On Love and Virtue: Theological Essays*
Michael S. Sherwin, O.P.

*Aquinas on Beatific Charity and the Problem of Love*
Christopher J. Malloy

*Christ the Logos of Creation: Essays in Analogical Metaphysics*
John R. Betz

*The One Church of Christ: Understanding Vatican II*
Stephen A. Hipp

*O Lord, I Seek Your Countenance:*
*Explorations and Discoveries in Pope Benedict XVI's Theology*
Emery de Gaal

*The Trinitarian Wisdom of God:*
*Louis Bouyer on the God-World Relationship*
Keith Lemna

*One of the Trinity Has Suffered:*
*Balthasar's Theology of Divine Suffering in Dialogue*
Joshua R. Brotherton

*Vessel of Honor: The Virgin Birth and the Ecclesiology of Vatican II*
Brian Graebe

*The Love of God Poured Out:*
*Grace and the Gifts of the Holy Spirit in St. Thomas Aquinas*
John Meinert

*Conforming to Right Reason: On the Ends of the Moral Virtues*
*and the Roles of Prudence and Synderesis*
Ryan J. Brady

# A Living Sacrifice

# A LIVING SACRIFICE

## Liturgy and Eschatology in Joseph Ratzinger

ROLAND MILLARE

EMMAUS
ACADEMIC
Steubenville, Ohio
www.emmausacademic.com

## EMMAUS
### ACADEMIC

Steubenville, Ohio
www.emmausacademic.com
A Division of The St. Paul Center for Biblical Theology
Editor-in-Chief: Scott Hahn
1468 Parkview Circle
Steubenville, Ohio 43952

Library of Congress Cataloging-in-Publication Data applied for
ISBN 978-1-64585-203-2 hardcover / 978-1-64585-204-9 paperback /
978-1-64585-205-6 ebook

Unless otherwise noted, Scripture quotations are taken from The Revised Standard Version Second Catholic Edition (Ignatius Edition) Copyright © 2006 by the Division of Christian Education of the National Council of the Churches of Christ in the United States of America. Used by permission. All rights reserved.

Excerpts from the Catechism of the Catholic Church, second edition, copyright © 2000, Libreria Editrice Vaticana—United States Conference of Catholic Bishops, Washington, D.C. Noted as "CCC" in the text.

Cover design and layout by Emily Demary
Cover image: Fra Angelico, *Last Judgment* (1429) Gemaldegalerie, Berlin

*Imprimatur*
Daniel Cardinal DiNardo
Archbishop of Galveston-Houston
December 8, 2020

*Nihil Obstat*
December 8, 2020

*To Veronica, my beloved bride*
*and a beautiful mother to our children.*

*Who can find a good wife?*
*She is far more precious than jewels.*
*The heart of her husband trusts in her,*
*and he will have no lack of gain.*
*(Proverbs 31:10–11)*

# TABLE OF CONTENTS

Foreword ....................................................................................................... xiii

Acknowledgments ........................................................................................ xvii

Abbreviations ................................................................................................. xix

Introduction ...................................................................................................... 1

    *Christocentrism* ............................................................................................ 2

    *The Structure of the Book* ........................................................................ 10

Chapter One:  Primacy of the *Logos* ............................................................ 15

    *Romano Guardini, the Christian* Weltanschauung, *and the*
    Logos *of the Liturgy* ................................................................................ 21

    *The Symphonic Harmony of Guardini and Ratzinger* .......................... 32

    *The Consistency and Centrality of the Logos in*
    *Ratzinger's Theology* ............................................................................... 43

    *Summary and Conclusion* ........................................................................ 55

Chapter Two: A Sacrificial People in the Incarnate *Logos* ......................... 57

    *Centrality of the Exodus* .......................................................................... 62

    *Temple Worship* ....................................................................................... 72

    *The* Grundgestalt *of the Holy Eucharist* ............................................... 87

    *Pro-Existence* ............................................................................................ 94

    *Summary and Conclusion* ...................................................................... 106

Chapter Three: Eucharistic *Communio* in a *Logos*-centric Key ............... 109

    *The* Logos *of* Communio ........................................................................ 112

    *Ecclesiology and Liturgy* ....................................................................... 129

    *Hope and Eschatology* ........................................................................... 135

    *Ratzinger's* Logos-*Centric Hope* .......................................................... 150

    *Summary and Conclusion* ...................................................................... 160

Chapter Four: *Logikē Latreia* and an *Ethos* of Charity ............................................. 163

    *Communion and Mission* ........................................................................................ 165

    *Liturgy as* Logikē Latreia ....................................................................................... 171

    Sacramentum Caritatis ........................................................................................... 183

    *Summary and Conclusion* ..................................................................................... 196

Chapter Five: The *Logos*-centric Beauty of Heavenly Worship ......................... 199

    *Conversi ad Dominum* ........................................................................................... 201

    *Homo Adorans* ....................................................................................................... 213

    *Via Pulchritudinis* ................................................................................................. 227

    *Ars Celebrandi* ....................................................................................................... 235

    *Summary and Conclusion* ..................................................................................... 248

Conclusion: A Finished Movement within an Unfinished Symphony ............. 251

    *Eucharistic Personalism* ......................................................................................... 255

    *Christocentric Union* ............................................................................................. 257

    *A Logos-Centric Theology of Saints* .................................................................... 263

Selected Bibliography ....................................................................................................... 269

Index .................................................................................................................................. 295

# Foreword

WHEN THE HISTORY OF THEOLOGY in the twentieth and twenty-first centuries is written, Joseph Ratzinger will be remembered as one of the greatest theologians, one who dedicated himself consistently to the renewal of theology in service to the Church by his prodigious writings, homilies, and the witness of his charitable dialogue with others.[1] We hope that Ratzinger's work in dogmatic and fundamental theology will continue to influence a new generation of theologians committed to the revitalization of theology, which has been undermined by an overspecialization in a particular subject within sacred theology, the loss of unity between faith and reason, and simply the reduction of the scientific study of theology to historical theology.[2] Under the influence of Romano Guardini (1885–1968), Ratzinger has repeatedly insisted upon the primacy of the *logos* over *ethos* (*Der Primat des Logos vor dem Ethos*). In his theology, Ratzinger has consistently reminded his readers of the dangers of subordinating the truth (*logos*) to praxis (*ethos*).

Ratzinger's theology is rooted in the Word of God as it is understood with the aid of faith *and* reason. The Word of God, as it has been revealed in Sacred Scripture and Tradition and as it has been interpreted by the Fathers of the Church (especially St. Augustine), is foundational for his theology. In an interview with Peter Seewald, Ratzinger describes the purpose of his theological work:

---

[1] See Peter Seewald, *Benedikt XVI: Ein Leben* (München: Droemer Knaur, 2020); Siegfried Wiedenhofer, *Die Theologie Joseph Ratzingers/Benedikts XVI: Ein Blick auf das Ganz*, Ratzinger-Studien 10 (Regensburg: Frie drich Pustet, 2016).

[2] See Joseph Ratzinger, *The Nature and Mission of Theology: Approaches to Understanding Its Role in the Light of Present Controversy*, trans. Adrian Walker (San Francisco: Ignatius Press, 1995), 78–79.

I have never tried to create a system of my own, an individual theology. What is specific, if you want to call it that, is that I simply want to think in communion with the faith of the Church, and that means above all to think in communion with the great thinkers of faith. The aim is not isolated theology that I draw out of myself but one that opens as widely as possible into the common intellectual pathway of the faith. For this reason exegesis was always very important. I couldn't image a purely philosophical theology. The point of departure is first of all the word. That we believe the word of God, that we try really to get to know and understand it, and then, as I said, to think it together with the great masters of the faith.[3]

Despite the claim by Ratzinger that his theology has an "unfinished" or "fragmentary" character, whenever a person engages his writings, one discovers a dialogue with the entire history of theology and dogma from the Church Fathers to contemporary thinkers. Ratzinger models for theologians how we should engage in the study of this sacred wisdom.

The desert monk Evagrius (c. 346–399) exhorts us to remember that "the one who is a theologian, prays."[4] Ratzinger consistently develops a theology, which is the fruit of study, prayer, and contemplation. Consequently, his theology is characterized by the centrality of Jesus Christ, the *Logos* made flesh, whom we encounter above all within the celebration of the sacred liturgy. For this reason, Pope Benedict XVI requested that the inaugural volume of his collected works begin with his theology of liturgy. Benedict wanted to underscore his concern "about anchoring the liturgy in the foundational act of our faith and, thus, also about its place in the whole of human existence."[5] Publishing his volume on the liturgy reflects the decision of the Conciliar Fathers at Vatican II to publish first the Dogmatic Constitution on the Liturgy, *Sacrosanctum Concilium*.

---

[3]   Joseph Ratzinger (with Peter Seewald), *Salt of the Earth: The Church at the End of the Millennium*, trans. Adrian Walker (San Francisco: Ignatius Press, 1997), 66.

[4]   Evagrius Ponticus, *De Oratione,* in *Patrologiae Graecae*, 79, ed. J. P. Migne (Paris: Thibaut, 1865), §60.

[5]   Pope Benedict XVI, preface to *Theology of the Liturgy: The Sacramental Foundation of Christian Existence,* by Joseph Ratzinger, ed. Michael J. Miller, trans. John Saward, Kenneth Baker, S.J., Henry Taylor, et al., Collected Works 11 (San Francisco: Ignatius Press, 2014), xvi. Originally published as Joseph Ratzinger, *Theologie der Liturgie: Die sakramentale Begründung christlicher Existenz*, Gesammelte Schriften 11, ed. Gerhard Ludwig Müller (Freiburg im Breisgau: Herder, 2008).

Benedict himself comments in the preface to his volume on the Theology of Liturgy:

> What may superficially appear to be an accident proved, in view of the hierarchy of the themes and duties of the Church, to be intrinsically the right thing also. By starting with the theme of liturgy, God's primacy, the absolute precedence of the theme of God, was unmistakably highlighted. Beginning with the liturgy tells us: "God first." When the focus of God is not decisive, everything else loses its orientation.[6]

The centrality of God or Jesus Christ the *Logos* Incarnate is underscored within theology when we begin with the liturgy as the true *theologia prima*.

The primacy of the *logos* is highlighted by Roland Millare's excellent study of the relationship between the theology of the liturgy and eschatology. In his meticulous study of Ratzinger's thought, Millare utilizes this hermeneutical key from Guardini to unlock the unity within Ratzinger's theology that brings together Christology, ecclesiology, the theology of liturgy, theological anthropology, social doctrine, and eschatology into a symphony of truth. What is unique about Millare's work, among other books on the theology of Ratzinger, is his ability to demonstrate the inseparable relationship between the liturgy and eschatology by focusing on the *logos* of communion, which is both prefigured and achieved by the celebration of the liturgy. Subsequently, he consistently argues that an *ethos* of charity proceeds from this *logos* of communion.

The *Logos* is above all a Person, whom we are called to know and love so we may be able to enter into communion with both God and neighbor. This communion begins within the celebration of the liturgy itself and continues through a life of self-giving love. Millare's reading of Ratzinger will help the faithful people of God, students of theology, and scholars to understand how Benedict XVI makes the profound claim "A Eucharist which does not pass over into the concrete practice of love is intrinsically fragmented."[7]

We hope that Millare's work will help its audience to appreciate the unique theological contributions of one of the greatest theologians ever to occupy the Chair of St. Peter. In his time as professor of dogmatic and

---

[6] Pope Benedict XVI, preface to *Theology of the Liturgy*, xv.

[7] Pope Benedict, XVI, Encyclical Letter *Deus Caritas Est* [hereafter, *DCE*](Vatican City: Libreria Editrice Vaticana, 2005), §14.

fundamental theology at Freising, Bonn, Münster, Tübingen, and Regensburg, during his brief period as the Archbishop of Munich and Freising, throughout his long tenure as the Prefect for the Congregation for the Doctrine of the Faith, and finally as the 264th successor to St. Peter, Ratzinger/Benedict XVI has invited all people to become "fellow workers of the truth" (3 John 1:8). When we respond generously to this proposal, then we can embrace the call to communion, which we can only find in Jesus Christ, whom we encounter in the sacred liturgy, thus anticipating our eschatological end in his love.

Gerhard Cardinal Müller
Prefect of the Congregation for the Doctrine of Faith (2012–2017)
Editor of Joseph Ratzinger's *Complete Works I–XVI* (Regensburg: Friedrich Pustet 2008ff).

# Acknowledgements

THIS WORK BEGAN ORIGINALLY as my dissertation at the Liturgical Institute at the University of St. Mary (Mundelein, IL), so I am especially grateful to the members of my dissertation board. I am very thankful to my director, Dr. Matthew Levering, who gave me the advice and direction that brought discipline, clarity, and theological accuracy to my work; my second reader, Fr. Emery de Gaál, whose meticulous reading and expertise on the thought of Ratzinger has been invaluable; and my third reader, Dr. Denis McNamara, whose work on the theology of sacred architecture has impressed upon me one of the central ideas in this study: the intrinsic relationship between the liturgy and eschatology.

I would also like to thank various theologians who generously offered feedback and insight for various parts of this work during its numerous iterations: Dr. Tracey Rowland, Fr. Pablo Blanco Sarto, Fr. Ralph Weimann, Fr. Charles Hough III, Fr. Leo Sven Conrad, F.S.S.P, and Sr. Sara Butler, M.S.B.T. The imperfections and deficiencies in this book remain the fruit of my own efforts and not these generous souls. I certainly would not have been able to answer the call to pursue further study without these selfless individuals at Franciscan University of Steubenville, Notre Dame Graduate School at Christendom College, and the Liturgical Institute/Pontifical Faculty at the University of St. Mary of the Lake.

Every researcher and writer is indebted to the staff of libraries. I am forever grateful to the gracious assistance of the staff of the Feehan Memorial Library (University of St. Mary of the Lake in Mundelein, IL), the Cardinal Beran Library (St. Mary's Seminary in Houston, TX), and the Lanier Theological Library (Houston, TX). They were able to procure sources, assist with research, and patiently guide me in the editorial process. I am also grateful for the varying women and men who served as my teachers throughout my studies of sacred theology. All authors owe a debt of gratitude to the various editors who exercise patient and meticulous editorial skills to bring their work to its completion. Stephen Phelan and Dawn Eden Goldstein were very helpful with earlier versions of the manuscript. Finally, I am indebted to Caroline Rock, the editor of this book, and the staff at Emmaus Academic for their hard work in making the dream of this book a reality.

I would never have been able to pursue this vocation if it were not for the great sacrifices of my late parents, Roland and Perla, and the love and friendship of my beloved late sister, Michelle. I pray each day that they rejoice with the Lord in the heavenly liturgy. I am grateful to my in-laws, Bill and Virginia, for allowing me to experience the joys of family life in the absence of my immediate family. I have the greatest gratitude for my beloved wife, Veronica. She has made countless sacrifices to support my studies in Front Royal, VA, and Mundelein, IL; and the hours of reading, writing, research, revising, and indexing. Without her constant care, kindness, patience, and love, this work would have never been completed. I am also thankful to our beautiful daughters, Gabriella and Karolina, for always reminding me of why I love the vocation of fatherhood.

# Abbreviations

| | |
|---|---|
| BPO | *Behold the Pierced One* |
| CCC | *Catechism of the Catholic Church* |
| CEP | *Church Ecumenism and Politics* |
| CIV | *Caritas in Veritate* |
| CTC | *Called to Communion* |
| DCE | *Deus Caritas Est* |
| DH | Denzinger-Hünermann (43rd edition) |
| DP | *Dogma and Preaching* |
| EMW | *End of the Modern World* |
| FSFD | *Fundamental Speeches from Five Decades* |
| GS | *Gaudium et Spes* |
| GSL | *Spirit of the Liturgy* (Guardini) |
| IC | *Introduction to Christianity* |
| ITB | *In the Beginning* |
| JN I | *Jesus of Nazareth: From the Baptism in the Jordan to the Transfiguration* |
| JN II | *Jesus of Nazareth: Holy Week: From the Entrance into Jerusalem to the Resurrection* |
| JN III | *Jesus of Nazareth: The Infancy Narratives* |
| JRCW | Joseph Ratzinger Collected Works |
| JRGS | Joseph Ratzinger Gesammelte Schriften |
| LG | *Lumen Gentium* |
| LLC | *Letters from Lake Como* |
| MM | *Milestones: Memoirs 1927–1977* |
| MROC | *Many Religions—One Covenant* |

| | |
|---|---|
| *NMT* | *The Nature and Mission of Theology* |
| *NSL* | *New Song for the Lord* |
| *PCT* | *Principles of Catholic Theology* |
| *PG* | *Patrologia Graeca* |
| *SC* | *Sacrosanctum Concilium* |
| *Sca* | *Sacramentum Caritatis* |
| *SS* | *Spe Salvi* |
| *ST* | *Summa Theologiae* |
| *TT* | *Truth and Tolerance* |

# Introduction

THE CELEBRATION OF THE SACRED LITURGY enables the faithful in pilgrimage here below to enter into the reality of worship above with the heavenly court. Commenting upon the theology of Pseudo-Dionysius the Areopagite during a General Wednesday Audience, Benedict XVI notes:

> God is found above all in praising him, not only in reflection; and the liturgy is not something made by us, something invented in order to have a religious experience for a certain period of time; it is singing with the choir of creatures and entering into the cosmic reality itself.[1]

The liturgy, above all else, is the work of God (the *opus Dei*). Joseph Ratzinger[2] consistently reechoes the emphasis of the Second Vatican Council, which renewed the Church's focus on the eschatological character of

---

[1] General Audience, May 14, 2008, "Pseudo-Dionysius, the Areopagite," in *The Fathers*, vol. 2 (Huntington, IN: Our Sunday Visitor Press, 2010), 30.

[2] Throughout this work, I will use "Joseph Ratzinger" to refer to any pre-papal writings, and I will use "Benedict XVI" when quoting or citing papal writings. In the case of the three volumes of *Jesus of Nazareth*, I will refer to Pope Benedict XVI by his given name, Joseph Ratzinger. The three volumes of *Jesus of Nazareth* are the fruit of his own private work as an individual theologian: "[These books are] in no way an exercise of the magisterium, but [they are] solely an expression of my personal search 'for the face of the Lord' (cf. Ps 27:8)." Joseph Ratzinger, *Jesus of Nazareth: From the Baptism in the Jordan to the Transfiguration* [hereafter, *JN* I], trans. Adrian J. Walker (New York: Doubleday, 2007), xxiii. The subsequent volumes: *Jesus of Nazareth: Holy Week: From the Entrance into Jerusalem to the Resurrection* [hereafter, *JN* II], trans. Vatican Secretariat of State (San Francisco: Ignatius Press, 2011) and *Jesus of Nazareth: The Infancy Narratives* [hereafter, *JN* III], trans. Philip J. Whitmore (New York: Image, 2012).

the liturgy.[3] In light of this eschatological impetus highlighted by the Council, Ratzinger maintains the "essence of the Liturgy" is found in the prayer contained in the writings of St. Paul (1 Cor 16:22) and in the *Didache* (10:6): "Maranatha—Our Lord is here—Our Lord, come!"[4]

The liturgy and eschatology are intrinsically connected. Modern theological scholarship has laid the foundation for a retrieval of the correlation between these two subjects within dogmatic theology. Throughout this book, I will argue that Ratzinger maintains a unified focus on the relationship between liturgy and eschatology by his consistent emphasis on the primacy of *logos* and the centrality of Christ within his theology.[5]

## CHRISTOCENTRISM

Most scholarship on Ratzinger's theology has rightly underscored the theme of Christocentrism in his writings, and some recent works along

---

[3] In the words of the Council Fathers, the Church is "participating by anticipation in the heavenly [liturgy]" through the celebration of the sacred liturgy. *Sacrosanctum Concilium* [hereafter, *SC*], §8. Unless otherwise noted, translations of conciliar documents will come from Norman P. Tanner, ed., *Decrees of the Ecumenical Councils*, 2 vols. (Washington, DC: Sheed & Ward and Georgetown University Press, 1990); slight modifications are my own. Aidan Nichols highlights the unique "eschatological orientation" in *Sacrosanctum Concilium*. See Aidan Nichols, O.P., *Concilar Octet: A Concise Commentary on the Eight Key Texts of the Second Vatican Council* (San Francisco: Ignatius Press, 2019), 24–27.

[4] Joseph Ratzinger, *Theology of the Liturgy: The Sacramental Foundation of Christian Existence* [hereafter, *JRCW11*], ed. Michael J. Miller, trans. John Saward, Kenneth Baker, S.J., Henry Taylor, et al., Collected Works 11 (San Francisco: Ignatius Press, 2014), 557; Joseph Ratzinger, *Theologie der Liturgie: Die sakramentale Begründung christlicher Existenz* [hereafter, *JRGS11*], Gesammelte Schriften 11, ed. Gerhard Ludwig Müller (Freiburg im Breisgau: Herder, 2008), 656. I will cite both the English and German texts of Ratzinger's completed works when I have been able to access them; slight modifications of the English translations are my own. Elsewhere, Ratzinger deals with the meaning of the prayerful invocation "*maranatha*." See his *Eschatology: Death and Eternal Life*, ed. Aidan Nichols, O.P., trans. Michael Waldstein, 2nd ed. (Washington, DC: The Catholic University of America Press, 2007), 5–15.

[5] I will use uppercase "Logos" when I am making reference to Jesus Christ whereas I will use lowercase "logos" when I am making reference to this term understood by Ratzinger as "reason," "word," or "meaning." Joseph Ratzinger, preface to the 2004 edition of *Introduction to Christianity* [hereafter, *IC*], trans. J. R. Foster (San Francisco: Ignatius Press, 2004), 26–29; Joseph Ratzinger, *Einführung in das Christentum: Bekenntnis—Taufe—Nachfolge*, Joseph Ratzinger Gesammelte Shriften 4, [hereafter, *JRGS4*] ed. Gerhard Ludwig Müller (Freiburg: Herder, 2014), 50–53.

these lines have developed specific aspects of his ecclesiology.[6] Although there are works on Ratzinger that highlight his Christocentrism and his primacy of *logos*, the study of his theology of the liturgy merits a work focused exclusively on the intrinsic relationship between the liturgy and eschatology.[7] Among the numerous studies of his theology of the liturgy

---

[6] On the ecclesiology of Ratzinger, see Santiago Madrigal, *Iglesia es caritas: La eclesiología teológica de Joseph Ratzinger—Benedicto XVI* (Santander: Sal Terrae, 2008); Maximilian Heinrich Heim, O. Cist., *Joseph Ratzinger: Life in the Church and Living Theology*, trans. Michael J. Miller (San Francisco: Ignatius Press, 2007); Thomas Weiler, *Volk Gottes—Leib Christi: Die Ekklesiologie Joseph Ratzingers und ihr Einfluss auf das Zweite Vatikanische Konzil* (Mainz: Matthias-Grünewald, 1997); James Massa, S.J., "The Communion Theme in the Writings of Joseph Ratzinger: Unity in the Church and in the World through Sacramental Encounter" (PhD diss., Fordham University, 1996); Seán Corkery, *A Liberation Ecclesiology?: The Quest for Authentic Freedom in Joseph Ratzinger's Theology of the Church* (Bern: Peter Lang, 2015). For a work on the theology of politics of Ratzinger, see D. Vincent Twomey, S.V.D., *Pope Benedict XVI: The Conscience of Our Age—A Theological Portrait* (San Francisco: Ignatius Press, 2007). For an overview of the biblical theology of Ratzinger, see Scott Hahn, *Covenant and Communion: The Biblical Theology of Pope Benedict XVI* (Grand Rapids, MI: Brazos Press, 2009).

[7] On Ratzinger's theology of liturgy, see José Aldazábal, "La Liturgia es ante todo obra de Dios," *Phase* 236 (2000): 181–86; Pedro Farnés, "Una Obra importante sobre la liturgia que debe leerse en su verdadero contexto," *Phase* 247 (2002): 55–76; John F. Baldovin, S.J., "Cardinal Ratzinger as Liturgical Critic," in *Studia Liturgica Diversa: Essays in Honor of Paul F. Bradshaw*, eds. Maxwell Johnson and Edward Phillips (Portland: Pastoral Press, 2004): 211–27; Baldovin, *Reforming the Liturgy: A Response to the Critics* (Collegeville: MN, 2009), 65–89; Joseph Murphy, "Joseph Ratzinger and the Liturgy: a Theological Approach," in *Benedict XVI and the Sacred Liturgy: Proceedings of the First Fota International Liturgical Conference*, ed. Janet Elaine Rutherford and Neil Roy (Dublin: Four Courts Press, 2008), 132–155; Alcuin Reid, "The Liturgical Reform of Pope Benedict XVI, in *Benedict XVI and the Sacred Liturgy*, 156–180; Rudolf Voderholzer, ed., *Der Logos-gemäße Gottesdienst: Theologie der Liturgie bei Joseph Ratzinger* (Regensburg: Friedrich Pustet, 2009); Helmut Hoping, "Kult und Reflexion: Joseph Ratzinger als Liturgietheologe," in *Der Logos-gemäße Gottesdienst*, 12–25; Josip Gregur, "Fleischwerdung des Wortes—Wortwerdung des Fleisches: Liturgie als *logikē latreia* bei Joseph Ratzinger," in *Der Logos-gemäße Gottesdienst*, 46–76; Gunda Brüske, "Spiel oder Anbetung? Romano Guardini und Joseph Ratzinger über den Sinn der Liturgie," in *Der Logos-gemäße Gottesdienst*, 91–110; Michael Kunzler, "Die kosmische Dimension der Eucharistiefeier: Zu Fragen ihrer liturgischen Gestalt bei Joseph Ratzinger," in *Der Logos-gemäße Gottesdienst*, 172–204; Eamon Duffy, "Benedict XVI and the Liturgy," in *The Genius of the Roman Rite: Historical, Theological, and Pastoral Perspectives on Catholic Liturgy*, ed., Uwe Michael Lang (Chicago: Hillenbrand Books, 2010), 1–21; Anselm J. Gribbin, O. Praem, *Pope Benedict XVI and the Liturgy: Understanding Recent Liturgical Developments* (Herefordshire: Gracewing, 2011); Nichola Bux, *Benedict XVI's Reform: The Liturgy between Innovation and Tradition*,

or his eschatology, none has focused solely upon his understanding of relationship between eschatology and liturgy in light of his insistence upon the primacy of *logos* over *ethos*.[8]

The primacy of *logos* over *ethos* is the hermeneutical key to understanding the unique vision of Ratzinger's Christocentric liturgical theology and eschatology (chapter one). The *logos* ("word," "meaning," or "reason") of a culture forms or directs the *ethos* ("habit," "custom," or "moral values") of individual people within a given society. In the twentieth century, many theologians identified the authentic Christian *logos* as *communio* and selfless love as its corresponding *ethos*. Because of Ratzinger's consistent appreciation of the primacy of the *logos*, he establishes the significance of sacrifice in forming the Church and her worship (chapter two), the Church as a *communio* and the hope rooted in her in contradistinction with the world (chapter three), rational worship (*logikē latreia*) and the Church's mission of charity (chapter four), and the orientation of the Church's worship (and all space and all time within it) towards the incarnate *Logos* as a central theme within Ratzinger's theology of liturgy (chapters five).

The Irish theologian James Corkery has argued that the priority of *logos* over *ethos* is one of the main features of Ratzinger's theology. Corkery argues that the primacy of *logos* "lies at the heart and centre of Joseph

---

trans. Joseph Trabbic (San Francisco: Ignatius Press, 2012); Manfred Hauke, "The 'Basic Structure' (*Grundgestalt*) of the Eucharistic Celebration according to Joseph Ratzinger," in *Benedict XVI and the Roman Missal: Proceedings of the Fourth Fota International Liturgical Conference*, ed. Janet Elaine Rutherford and James O'Brien (Dublin: Four Courts Press, 2013), 70–106; and Mariusz Biliniewicz, *The Liturgical Vision of Pope Benedict XVI: A Theological Inquiry* (Bern: Peter Lang, 2013). On the eschatology of Ratzinger, see Gerhard Nachtwei, *Dialogische Unsterblichkeit: eine Untersuchung zu Joseph Ratzingers Eschatologie und Theologie* (Leipzig: St. Benno-Verlag, 1986); *Hoffnung auf Vollendung: Zur Eschatologie von Joseph Ratzinger*, ed. Gerhard Nachtwei (Regensburg: Verlag Friedrich Pustet, 2015); Thomas Marschler, "Perspektiven der Eschatologie bei Joseph Ratzinger," in *Joseph Ratzinger: Ein theologisches Profil*, ed. Peter Hofman, (Paderborn: Ferdinand Schöningh),161–188. Marschler's work offers a general overview of Ratzinger's eschatology.

8 Mariusz Biliniewicz briefly highlights the eschatological nature of Ratzinger's theology of liturgy. According to Biliniewicz, Ratzinger's theology of liturgy works on three levels: "historical (once-for-all event of Christ's Paschal Mystery), sacramental (entering of Divine, eternal reality into contemporariness, through liturgy) and eschatological (expected completion of the process of divinization, already started in liturgy and sacramental acts but not yet fulfilled). This third, eschatological level has some important moral and practical implications in Ratzinger's theology." *The Liturgical Vision of Pope Benedict XVI*, 44–45.

Ratzinger's theological synthesis."[9] Corkery repeatedly notes that this position highlights the Neoplatonic-Augustinian influence upon Ratzinger's theology. Corkery concludes that this Platonic outlook leads Ratzinger to be critical of the world and praxis.[10] Contrary to the thesis of Corkery, this work demonstrates that Ratzinger's theology is oriented *to* the world as it is directed to communion with the incarnate *Logos*, through and for whom the world has been created. The prioritization of *logos* strengthens the praxis of charity because the *Logos* is the Person of Jesus Christ and not simply an abstract idea. Ratzinger's understanding of the relationship between the Church and the world is inseparable from an appreciation of the relation between his Christology, theology of liturgy, and eschatology.

The primacy of *logos* for Ratzinger establishes an inseparable link between the liturgy and Christology. Emery de Gaál has maintained that this inseparable link also includes eschatology: "Ratzinger's eschatology is eminently Christological, and it contains a rarely reached intensification toward Christ."[11] By contrast, some eschatologies are characterized by an exclusive focus on the human person that overshadows the importance and role of Jesus Christ in favor of a political or social agenda directed towards alleviating the plight of the suffering.[12] Ratzinger's Christocentric

---

9   James Corkery, S.J., *Joseph Ratzinger's Theological Ideas: Wise Cautions and Legitimate Hopes* (Mahwah, NJ: Paulist Press, 2009), 31.

10   See Corkery, *Joseph Ratzinger's Theological Ideas*, 69–80. Corkery develops this thesis by examining the thought of Ratzinger in tension with Walter Kasper and Gustavo Gutiérrez. Also see Corkery, "Reflection on the Theology of Joseph Ratzinger (Pope Benedict XVI)," *Acta Theologica* 32, no. 2 (2012): 19–26. Kasper argues that the Platonic Idealism is an underlying issue in Ratzinger's *Introduction to Christianity*. See Walter Kasper, "Das Wesen des Christlichen," *Theologische Revue* 65, no. 3 (1969): 182–188. Cf. Joseph Ratzinger, "Glaube, Geschichte und Philosophie Zum Echo auf meine *Einführung in das Christentum*," and "Schlussword zu der Discussion mit Walter Kasper," in JRGS4, 323–342.

11   Emery de Gaál, *The Theology of Pope Benedict XVI: The Christocentric Shift* (New York: Macmillan Palgrave, 2010), 276. My understanding and appreciation of the Christocentric thread that connects the thought of Ratzinger has been influenced by the work of de Gaál. Also see Thomas Marschler, "Perspektiven der Eschatologie bei Joseph Ratzinger," 186–88. Marschler concludes his article with an overview of Ratzinger's eschatology with a section on eschatology as a concrete Christology.

12   See Congregation for the Doctrine of the Faith, *Libertatis Conscientia* Instruction on Christian Freedom and Liberation, (Vatican City: Libreria Editrice Vaticana, 1986); Congregation for the Doctrine of the Faith, *Libertatis Nuntius* Instruction on Certain Aspects of the "Theology of Liberation," (Vatican City: Libreria Editrice Vaticana, 1984). Also see Joseph Ratzinger, "Freedom and Liberation: The Anthropological Vision of the Instruction *Libertatis conscientia*," in *Joseph Ratzinger in Communio*, vol. 2,

eschatology enables him to navigate between various systems of eschatology that focus too much on the present ("already") or too much on the future ("not yet"). At the same time, his focus on Christ enables him to develop an eschatology that affirms the twofold commandment to love God and neighbor. Hence, he achieves a balance with respect to eschatology that affirms the transcendent ("not yet") and recognizes the urgency of the imminent ("already") because he establishes a close relationship between eschatology and liturgy rooted in the primacy of the incarnate *Logos*.

---

*Anthropology and Culture*, trans. Stephen Wentworth Arndt, eds. David L. Schindler and Nicholas J. Healy (Grand Rapids, MI: Eerdmans Publishing, 2013), 52–69. Cf. Juan Luis Segundo, S.J., *Theology and the Church: A Response to Cardinal Ratzinger and a Warning to the Whole Church*, trans. John W. Diercksmeier (Minneapolis, MN: Winston Press, 1985). Segundo offers a systematic response to the documents published by the CDF and the critiques espoused by Ratzinger relating to certain features that have become prominent in liberation theology. For an overview of Ratzinger's engagement with liberation theology, see Siegfried Wiedenhofer, "Politische Utopie und christliche Vollendungshoffnung: Joseph Ratzingers Auseinandersetzung mit Politischer Theologie und Befreiungstheologie," in *Hoffnung auf Vollendung: Zur Eschatologie von Joseph Ratzinger*, ed. Gerhard Nachtwei (Regensburg: Friedrich Pustet, 2015), 186–245; Veit Neumann, "Ideologiekritik und Befreiungstheologie: Der Schutz des Glaubens vor einem totalisierenden System des Geistes, das sich als 'Praxis' versteht," in *Hoffnung auf Vollendung*, 246–58; Hansjürgen Verweyen, *Joseph Ratzinger—Benedikt XVI: Die Entwicklung seines Denkens* (Darmstadt: Primus Verlag, 2007), 117–125. Cf. Corkery, *Joseph Ratzinger's Theological Ideas*, 74–80. Whereas the work of Wiedenhofer and Neumann focus on the breadth of Ratzinger's engagement with political theology and liberation theology, Corkery will narrow his concern to address Ratzinger's treatment of Gustavo Gutiérrez. Without mincing words, Corkery in his assessment of Ratzinger's engagement with liberation theology vis-à-vis the theology of Gutiérrez contends, "Overall, I consider that Ratzinger's critiques—and I include here documents of his Congregation—gave space to people who have no concern for changing the mechanisms that cause poverty and keep the poor in poverty, to assume that they had an easy ally in the Church authorities, in spite of how the Instructions of 1984 and 1986 attempted to support the aspiration of the poor to liberation. Also, due to deficiencies in how the dialogue with liberation theologians was undertaken, the critiques proved overly subduing, even stifling. Views on this differ, of course, but I recall that it was an era in which many theologians were very discouraged." *Joseph Ratzinger's Theological Ideas*, 80. What Corkery and other critics of Ratzinger fail to account for is the theology of liberation that is at the heart of Ratzinger's theology of liturgy. The end goal of Ratzinger's theology of liturgy is freedom *in* Christ. For a discussion of freedom in the theology of Ratzinger, see Peter John McGregor, *Heart to Heart: The Spiritual Christology of Joseph Ratzinger* (Eugene, OR: Pickwick Publications, 2016), 242–278. I am grateful to Tracey Rowland for directing me to McGregor's work. For a brief and very insightful analysis of the contrasting views of Ratzinger and Gutiérrez, see Karl-Heinz Menke, *Der Leitgedanke Joseph Ratzingers: Die Verschränkung von vertikaler und horizontaler Inkarnation* (Paderborn: Schöningh, 2008), 63–68.

English theologian Aidan Nichols characterizes liturgy for Ratzinger as "essentially proleptic," meaning "it works by anticipation of our destiny."[13] Consequently, Ratzinger emphasizes that "every Eucharist is Parousia." Ratzinger continues, "In the Liturgy the Church should, as it were, in following [Christ], prepare for him a dwelling in the world."[14] The sacraments prepare and anticipate the Parousia of Jesus Christ. A clear understanding of Christology and eschatology are therefore necessary in order to comprehend the Church's liturgy.[15]

Ratzinger in *A New Song for the Lord* includes two papers on the Church's faith in Christ (Christology) and one paper on the hope that is grounded in Christ (eschatology) prior to the main section, which is focused on the liturgy. In the book's preface, he comments on the rationale for the inclusion of these papers as the first part of a work that is dedicated to his theology of liturgy:

> Rereading these texts [on Christology and eschatology] after an interval of several years, I became aware that our entire search for the criteria of liturgical renewal ultimately culminates in one question: Who do people say that the Son of Man is? (Matt. 16:4f.). Hence, this first section seems to me to be imperative for placing liturgical questions in the right context. *Only a close connection with Christology can make possible a productive development of the theology and practice of liturgy.*[16]

---

[13] Aidan Nichols, O.P., *The Thought of Benedict XVI: An Introduction to the Theology of Joseph Ratzinger* (New York, NY: Burn & Oates, 2005), 232.

[14] Ratzinger, *Eschatology*, 204.

[15] On the role of the Parousia in the liturgy of the Church, see Paul O'Callaghan, *Christ Our Hope: An Introduction to Eschatology*, (Washington, DC: The Catholic University of American Press, 2011), 66–71. Ratzinger's eschatology can also be characterized as a *Präsentische Eschatologie* ("realized eschatology") with his assertion that the Parousia is made present with the liturgy. See Ludwig Weimer, "Die Baugesetze der Geschichtstheologie Joseph Ratzingers," in *Hoffnung auf Vollendung*, 55–74, especially 61–65. Weimer highlights the significance of *Präsentische Eschatologie* in Ratzinger's thought.

[16] Joseph Ratzinger, *A New Song for the Lord: Faith in Christ and Liturgy Today* [hereafter, *NSL*], trans. Martha M. Matesich (New York: The Crossroad Publishing Company, 1997), x; emphasis added. These two papers are not contained in the volume on the liturgy in the collected works of Joseph Ratzinger, which is a significant lacuna in light of Ratzinger's claim within the preface that "only a close connection with Christology can make possible a productive development of the theology and practice of liturgy." The first paper, "Jesus Christ Today" ("*Jesus Christus heute*"; *NSL*, 3–28), is found in Ratzinger's second Christology volume of his collected works. See Joseph Ratzinger, *Jesus von Nazareth: Beiträge zur Christologie*, Joseph Ratzinger Gesammelte Schriften

The eschatology and liturgy developed by many contemporary theologians reflect a Christology that places an emphasis on Christ's human nature to the point where it seems separated from his divine nature (the *Logos*). Both the understanding of eschatology and the celebration of the liturgy suffer when they lack a clear understanding of who Jesus Christ is as the incarnate Word.

According to Nichols, Ratzinger has been of the opinion that eschatology was the main issue in the New Testament since he wrote his *Habilitationsschrift* on Bonaventure.[17] Ratzinger's *Eschatology: Death and Eternal Life* is among the most developed and systematic of his writings; indeed, Ratzinger himself describes it as his "most thorough work."[18] His *The Spirit of the Liturgy* treats the nature of the liturgy with a similar level of depth and insight. Among the volumes in the collected writings of Joseph Ratzinger, his *Theology of Liturgy* was published first, which underscores the significant place of the liturgy within his theology.[19] Theologians such

---

6/2 [hereafter, JRGS6/2], ed. Gerhard Ludwig Müller (Freiburg: Herder, 2013), 966–988; the first part of this volume will be cited as JRGS6/1.

[17] Nichols, *The Thought of Benedict XVI*, 110. In the foreword to the American edition of his *Habilitationsschrift*, Ratzinger's study of Bonaventure's thought had a significant impact upon his engagement of the relationship between revelation, history, and metaphysics. As a result of this study, Ratzinger concludes that "Bonaventure's theology of history presents a struggle to arrive at a proper understanding of eschatology." Joseph Ratzinger, *The Theology of History in St. Bonaventure*, trans. Zachary Hayes, O.F.M (Chicago: Franciscan Herald Press, 1989), xiii. On the significance of his *Habilitationsschrift* upon his theology, see Hansjürgen Verweyen, *Ein unbekannter Ratzinger: Die Habilitationsschrift von 1955 als Schlüssel zu seiner Theologie* (Regensburg: Friedrich Pustet, 2010). Also see Kurt Koch, "Benedict XVI und Bonaventura: Einführung in die theologischen Wurzeln des Denkens des Papstes," in *Das Geheimnis des Senfkorns: Grundzüge des theologischen Denkens von Papst Benedikt XVI* (Regensburg: Friedrich Pustet, 2010), 45–68; Peter Hofmann, "Jesus Christus als Mitte der Geschichte: Der Einfluss Bonaventuras auf das Denken Joseph Ratzingers/Benedikts XVI. Und dessen Bedeutung für die aktuelle Fundamentaltheologie," in *Zur Mitte der Theologie im Werk von Joseph Ratzinger/Benedikt XVI*, ed., Maximilian Heim and Justinus C. Pech (Regensburg: Friedrich Pustet, 2013), 79–92.

[18] Joseph Ratzinger, *Milestones: Memoirs 1927–1977* [hereafter, *MM*], trans. Erasmo Leiva-Merikakis (San Francisco: Ignatius Press, 1998), 150.

[19] In his explanation for why his writings on the liturgy were chosen for the initial volume published among his collected works, Pope Benedict XVI maintains that he was following the lead of the Second Vatican Council. The first document that was promulgated by the Council Fathers was on the sacred liturgy giving primacy to God: "By starting with the theme of liturgy, God's primacy, the absolute precedence of the theme of God was unmistakably highlighted. Beginning with the liturgy tells us: 'God first.' When the focus on God is not decisive, everything loses orientation." JRCW11, xv [JRGS11, 5].

as Michael Schmaus (1897–1993), Gottlieb Söhngen (1892–1971), Josef Pascher (1893–1979), and Romano Guardini (1885–1968) have influenced him to make the liturgy the heart of his theological works.[20]

Ratzinger's ultimate conclusions regarding the liturgy—particularly regarding the orientation of the celebrant, the various *ars celebrandi*, and the full implications for his understanding of the Pauline *logikē latreia* ("worship according to the *logos*")—are influenced by his eschatology. But Ratzinger does not limit his interest in the theology of the liturgy to the "specific problems of liturgical studies." He grounds the study of the liturgy in its ultimate context rooted in the act of faith in God, which culminates in the eschaton.[21] Therefore, Ratzinger's liturgical writings should be read in tandem with his eschatology while keeping in mind the centrality of Christ and the primacy of *logos* in his theology.

The liturgy is inherently eschatological in Ratzinger's theology. The close relationship between the liturgy and eschatology in Ratzinger could be called a liturgical eschatology or an eschatological theology of liturgy. Ratzinger's commitment to an eschatological theology of liturgy is demonstrated by his repeated calls to consider the purpose of worship *ad orientem*, which dates back to the early Church. Liturgical celebrations in the ancient Church were characterized by consideration of the need to prepare for the Lord's Parousia. The ancient liturgical use of *Maranatha* as a prayer was understood as a petition for the Parousia and preparation for the coming of the Lord in his Eucharistic presence.[22]

---

[20] "Die Liturgie der Kirche war für mich seit meiner Kindheit zentrale Wirklichkeit meines Lebens und ist in der theologischen Schule von Lehrern wie Schmaus, Söhngen, Pascher, Guardini auch Zentrum meines theologischen Mühens geworden." JRGS11, 6 (JRCW11, xvi). Schmaus, Söhngen, and Pascher were Ratzinger's professors during his time of theological study in Munich. Ratzinger, *MM*, 98. Incidentally, Guardini was an acquaintance of Söhngen, whereas Pascher and Schmaus "were very closely connected" to him. Pope Benedict XVI (with Peter Seewald), *Last Testament: In His Own Words*, trans. Jacob Philips (New York: Bloomsbury, 2016), 84. On the work of Pascher, see Markus Roth, *Joseph Maria Pascher (1893–1979): Liturgiewissenschaftler in Zeiten des Umbruchs* (Erzabtei, St. Ottilien: EOS, 2011). For a comprehensive treatment of the theological influences upon Ratzinger's theology of liturgy, see Leo Sven Conrad, F.S.S.P., "Liturgie und Eucharistie bei Joseph Ratzinger: Zur Genese seiner Theologie während der Studien und Professorenzeit" (PhD diss., Europa-Universität Flensburg, 2016).

[21] Benedict XVI, JRGS11, 6 (JRCW11, xvi).

[22] See Geoffrey Wainwright, *Eucharist and Eschatology* (New York: Oxford University Press, 1981), 68–70. Anticipation of the return of Jesus Christ in his Second Coming was made present liturgically through the celebration of the liturgy of the Eucharist towards the east (*ad orientem*). St. John Damascene (ca. 650–ca. 750) enumerates

## THE STRUCTURE OF THE BOOK

The primacy of *logos* and the centrality of Christ is the unifying thread connecting Ratzinger's theology of liturgy and eschatology. Hence, this book is divided into two main parts. In the first part (Chapters 1–3), I will address the fundamental foundation of Ratzinger's liturgical eschatology by examining his emphasis upon the role of the *logos* in theology, Christology, and ecclesiology. This will be coupled with a study of Ratzinger's spiritual Christology, with a focus on how it influences his theology of liturgy and eschatology through the notions of participation and communion in Christ's sacrificial love. In the second part of this work (Chapters 4–5), I will examine Ratzinger's theology of hope, charity, and beauty, as well as his understanding of active participation in relationship to the eschatological and cosmic characteristics of the sacred liturgy.

In chapter one, I will underscore Guardini's influence upon the primacy of *logos* over *ethos* in Ratzinger's thought. Here I will emphasize the *logos*-centrism found throughout Ratzinger's works and how this connects

---

four reasons for Christian worship in the eastern direction: (1) The title of Christ as "Sun of Righteousness" associated with the Sun rising in the east, (2) Christ's ascension towards the east, (3) the anticipation of the Parousia from the east, and (4) Eden's eastward orientation (cf. Gen 2:8; 3:24). *Eucharist and Eschatology*, 78–79. Also see Uwe Michael Lang, *Turning towards the Lord: Orientation in Liturgical Prayer* (San Francisco: Ignatius Press, 2004), 54–55. There, Lang quotes the text of St. John of Damascus summarized by Wainwright in full. In the celebration of the ancient liturgy, there are summons by the deacon in the liturgy to look towards the east. According to the Coptic anaphora of St. Basil, the deacon exhorts the people with these words: "You who are sitting, stand up. Look eastward." Wainwright, *Eucharist and Eschatology*, 80. Wainwright maintains that this diaconal summons is used in other liturgies such as the Alexandrian Greek liturgy of *St. Basil*, the Greek liturgy of *St. Mark*, the Coptic liturgy of *St. Cyril*, and in the Ethiopian *Anaphora of the Apostles*. Also see Stefan Heid, "Gebetshaltung und Ostung in der frühchristlichen Zeit," *Rivista di Archeologia Christiana* 72 (2006): 386–391; Lang, *Turning towards the Lord*, 49–51; Lang, "The Direction of Liturgical Prayer," in U. M. Lang, ed., *Ever Directed towards the Lord: The Love of God in the Liturgy of the Eucharist Past, Present, and Hoped For* (Edinburgh: T & T Clark, 2007), 95; Louis Bouyer, *Liturgy and Architecture* (Notre Dame, IN: University of Notre Dame Press, 1967), 52–60. Cf. John Baldovin, *Reforming the Liturgy*, 111. On the one hand, Baldovin acknowledges there is "evidence of the people being commanded to turn east in both the Byzantine and North African traditions." Baldovin nuances his view as he opines, "It is not really possible to know for sure whether the people actually turned to face east during the eucharistic prayer or whether the command was a spiritual exhortation along the lines of 'Lift up your hearts.'" *Reforming the Liturgy*, 111. It is difficult to comprehend how Baldovin could voice such an opinion when the liturgical and historical evidence seems to clearly suggest that the call to "Look eastward" during the celebration of the liturgy was more than simply a "spiritual exhortation."

his eschatology and theology of liturgy. The primacy and centrality of the *logos* is foundational for Ratzinger in outlining the person's relationship to God and other people. His eschatology emphasizes the need to overcome the temptation towards an immanentized view of salvation (which results from subordinating the *logos* to *ethos*), whereas his liturgical theology stresses that the liturgy is above all an *actio Dei*.

This outline of the relationship between eschatology and liturgy in light of the primacy of *logos* will lead to a study of Ratzinger's liturgical understanding of sacrifice in chapter two. Ratzinger explores the true significance of the Exodus narrative as well as the identity of Christ as the new Temple and the new Lamb, with the aim of fostering an appreciation of the unity of liturgy and eschatology. An examination of this aspect of Ratzinger's theology will lead to an understanding of how he holds sacrifice as the true *Grundgestalt* ("basic form") of the Eucharist. This sacrifice-centered notion will be contrasted with Romano Guardini's understanding of the Eucharist primarily as a meal. A comprehensive reading of the role of sacrifice in Ratzinger's theology can be appreciated through an understanding of his spiritual Christology, the significance of vicarious representation (*Stellvertretung*), and by the worshippers' participation in the life and mission of Christ.

Chapter three develops the centrality of the theme of *communio* in Ratzinger's ecclesiology in light of his Christocentric vision. This centrality influences his understanding of the relationship of the Church to the liturgical celebration of the Eucharist. My analysis of Ratzinger's ecclesiology will further clarify the relationship of eschatology to his theology of liturgy. The human person cannot be understood simply as an autonomous individual as he approaches the eschaton or as he fully participates in the liturgy. As Mystical Body ecclesiology influenced the early thinkers in the liturgical movement, so, too, *communio* ecclesiology would be a development that would guide Ratzinger's theology of liturgy.

*Communio* ecclesiology affects Ratzinger's approach to eschatology in that the person is saved not simply as an individual; rather, people experience the gift of salvation in communion with the entire Body of Christ. The chapter concludes by contrasting the theology of hope developed by Ratzinger under the influence of Josef Pieper in contrast with the theology of hope and politics developed by Moltmann and Metz. A consequence of Ratzinger's Eucharistic ecclesiology is the emphasis he places upon the realization of eschatological hope.

Chapter four explores the *ethos* of charity, which precedes from the *logos* of communion examined in chapter three. I will examine the Pauline scholarship on the liturgy as *logikē latreia* according to Romans 12:1, and I will highlight the centrality of this phrase for Ratzinger's understanding of the liturgy. The chapter emphasizes that despite the critiques of his ecclesiology as being narrowly focused on the vertical communion, Ratzinger clearly highlights the horizontal mission of charity that proceeds from the love of God expressed fully in the liturgy.[23] My analysis of his understanding of the liturgy in light of the primacy of the *logos* will culminate in an examination of his presentation of the Eucharist as a *sacramentum caritatis*.

In chapter five, I discuss the orientation of the celebrant during the celebration of the liturgy, a topic that, for Ratzinger, relates to eschatology. What is most important for Ratzinger is the eschatological and cosmic symbolism of the celebrant offering the liturgy in anticipation of Christ's advent. Ratzinger presents the human person as a *homo adorans*; hence, every human gesture and posture during the liturgy can become a form of discipline that prepares the entire person for the eschaton. I will also probe Ratzinger's understanding of how beauty directs the faithful towards the anticipation of the eschaton, which is inherent in the celebration of liturgy.

---

[23] On the relationship between the vertical and horizontal communion within the Church, Ratzinger opines, "It is vertical unification, which brings about the union of man with the triune love of God, thus also integrating man in and with himself. But because the Church takes man to the point toward which his entire being gravitates, she automatically becomes horizontal unification as well: only by the impulse power of vertical unification can horizontal unification, by which I mean the coming together of divided humanity, also successfully take place." Joseph Ratzinger, *Called to Communion* [hereafter, *CTC*], trans. Adrian Walker (San Francisco: Ignatius Press, 1996), 76; *Zeichen unter den Völkern: Schriften zur Ekklesiologie und Ökumene*, Gesammelte Schriften 8/1 [hereafter, JRGS8/1], ed. Gerhard Ludwig Müller, (Freiburg: Herder, 2010), 519–20; the second part of this volume will be cited as JRGS8/2. This fundamental idea in the ecclesiology of Ratzinger can be summarized by the assertion of Cardinal Jean Jérôme Hamer, O.P. (1916–1996): "In communion (κοινωνία) the horizontal dimension depends on the vertical and can only be understood on that basis" (Hamer, 1976); quoted in *Behold the Pierced One: An Approach to Spiritual Christology* [hereafter, *BPO*], trans. Graham Harrison (San Francisco: Ignatius Press, 1986), 83 (JRGS8/1, 317). On the relationship between the vertical and horizontal communion, which is rooted in the Christocentric thought of Ratzinger, see Karl-Heinze Menke *Der Leitgedanke Joseph Ratzingers*. In Menke's analysis of the implications of Ratzinger's theology of incarnation, he examines the relationship between reason, religion, and faith, the universal and the particular church, the soul and the body, and politics and liberation. This brief work offers insight into understanding the cause of tension between the theology of Ratzinger and the theologies of Walter Kasper, Johann Baptist Metz, and Gustavo Gutiérrez.

Finally, I will draw out the liturgical and eschatological implications of Ratzinger's theology of beauty and his emphasis on the primacy of *logos*.

In the liturgy, the eschaton is realized and anticipated; it is "already" present, but at the same time, "not yet" fulfilled. For Ratzinger, the source of renewal for the Church and modern culture is the proper celebration of the liturgy. The faithful gather together in worship to participate in and to experience a foretaste of the eschatological *communio* that God desires for all of humanity. This *communio* is founded upon the primacy of *logos*.

The priority of *logos* over *ethos* assists the Church and all her members in being who they are called to be as adopted sons and daughters of God. The Incarnation is the beginning of *the end*. Jesus Christ is one divine Person with two natures: human and divine. This communion of natures, unique though it is in Christ (who alone enjoys the hypostatic union), in a certain sense represents the end for which every human person is created and which all the blessed are destined to enjoy in the communion of saints. Divinization marks the beginning of a human person's life in intimate communion with Christ through grace. The liturgy is the foretaste and anticipation of this communion that the human person has been created for and that impels the person to go forth on a mission to draw others to this communion through a life of love.

# CHAPTER 1

# Primacy of the *Logos*

ONE OF RATZINGER'S CENTRAL THESES in an article titled "Preaching God Today" is that "God should be preached as *Logos*."[1] Ratzinger defends this thesis, which he received from the Italian-German theologian Romano Guardini, on the following grounds: "In the beginning was not the 'deed' [*ethos*] but, rather, the Word [*Logos*]; it is mightier than the deed. Doing does not create meaning; rather, meaning creates doing."[2]

The liturgy and eschatology become subject (if such were possible) to the creation of the community, and they cease to be the *opus Dei*, when the primacy of *ethos* is asserted. Establishing the primacy of the *logos* within Ratzinger's theology in this chapter is critical to the overall thesis of this work, which is that the liturgy is inherently eschatological and that the realized eschatology of Ratzinger begins with the liturgy. Ratzinger's claim for the priority and centrality of the incarnate *Logos* establishes the relationship between the liturgy and eschatology.[3]

---

[1]  See Joseph Ratzinger, *Dogma and Preaching: Applying Christian Doctrine to a Daily Life* [hereafter, *DP*], trans. Michael J. Miller (San Francisco: Ignatius Press, 2011), 93–95.

[2]  Ratzinger, *DP*, 94. Elsewhere, Ratzinger addresses the significance of Guardini's thesis concerning the priority of *logos* over *ethos*: "In the early 1920s, Romano Guardini spoke of the primacy of *logos* over *ethos*, intending thereby to defend the Thomistic position of *scientia speculativa:* a view of theology in which the meaning of christocentrism consists in transcending oneself and, through the *history* of God's dealings with mankind, making possible the encounter with the *being* of God himself. I admit that it has become clear to me only through the developments of recent years how fundamental this question actually is." Joseph Ratzinger, *Principles of Catholic Theology: Building Stones for a Fundamental Theology* [hereafter, *PCT*], trans. Sister Mary Frances McCarthy, S.N.D. (San Francisco: Ignatius Press, 1987), 319; emphasis in the original.

[3]  See Michael Schneider, "Primat des Logos vor dem Ethos—Zum theologischen Diskurs bei Joseph Ratzinger," in *Joseph Ratzinger: Ein theologisches Profil*, ed. Peter Hofmann (Paderborn: Ferdinand Schöningh, 2008), 15–45. Schneider surveys briefly this theme

Ratzinger comments that as a result of the subordination of *logos* to *ethos*, eschatology "is no longer seen within the theology of creation but, rather, replaces creation: the real world worth living in is yet to be created, namely, by man himself, contrary to what he finds already in place."[4] In such a case, eschatology becomes a highly dangerous force, to which lives are sacrificed for an impossible dream of self-creation and self-perfection. In the celebration of the liturgy, similarly, the golden calf is a symbol for false worship that is characterized by the primacy of *ethos* because it is a "self-generated cult," a "festival of self-affirmation," or a "circle closed in on itself."[5] Although humans are continually making idolatrous pseudo-liturgies, Ratzinger asserts that the true "liturgy cannot be 'made.' This is why it has to be simply received as a given reality and continually revitalized."[6]

This chapter establishes the definition of the *logos* for Ratzinger and

---

throughout Ratzinger's theology with an emphasis on Ratzinger's spiritual Christology and theology of liturgy. The introduction highlighted how the Council of Chalcedon was important in influencing the contours of Ratzinger's arguments for Christocentrism as a point of departure for modern theology. Schneider, as we have seen with Pablo Blanco above, also notes the importance of Chalcedonian Christology. See Schneider, "Primat des Logos vor dem Ethos," 24. The discussion of the primacy of the *logos* influences Ratzinger's ecumenical concerns. Commenting upon what he refers to as the "so-called consensus ecumenism," Ratzinger maintains, "It is not, they say, truth that creates consensus but consensus that is the only concrete and realistic court of judgment to decide what shall now hold good. The confession of faith, too, would not then express the truth but would have significance as an achievement of consensus. Yet thereby the relationship between truth and action ("praxis") is also reversed. Action becomes the standard for truth." Further on, Ratzinger expresses his concern regarding this new paradigm for ecumenism that upholds various notions of justice for different (and at times contradictory) causes: "Ethos without logos cannot endure; that much the collapse of the socialist world, in particular, should have taught us." Joseph Ratzinger, *Pilgrim Fellowship of Faith: The Church as Communion* [hereafter, *PFF*], ed. Stephan Otto Horn and Vinzenz Pfnür, trans. Henry Taylor (San Francisco: Ignatius Press, 2005), 262; In Ratzinger's estimation, we must begin with a unified *logos* to guide our *ethos*. On the critique of the priority of an "ethos without logos" in ecumenism, see Maximilian Heinrich Heim, O. Cist., *Joseph Ratzinger: Life in the Church and Living Theology*, trans. Michael J. Miller (San Francisco: Ignatius Press, 2007), 436–440.

4  Ratzinger, *DP*, 380.

5  Joseph Ratzinger, *Theology of the Liturgy: The Sacramental Foundation of Christian Existence* [hereafter, JRCW11], ed. Michael J. Miller, trans. John Saward, Kenneth Baker, S.J., Henry Taylor, et al., Collected Works 11 (San Francisco: Ignatius Press, 2014), 12; *Theologie der Liturgie: Die sakramentale Begründung christlicher Existenz* [hereafter, JRGS11], Gesammelte Schriften 11, ed. Gerhard Ludwig Müller (Freiburg im Breisgau: Herder, 2008), 39–40.

6  Ratzinger, JRCW11, 323 (JRGS11, 387).

its relation to the *ethos* of self-giving love. First, there is a harmony between Guardini and Ratzinger on primacy of *logos*. Guardini's influence upon Ratzinger's view of the *logos* will become evident as the consistency of this theme becomes evident throughout Guardini's writings.[7] Second, the parallels in the thought of Guardini and Ratzinger through their shared insistence upon the primacy of *logos* and their mutual interest in developing a strong relationship between the liturgy and Christology will underscore the clear affinity between them. Third, the primacy of the *logos* has long been the central theme for Ratzinger, beginning with his inaugural lecture as a professor of theology at the University of Bonn in 1959 and leading to his address as pope at the University of Regensburg in 2006. As a result of the consistent *logos*-centrism in Ratzinger's theology, the relationship between the liturgy and eschatology cannot be fully understood without a proper definition of *logos*; neither can it be understood by subordinating *logos* to *ethos*.

Foremost for Ratzinger, the *Logos* is the person of Jesus Christ, who is fully God and fully man. However, Ratzinger does use the other meanings of *logos*: "mind," "reason," "meaning," "discourse," and "word."[8] He argues that "divine worship in accordance with *logos*," or *logikē latreia*, is

---

[7]  On the influence of Guardini's theme of the primacy of the *logos* over *ethos*, see Stephan Otto Horn, "Zum existentiellen und sakramentalen Grund der Theologie bei Joseph Ratzinger—Papst Benedikt XVI," *Didaskalia* 38, no. 2 (2008): 301–10. In this article, Horn describes what we have termed as a sacramental *logos* in Ratzinger's thought. Also see Franz-Xavier Heibl, "Theologische Denker als Mitarbeiter der Wahrheit: Romano Guardini und Papst Benedikt XVI," in *Symphonie des Glaubens: Junge Münchener Theologen im Dialog mit Joseph Ratzinger/Benedict XVI*, ed. Michaela C. Hastetter, Christoph Ohly, and Georgios Vlachonis (St. Ottilien: EOS, 2007), 77–101. Heibl's essay offers a very thorough article demonstrating consistently the influence of Guardini upon the various theological themes of Ratzinger's pre-papal and papal writings.

[8]  See Joseph Ratzinger, *Introduction to Christianity* [hereafter, *IC*], trans. J. R. Foster (San Francisco: Ignatius Press, 2004), 26–29; *Einführung in das Christentum: Bekenntnis—Taufe—Nachfolge*, Joseph Ratzinger Gesammelte Shriften 4, [hereafter, JRGS4] ed. Gerhard Ludwig Müller (Freiburg: Herder, 2014), 50–53. Also see *IC*, 151–161 (JRGS4, 148–156); and *DP*, 93–95. I will rely upon Ratzinger's understanding of *logos* and its relation to *ethos* throughout this work. For a detailed analysis of the concept of *logos*, see Christos Yannaras, *Person and Eros*, trans. Norman Russell (Brookline, MA: Holy Orthodox Press, 2007), 159–172. For a brief survey of *logos* as both reason and Christ in the writings of the Church Fathers, see Brian Daley, S.J., "*Logos* as Reason and *Logos* Incarnate: Philosophy, Theology and the Voices of Tradition," in *Theology Needs Philosophy: Acting against Reason is Contrary to the Nature of God*, ed. Matthew L. Lamb (Washington, DC: The Catholic University of America Press, 2016), 91–115. Also see Michael Maria Waldstein, "The Self-Critique of the Historical-Critical Method: Cardinal Ratzinger's Erasmus Lecture," *Modern Theology* 28:4 (October 2012): 732–747.

the "most appropriate way of expressing the essential form of Christian liturgy."[9] In Ratzinger's view, other definitions or descriptions of the Eucharist, such as an assembly or a meal, fall short because they touch upon an individual aspect of the Eucharist and not the entire reality. By contrast, the idea of *logikē latreia* demonstrates how the "*logos* of creation, the *logos* in man, and the true and eternal *Logos* made flesh, the Son, come together."[10]

The *Logos* is the divine Person of Jesus Christ, who reveals the *logoi* of creation and of the human person. Drawing upon the patristic tradition, Benedict XVI emphasizes that in Jesus Christ, "*the word was 'abbreviated.'*"[11] Throughout this work, the centrality of the incarnate *Logos* in revealing the authentic *logos* that defines the liturgy and eschatology while simultaneously effecting their intrinsic relationship becomes irrefutable.

Romano Guardini explored the dynamic relationship between *logos* and *ethos* throughout his writings. Undoubtedly, Guardini's affirmation of the primacy of *logos* over *ethos* and his critique of the modern world's *logos*, characterized by the dominance of *technē*, greatly influenced Ratzinger's theology.[12] In his pre-papal, papal, and post-papal writings, Ratzinger

---

9   Ratzinger, JRCW11, 30 (JRGS11, 61).

10  Ratzinger, JRCW11, 30 (JRGS11, 61).

11  Benedict XVI, Post-synodal Apostolic Exhortation *Verbum Domini* (Vatican City: Libreria Editrice Vaticana, 2010), §12: "The Fathers of the Church found in their Greek translation of the Old Testament a passage from the prophet Isaiah that St. Paul also quotes in order to show how God's new ways had already been foretold in the Old Testament. There we read: 'The Lord made his word short, he abbreviated it' (*Is* 10:23; *Rom* 9:28). . . . The Son himself is the Word, the *Logos*; the eternal word became small— small enough to fit into a manger. He became a child, so that the word could be grasped by us.' Now the word is not simply audible; not only does it have a *voice*, now the word has a *face*, one which we can see: that of Jesus of Nazareth."

12  A number of scholars have highlighted the following remarkable parallels between Ratzinger and Guardini: Both wrote a doctoral thesis concerning the work of St. Bonaventure, both wrote books outlining the main contours of the Christian faith, both wrote books on the liturgy, and both have written their own theological reflections on the person of Jesus Christ. See Rowland, *Benedict XVI: A Guide for the Perplexed* (New York: T & T Clark, 2010), 17–19; Emery de Gaál, *The Theology of Pope Benedict XVI: The Christocentric Shift* (New York: Macmillan Palgrave, 2010), 39–43; and Nichols, "Romano Guardini and Joseph Ratzinger on the Theology of Liturgy," in Aidan Nichols O.P. *Lost in Wonder: Essays on Liturgy and the Arts* (Burlington, VT: Ashgate Publishing Company, 2011), 21–25. The Italian theologian Elio Guerriero surmises that Ratzinger began to follow Guardini's intellectual path explicitly in the aforementioned works focused on the liturgy, the life of Jesus, and finally the Church after he developed a series of retreats for the priests associated with the ecclesial movement Communio e liberazione. This retreat was published in English as Joseph

worked tirelessly to proclaim the primacy of Christ as the living *Logos* with the further intention of redirecting contemporary culture towards an *ethos* of love for God and neighbor. According to Ratzinger, this twofold love is authentic worship in accordance with the *Logos* (*logikē latreia*).[13] Many

---

Ratzinger, *To Look on Christ: Exercises in Faith, Hope, and Love*, trans. Robert Nowell (New York: The Crossroad Publishing Company, 1991). The inspiration for the theme of these retreat conferences, which was focused on the theological virtues, was the philosopher Josef Pieper (1904–1997), a student of Romano Guardini. See Guerriero's *Benedict XVI: His Life and Thought*, trans. William J. Melcher (San Francisco: Ignatius Press, 2018), 353–357. In addition to Pieper, Guardini was also influential in the thought of Hans Urs von Balthasar; both Pieper and von Balthasar would impact the thought of Ratzinger. Rowland, *Benedict XVI*, 19. Incidentally, Pieper urged Ratzinger to get in touch with Karol Wojtyla. "Ratzinger and Wojtyla began exchanging books; the Polish cardinal [Wojtyla] made use of Ratzinger's *Introduction to Christianity* in preparing the Lenten retreat he preached for Paul VI and the Curia in 1976, and they met briefly at the Synod of Bishops in 1977." George Weigel, *God's Choice: Pope Benedict XVI and the Future of the Catholic Church* (New York: Harper Collins Publishing, 2005), 178. For an account of Guardini's influence on Pieper, see Alberto Berro, "Pieper y Guardini en Rothenfels: un encuentro fecundo," *La Plata* 59, no. 216 (2004): 339–357. Pieper himself writes briefly about his encounter with Guardini in his autobiography, *No One Could Have Known: An Autobiography: The Early Years, 1904–1945*, trans. Graham Harrison (San Francisco: Ignatius Press, 1987), 34–39. For more on the impact that Guardini had on von Balthasar, see Hans Urs von Balthasar, *Romano Guardini: Reform from the Source* (San Francisco: Ignatius Press, 2010). In his description of his studies as a seminarian in Freising, Ratzinger writes, "In the domain of theology and philosophy, the voices that moved us *most directly* were those of Romano Guardini, Josef Pieper, Theodor Häcker, and Peter Wust." *Joseph Ratzinger, Milestones: Memoirs 1927–1977 [hereafter, MM]*, trans. Erasmo Leiva-Merikakis (San Francisco: Ignatius Press, 1998), 43; emphasis added. On the influence of Guardini as one of Ratzinger's primary teachers, see Blanco Sarto, *La Teología de Joseph Ratzinger: Una Introducción* (Madrid: Ediciones Palabra, 2011), 18–23. Also, see the previously cited article of Franz-Xavier Heibl, "Theologische Denker als Mitarbeiter der Wahrheit: Romano Guardini und Papst Benedikt XVI," in *Symphonie des Glaubens*, 77–101. Heibl stresses the unity between the liturgy and Christology, which Ratzinger judges as one of the most significant contributions of Guardini. See "Romano Guardini im Urteil Papst Benedikts," in *Symphonie des Glaubens*, 87–91.

13   Romans 12:1–2. Chapter four describes how this Pauline passage has a central role in Ratzinger's liturgical theology. "Far from being a mere liturgical game or ritual, it is 'λογικὴ λατρεια,' *logikē latreia*,' *Logos*-filled worship that transforms human existence in the Logos, allowing the Christian's interior to become contemporaneous with Christ." De Gaál, *The Theology of Pope Benedict XVI*, 240. For a succinct overview of the notion of the *logikē latreia* in Ratzinger's theology of liturgy, see Michael Schneider, "Zur Erneuerung der Liturgie nach dem II. Vatikanum: Ihre Beurteilung in der Theologie Joseph Ratzingers auf dem Hintergrund seiner Reden in der Abtei Fontgombault," in *Der Logos-gemäße Gottesdienst: Theologie der Liturgie bei Joseph Ratzinger*, ed. Rudolf

theologians of the twentieth century have worked to establish the primacy of the *logos* of *communio* and the *ethos* of self-giving love in contradistinction with modernity's *logos* of mechanistic autonomy (*technē*), hedonistic utilitarianism, and radical pragmatism. Ratzinger is one of the most recent thinkers to adopt consistently the Guardinian tension between *logos* and *ethos* as a major theological and pastoral theme throughout his works.[14]

The authentic meaning and relationship between *logos* and *ethos* has important implications for our modern culture, which is characterized by a materialistic and secular *logos*. In his analysis of cultural development, the American theologian David L. Schindler concludes that "every *ethos* always needs a *logos* that precedes it and gives it meaning."[15] He describes

---

*Voderholzer (Regensburg: Friedrich Pustet, 2009), 146–52*. Also see Michaela Christine Hastetter, "Liturgie—Brücke zum Mysterium: Grundlinien des Liturgieverständnisses Benedikts XVI," in *Symphonie des Glaubens*, 131–50, especially 140–42; Josip Gregur, "Fleischwerdung des Wortes—Wortwerdung des Fleisches: Liturgie als *logikē latreia* bei Joseph Ratzinger," in *Der Logos-gemäße Gottesdienst*, 46–76. Gregur's essay is very insightful in offering the philosophical and scriptural context to understand the implications of Ratzinger's use of the Pauline *logikē latreia* to describe the liturgy.

[14] In his article "Preaching God Today," Ratzinger presents various theses relating to how God should be preached. Following his second thesis that "God should be proclaimed as Creator and Lord" and preceding the fourth thesis that "God should be proclaimed in Jesus Christ," he presents his third thesis: "God should be preached as Logos." After giving credit to Guardini for asserting the primacy of the *logos*, Ratzinger argues, "Above all, however, this [primacy of the *logos* over *ethos*] means that Christian faith essentially and originally has to do with the truth. What a man believes is not a matter of indifference to him; the truth cannot be replaced by a 'good opinion.' The loss of the truth cannot be replaced by a 'good opinion.' The loss of the truth corrupts even good opinions. It also corrupts love, which without truth is blind and, hence, cannot fulfill its real purpose [*Sinn*]: to will and to do for the other what is truly good. Only when I know what man is in truth and the world is in truth can I also be truly good. Goodness without truth can bring about subjective justification but not salvation. God is the Truth—this statement is a program, a fundamental orientation for human existence, which finds verbal expression in the belief in creation." Ratzinger, *DP*, 94.

[15] David L. Schindler, "Grace and the Form of Nature and Culture," in *Catholicism and Secularization in America: Essays on Nature, Grace and Culture*, ed. David L. Schindler (Huntington, IN: Our Sunday Visitor, 1990), 30. According to Tracey Rowland, Schindler's insistence on the relationship between *logos* and *ethos* is influenced by the thought of Hans Urs von Balthasar. See her "Theology and Culture," in *Being Holy in the World: Theology and Culture in the Thought of David L. Schindler*, ed. Nicholas J. Healy, Jr. and D. C. Schindler (Grand Rapids, MI: Eerdmans Press, 2011), 56. For an overview of Schindler's understanding of modern culture's mechanistic *logos* in contrast to the *logos* of *communio*, see Michael Hanby, "Beyond Mechanism: The Cosmological Significance of David L. Schindler's *Communio* Ontology," in *Being Holy in the World: Theology and Culture in the Thought of David L. Schindler*, ed. Nicholas J. Healy, Jr. and

the effect of the contemporary mechanistic and materialistic *logos* on modern culture as he maintains that sexual relations are reduced to lustful manipulation; political relations become "brutal power"; market relations become "hedonistic consumerism"; and music and architecture, in light of such market relations, become "noise and harsh ugliness."[16]

Within Ratzinger's theology, the *logos* is sacramental insofar as the unity between the *Logos* incarnate and the *logoi* is reflected in all of creation. The world is sacramental in that it reflects the glory and beauty of the *Logos*, but it should not be conflated with the *Logos* himself. Modern culture divorces the *logoi* of creation from the *Logos*, which has had detrimental effects upon how people understand the *logos* of the human person and of the world, as modern culture defines reality ultimately by what is materialistic. Subsequently, the truth (*logos*) is reduced to what is empirically verifiable. What is good or ethical (*ethos*) is determined by the law of utility or expediency. The modern *ethos* has been shaped by either a materialistic *logos* and/or the subordination of *logos* to *ethos*.

## Romano Guardini, the Christian *Weltanschauung*, and the Logos of the Liturgy[17]

Romano Guardini's first encounter with the liturgical movement took place in 1906, when he was visiting a friend at the Benedictine Abbey of Beuron, which was founded by monks from the Abbey of Solesmes.[18] This

---

D. C. Schindler (Grand Rapids, MI: Eerdmans Press, 2011), 162–189.

[16] David L. Schindler, "Grace and the Form of Nature and Culture," 19.

[17] A previous version of this section on Guardini has been published: Roland Millare, "The Primacy of *Logos* over *Ethos*: The Influence of Romano Guardini on Post-Conciliar Theology," *Heythrop Journal* 57, no. 6 (November 2016): 974–83. The author is grateful to *Heythrop Journal* and Wiley-Blackwell publishers for permission to re-publish this material.

[18] Robert Krieg, C.S.C., *Romano Guardini: A Precursor of Vatican II* (Notre Dame, IN: University of Notre Dame Press, 1997), 74. Krieg's work is the only substantial secondary source published in English besides a volume of essays, see Robert Krieg, ed., *Romano Guardini: Proclaiming the Sacred in the Modern World* (Chicago, IL: Liturgical Training Press, 1995). There are a number of significant secondary works on Guardini: Albino Babolin, *Romano Guardini-Filosofo dell'alterità*, 2 vols. (Bologna: Zanichelli, 1968); Hanna Barbara Gerl, *Romano Guardini 1885–1968* (Mainz: Matthias Grünewald, 1985); and Joseph Ratzinger, ed., *Wege zur Wahrheit: die bleibende Bedeutung von Romano Guardini* (Düsseldorf: Patmos, 1985). A number of Guardini's own works have not been published in English or are out of print. For an exhaustive bibliography of Guardini's work, see Hans Merker and the Katholische Akademie in Bayern, eds., *Bibliographie Romano Guardini (1885–1968)* (Paderborn: Ferdinand Schöningh, 1978). For a selective bibliography of Guardini's works, see Hans Urs von

first encounter led to his making a series of visits to the abbey during his student years in Tübingen from 1906 to 1908.[19] The experiences of the liturgy at Beuron led to the development of his 1918 book, entitled *The Spirit of the Liturgy*, which was the first book published by Abbot Ildefons Herwegen (1874–1946) in a series titled *Ecclesia Orans*.[20]

In Ratzinger's estimation, Guardini's *The Spirit of the Liturgy* "may rightly be said to have inaugurated the liturgical movement in Germany."[21] This text enabled many people to encounter the living beauty and centrality of the liturgy. One cannot fully comprehend Guardini's thesis in this work without first understanding his critique of modern culture. Guardini contrasts the primacy of *logos* for Christianity with the subordination of *logos* to *ethos* in modernity. The modern and postmodern worlds each operate from a completely different *logos* in Guardini's work, which the section below describes.

Whereas Christ unites the faith and the world for Guardini's Christian worldview (*Weltanschauung*), the modern worldview departs from this unity. This departure lays the foundation for a completely secular order. Guardini's insight into this shift is expressed most poignantly in his two works: *The End of the Modern World*[22] and *Letters from Lake Como: Explorations in Technology and the Human Race*.[23] While the latter work is less systematic in its treatment, nevertheless it remains an important complement to the former because both outline the main contours of the *logos* of modernity and postmodernity relative to previous ages.

In *The End of the Modern World*, Guardini divides history into three ages: (1) the medieval world, (2) the modern world, and (3) the coming age after the modern world (what would now be described as postmodern). Although the book was originally published in 1956, Guardini foresaw the end of modernity on the horizon in light of his observations of cultural trends. The medieval period, he maintained, built its worldview on the foundation of classical philosophy and culture, culminating above all in the recognition of transcendence and the ultimate authority

---

Balthasar, *Romano Guardini*, 107–112.

[19] Krieg, *Romano Guardini: A Precursor of Vatican II*, 74–75.

[20] Krieg, *Romano Guardini: A Precursor of Vatican II*, 74. In 1921, Herwegen founded one of the prominent journals on liturgical theology, *Das Jahrbuch für Liturgiewissenschaft*.

[21] Ratzinger, JRCW11, 3 (JRGS11, 30).

[22] Romano Guardini, *The End of the Modern World* [hereafter, *EMW*], trans. Joseph Theman and Herbert Burke (Wilmington, DE: ISI Books, 2001).

[23] Romano Guardini, *Letters from Lake Como: Explorations in Technology and the Human Race* [hereafter, *LLC*], trans. Geoffrey W. Bromiley (Grand Rapids, MI: Eerdmans, 1994).

of revelation.[24] Under the influence of St. Augustine, medieval culture embraced a view governed by the perspective of salvation history. Guardini described it this way: "The world, time, history had begun with Creation; they reached apotheosis in the Incarnation of the Son of God . . . and all shall end with the destruction of the world and the Last Judgment."[25] History was radically transformed with the Incarnation marking the center of human history.

Through the Incarnation, the Eternal Word became flesh and affected every aspect of nature. Consequently, the Christian faith shaped every aspect of human life: architecture, artwork, annual seasons, literature, and the very structure of society. Above all, the medieval world was governed by a sense of unity rooted in the truth. For Guardini, this medieval unity was embodied in the varying *Summae* because this method of theology highlighted the "truth that reality itself was ordered harmoniously in being, that it could be formed and fashioned by the artistic genius of man."[26] In the medieval world, harmony was reflected in the architecture of the Church's cathedrals and the very structure of its theological writings. This unity built up by the use of faith and reason would soon be dissolved with the birth of modernity.

In Guardini's estimation, the disharmony between faith and reason began during the fourteenth century, and it culminated in its ultimate dissolution by the seventeenth century.[27] Whereas the medieval worldview was characterized by an orientation towards unity and harmony, the modern world was overshadowed by division and autonomy. The view of society as a communal, harmonious body was displaced by the individual, autonomous subject. On the origins of the modern concern revolving around the self, Guardini posits, "With the new consciousness of self, however, which arose late in the Middle Ages and especially in the Renaissance, man became important to himself. The 'I' . . . became the measure by which all human life was judged."[28] This triumph of the subjectivity for the autonomous person would lead to a view characterized by dominance in man's relation to the universe and culture. Consequently, Guardini characterizes modernity's view of culture as essentially the work of the person—"independent of the Work of God."[29] Whereas the medieval

---

[24] Guardini, *EMW*, 14–18.
[25] Guardini, *EMW*, 19.
[26] Guardini, *EMW*, 26.
[27] Guardini, *EMW*, 28.
[28] Guardini, *EMW*, 39.
[29] Guardini, *EMW*, 42.

world was oriented towards sacramental transcendence characterized by the communion of the "we," modernity is shaped by a secular immanence marked by the autonomy of the "I."

To facilitate an understanding of Guardini's argument, it is necessary to outline the essential aspects of modernity and its fundamental orientation towards progress for the sake of progress in order. The three characteristics of modernity include "a Nature subsisting in itself, an autonomous personality of the human subject, [and] a culture self-created out of norms intrinsic to its own essence."[30] It is inevitable that a world marked by such dissolution would move beyond modernity, as described in the final part of Guardini's *End of the Modern World*. As a result of its subsistence, the human person becomes alienated from nature. Governed by a *logos* ordered by *technē*, "man's relations with nature," Guardini surmises, "have reached the point of final crisis: man will either succeed in converting his mastery into good—then his accomplishment would be immense indeed—man will either do that or man himself will be at an end."[31] In an endless drive to conquer nature, which governs endless progress, the person may consequently be conquered.

In practice, the *logos* of *technē* is oriented towards an *ethos* of power and domination. Power exceeds the order and structure that the person tries to give it through his progress in technology. According to Guardini, power "unfolds independently from the continuous logic of scientific investigations, from technical problems, from political tensions. The conviction grows that power simply demands its own actualization."[32] Everything becomes subordinated to the drive for power, which ultimately leads to the subordination of the person himself. Guardini draws upon his experience of modernity to outline the logical consequences of the "end of the modern world," which is a fruit of this new *logos* and *ethos*.

The coming culture is, according to Guardini, a "non-cultural culture," which will be accompanied by a "non-human" man and a "non-natural nature."[33] Reflecting upon this same time period, the English apologist C. S. Lewis (1898–1963) aptly described the fruit of modern culture as the "abolition of man." Culture, severed from its orientation towards transcendence, ceases to be a culture *for* the authentic good of the person. Freedom divorced from responsibility and the guidance of truth leads society on a perilous course towards the destruction of human life at all stages.

---

[30] Guardini, *EMW*, 50.

[31] Guardini, *EMW*, 56.

[32] Guardini, *EMW*, 83.

[33] Guardini, *EMW*, 88.

In Guardini's view, the central issue is power: "Every decision faced by the future age—those determining the welfare or misery of humanity and those determining the life or death of mankind itself—will be decisions centered upon the *problem of power*. Although it will increase automatically as time moves on, the concern will not be its increase but *first restraint* and then the *proper use of power*."[34] Unbridled power will continue to wreak havoc, but there must be a rationale (*logos*) that restrains its use and guides the appropriate exercise of such power. Guardini would never advocate a return to medieval Christendom; however, what is necessary to prevent or to reverse the onslaught of a culture of dissolution (a culture of death or a throwaway culture) is to reorient the person towards the truth of Revelation, the incarnate *Logos*. This redirection will require the recovery of the sense of transcendence that leads to God, who is the object of faith.

Only faith can preserve culture because it allows the human person to *realize* or *fully develop* his nature.[35] Despite what seems to be an inevitable trend towards an ever-growing dissolution in postmodern culture, Guardini places his hope in the faithful, who will continue to enter into communion

---

[34] Guardini, *EMW*, 91; emphasis added. In *Power and Responsibility*, his sequel to *The End of the Modern World*, Guardini writes, "The core of the new epoch's intellectual task will be to integrate power into life in such a way that man can employ power without forfeiting his humanity. For he will have only two choices: to match the greatness of his power with the strength of his humanity, or to surrender his humanity to power and perish. The very fact that we can define these alternatives without seeming utopian or moralistic—because by so doing we but voice something of which the public is more or less aware—is a further indication that the new epoch is overtaking the old." Guardini, *Power and Responsibility: A Course of Action for the New Age*, trans. Joseph Theman and Herbert Burke (Wilmington, DE: ISI Books, 2001), 119. While the *End of the Modern World* and *Power and Responsibility* were originally translated into English and published by Regnery Press as two separate works, ISI Press has published them together in one volume.

[35] Guardini, *EMW*, 98; emphasis added. Many of the theologians who were influenced by the Romantic movement would have understood culture in the three German senses of the word: (1) *Kultur* or civilization, (2) *Geist* or the *ethos* of an institution, and (3) *Bildung* or self-cultivation/education. Rowland, *Benedict XVI*, 25. Also see Rowland, *Culture and the Thomist Tradition*, 21; Rowland, "Culture in the Thought of John Paul II and Benedict XVI," in *The Culture of the Incarnation* (Steubenville, OH: Emmaus Academic, 2017), 89–103. For more details on the history and etymology of the word "culture," see Kathryn Tanner, *Theories of Culture: A New Agenda for Theology* (Minneapolis, MN: Fortress Press, 1997), 3–24. It is clear that Guardini is appealing to culture as *Bildung* when describing the development of the person that can only come from embracing the faith. For the influence of the Romantic movement on German theologians, see Thomas F. O' Meara O.P., *Romantic Idealism and Roman Catholicism: Schelling and the Theologians* (Notre Dame, IN: University of Notre Dame, 1982).

with Christ. In Guardini's estimation, "This free union of the human person with the Absolute through unconditional freedom will enable the faithful to stand firm—God-centered—even though placeless and unprotected. . . . It will permit him to remain a vital person within the mounting loneliness of the future."[36] This Christocentric communion gives the person the strength to overcome the alienation that is experienced within a culture that values the triumphs of science and technology over the good of the person.

In *Letters from Lake Como*, Guardini offers a beautiful narrative description of the transformation of human culture, which has occurred through the dominance of technological progress. Guardini saw the advances of technology in the modern world as a means of subordinating the human person and human culture: "I saw machines invading the land that had previously been the home of culture. I saw death overtaking a life of infinite beauty, and I felt that this was not just an external loss that we could accept and remain who we were."[37]

Culture is affected by how the person relates to nature. The effect of technological advancement is that it further removes the person from his proximity to nature, as Guardini himself emphasizes:

> Every technical action involves the possessing, using, and shaping of nature. Nature becomes culture. Nature is what is there on its own; culture is what we humans make of it. In the course of history, the culture factor in existence has become stronger, while the natural factor has become weaker. With the coming of the machine this process has reached a new stage. Nature has been seized and made ready for use. Human beings take a cultural attitude to nature when they go to it.[38]

From the *beginning*, the person has been entrusted with dominion over the earth (see Gen 1:28). Nature can relate to the person when he begins to dwell in it as a result of his vocation to be its steward; and subsequently, "culture begins in it. . . . The human world is putting natural things and relations in a different sphere, that of what is thought, willed, posited, and created, and always in some way remote from nature—the sphere of the cultural."[39]

---

[36] Guardini, *EMW*, 108.
[37] Guardini, *LLC*, 5.
[38] Guardini, *LLC*, 109.
[39] Guardini, *LLC*, 10.

Guardini describes the dynamic between human creativity and nature: "Culture develops when we press on from what is simply there [in nature] to what is meaningful and essential."[40] Machines have been useful in the person's work with nature and have led to various advancements in the culture that have served the good of the human person. In a culture that has limited its view of reality to an immanent materialism, however, machines, which are meant to serve and advance life for the human person, at times seem to threaten his existence. The advent of modernity has brought about a mechanized view whereby only what a person can apprehend with the senses truly exists; consequently, people are valued for what they are able to do.

A culture dominated by the *logos* of *technē* will undermine the practice of the faith. In his diagnosis of Western culture in the early twentieth century, Guardini opines, "It is no accident that the worldview which sees in the machine the symbol of fulfilled culture—namely materialistic communism—is trying systematically to destroy religious life."[41] Unbridled progress, without any transcendent end, leads to the view that the perfect utopia, governed by justice, can be established in the present time, with the aid of science and technology to secure this kingdom. This *logos* will lead to a destructive *ethos* that will ultimately reduce human beings to mere things subject to the capricious use of others. With his prophetic clarity, Guardini gives humanity this warning: "Everywhere we see true culture vanishing, and our first reaction tells us that what is replacing it is barbaric. Only further reflection and a more profound reaction indicate the possibility of a new order in what is now chaotic in its effects, an order of different proportions and with a different basic attitude."[42] Society needs direction to reorient it back towards its proper end; otherwise, it faces the absurdity of violent destruction as a result of the unquenchable thirst of progress for its own sake. Clearly the answer to this problem, which plagues all of humanity, cannot be found in that which is immanent or material. Guardini directs the world to the transcendent *Logos*, whom the Church encounters in the liturgy.

Modernity and postmodernity have been marked by a mechanistic *logos*, which has resulted in a utilitarian *ethos*. Christianity needs to propose to the world a sacramental or, specifically, a Eucharistic *logos* directed to an *ethos of* self-giving love. Consequently, the need for culture to be re-formed by the source and summit of the *Logos* present in the

---

[40] Guardini, *LLC*, 21.
[41] Guardini, *LLC*, 111.
[42] Guardini, *LLC*, 48.

celebration of the liturgy underscores the importance of Guardini's *The Spirit of the Liturgy*.[43]

In Guardini's view, the liturgy "is primarily occupied in forming the fundamental Christian temper [*logos*]. By it, man is to be induced to determine correctly his essential relation to God. . . . As a result of this spiritual disposition, it follows that when action [*ethos*] is required of him he will do what is right."[44] Under this *logos*, the person views himself as the creator with limitless power and freedom. His sole concern is an ongoing progress, which he can only measure materially with an increase in money, influence, pleasure, or simply the accumulation of any material good. The *ethos* of such a worldview must necessarily be based on a utilitarian perspective—the greatest good for the greatest number. Further, modernity and postmodernity have subordinated *logos* to *ethos*.[45] A proper understanding of the mystery of the liturgy can help recover the proper ordering of culture.

Modernity embraced two different extremes in relation to the person that have had deleterious effects on the perception of the dignity of the person. On the one hand, the person has been reduced to an autonomous individual. On the other hand, the individual person is subordinated to what Guardini has described as "mass man." The former rejects the person's solidarity with other people, while the latter undermines each person's individuality and incommunicability. The liturgy allows for an anthropological balance because worship is transcendently directed towards God. Whereas the liturgy consists of individuals gathered together in common for worship, Guardini maintains that "the primary and exclusive aim of the liturgy is not the expression of the individual's reverence and worship for God."[46] His view of the liturgy gives primacy to the communion of believers over the individual, without diminishing the latter. For Guardini, "The liturgical entity consists rather of the united body of the faithful as such—the Church—a body which infinitely outnumbers the mere congregation."[47] In truth, the "liturgy does not say 'I,' but 'We.' . . . The liturgy is not celebrated by the individual, but by the body of faithful."[48] There is no room for a selfish autonomy in the liturgy; hence the individual must humbly embrace the corporate identity of the one Body of Christ over the

---

43  Romano Guardini, *The Spirit of the Liturgy* [hereafter, GSL], trans. Ada Lane (New York: The Crossroad Publishing Company, 1998).

44  Guardini, GSL, 86.

45  Guardini, GSL, 88.

46  Guardini, GSL, 19.

47  Guardini, GSL, 19.

48  Guardini, GSL, 36.

individual self. According to Guardini, "The individual has to renounce his own ideas and his own way. He is obliged to subscribe to the ideas and to follow the lead of the liturgy."[49] The liturgy forms the individual person by subordinating the "I" to the larger "we" of the Church. Guardini emphasizes that within the celebration of the liturgy itself, the "subordination of the self is actually facilitated."[50] Contrary to the mechanistic *logos* of postmodernity, the human person cannot simply create or manufacture liturgical worship in accordance with his personal preferences. Rather, the celebration of the liturgy is characterized by a different type of *logos*, which is oriented towards receptivity and communion. The liturgy receives and is directed towards an objective order that is not man-made, and therefore understanding and articulating its essence properly is a fundamental mission of the Church.

Guardini argues that the *"first and most important lesson"* which the liturgy has to teach is that the prayer of a corporate body must be sustained by thought. The prayers of the liturgy are entirely governed by and interwoven with dogma."[51] These statements are a reiteration of the axiom of Prosper of Aquitaine (d. after 455): *lex orandi statuat legem credendi*—"the law of prayer constitutes the law of belief."[52] In other words, Guardini wants to highlight the primary truth that the liturgy is "nothing else but truth expressed in terms of prayer."[53] Liturgy provides culture with its proper orientation because it enables every human person to engage in the highest act of religion: worship or *cultus*, from which the English word "culture" is derived. The celebration of the liturgy is first and foremost an *actio Dei* and not the work of man (*opus hominum*).[54] Guardini emphasizes, "When the liturgy is rightly regarded, it cannot be said to have a purpose, because it does not exist for the sake of humanity, but for the sake of God. In the liturgy man is no longer concerned with himself; his gaze is directed towards God."[55]

---

[49] Guardini, GSL, 38.

[50] Guardini, GSL, 40.

[51] Guardini, GSL, 21; emphasis in the original.

[52] Heinrich Denzinger, *Enchiridion symbolorum definitionum et declarationum de rebus fidei et morum: Compendium of Creeds, Definitions and Declarations on Matters of Faith and Morals* [hereafter, DH], ed., Peter Hünermann, 43rd ed. (San Francisco: Ignatius Press, 2012), 246. For a brief overview of the historical context and theological significance of this patristic adage, see Helmut Hoping, *My Body Given for You: History and Theology of the Eucharist*, trans. Michael J. Miller (San Francisco: Ignatius Press, 2019), 23–25.

[53] Hoping, *My Body Given for You*, 24.

[54] This is a major theme in Ratzinger's theology of liturgy presented throughout this work.

[55] Guardini, GSL, 66.

Liturgy directs the person towards an order that transcends nature. In what Guardini describes as the "playfulness" of the liturgy, the person learns to "abandon, at least in prayer, the restlessness of purposeful activity."[56] Unlike the mechanistic *logos*, the liturgical or sacramental *logos* is not concerned with usefulness or utility alone. Liturgy actualizes the highest form of leisure by leading the person to *rest* in God's presence through entering into the communal worship of the Body of Christ. Every aspect of liturgical celebration is a part of this *logos*. Guardini explains: "The Church has not built up the *Opus Dei* for the pleasure of forming beautiful symbols, choice language, and graceful, stately gestures, but she has done it . . . for the sake of our desperate spiritual need."[57] While a mechanized worldview is concerned with material satisfaction, the liturgy satisfies the full desires of the human person, which includes his spiritual nourishment.

The modern and, subsequently, the postmodern worlds have inverted the proper order between *logos* and *ethos*. As a result of the nominalist emphasis on the superiority of the will (voluntarism), *ethos* has received a primacy over *logos*. Liturgy helps to maintain the contemplation (*logos*) that fruitful action (*ethos*) presupposes. Guardini maintains, "No matter how great the energy of the volition and action and striving may be, it must rest on the tranquil contemplation of eternal, unchangeable truth."[58] There is no greater action that indicates that a person takes the needs of the world around him seriously than for him to enter consistently and faithfully into the authentic and full worship offered within the liturgy. The *logos* of the liturgy has the potential to redirect the human person away from an *ethos* of power divorced from responsibility that is driven by a thirst for domination, which Guardini boldly describes as "demonic." In Guardini's estimation, "Once action [*ethos*] is no longer sustained by personal awareness, is no longer morally answerable, a peculiar vacancy appears in the actor. He no longer has the feeling that *he*, personally, is acting; that since the act originates with him, he is responsible for it."[59]

The modern person abdicated any sense of responsibility when *logos* was subordinated to *ethos* in the nominalist shift. As a result, the fate of the dignity of the person has been entrusted to the "will to power" of the majority. Guardini, with prophetic clarity, asks the key question, which the

---

[56] Guardini, GSL, 71.

[57] Guardini, GSL, 82.

[58] Guardini, GSL, 94.

[59] Guardini, *Power and Responsibility*, 125.

Second Vatican Council would try to answer: "Man is acquiring ever more power over man, an ever profounder influence over him physically, intellectually, spiritually; but how will he direct that influence?"[60] The answer to this question is determined by what type of *logos* precedes a given *ethos*.

There are many similarities in how Guardini and Ratzinger outline the genealogy of modernity and how they underscore the importance of a proper theology of culture. Above all, they share an interest in identifying the living spirit of the liturgy as the key to redirecting the modern person back to the authentic worship of God. The following assessment of Ratzinger's concerning the Church in the modern world could easily be attributed to Guardini:

> I am convinced that the crisis in the Church that we are experiencing today is to a large extent due to the disintegration of the liturgy, which at times has even to be conceived of *etsi Deus non daretur*: in that it is a matter of indifference whether or not God exists and whether or not he speaks to us and hears us. But when the community of faith, the worldwide unity of the Church and her history, and the mystery of the living Christ are no longer visible in the liturgy, where else, then, is the Church to become visible in her spiritual essence? Then the community is celebrating only itself, an activity that is utterly fruitless.[61]

A self-referential Church and a self-enclosed world are on a dead-end road, and therefore Ratzinger contends that "we need a new Liturgical Movement, which will call to life the real heritage of the Second Vatican Council."[62]

In light of the themes in the work of Romano Guardini related to modern culture and the liturgy, the contours of Ratzinger's liturgical theology can be outlined. His views on the liturgy are the core of his theology of culture and offer insight into his clarion call for a liturgical movement that is *new*. Further, Ratzinger shaped his theology of liturgy and eschatology under the influence of Guardini's writings. The primacy of *logos* is fundamental for Ratzinger's approach to these areas of theology.

As demonstrated above, Guardini outlined the general cultural shift that takes place with the of subordination *logos* to *ethos*. A secular *logos* is characteristically materialistic, whereas as the Christian *logos*, developed

---

[60] Guardini, *Power and Responsibility*, 176.
[61] Ratzinger, *MM*, 149.
[62] Ratzinger, *MM*, 149.

by theologians such as Ratzinger and Guardini, is sacramental. The implications of Guardini's ideas on Ratzinger's theology become clear when one considers Guardini's eschatology. A materialist ontology forms an immanentized eschatology. If liturgy is inherently eschatological, then this will have logical consequences for the manner in which the sacred liturgy is celebrated. The most significant insight that one gains for understanding Ratzinger's theology of liturgy is its inseparability from his eschatology.

## THE SYMPHONIC HARMONY OF GUARDINI AND RATZINGER[63]

Joachim Cardinal Meisner (1933–2017), the Archbishop of Cologne, has referred to Joseph Ratzinger as the "Mozart of Theology" because of his great gift of weaving various aspects of theology into a unified and joyful symphony.[64] As a master composer of theological erudition, Ratzinger unifies Christology, ecclesiology, anthropology, eschatology, and his theology of liturgy. The Guardinian theme of the priority of *logos* over *ethos* assists Ratzinger in bringing about this symphonic harmony.

---

[63] The following sections within this chapter have been published as Roland Millare, "The Hermeneutic of Continuity and Discontinuity between Romano Guardini and Joseph Ratzinger: The Primacy of *Logos*," *Nova et Vetera* (English) 18, no. 2 (Spring 2020): 521–564.

[64] Although the above is my general interpretation for Cardinal Meisner's usage of this analogy, Tracey Rowland suggests that the analogy reflects Ratzinger's theological method insofar as he does not "jettison the classical repertoire" and integrates it with the influence of the German Romantic movement. Rowland, *Benedict XVI: A Guide for the Perplexed,*, 23–24: "Cardinal Joachim Meisner has suggested that Ratzinger is the 'Mozart of theology,' and while it is true that Ratzinger does not jettison the classical repertoire, given the influence of the Romantic movement on German theology, coupled with Ratzinger's recognition that the failure to provide an adequate account of the mediation of history in the realm of ontology represented the single greatest crisis for Catholic theology in the twentieth century, a more appropriate analogy might be that of a more romantically-inclined composer, such as Carl Maria von Weber or Bruckner. Nonetheless, Ratzinger's work does have the luminosity and directness of Mozart, and of course, a Mozart composition like the 40th symphony in G minor has its romantic movements." De Gaál, also commenting on the analogy of Ratzinger's theology to Mozart, adds, "Like Mozart, he does not delight in dark problematizations. He is charming and always cheerful in a quiet way." *The Theology of Pope Benedict XVI*, 45. For a treatment of Ratzinger's theology in conjunction with this well-known and deserved appellation as the "Mozart of theology," see the essay by the German theologian Michaela Christine Hastetter, "Einheit Aller Wirklichkeit: Die Bedeutung des symphonischen Denkens des "Mozarts der Theologie" für die Pastoral," in *Symphonie des Glaubens*, 15–50, especially 16–21.

On February 2, 1985, Ratzinger gave an address on the occasion of the hundreth anniversary of Guardini's birth in which he traced the contours of the German-Italian author's theological thought.[65] Guardini's basic theological approach parallels the methodology adopted by Ratzinger. For both thinkers, theology reaches its culmination in the liturgy, which is celebrated properly in accord with the *logos* (*logikē latreia*). Liturgy allows the human person to enter into the dialogue (*dia-logos*) of love that Jesus Christ has with the Father in the Holy Spirit. In his analysis of Guardini's thought, Ratzinger discusses the unity between liturgy and Christology. This unity is also retraced throughout the oeuvre of Ratzinger as the *logos* is the consistent thread that unifies his symphonic thought.

According to Ratzinger, Guardini desired to address the modern world, which was marked by a total separation between God and the human person. This chasm, which was characteristic of modernity, resulted in an alienation that reduced nature to "mere materiality."[66] Liturgy enables the human person to appreciate the sacramental or symbolic nature of the world. Ratzinger contends that for Guardini, "liturgical action is more specifically symbolic action that is capable of grasping the world and its own being as symbol, because the symbol is the real epitome of the unity of spirit and the matter, the spirituality of matter and the materiality of the spirit."[67] There is an inherent transcendence in nature by the mere fact that it is an effect of the Creator's love. In the words of St. Bonaventure, God created everything "not to increase his glory, but to show it forth and to communicate it."[68] The rites of the various liturgies involve the use of created things such as water, oil, bread, and wine.

---

[65] Joseph Ratzinger, *Fundamental Speeches from Five Decades*, [hereafter, *FSFD*], ed. Florian Schuller, trans. Michael J. Miller, J. R. Foster, and Adrian Walker (San Francisco: Ignatius Press, 2012), 230–258; *Jesus von Nazareth: Beiträge zur Christologie*, Joseph Ratzinger Gesammelte Schriften 6/2 [hereafter, *JRGS6/2*], ed. Gerhard Ludwig Müller (Freiburg: Herder, 2013), 719–741.

[66] Ratzinger, *FSFD*, 233 (JRGS6/2, 721).

[67] Ratzinger, *FSFD*, 234 (JRGS 6/2, 722). The sacramentality of the world is a dominant theme in the thought of the Eastern Orthodox theologian Alexander Schmemann (1921–1983). See his work *For the Life of the World: Sacraments and Orthodoxy* (Crestwood, NY: St. Vladimir's Seminary Press, 1982). For a summary and commentary on Schmemann's writings on the "ontological sacramentality" of the created order, see David Schindler, *Ordering Love: Liberal Societies and the Memory of God* (Grand Rapids, MI: Eerdmans, 2011), 288–309.

[68] St. Bonaventure, *In II Sent.* I, 2, 2, 1, quoted in the *Catechism of the Catholic Church*, 2nd ed. (Washington, DC: Libreria Editrice Vaticana-United States Conference of Catholic Bishops, 2000), 293; cited henceforth as *CCC*.

These worldly gifts reach their supernatural end in the celebration of the liturgy. This dynamic between the material and the spiritual within the liturgy points towards the world's symbolic nature that cannot remain on the level of "mere materiality."

In Guardini's theology, "freedom is truth," meaning that the human person discovers freedom by living in conformity with his God-given nature (being or *logos*).[69] The liturgy is the primary means through which the human person realizes his nature to worship God. Ratzinger emphasizes the interrelationship between truth and worship: "The freedom *for* the truth and the freedom *of* the truth cannot exist without the acknowledgement and worship of the divine."[70] Every human person shares a fundamental characteristic—a call to the adoration of God. Adoration is a concrete recognition on the part of the human person that he is not self-sufficient or autonomous. It is a humble act that recognizes God as the source of all existence. This is why Guardini defines adoration as "the obedience of being."[71] The nature of the human person finds its fulfilment in worship.

Guardini goes on to state, "Adoration is the primary obedience that serves as the foundation for all the rest: the obedience of our being to the being of God. If a being is in truth, then it itself is nothing but truth."[72] This anthropological truth lays the foundation for one of the key concepts in the thought of Guardini: the primacy of *logos* over *ethos*, which is an idea that must be rediscovered for the sake of the renewal of theology.[73]

---

[69] Romano Guardini, *Auf dem Wege* (Mainz: Matthias Grünewald, 1923), 20, quoted in Ratzinger, *FSFD*, 247 (JRGS6/2, 732). This dynamic between freedom and truth has been emphasized by the moral theologian Servais Pinckaers as a "freedom for excellence." See Servais Pinckaers, O.P., *The Sources of Christian Ethics*, trans. Sister Mary Thomas Noble, O.P. (Washington, DC: The Catholic University of America Press, 1995), 354–378.

[70] Ratzinger, *FSFD*, 190; emphasis added. For a development of this theme on the relationship between truth and freedom, see Joseph Ratzinger, "Truth and Freedom," *Communio* 23, no. 1 (1996): 16–35.

[71] Ratzinger, *FSFD*, 247 (JRGS6/2, 732). Josef Pieper, who was also influenced by Guardini, speaks of adoration in the form of festivity or liturgical worship as a commemoration of the truth of the person's creation by God. See his *In Tune with the World: A Theory of Festivity*, trans. Richard and Clara Winston (South Bend, IN: St. Augustine's Press, 1999), 44–51. Ratzinger cites this text of Pieper as he develops the theological basis of prayer and liturgy. Joseph Ratzinger, *The Feast of Faith: Approaches to a Theology of Liturgy*, trans. Graham Harrison (San Francisco: Ignatius Press, 1986), 26–27. Also see Pieper, *Leisure: The Basis of Culture*, trans. Alexander Dru (San Francisco: Ignatius Press, 2009), 65–75.

[72] Guardini, *Auf dem Wege*, 21, quoted in Ratzinger, *FSFD*, 247 (JRGS6/2, 732).

[73] As explained earlier, Guardini's purpose in articulating this primacy, in Ratzinger's

Guardini's assertion of the primacy of *logos* represents a recovery of theology's proper method, which is distinguished from other approaches to theological questions insofar as they give priority to *ethos*.[74] Ratzinger highlights this famous idea of Guardini's as a hermeneutical key to differentiate Guardini's approach to the liturgical movement from the method employed by the Benedictine monastery of Maria Laach in Germany's Eifel region. Whereas Guardini embraced the metaphysics of being in medieval thought, Odo Casel (1886–1948) and the monks of Maria Laach subordinate the use of philosophical thought and logic in favor of seeking the form (*eidos*) of mystery.[75] In Ratzinger's estimation, this approach "resulted in a certain narrowness that had no sense of extra-liturgical piety and bore within itself a tendency to archaeological investigation aimed at a pristine *restoration* of an earlier age."[76] Guardini's method was aimed at the larger question of *being*, which is found in the pursuit of the truth or the *logos*. Ratzinger, under the influence of Guardini, will develop an outline of the authentic spirit of the liturgy with this same end in mind. Ratzinger contends that "truth and worship stand in an indissociable relationship to each other; one cannot flourish without the other, however often they have gone their separate ways in the course of history."[77] The innate search for truth finds its fulfillment in divine worship. The true being or *logos*, whom every person seeks, is above all a living person that invites each person into a dialogue (*dia-logos*) of love.

Throughout his work Ratzinger emphasizes that *logos* is no mere abstraction or proposition, for the *Logos* has become flesh in the person

---

estimation, was "to defend the Thomistic position of *scientia speculativa:* a view of theology in which the meaning of christocentrism consists in transcending oneself and, through the *history* of God's dealings with mankind, making possible the encounter with the *being* of God." Ratzinger, *PCT,* 319.

[74] Ratzinger, *PCT,* 320: "Theology has to do with God, and it conducts its inquiry in the manner of philosophy. The challenge and the difficulty of such a concept will have become clear by now. Such a metaphysical (ontological) alignment of theology is not, as we have long feared, a betrayal of salvation history. On the contrary, if theology will remain true to its historical beginnings, to the salvation event in Christ to which the Bible bears witness, it must transcend history and speak ultimately of God himself. If it will remain true to the *practical Scientia speculativa*; it cannot start by being a *Scientia practica*. It must preserve the primacy of truth that is self-subsistent and that must be discovered in its self-ness before it can be measured in terms of its usefulness to mankind."

[75] Ratzinger, *FSFD,* 249 (JRGS6/2, 733–734).

[76] Ratzinger, *FSFD,* 249 (JRGS6/2, 734).

[77] Joseph Ratzinger, *The Nature and Mission of Theology*: *Approaches to Understanding Its Role in the Light of the Present Controversy* [hereafter, *NMT*], trans. Adrian Walker (San Francisco: Ignatius Press, 1995), 40.

of Jesus Christ. Ratzinger notes in his summary of Guardini's liturgical theology, philosophy, and Christology, "Man is open to the truth, but the truth is not out there somewhere; rather, it is in concrete existence, in the figure of Jesus Christ."[78] Faith is not merely an assent to set of propositions; it is a personal communion that the human person enters into through the Person of the incarnate *Logos*.[79]

Guardini himself stresses that the person of Jesus Christ is the central message of Christianity, a theme which will be emphasized by Ratzinger throughout his work. He maintains:

> This *Logos*, which is perfectly simple and yet immeasurably rich, is no order of forms and laws, no world of prototypes and arrangements, but *Someone*, He is the living son of the eternal Father. We can stand before Him, face to face. We can speak to Him and He answers, indeed, He Himself gives us the power to stand before Him and He can grant our request. We can love Him and He is able to give us a communion which reflects the intimacy in which He lies upon the bosom of the Father, and which St. John experienced when His Master permitted him to lay his head upon His heart. This fact established a contrast to everything which natural philosophy and piety can experience or invent. This *Logos*, this one and all, steps into history and becomes man.[80]

---

[78] Ratzinger, *FSFD*, 254 (JRGS6/2, 738). In his commentary on the Johannine characterization of the Lord as *Logos*, Ratzinger maintains that "the concept of *logos* acquires a new dimension. It no longer denotes simply the permeation of all being by meaning; it characterizes this man: he who is here is 'Word.' The concept of *logos*, which to the Greeks meant 'meaning' (*ratio*), changes here into 'word' (*verbum*). He who is here is Word; he is consequently 'spoken' and, hence, the pure relation between the speaker and the spoken to. Thus *logos* Christology, as 'word' theology, is once again the opening up of being to the idea of relationship. For again it is true that 'word' comes essentially 'from someone else' and 'to someone else'; word is an existence that is entirely way and openness." Ratzinger, *IC*, 189 (JRGS4, 180). Elsewhere, Ratzinger maintains a similar argument in Ratzinger, *DP*, 94: "Logos in the Johannine sense means not only *ratio*, but also *verbum*—not only 'mind,' but also 'discourse.' That is to say: the Christian God is not just reason, objective meaning, the geometry of the universe, but he is speech, relation, Word, and Love. He is sighted reason, which sees and hears, which can be called upon and has a personal character. The 'objective' meaning of the world is a subject, in relation to me."

[79] For a summary of Ratzinger's emphasis on the *Logos* as the Person of Jesus Christ, see Christopher S. Collins, *The Word Made Love: The Dialogical Theology of Joseph Ratzinger/Benedict XVI* (Collegeville, MN: Liturgical Press, 2013), 74–79.

[80] Romano Guardini, *The Word of God: On Faith, Hope and Charity*, trans. Stella Lange

This Christocentric approach in the writings of Guardini is characteristic of much of the theological work of the twentieth century. Ratzinger's theology is no exception of this characteristic in light of the influence of Guardini upon his thought. Communion with Jesus Christ restores the communion that the human person enjoyed in the beginning with the gift of sanctifying grace.

Pablo Blanco Sarto writes that, as a consequence of the absolute priority of the *logos* in the thought of Ratzinger, Ratzinger's thought is characterized by a certain *logos*-centrism (*logocentrismo*).[81] One of the fundamental truths about creation is that it was brought about by the word (the *Logos*), which has existed from the beginning (Gen 1:1; cf. John 1:1). Nature reflects the beauty of the *logos* because its very being originates from the Creator. The modern shift, which has been traced back to the univocal conception of being, according to Blessed Duns Scotus, is the beginning of the shift towards a desacramentalization of nature, according to many contemporary thinkers.[82]

Hans Boersma maintains that in light of Scotus's influence, "it became possible to deny the sacramentality of the relationship between

(Chicago: Henry Regnery, 1963), 28.

[81] Blanco Sarto, *La Teología de Joseph Ratzinger*, 161.

[82] This view was espoused by the pope emeritus, Benedict XVI. See his The Regensburg Lecture, no. 25. The citations for the text of this speech, which is known colloquially as "The Regensburg Lecture," will come from the official English translation of the Vatican, which is printed in James V. Schall, S.J., *The Regensburg Lecture* (South Bend, IN: St. Augustine's Press, 2007), 130–148. I will employ the numbers used by Schall and cite the text as "The Regensburg Lecture." Scotus opted for a univocal conception of being over Aquinas's analogical understanding. In the metaphysics of Scotus, there is no distinction between the being of God and the human person. Hence, the Creator and creature belong to the same basic metaphysical category. Whereas for St. Thomas, human creatures through their being participate in the divine nature, which for St. Thomas is a sheer act of to-be itself (*ipsum esse subsistens*); Scotus effectively separates the natural from the supernatural, which comes to fruition in the thought of Ockham. Robert Barron, *The Priority of Christ: Toward a Postliberal Catholicism* (Grand Rapids, MI: Brazos Press, 2007), 13–14. Also see David Burrell, C.S.C., *Analogy and Philosophical Language* (New Haven, CT: Yale University Press, 1973), 171–193; Louis Dupré, *Passage to Modernity: An Essay in the Hermeneutics of Nature and Culture* (New Haven, CT: Yale University Press, 1993), 170–176; John Milbank, *Theology and Social Theory: Beyond Secular Reason* (Cambridge, MA: Blackwell Publishers, 1995), 302–325; Catherine Pickstock, *After Writing: On the Liturgical Consummation of Philosophy* (Cambridge MA: Blackwell Publishers, 1998), 122–131; and Brad S. Gregory, *The Unintended Reformation: How a Religious Revolution Secularized Society* (Cambridge, MA : Harvard University Press, 2012), 36–38.

earthly objects and the Logos as their eternal archetype."[83]   If every created being is univocal, then each being possesses its own nature apart
from God. Boersma concludes that the "loss of analogy meant the loss
of sacramentality."[84] The world is perceived as a purely materialistic and
mechanistic reality in the modern world. This mentality has resulted in a
great alienation in the created order wherein the human person is at odds
with nature itself, other people, and God.

Ratzinger argues for a sacramental *logos* in order to uphold the analogy between creation and the Creator. The great difficulty of the twentieth
century has been what Ratzinger describes as a "crisis of sacramentality."[85]
In Ratzinger's estimation, the majority of people in modern culture have
"grown accustomed to seeing in the substance of things nothing but the
material for human labor—when, in short, the world is regarded as matter
and matter as material—initially there is no room left for that symbolic
transparency of reality toward the eternal on which the sacramental
principle is based."[86] In other words, there is only room for an immanentization for all created reality. Hence the modern *logos*, as described at the
beginning of this chapter by David L. Schindler, results in the reduction
of politics to power, sexuality to hedonistic lust, and so forth. This view
will also affect the understanding of liturgy and eschatology because the
presupposition of secular modernity precludes transcendence.

As a result of the dominance of an immanentized secular *logos* in
modernity, liturgy is reduced to a product that can be manipulated by the

---

[83]   Hans Boersma, *Heavenly Participation: The Weaving of a Sacramental Tapestry* (Grand
Rapids, MI: Eerdmans Publishing Company, 2011), 75. The self-sufficiency of the
individual, which results from the univocal conception of being, will lead to alienation between the person and God because the intimate union between every created
being with one another and God is severed. In the analogous conception of being, every
created being participates in the eternal logos of God. Boersma expands upon the consequences of the nominalist shift towards the univocity of being from the *analogia
entis*: "Nominalism deeply affects human beings' vertical and horizontal relationships.
The christological anchor of the Great Tradition had ensured the vertical link between
God and humanity: human beings received their being by participation in the eternal
Logos [the *analogia entis*]. This vertical link with the Word of God means that, in turn,
all human beings were horizontally related to one another: they all participated in a
common humanity. The realism of the Platonist-Christian ontology meant that what
united human beings was much more important than what divided them. Their common participation in the Logos provided unity and prevented fragmentation." Boersma,
*Heavenly Participation*, 89.

[84]   Boersma, *Heavenly Participation*, 75.

[85]   Ratzinger, JRCW11, 153 (JRGS11, 197).

[86]   Ratzinger, JRCW11, 153 (JRGS11, 198).

people. Eschatology is focused on the building of the kingdom of God here below. The disavowal of the existence of a transcendent logically stresses what is immanent. Ratzinger addresses both areas repeatedly by emphasizing the primacy of *logos*, which has been subordinated to *ethos*. With respect to the notion of *logos*, Ratzinger affirms the need to recover a truly sacramental *logos* (*communio*) over and above the dominant materialistic secular logos (*technē*). He characterizes the latter as a "de-sacramentalized [*entsakramentalisierte*] technological world."[87] Consistently, Ratzinger develops a truly sacramentalized view in his theology of liturgy and eschatology that is centered on Christ, the incarnate *Logos*, instead of the de-sacramentalized view with its focus on the centrality of the person.

A major theme in Ratzinger's theology of the liturgy is that the liturgy is the *actio Dei* and not merely a product to be manipulated according to the varying whims of the individual person. In "The Theology of the Liturgy," a lecture given at the Benedictine abbey in Fontgombault in 2001, Ratzinger cites the Second Vatican Council's definition of the liturgy as "an action of Christ the Priest and of his Body, which is the Church."[88] For Ratzinger, the "action of Christ" refers to the Paschal Mystery on the one hand and the celebration of the liturgy itself on the other. In both instances, he underscores the work of redemption and the liturgy as actions of God and not mere human actions.[89]

Consistent with his insistence upon the primacy of the *logos*, Ratzinger insists that the liturgy is the *opus Dei* or *actio Dei* and not the work of man. The false icon that embodies this perversion of worship on the part of the human person is the construction of the golden calf in the book of Exodus. Ratzinger defines the idolization of the golden calf as a "self-generated cult," whereby worship "becomes a feast that the community gives itself, a festival of self-affirmation."[90] Authentic worship is directed towards God and created by him, whereas this anti-worship is the product of the person. Elsewhere, Ratzinger writes, "Liturgy is God's work or it does not exist at all."[91] Unlike the golden calf, liturgy is not made by the human person

---

[87] Ratzinger, JRCW11, 156 (JRGS11, 200).

[88] *SC*, §7.

[89] Ratzinger underscores the tension between Jesus and history: "Thus in the liturgy, the present historical moment is transcended, leading into the permanent divine-human act of redemption. In it, Christ is really the responsible subject: it is the work of the Christ; but in it he draws history to himself, into this permanent act which is the locus of salvation." Ratzinger, JRCW11, 542 (JRGS11, 640).

[90] Ratzinger, JRCW11, 12 (JRGS11, 39–40).

[91] Ratzinger, JRCW11, 466, (JRGS11, 555).

alone. Ratzinger asserts that the "liturgy cannot be 'made.' This is why it has to be simply received as a given reality and continually revitalized."[92]

The primacy of God's work is fundamental for Ratzinger's theology of liturgy; liturgy is an *opus Dei* and thus "all *opera hominum* [must] come to an end."[93] Commenting on Guardini's *The Church of the Lord*, Ratzinger asserts that Guardini learned to see in the Incarnation

> the presence of the Lord who has made the Church his body. Only if that is so is there a simultaneity of Jesus Christ with us. And only if it this exists is there real liturgy which is not a mere remembrance of the Paschal Mystery but its true presence. Once again, only if this is the case is liturgy a participation in the trinitarian dialogue between Father, Son, and Holy Spirit. Only in this way is it not our "doing" but the *opus Dei*—God's action in and with us.[94]

The Church enters into the prayer of Jesus Christ the High Priest, who offers himself to the Father in the Holy Spirit. Through the celebration of the liturgy, the Church actualizes her identity as a visible communion, which reflects the communion of love of the triune God. This visible communion is also an anticipation of the communion that awaits all of humanity in the eschaton.

That Ratzinger maintains that the work of eschatology is first and foremost an *opus Dei* supports our fundamental thesis concerning the primacy of *logos* in Ratzinger's theology. Ratzinger argues that "Jesus is opposed to any form of righteousness, whether political or ethical, that tries to achieve the Kingdom of God by its own volition."[95] Christians,

---

[92] Ratzinger, *Feast of Faith*, 66.

[93] Ratzinger, JRCW11, 206 (JRGS11, 256–257).

[94] Ratzinger, *Joseph Ratzinger in Communio*, vol. 1, *The Unity of the Church*, ed. David L. Schindler and Nicholas J. Healy (Grand Rapids, MI: Eerdmans, 2010), 33. In light of Ratzinger's emphasis on the liturgy as the *opus Dei* or *actio Dei*, Mariusz Biliniewicz summarizes Ratzinger's understanding of active participation (*participatio actuosa*) as "being a part of the action." Biliniewicz explains, "'The action' in the liturgy is not the action of a human, but the action of God. Therefore, we are a part of that action (we participate) when we are included in the act that God himself performs in the sacrifice of the Eucharist." Mariusz Biliniewicz, *The Liturgical Vision of Pope Benedict XVI: A Theological Inquiry* (Bern: Peter Lang, 2013), 57.

[95] Joseph Ratzinger, *Eschatology: Death and Eternal Life*, ed. Aidan Nichols, O.P., trans. Michael Waldstein, 2nd ed. (Washington, DC: The Catholic University of America Press, 2007), 31; Joseph Ratzinger, *Auferstehung und ewiges Leben: Beiträge*

through the gift of grace received from the sacraments, are called to respond to their vocation as a relational being to enter into communion with God and neighbor. This relationality, which is initiated in Baptism, is strengthened by the Holy Eucharist and fully realized in the eschaton. Ratzinger describes heaven as the full realization of the "integration of the 'I' into the body of Christ."[96]

The transformation of the individual "I" into the communal (ecclesial) "we," through his communion with the Infinite "Thou," is a constant theme throughout the works of Ratzinger. This unity can be fully realized only by God. Communion with the incarnate *Logos* enables the human person to be drawn into Jesus Christ's "being for all."[97] The celebration of the liturgy brings about what Ratzinger describes as an "eschatological realism." In an interview with Peter Seewald, Pope Benedict XVI maintains that the eschaton is not a "*fata morgana* or some kind of fictitious utopia, but [corresponds] exactly to reality."[98] A more detailed account of the profound implications of this statement become clearer in examining the relationship between the liturgy and eschatology.

It is clear in the words cited above and in the rest of his comments in addressing Seewald's question regarding "eschatological realism" that Benedict maintains the view that Jesus instituted the Last Supper as "the sacrament of inaugurated eschatology," to borrow a phrase from the work of the Scripture scholar Brant Pitre. The recent work of Pitre offers insight into the radical nature of Ratzinger's claim as he argues that the Last Supper was the beginning of a new exodus, wherein *"Jerusalem is the point of departure and the kingdom of God is the ultimate destination."*[99]

---

zur Eschatologie und zur Theologie der Hoffnung [hereafter, JRGS10], Gesammelte Schriften 10, ed. Gerhard Ludwig Müller (Freiburg: Herder, 2012), 61.

[96] Ratzinger, *Eschatology*, 235 (JRGS10, 235).

[97] See Pope Benedict XVI, Encyclical Letter *Spe Salvi* [hereafter, *SS*] (Vatican City: Libreria Editrice Vaticana, 2007), 28.

[98] Benedict XVI, *Light of the World: The Pope, the Church, and the Signs of the Times: A Conversation with Peter Seewald*, trans. Michael J. Miller and Adrian J. Walker (San Francisco: Ignatius Press, 2010), 180.

[99] See Brant Pitre, *Jesus and the Last Supper* (Grand Rapids, MI: Eerdmans, 2015), 444–512, here 511–12; emphasis in the original. The phrase "the sacrament of inaugurated eschatology" is a modification of the words used by the English exegete C. H. Dodd, who described the Eucharist as a "sacrament of realized eschatology." C. H. Dodd, *The Parables of the Kingdom* (New York: Scribner, 1961), 164. Commenting upon Dodd's notion, Ratzinger maintains, "From his starting point in modern exegesis, Dodd thus recreated that synthesis whereby the faith of the Church throughout the centuries has interpreted the relation of past, present and future, in the eschatological message of

Every celebration of the Eucharist is both a realization and foretaste of the eschaton insofar as Jesus Christ does truly come back again. Further, Jesus offers the grace to each recipient to grow in the freedom that is characteristic of the kingdom of God, which anticipates the ultimate freedom to be realized in the kingdom in heaven. The Eucharist is both anticipation and realization of the eschatological kingdom. According to Ratzinger, "This eschatological realism becomes present in the Eucharist: we go out to meet him—as the One who comes—and he comes already now in anticipation of this hour, which one day will arrive once and for all."[100] In the liturgy, the Church is able to hear the *logos* proclaimed and meet the *Logos* in his sacramental form, which is a both a foretaste and realization of the coming of the incarnate *Logos* in the Parousia.

Ratzinger thus develops his theology of liturgy and eschatology in a Guardinian key. He hopes to address the gap between God and humanity that has been created by the modern materialistic conception of the *logos*. The subordination of *logos* to *ethos* contributes to the overshadowing of sacramentality. Ultimately both Guardini and Ratzinger, in emphasizing the need to understand the authentic "spirit of the liturgy," seek to affirm the liturgy as first and foremost the work of God.

At the center of the liturgy's essence is Jesus Christ himself, who enables the individual human person ("I") to enter into communion with others ("thou"). This communion of every person as a "we" in Christ is a realization and anticipation of the unity of the eschaton. In order to understand fully the significance of the *logos'* primacy for Ratzinger, the section below will highlight some of the themes primarily from his Regensburg Address as Pope Benedict XVI, which is a culmination and summary of his persistent thesis concerning the primacy of the *logos* over *ethos* and an outline of the consequences of subordinating *logos* to *ethos* that extend beyond its effects on the theology of liturgy.

---

the New Testament. In German language exegetical studies, and the theology which took its cue from them, such a view could find neither house nor home. Admittedly, the methodological basis of this mediation of the Church's synthesis needs to be thought out afresh. Yet is should be clear that the native power of Christianity, something which will outlive all the ideas of the academics, draws its strength from just this synthesis. This synthesis is what binds together faith and life in a real and effective manner, whereas neither the actualism of the early Barth, nor Bultmann's theological Existentialism, nor a theology with the formal structure of salvation history but deprived of this life-giving background will ever be more than somebody's compilation." Ratzinger, *Eschatology*, 56 (JRGS10, 83).

[100] Benedict XVI, *Light of the World*, 180.

## THE CONSISTENCY AND CENTRALITY OF THE LOGOS IN RATZINGER'S THEOLOGY

The key to understanding Ratzinger's use of the word *logos* throughout his works is realizing that *logos* is to be understood as truth *and* love.[101] In light of his emphasis of Christ as the eternal "I," who lives in eternal relation to the Father (the eternal "Thou"), Ratzinger claims it "is the identity of *logos* (truth) and love and thus makes love in the *logos*, the truth of human existence."[102] Jesus Christ's very being is derived from the love of the Father. Consequently, truth and love coincide with one another. Reason has certain limitations because truth is a person and not simply an abstract idea. Love alone can overcome the shortcomings of reason.[103]

In a paper given at a conference commemorating the twenty-fifth

---

[101] On the relationship between truth and love, see Pope Francis, Encyclical Letter *Lumen Fidei* (Vatican City: Libreria Editrice Vaticana, 2013), §§ 26–28. A strong argument can be made for the influence of Benedict XVI on this particular excerpt. Also see Kurt Koch, *Das Geheimnis des Senfkorns: Grundzüge des theologischen Denkens von Papst Benedikt XVI* (Regensburg: Friedrich Pustet, 2010), 14–44.

[102] Ratzinger, *IC*, 208 (JRGS4, 195).

[103] On this theme, see Ratzinger's comments on the theology of St. Bonaventure in Ratzinger, *NMT*, 26–27. Ratzinger outlines the relationship between truth and love and the implication this has for theology and philosophy. Also see Pope Benedict XVI, General Audience, March 3, 2010, "St. Bonaventure," in *Doctors of the Church* (Huntington, IN: Our Sunday Visitor, 2011) 175–193. In one of his Wednesday audiences on the Doctors of the Church, Benedict focuses his attention on the theology of Bonaventure wherein he highlights the primacy of love for Bonaventure: "For St. Bonaventure the ultimate destiny of the human being is to love God, to encounter him, and to be united in his and our love." Benedict XVI, "St. Bonaventure," 190. St. Bonaventure, under the influence of Pseudo-Dionysius, emphasizes love's ability to exceed the capacity of reason in the assent towards the truth. Further, in the text used for his General Audience, Benedict asserts, "Whereas for St. Augustine the *intellectus*, the seeing with reason and the heart, is the ultimate category of knowledge, Pseudo-Dionysius takes a further step: in the ascent toward God one can reach a point in which reason no longer sees. But in the night of the intellect love still sees; it sees what is inaccessible to reason. Love goes beyond reason, it sees further, it enters more profoundly into God's mystery." Benedict XVI, "St. Bonaventure," 192. Pseudo-Dionysius had a strong influence on the development of medieval theology in Benedict's estimation. See Pope Benedict XVI, General Audience, May 14, 2008, "Pseudo-Dionysius, the Areopagite," in *The Fathers,* vol. 2 (Huntington, IN: Our Sunday Visitor Press, 2010), 27–32. In addition to St. Bonaventure, the theology of Pseudo-Dionysius would influence other medieval theologians such as St. Bernard (1090–1153), William of Saint-Thierry (d. ca. 1148), Isaac d'Étoile (d. ca. 1169), Robert Grosseteste (1168–1253), and St. Albert the Great (d. 1280). William Riordan, *Divine Light: The Theology of Denys the Areopagite* (San Francisco: Ignatius Press, 2008), 61. Riordan's work is an excellent introduction to the thought of Denys the Areopagite (Pseudo-Dionysius).

anniversary of Pope Pius XII's encyclical on the devotion to the Sacred Heart, *Haurietis Aquas*, Ratzinger addresses the inadequacies of using reason alone in the pursuit of truth.[104] He cites various texts to highlight love's ability to see what reason is unable to see: "Gregory the Great's *'Amor ipse notitia est'* (Love is knowledge itself); Hugh of St. Victor's *'Intrat dilectio et appropinquat, ubi scientia foris est'* (Love enters and comes close where knowledge has been left outside); or Richard of St. Victor's beautiful formulation: *'Amor oculus est et amare videre est'* (Love is the eye, and to love is to see)."[105]

*Logos* finds its full meaning in love, which only Christ fully reveals to all of humanity. Ratzinger points out that Christianity moves beyond the God of philosophy, who is described as pure thought: "The *logos* of the whole world, the creative original thought, is at the same time love; in fact this thought is creative because, as thought, it is love, and, as love, it is thought."[106] Love and truth are identical for Ratzinger; thus, grasping this point is fundamental for appreciating his theology of the Sacred Heart, which becomes a central component of his Christology.[107] His

---

[104] Joseph Ratzinger, *Behold the Pierced One: An Approach to Spiritual Christology* [hereafter, *BPO*], trans. Graham Harrison (San Francisco: Ignatius Press, 1986), 47–69 (JRGS6/2, 672–690). This address is also published as Joseph Ratzinger, "The Paschal Mystery as Core and Foundation of Devotion to the Sacred Heart," in *Towards a Civilization of Love: A Symposium on the Scriptural and Theological Foundations of Devotion to the Heart of Jesus*, trans. Erasmo Leiva-Merikakis (San Francisco: Ignatius Press, 1981), 145–165. See the parallels of thought in Hans Urs von Balthasar, *Theo-Logic*, vol. 2, *Truth of God*, trans. Adrian J. Walker (San Francisco: Ignatius Press, 2004), 27–33, here 28: "Thus, where one defines God (Thomas Aquinas) or Christ (Bonaventure) as the formal object of theology, the first thing this object demands is to be loved." Also see Pierre Rousselot, S.J. "Spiritual Love and Apperceptive Synthesis," in *Essays on Love and Knowledge*, ed. Andrew Tallon and Pol Vandevelde, trans. Andrew Tallon, Pol Vandevelde, and Alan Vingelette (Milwaukee, WI: Marquette University Press, 2008), 119–134; Rousselot, *Eyes of Faith*, trans. Joseph Donceel, S.J. (New York: Fordham University Press, 1990), 49–61. Rousselot argues for the mutual need for both knowledge and love in the act of faith.

[105] Ratzinger, *BPO*, 55 [Ratzinger, JRGS6/2, 678–679]. Pope Benedict XVI speaks of "a heart which sees." *Encyclical Letter Deus Caritas Est* [hereafter, *DCE*] (Vatican City: Libreria Editrice Vaticana, 2005), §31. The Patristic theme of love as form of knowledge is repeated throughout the writings of Ratzinger/Benedict.

[106] Ratzinger, *IC*, 148 (JRGS4, 145). Also see Ratzinger, *IC*, 158–61 (JRGS4, 154–161).

[107] Peter John McGregor, *Heart to Heart: The Spiritual Christology of Joseph Ratzinger* (Eugene, OR: Pickwick Publications, 2016), 62–98; 279–335. McGregor's work is a great contribution to the understanding of Ratzinger's Christology. He is able to demonstrate the significance of Ratzinger's spiritual Christology within Ratzinger's theological oeuvre. McGregor is able to substantiate the importance of Neo-Chalcedonian Christology

Christology forms the foundation for his anthropology, his theology of liturgy, and his eschatology.[108]

Due to his interest in preserving the primacy of *logos*, one of Ratzinger's main intellectual pursuits concerns the relationship between the God of philosophy and the God of faith, which was the subject of his inaugural lecture as a professor of fundamental theology at the University of Bonn in 1959.[109] He has always been interested in the relationship and the affinity

---

in Ratzinger's thought. Also see Sara Butler, M.S.B.T., "Benedict XVI: Apostle of the 'Pierced Heart of Jesus,'" in *The Pontificate of Benedict XVI: Its Premises and Promises*, ed. William G. Rusch (Grand Rapids, MI: Eerdmans Publishing, 2009), 144–167. For a brief treatment of various Christologies among Protestant and Catholic thinkers who relate Christology with the heart, see Edward T. Oakes, S.J., *Infinity Dwindled to Infancy: A Catholic and Evangelical Christology* (Grand Rapids, MI: Eerdmans Publishing, 2011), 271–300. Also see Bertrand de Margerie, S.J., *Christ for the World: The Heart of the Lamb: A Treatise on Christology*, trans. Malachy Carroll (Chicago, IL: Franciscan Herald Press, 1973). De Margerie focuses on Christology with the hope of highlighting the co-redemptive role the Church has in communion with the eucharistic or Sacred Heart of Jesus.

[108] See Helmut Hoping, "Gemeinschaft mit Christus: Christologie und Liturgie bei Joseph Ratzinger," *Internationale Katholische Zeitschrift Communio* 35 (2006): 557–572. Hoping argues that spiritual Christology is the foundation for Ratzinger's theology of liturgy. Also see Hoping, "Christologie und Liturgie bei Joseph Ratzinger/Benedikt XVI," in *Zur Mitte der Theologie im Werk von Joseph Ratzinger/Benedikt XVI*, eds. Maximilian Heim and Justinus C. Pech (Regensburg: Friedrich Pustet, 2013), 109–121. Hoping reiterates the same thesis in his article from *Communio*.

[109] This lecture has been published with a commentary by Heino Sonnemans, ed., *Joseph Ratzinger-Benedikt XVI, Der Gott des Glaubens und der Gott der Philosophen. Ein Beitrag zum Problem der theologia naturalis* (Leutesdorf: Johannes, 2005). For a summary and further commentary on this inaugural lecture, see de Gaál, *The Theology of Pope Benedict XVI*, 73–77; Emery de Gaál, *O Lord, I Seek Your Countenance: Explorations and Discoveries in Pope Benedict XVI's Theology* (Steubenville, OH: Emmaus Academic, 2018), 71–81; Hansjürgen Verweyen, *Joseph Ratzinger—Benedikt XVI: Die Entwicklung seines Denkens* (Darmstadt: Primus Verlag, 2007), 28–30; Guerriero, *Benedict XVI*, 124–130. Also see James Corkery, S.J., *Joseph Ratzinger's Theological Ideas: Wise Cautions and Legitimate Hopes* (Mahwah, NJ: Paulist Press, 2009), 30–31. Corkery argues that the unity between the God of philosophy and faith is the first facial feature of Ratzinger's theology. The pope emeritus himself comments that the subject of this lecture originated with his study of Pascal in a seminar with Gottlieb Söhngen in which they read Romano Guardini's book on Pascal. The work by Guardini focused on Pascal's *Memorial*, which Benedict XVI notes is about the "'God of faith,' the 'God of Abraham, Isaac and Jacob,' as a contrast to the 'God of the philosophers.'" Pope Benedict XVI (with Peter Seewald), *Last Testament: In His Own Words,* trans. Jacob Philips (New York: Bloomsbury, 2016), 104. On Guardini's work on Pascal, *Christliches Bewußtsein: Versuche über Pascal*, see von Balthasar, *Romano Guardini*, 69–73. On the larger theme of faith (God of Abraham) and reason (God of philosophy), see Ralph Weimann, *Dogma*

between reason and faith.[110] His former student Vincent Twomey comments, "For Ratzinger, 'reason' is our capacity for truth (and, therefore, for God). Like language, reason is at the same time both personal and communal by nature. Indeed, so is revelation, the social dimension of which is found in the human-divine complex of tradition/Church."[111]

Throughout his theological work Ratzinger has demonstrated the unity between reason and faith. As discussed above, faith purifies reason and enables him to identify *logos* with love: "The primacy of the Logos and the primacy of love proved to be identical. The *Logos* was seen to be, not merely a mathematical reason at the basis of all things, but a creative love taken to the point of becoming sympathy, suffering with the creature."[112] Authentic *logos* is reason that is truly liberated and elevated by faith; philosophy is made complete by theology. The god of philosophers—an object of reason—can become an object of idolatry, unlike the God of Abraham. Consistently throughout his work, Ratzinger draws our attention to the primacy of *logos* to reorient the human person to the truth about himself, God, culture, and the world.

The *logos*, which the Christian faith has received from its Hellenic influence, is crucial for fully comprehending the human person. Ratzinger

---

*und Fortschritt bei Joseph Ratzinger* (Paderborn: Schöningh, 2012), 79–117; Verweyen, *Joseph Ratzinger—Benedikt XVI*, 99–105. On the unity of the God of faith (faith) and the God of philosophers (reason) elsewhere in the writings of Ratzinger, see Ratzinger *IC*, 137–50 (JRGS4, 136–147); *NMT*, 13–29; *Faith and the Future*, trans. Ronald Walls (San Francisco: Ignatius Press, 2009), 61–85; *Truth and Tolerance* [hereafter, *TT*], trans. Henry Taylor (San Francisco: Ignatius Press, 2004), 138–209.

[110] See Aidan Nichols, O.P., *Conversation of Faith and Reason: Modern Catholic Thought from Hermes to Benedict XVI* (Chicago: Liturgy Training Publications, 2009), 190–206. Nichols underscores the relationship between faith and reason throughout Ratzinger's works with a particular focus on *Introduction to Christianity*, *Truth and Tolerance*, *The Nature and Mission of Theology*, and the *Regensburg Address*.

[111] D. Vincent Twomey, S.V.D., *Pope Benedict XVI: The Conscience of Our Age—A Theological Portrait* (San Francisco: Ignatius Press, 2007), 54.

[112] *TT*, 182. Elsewhere, Ratzinger maintains, "God is Logos. But there is a second characteristic. The Christian faith in God tells us also that God—eternal Reason—is Love. It tells us that he is not a being turned in on himself, without relation to others. Precisely because he is sovereign, because he is the Creator, because he embraces everything, he is Relation and he is Love. Faith in the Incarnation of God in Jesus Christ, and in his suffering and death for mankind, is the supreme expression of a conviction that the heart of all morality, the heart of being itself and its deepest principle, is love." Joseph Ratzinger, *Europe: Today and Tomorrow*, trans. Michael J. Miller (San Francisco: Ignatius Press, 2007), 97. Also see Joseph Ratzinger, *Values in a Time of Upheaval*, trans. Brian McNeil (San Francisco: Ignatius Press, 2006), 112–13.

affirms the centrality of *logos* in light of the writings of the Church Father Origen and the work of the historian Endre von Ivánka (1902–1974): "It is the Logos which is at the center of us all—without our knowing—for the center of man is the heart, and in the heart there is the ἡγεμονικόν—the guiding energy of the whole, which is the Logos."[113] In Ratzinger's view, the center of the human person is not the intellect but the heart. According to Ratzinger, who draws once again upon the thought of Ivánka, "Here the word 'heart' has expanded beyond the reason and denotes 'a deeper level of spiritual/intellectual existence where direct contact takes place with the divine.'"[114] Hence, it is the pierced Sacred Heart of Christ that allows Christians to enter into an intimate knowledge of the Lord, who is love itself. As a consequence of modernity's self-limiting divorce between reason and faith, and modernity's exercise of faith without the *logos*, the human person is unable to know and to love fully. It is the primacy of *logos* that Ratzinger is interested in reiterating in his papal address at the University of Regensburg.

On September 12, 2006, Pope Benedict XVI gave a lecture to the faculty of the University of Regensburg entitled "Faith, Reason and the University: Memories and Reflections" to highlight the essential unity between faith and its proper relation to *logos*, the potential consequences and implications of separating faith and reason, and the primacy of the *logos*.[115] Although Benedict's concern was to underscore the relationship between faith and *logos*, the media highlighted the following quotation from Byzantine Emperor Manuel II: "Show me just what Mohammed brought that was new, and there you will find things only evil and inhuman, such as his command to spread by the sword the faith he preached."[116]

---

[113] Ratzinger, *BPO*, 67 (JRGS6/2, 688).

[114] Ratzinger, *BPO*, 68 (JRGS6/2, 689). For a definitive and thorough philosophical exploration of the heart and affectivity, see Dietrich von Hildebrand, *The Heart: An Analysis of Human and Divine Affectivity*, ed. John F. Crosby (South Bend, IN: St. Augustine's Press, 2007).

[115] On January 17, 2008, as Supreme Pontiff, Benedict was supposed to give another public lecture on the theme of faith and reason at Rome's La Sapienza University. Hostile protests from members of the faculty and student body resulted in the cancellation of Benedict's appearance; nevertheless, the text of the speech was made available. For a summary of this text and its relation to the Regensburg Lecture, see Nichols, *Conversation of Faith and Reason*, 201–206. For a succinct history of theology (faith) and philosophy (reason) in relation to the mission of the university, see Alasdair MacIntyre, *God, Philosophy, Universities: A Selective History of the Catholic Philosophical Tradition* (New York: Rowan & Littlefield Publishers, Inc., 2009).

[116] Manuel II Paléologue, *Entretiens avec un Musulman. 7e Controverse, Sources Chrétiennes*

The focus on this quotation apart from the full context of the Regensburg Lecture misses the fundamental point, which Benedict makes as he draws upon the writings of Manuel II: "Violence is incompatible with the nature of God and the nature of the Soul."[117] In the words of Manuel II, "not acting reasonably (σὺν λόγω) is contrary to God's nature."[118] This is Benedict's main argument against the incompatibility between faith and violence. Acting with reason or *logos* precludes the use of force because it is

---

n. 115, ed. Theodore Khoury (Paris: Édition du Cerf, 1966), 240–41, quoted in *The Regensburg Lecture*, no. 12. In recognition of the tragic misunderstanding and misrepresentation of this quotation, Benedict writes this in a footnote added to a published version of his lecture: "In the Muslim world, this quotation has unfortunately been taken as an expression of my personal position, thus arousing understandable indignation. I hope that the reader of my text can see immediately that this sentence does not express my personal view of the Qur'an, for which I have the respect due to the holy book of a great religion. In quoting the text of the Emperor Manuel II, I intended solely to draw out the essential relationship between faith and reason. On this point I am in agreement with Manuel II, but without endorsing his polemic." Nevertheless, the fallout that occurred in the Muslim world led to a reopening of a dialogue that remains pertinent. In a response to the journalist Peter Seewald, Benedict affirms, "It became evident that Islam needs to clarify two questions in regard to public dialogue, that is, the questions concerning its relation to violence and its relation to reason. It [The Regensburg Lecture] was an important first step that now there was within Islam itself a realization of the duty and the need to clarify these questions, which has since led to an internal reflection among Muslim scholars, a reflection that has in turn become a theme of dialogue with the Church." Benedict XVI, *Light of the World*, 98. For commentary on the relationship between freedom and religion as it relates to the Regensburg Lecture specifically and the treatment of this topic in light of both Christian and Islamic theology, see Martin Rehak, "Die Freiheit der Religion: Nachbetrachtungen zur Regensburger Vorlesung," in *Symphonie des Glaubens*, 171–218.

[117] *The Regensburg Lecture*, no. 13.

[118] Manuel II Paléologue, *Entretiens*, 144–45, quoted in *The Regensburg Lecture*, no. 13. God's very nature is *logos*, which is characterized as both reasonable and loving. In an earlier address, prior to his papacy, Ratzinger states, "God is Logos. But there is a second characteristic. The Christian faith in God tells us also that God—eternal Reason—is Love. It tells us that he is not a being turned in on himself, without relation to others. Precisely because he is sovereign, because he is the Creator, because he embraces everything, he is Relation and he is Love. Faith in the Incarnation of God in Jesus Christ, and in his suffering and death for mankind, is the supreme expression of a conviction that the heart of all morality, the heart of being itself and its deepest principle, is love. This affirmation is the most resolute refusal of every ideology of violence; it is the true *apologia* for man and for God." Ratzinger, *Europe*, 97. This text comes from a conference given by Ratzinger at the Church of Saint-Étienne in Caen, June 5, 2004, on the occasion of the sixtieth anniversary of the landing of the Allied forces in France during World War II.

opposed to God's very nature. The use of irrational violence as a result of the separation of faith from *logos* represents an extreme form of immanentizing the eschaton. In the absence of the *logos*, the human person becomes the uncreated, and casts judgment upon others in the name of religion using terror and violence.

Christianity is formed in part by the unity between the reason of the Greeks and the faith of the Jews. Benedict accentuates the use of *logos* in the Johannine tradition as representative of the "profound harmony between what is Greek in the best sense of the word and the Biblical understanding of faith in God."[119] According to St. John, the *logos* has existed from the beginning, and this *Logos* is God.[120] A synthesis between faith and reason developed early in the Church only to be severed, in Benedict's estimation, by late medieval theology, beginning with the voluntarism of Duns Scotus.[121] In response to the developments in theology following Scotus, Benedict avers, "God does not become more divine when we push him away from us in a sheer, impenetrable voluntarism; rather, the truly divine God is the God who has revealed himself as *logos* and, as *logos*, has acted and continues to act lovingly on our behalf."[122] God's acts of love flow from his being as the *Logos*. Consequently, Benedict affirms once again with St. Paul that Christian worship is *logikē latreia*.[123] Christians offer true worship in accordance with the *logos* and not in spite of it.

The nominalism and the voluntarism of the fourteenth century laid the foundation for various forms of dehellenization, which emerged in the Reformation in the sixteenth century and the liberal theology of the

---

[119] *The Regensburg Lecture*, no. 17.

[120] *The Regensburg Lecture*, no. 18. The Prologue of St. John (John 1:1–18) will serve as a fundamental Scripture passage as Pope Benedict develops a theology of the *Logos* in his Apostolic Exhortation *Verbum Domini*. See *The Regensburg Lecture*, no. 5: "[The Prologue of St. John] is a magnificent text, one which offers a synthesis of the entire Christian faith." Later in the Exhortation, Benedict notes that the "*Logos* is truly *eternal*, and from eternity *is himself God*. God was never without his *Logos*. The Word exists before creation. Consequently at the heart of the divine life there is communion, there is absolute gift" (no. 6).

[121] *The Regensburg Lecture*, no. 25. On the effect of the primacy of freedom and the will in the thought of Scotus on medieval thought, see Josef Pieper, *Scholasticism: Personalities and Problems of Medieval Philosophy*, trans. Richard and Clara Winston (South Bend, IN: St. Augustine's Press, 2001), 136–151. Pieper outlines the consequences for the relationship between faith and reason in light of the *via Scoti* and the influence his writings will have on William of Ockham.

[122] *The Regensburg Lecture*, no. 27.

[123] *The Regensburg Lecture*, no. 28.

nineteenth and twentieth centuries, as represented by the Lutheran theologian Adolf von Harnack (1851–1930).[124] The latter form is the focus of
the remainder of Benedict's address. This second type of dehellenization is
rooted in Kant's "self-limitation of reason."[125] Reason is limited by what can
be measured empirically because matter or nature is limited to what is visible. Benedict explains the dire consequences of this misguided and limited
*logos*: "The subject then decides on the basis of his experiences, what he considers tenable in matters of religion, and the subjective 'conscience' becomes
the sole arbiter of what is ethical."[126] The radical autonomy of the individual
and an ethic based on utility, power, and pleasure remains the "moral" norm
in contemporary secular culture. Consequently, *logos* becomes subordinated
to the *ethos* of the person's capricious will. The Regensburg Lecture is simply
one of the many addresses in which Benedict expresses his invitation for all
of humanity to enter into dialogue with the incarnate *Logos*. The *dia-logos* is
fundamental for a fully developed human person.

In Benedict's view, the key to understanding the inherently eschatological nature of the liturgy is to emphasize the dialogical nature of the
human person. The emphasis on dehellenization within theology, which
began with Adolf von Harnack, has contributed to an emphasis upon the
primacy of *ethos*. It is evident to Benedict in the Regensburg Address that

---

[124] According to Benedict, he has dealt with the theme of Hellenization in more detail in
his inaugural lecture as a newly appointed professor at the University of Bonn in 1959.
Also see Ratzinger's comments on Hellenization in *TT*, 90–95.

[125] *The Regensburg Lecture*, no. 40. Ratzinger explains the self-limitation imposed by Kantian epistemology: "According to Kant, man cannot perceive the voice of being in itself;
he can hear it only indirectly, in the postulates of practical reason, which remain so to
say as the last narrow slit through which contact with the really real, with his eternal
destiny, can still reach him. For the rest, for what the activity of his reason can substan-
tively grasp, man can go only so far as the categorical allows. He is therefore limited to
the positive, to the empirical, to "exact" science, in which by definition something or
someone Wholly Other, a new beginning from another plane has no room to occur."
Joseph Ratzinger, "Biblical Interpretation in Conflict: On the Foundations and the
Itinerary of Exegesis Today," in *Opening Up the Scriptures: Joseph Ratzinger and the
Foundations of Biblical Interpretation*, ed. José Granados, Carlos Granados, and Luis
Sánchez-Navarro (Grand Rapids, MI: Eerdmans Publishing Company, 2008), 18. The
predominance of Kantian presuppositions in the interpretation of Sacred Scripture has
resulted in a secularized hermeneutic. In response to this limited method, Benedict
calls for the use of a hermeneutic of faith and the harmony of faith and reason in the
interpretation of the Scriptures. See Benedict XVI, *Verbum Domini*, §§29–36. For
more commentary on the effect of Kant on the relationship between faith and reason in
general, see Ratzinger, *TT*, 130–137; and Ratzinger, *NMT*, 13–41.

[126] *The Regensburg Lecture*, no. 48.

this dehellenization has implications for the relationship between faith and reason. In addition, it is important to note that dehellenization has affected the unity between salvation history and metaphysics, which forms the "fundamental crisis" of our age. True worship will always be in accordance with the *logos*, and eschatology must always begin with asserting the primacy of *logos*.

The liturgy and eschatology cannot be fully understood without a proper definition of *logos* or by subordinating *logos* to *ethos*. A materialist ontology guides the modern world. In practice, this ontology can reduce the liturgy to a display of the person's creative abilities or make it subject to the personal preferences of the individual community of believers.[127] As it has been established above, the liturgy enables every individual believer (the "I") to worship Jesus Christ, the source of authentic freedom, as part of the ecclesial "we." Ratzinger maintains that every person finds his authentic liberation as a result of the "being-taken-out-of-himself that goes beyond reflection—not in continuing to be himself, but in going out from himself."[128]

There is never truly an individual "I" in the celebration of the liturgy, as demonstrated above with the thought of Guardini and reechoed in the theology of Ratzinger. The "I" used in the prayers of the liturgy refers to communal "I" of the Body of Christ. At the same time, the liturgical encounter with the eschaton points to the reality that individuals united to the incarnate *Logos* in prayer are meant to experience the gift of salvation as a unified group. Whereas the materialist ontology affirms an autonomous individual, the sacramental ontology emphasizes the relational communion that should be the true end of human existence. God's eschatological action, as exhibited by the Resurrection, highlights the communal existence for all of humanity in Ratzinger's view: "The Resurrection has both a cosmic and a future-oriented character and that the corresponding Christian faith is a faith of hope in the fullness of a promise that encompasses the whole cosmos."[129]

---

[127] Again in his interview with Peter Seewald, Benedict XVI clearly states, "[The liturgy] is not about our doing something, about our demonstrating our creativity, in other words, about the displaying everything we can do. Liturgy is precisely not a show, a piece of theater, a spectacle. Rather, it gets its life from the Other. This has to become evident, too. This is why the fact that the ecclesial form has been given in advance is so important. It can be reformed in matters of detail, but it cannot be reinvented every time by the community. It is not a question, as I said, of self-production. The point is to go out of and beyond ourselves, to give ourselves to him, and to let ourselves be touched by him." Benedict, *Light of the World*, 156.

[128] Ratzinger, *PCT*, 171.

[129] Ratzinger, *PCT*, 187.

The significance of this "cosmic" and "future-oriented character" of the Resurrection in Ratzinger's thought means "a rejection of the individualization of [the person], the ordering of the "I" to the "we," the orientation of Christianity to the future as much as to the past."[130] The modern view of liturgy and eschatology, under the influence of a culture which emphasizes the autonomy of the "rugged individual," leads to alienation of the person with himself and others. The lack of full transcendence in the reigning materialist or secular ontology leads to a view that emphasizes action (*ethos*) over and above *logos*.

Ratzinger's *logos*-centrism is an example of what Father Matthew Lamb describes as "wisdom (or sapiential) eschatology."[131] Contrary to the self-imposed limitations upon reason, Ratzinger maintains that the human *logos* finds its fulfillment in an illuminated faith directed towards the incarnate *Logos*. Reason alone is insufficient, and faith expressed by the Creed is fully realized in *cultus*. Cultic worship, which has been established throughout our work, is most aptly described by the Pauline *logikē latreia* (cf. Rom 12:1). Sacramental communion with God in Jesus Christ leads to communion with one's neighbor in love. This is a foretaste of the eschatological communion that is realized for the Church triumphant.

Worship is foundational for a proper *ethos* of charity. Ratzinger emphasizes this point: "It is only, therefore, when man's relationship with God is right that all of his other relationships—his relationships with his fellowmen, his dealings with the rest of creation—can be in good order."[132] The *logos*, achieved in authentic worship, precedes any authentic *ethos*. As indicated previously, the false form of worship is exemplified by the building and worship of the golden calf in Ratzinger's view: "The worship of the golden calf is a self-generated cult. . . . Worship becomes a feast that the community gives itself, a festival of self-affirmation."[133] Preference is given to the *ethos* of

---

[130] Ratzinger, *PCT*, 187.

[131] See Matthew L. Lamb, "Wisdom Eschatology in Augustine and Aquinas," in *Aquinas the Augustinian*, ed. Michael Dauphinais, Barry David, and Matthew Levering (Washington, DC: The Catholic University of America Press, 2007), 259. Lamb uses the term "wisdom eschatology" because in his view, "eschatology depends upon a faith-illumined knowledge and wisdom of the *telos* or end of the whole of redeemed creation."

[132] Ratzinger, JRCW11, 10 (JRGS11, 38).

[133] Ratzinger, JRCW11, 12 (JRGS11, 39–40). Unlike the golden calf, liturgy is not made by the human person. Ratzinger asserts that the "liturgy cannot be 'made.' This is why it has to be simply received as a given reality and continually revitalized." Ratzinger, *Feast of Faith*, 66. Commenting on Guardini's work *The Church of the Lord*, Ratzinger asserts that Guardini learned to see in the Incarnation "the presence of the Lord who

the human person over the *logos* of God. The assessment of the philosopher Gabriel Marcel (1889–1973) is an apt summary of this type of false worship: the value of "doing" replaces that of "being." As a consequence, Ratzinger concludes that "instead of being worship of God, it becomes a circle closed in on itself: eating, drinking, and making merry."[134]

An *ethos* of self-seeking pleasure is an antithesis to the authentic worship of God. Authentic worship leads to an *ethos* of charity for one's neighbor. This type of *ethos* is a sign of eschatological faith that was evident in the life of the Church from its apostolic beginnings. Theologian Matthew Levering draws upon the Acts of the Apostles to highlight the essential marks of eschatological faith in the apostolic Church: "Apostolic teaching and fellowship, and the liturgical celebration of the Eucharist."[135] Regular participation in the liturgy led to and presupposed charitable concern for one's neighbor. Levering, continuing to cite Acts, goes on to say that the "eschatological community is also known by its sharing of possessions so that all have a sufficiency: 'And all who believed were together and had all things in common; and they sold their possessions and goods and distributed them to all, as any had need' (Acts 2:44–45; cf. 4:32–35)."[136]

Love of God expressed in liturgical worship is not mutually exclusive of love of neighbor. The latter is a realization and anticipation of eschatological communion. Drawing upon the Pauline corpus, particularly 1 Corinthians, Levering highlights the eschatological marks of the apostolic Church emphasizing the participation in the Eucharist as the means by which the community participates in the Pasch of Jesus Christ. This participation, he writes, likewise shows that the apostolic Church embraced selfless generosity with one's neighbor as part of her eschatological mission.[137] Self-giving, which Christians experienced in the "breaking of the bread," was translated into their everyday giving of bread to others.

---

has made the Church his body. Only if that is so is there a simultaneity of Jesus Christ with us. And only if it this exists is there real liturgy which is not a mere remembrance of the paschal mystery but its true presence. Once again, only if this is the case is liturgy a participation in the trinitarian dialogue between Father, Son, and Holy Spirit. Only in this way is it not our 'doing' but the *opus Dei*—God's action in and with us." *Joseph Ratzinger in Communio*, vol. 1, *The Unity of the Church*, trans. Stephen Wentworth Arndt, eds. David L. Schindler and Nicholas J. Healy (Grand Rapids, MI: Eerdmans Publishing, 2013), 33.

[134] Ratzinger, JRCW11, 10 (JRGS11, 39–40).

[135] Matthew Levering, *Jesus and the Demise of Death: Resurrection, Afterlife, and the Fate of the Christian* (Waco, TX: Baylor University Press, 2012), 66. He quotes from Acts 2:42.

[136] Levering, *Jesus and the Demise of Death*, 66.

[137] Levering, *Jesus and the Demise of Death*, 71–72.

The *logos* of the liturgy should transform the existence of the Christian. Ratzinger maintains that the liturgy should be a "*logikē latreia*, the 'logicizing' [*Logisierung*] of my existence, my interior simultaneously together with the sacrifice of Christ."[138] The bodies of Christians can become a "living sacrifice" through the generous self-gift that unfolds as they love others, particularly those in need. The primacy of *logos* leads to Ratzinger's emphasis on the primacy of the vertical relationship of love, which the person offers to God in the sacred liturgy. At the same time, worship does not preclude love, which the faithful believer must have in his horizontal relationships of love for his neighbor. In *Jesus of Nazareth: Holy Week: From the Entrance into Jerusalem to the Resurrection*, Ratzinger maintains:

> "*Caritas*," care for the other, is not an additional sector of Christianity alongside worship; rather, it is rooted in it and forms part of it. The horizontal and the vertical are inseparably linked in the Eucharist, in the "breaking of the bread." In this dual action of praise/thanksgiving and breaking/distributing that is recounted at the beginning of the institution narrative, the essence of the new worship established by Christ through the Last Supper, Cross, and Resurrection is made manifest: here the old Temple worship is abolished and at the same time brought to its fulfillment.[139]

---

[138] Ratzinger, JRCW11, 34 (JRGS11, 65–66).

[139] Joseph Ratzinger, *Jesus of Nazareth: Holy Week: From the Entrance into Jerusalem to the Resurrection* [hereafter, *JN* II], trans. Vatican Secretariat of State (San Francisco: Ignatius Press, 2011), 129–30; Joseph Ratzinger, *Jesus von Nazareth: Beiträge zur Christologie*, Joseph Ratzinger Gesammelte Schriften 6/1 (hereafter, JRGS6/1), 515–516. Also see Joseph Ratzinger, *God Is Near Us: The Eucharist, The Heart of Life*, ed. Stephan Otto Horn and Vinzenz Pfnür, trans. Henry Taylor (San Francisco: Ignatius Press, 2003), 121–29: "Christ shares himself with us. Let us take this to heart again and again, so that we may share him out; it is immediately clear that we can devote ourselves to the breaking of bread only if we ourselves become breakers of bread in the fullest sense. Hence the Eucharist is the true motive power for all social transformation in the world. From Elizabeth of Hungary, by way of Nicholas of Flüe and Vincent de Paul, right up to Mother Teresa, it is evident that wherever the gestures of the Lord, the breaker of the bread, are accepted, then the breaking of the bread must be carried on right into everyday life. There is no longer any stranger there who means nothing to me; rather, there is a brother there who calls on me and who is waiting for the broken bread, to find a resting place in his love" (here, 127–28). Also see Joseph Ratzinger, *Called to Communion*, trans. Adrian Walker (San Francisco: Ignatius Press, 1996), 43; *Zeichen unter den Völkern: Schriften zur Ekklesiologie und Ökumene*, Gesammelte Schriften 8/1, ed. Gerhard Ludwig Müller, (Freiburg: Herder, 2010), 239: "The designation of the sacrament as the 'breaking of the bread' expresses the social requirement of the Eucharist, which is not

Worship includes both love of God and love of neighbor. This type of new worship is eschatological and centered upon the Christian finding his identity first and foremost in the incarnate *Logos*.

The tension between history and ontology, reason and revelation, nature and grace, and ultimately between the human person and God is sustained throughout Ratzinger's thought because the incarnate *Logos* maintains the tension between the natural and supernatural. Divorced from the *logos*, both liturgy and eschatology can cease to be the *actio Dei*; the former can become a product of the creative human person, whereas the latter can be driven by utopian ideology.

## SUMMARY AND CONCLUSION

Under the influence of Romano Guardini, Ratzinger favors the primacy of *logos* over *ethos*. This will have implications for Ratzinger in his approach to the liturgy and eschatology. Regarding the liturgy, Ratzinger's emphasis on the primacy of *logos* drives one of his fundamental refrains within his theology: that the liturgy is the *opus Dei*. A subordination of *logos* to *ethos* subjects the liturgy to be manipulated or changed solely at the discretion of the people. The primacy of *logos* ensures that the proper nuances are given to the definition of the liturgy as the "work of the people."[140] In eschatology, the concern of Ratzinger regarding the subordination of the *logos* to *ethos* (or theory to praxis) is that political theology, theology of hope, and liberation theology advocate social action without receiving their proper orientation from the *logos* of the liturgy.[141] In practice, eschatology can easily be characterized like the liturgy solely as a caricature of the authentic "work of the people," placing great stress upon the role of politics and social justice.

Romano Guardini has clearly impacted Ratzinger's presentation of the *logos*. Both theologians have a similar interest to critique modern culture, which attempts to separate itself from the influence of God in favor of human technocracy. Guardini and Ratzinger develop the harmony between liturgy and Christology, which offers a sacramental worldview

---

an isolated cultic act but a way of existence: life in sharing, in communion with Christ, who gives the gift of his very self."

[140] See the *CCC* §1069. The Church affirms that the liturgy is properly understood as "the participation of the People of God in 'the work of God.'"

[141] On the various relationships between theory (*logos*) and praxis (*ethos*), see Matthew Lamb, *Solidarity with Victims: Towards a Theology of Social Transformation* (New York: The Crossroad Publishing Company, 1982), 61–99.

that can bring the modern world back to its authentic *logos*. The true spirit of the liturgy is the communion that unites the individual "I" with other people in worship to form a "we." The remedy for the isolating *logos* of technē is the communion that is realized via the liturgy.

This chapter demonstrated the continuity in Ratzinger's thought in presenting the primacy of the *logos* from his days as a young professor of fundamental theology to his service as the Supreme Pontiff. A person will not be able to penetrate Ratzinger's thought with any depth if they do not take the significance of this position seriously. The next chapter describes how the significance of worshipping in accordance with the *logos* can only be fully explained by highlighting the significance of the Eucharist as a sacrifice, the purpose and relationship of sacrifice in salvation history and to temple worship, and the identity of Christ existing "for" (*pro*) others. Ratzinger asserts the primacy of *logos* over *ethos* in order to emphasize the call of the Christian to participate in the sacrificial love of the incarnate *Logos*, which is the authentic Christian *ethos*.

# CHAPTER 2

# A Sacrificial People in the Incarnate *Logos*

CHRISTIANS HAVE RECEIVED THEIR VOCATION in light of Christ's redemptive act to become a sacrificial people participating in the paschal sacrifice of the *Logos*. Ratzinger describes the change that takes place with our communion with Christ and our subsequent participation in his existence *for* others: "Our reflections have shown that Christian unity is first of all unity with Christ, which becomes possible where insistence on one's own individuality ceases and is replaced by pure, unreserved being 'from' and 'for.'"[1] The previous chapter demonstrated the significance of Romano Guardini's influence upon Ratzinger's understanding that *logos* has primacy over *ethos*. In the present chapter, the central focus is Ratzinger's emphasis on the relationship between the sacrifice and *logos* in his spiritual Christology.

Understanding the Exodus is essential to analyzing the strong relationship between sacrifice, worship, ethics, and *logos* in the thought of Ratzinger. Jesus is the new Lamb and the new Temple within Ratzinger's theology. This theology enables Ratzinger to define sacrifice *logos*-centrically as self-giving love, which is the authentic *ethos* for Christians. This chapter assesses Ratzinger's claims that sacrifice is the true *Grundgestalt* ("basic form") of the Eucharist, which will put his thought in tension with Guardini, who suggests that the meal aspect has primacy over the sacrificial nature of the Eucharist. In Ratzinger's view, the Church enters into the sacrificial prayer of the incarnate *Logos* through the Eucharist. Every Christian is called to participate in the self-giving identity (the

---

[1] Joseph Ratzinger, *Introduction to Christianity* [hereafter, IC], trans. J. R. Foster (San Francisco: Ignatius Press, 2004), 187; *Einführung in das Christentum: Bekenntnis—Taufe—Nachfolge*, Joseph Ratzinger Gesammelte Shriften 4, [hereafter, JRGS4] ed. Gerhard Ludwig Müller (Freiburg: Herder, 2014), 178.

"pro-existence") of the *Logos* by participating in the sacrifice of the Eucharist and engaging in an *ethos* of love.

Since Ratzinger defends the value of affirming the Eucharist primarily as a sacrifice—by contrast with the critical view of this traditional understanding of the Eucharist that has developed among theologians following the Second Vatican Council—it will be helpful to survey very briefly the magisterial teaching that has consistently and explicitly linked the Eucharist with the sacrifice of Christ on the Cross.[2] In its *Decree on the Sacrifice of the Mass*, the Council Fathers at Trent affirm this teaching: "In this divine sacrifice that is celebrated in the Mass, the same Christ who offered himself once in a bloody manner [cf. Heb 9:14, 27 f.] on the altar is contained and is offered in an unbloody manner." Trent continues, "For, the victim is one and the same: the same [victim] now offers himself through the ministry of priests who then offered himself on the Cross; only the manner of offering is different."[3] The sacrifice of Christ on the Cross and the offering celebrated in the Holy Eucharist are one and the same, but they differ in the manner in which the sacrifice is offered. Venerable Pope Pius XII (1876–1958) in *Mediator Dei* refers to the Tridentine doctrine

---

[2]  The magisterial teaching on the Eucharist as sacrifice, beginning with Trent, has received much critique. See for example, Robert J. Daly, S.J., "Robert Bellarmine and Post-Tridentine Eucharistic Theology," *Theological Studies* 61 (2000): 239–260. Building upon the historical research of Edward J. Kilmartin, Daly traces the theology of sacrifice articulated by Trent and subsequent magisterial teachings to Bellarmine. On the sacrificial nature of the Eucharist, see Matthew Levering, *Sacrifice and Community: Jewish Offering and Christian Eucharist* (Malden, MA: Blackwell Publishing, 2005); Helmut Hoping, *My Body Given for You: History and Theology of the Eucharist*, trans. Michael J. Miller (San Francisco: Ignatius Press, 2019), 15–20, 411–21; Lawrence Feingold, *The Eucharist: Mystery of Presence, Sacrifice, and Communion* (Steubenville, OH: Emmaus Academic, 2018), 323–483; Michael McGuckian, *The Holy Sacrifice of the Mass: A Search for an Acceptable Notion of Sacrifice* (Chicago: Hillenbrand Books, 2005); Robert J. Daly, *Sacrifice Unveiled: The True Meaning of Christian Sacrifice* (New York: T & T Clark, 2009); Thomas Witt, *Repraesentatio sacificii: Das eucharistische Opfer und seine Darstellung in den Gebeten und Riten des Missale Romanum 1970: Untersuchungen zur darstellenden Funktion der Liturgie*, Paderborner theologische Studien 31 (Paderborn: Schöningh, 2002).

[3]  Ecumenical Council of Trent, Session XXII, "Doctrina de ss. Missae Sacrificio," chapter 2, in Heinrich Denzinger, Enchiridion symbolorum definitionum et declarationum de rebus fidei et morum: Compendium of Creeds, Definitions and Declarations on Matters of Faith and Morals [hereafter, DH], ed., Peter Hünermann, 43rd ed. (San Francisco: Ignatius Press, 2012), 1743. The Tridentine teaching on sacrifice is affirmed by the *Catechism of the Catholic Church*. See *CCC* §§1364–1368. The Council of Trent is cited explicitly in its teaching.

of Eucharistic sacrifice as he continues to affirm that Christ acts as High Priest at Calvary, and there is an ongoing offering of this "true and proper act of sacrifice" in the Mass.[4]

The identity between the sacrifice on the Cross and the sacrifice of the Mass was also reiterated at the Second Vatican Council and by Pope St. Paul VI (1897–1978) in his encyclical on the Eucharist, *Mysterium Fidei*.[5] This continuity strengthens the reception of the Tridentine doctrine in magisterial teaching. Citing the Council of Trent and the most recent *Catechism*, Pope St. John Paul II affirms the sacrificial nature of the Eucharist in his encyclical *Ecclesia de Eucharistia*: "The Eucharist is indelibly marked by the event of the Lord's passion and death, of which it is not only a reminder but the sacramental re-presentation. It is the sacrifice of the Cross perpetuated down the ages."[6] The Eucharist is a sacramental sacrifice that makes present the sacrifice of Christ.

John Paul II's encyclical emphasizes the notion of sacrifice.[7] The Eucharist also makes present the mystery of the Resurrection, which John Paul II refers to as the event which "crowned" the sacrifice of Christ.[8] Interestingly, John Paul highlights an aspect of the sacrificial gift of Christ that is often overlooked: "*first and foremost* [Christ's sacrifice is] *a gift to the*

---

4   Pope Pius XII, Encyclical Letter *Mediator Dei* (Boston: St. Paul Books & Media, 1947), §68.

5   See *Sacrosanctum Concilium,* in Norman P. Tanner, ed., *Decrees of the Ecumenical Councils*, 2 vols. (Washington, DC: Sheed & Ward and Georgetown University Press, 1990), §§6–8; Pope Paul VI, Encyclical Letter *Mysterium Fidei* (Vatican City: Libreria Editrice Vaticana, 1965), §§26–34. Once again, the Tridentine doctrine on Eucharistic sacrifice is referenced.

6   Pope John Paul II, Encyclical Letter *Ecclesia de Eucharistia* (Vatican City: Libreria Editrice Vaticana, 2003), §11. On John Paul's encyclical in relation to the thought of Aquinas, see Matthew Levering, "John Paul II and Aquinas on the Eucharist," in *John Paul II & St. Thomas Aquinas*, ed. Michael Dauphinais and Matthew Levering (Naples, FL: Sapientia Press, 2006), 209–31.

7   In his theological analysis of the encyclical, Richard Schenk, O.P., highlights John Paul's uses of the term "sacrifice" or "sacrificial" over seventy times, which does not include the use of various synonyms such as "blood poured out," "offering," or "paschal victim." Richard Schenk, O.P., "The Eucharist and Ecclesial Communion," in *At the Altar of the World: The Pontificate of Pope John Paul II through the Lens of L'Osservatore Romano and the Words of Ecclesia de Eucharistia*, ed. Daniel G. Callahan (Washington, DC: John Paul II Cultural Center, 2003), 85. Schenk also remarks that the encyclical is "characterized by its emphasis on the Eucharist as containing the work of Christ 'for' ['*pro*'] humankind (pro vobis et pro multis, for those receiving Communion and for those others whose needs are prayed for by a Church united to Christ's own sacrifice 'for' the world in the Eucharist)." Schenk, "The Eucharist and Ecclesial Communion," 85.

8   *John Paul II, Ecclesia de Eucharistia*, §14; §15.

*Father.*"[9] It should come as no surprise that John Paul would apply his concept of the law or the hermeneutic of the gift to Christ's sacrifice. Consistent with this theological notion of self-gift at the heart of John Paul's thought, he affirms that the full efficacy of this sacrificial gift is realized only in communion. Gift and communion are inseparable ideas in the theology of John Paul II.[10] This interconnection and the language of self-gift will lay a foundation for further development in the magisterial teaching relating to Eucharistic sacrifice with the theology of Pope Benedict XVI.

Understanding the continuity within the magisterial teaching on Eucharistic sacrifice is necessary to engage Ratzinger's theology of sacrifice, which is developed in part to address theologians and liturgists who espouse views regarding the Eucharist that have more in common with Martin Luther than they do with the teaching on Trent.[11] In light of the rejection of the Tridentine teaching (and subsequently any magisterial teaching that builds upon Trent's foundation) on the Eucharist as a sacrifice, the Mass is reduced to a "farewell meal that included an eschatological perspective."[12] Benedict XVI highlights a unique aspect of the sacrificial gift of Christ, as he refers to the "radical newness of Christian worship."[13]

---

[9]   *John Paul II, Ecclesia de Eucharistia,* §13.

[10]   On the themes of gift and communion in the writings of John Paul II, see Jaroslaw Kupczak, O.P., *Gift and Communion: John Paul II's Theology of the Body* (Washington, DC: The Catholic University of America Press, 2014).

[11]   See Joseph Ratzinger, *Theology of the Liturgy: The Sacramental Foundation of Christian Existence* [hereafter, JRCW11], ed. Michael J. Miller, trans. John Saward, Kenneth Baker, S.J., Henry Taylor, et al., Collected Works 11 (San Francisco: Ignatius Press, 2014), 542–57, here, 544; *Theologie der Liturgie: Die sakramentale Begründung christlicher Existenz* [hereafter, JRGS11], Gesammelte Schriften 11, ed. Gerhard Ludwig Müller (Freiburg im Breisgau: Herder, 2008), 640–48, 642: "A sizeable party of Catholic liturgists seems to have arrived in practice at the conclusion that Luther, rather than Trent, was substantially right in the sixteenth century debate; one can detect much the same position in the post-conciliar discussions on the priesthood." Among the theologians who espouse this view, Ratzinger explicitly cites Harald Schützeichel, David N. Power, and Reinhard Messner. See Schützeichel, *Die Feier des Gottesdienstes: Eine Einführung* (Düsseldorf: Patmos, 1996); Power, *The Sacrifice We Offer: The Tridentine Dogma and Its Reinterpretation* (New York: The Crossroad Publishing Company, 1987), 141ff; Schnitker, review of the American *Book of Prayer,* in *Theologische Revue* 78 (1982): 265–72; and Reinhard Messner, *Die Messreform Martin Luthers und die Eucharistie der Alten Kirche,* Innsbrucker Theologische Studien 25 (Innsbruck: Tyrolia, 1989).

[12]   Ratzinger, JRCW11, 545 (JRGS11, 643).

[13]   Pope Benedict XVI, Post-synodal Apostolic Exhortation *Sacramentum Caritatis* [hereafter, *SCa*] (Vatican City: Libreria Editrice Vaticana, 2007), §11.

The "radical newness" lies in the idea that Christians throughout the centuries have the ability to participate in the one sacrifice of the incarnate *Logos*. In *Deus Caritas Est*, Benedict describes the radical transformation brought about by the Eucharist: "The Eucharist draws us into Jesus's act of self-oblation. More than just statically receiving the incarnate *Logos*, we enter into the very dynamic of his self-giving."[14]

The key contribution of Ratzinger to the discussion of sacrifice in theology has been to emphasize the Augustinian understanding of self-giving love as the authentic *logos* of sacrifice.[15] The common view reduces sacrifice to an act involving destruction.[16] True sacrifice involves a surrender that hands over to God what already belongs to him. This type of sacrifice is a "belonging to God [that] has nothing to do with destruction or non-being: it is rather a way of being. It means emerging from the state of separation, of apparent autonomy, of existing only for oneself and in oneself."[17] In other words, existence coincides with self-gift. Ratzinger affirms the Augustinian notion that authentic sacrifice is the city of God, a "love-transformed mankind," or the "divinization of creation and the surrender of all things to God."[18] Ratzinger asserts that creation and worship have the same goal of divinization, which results from the *communio* between God, the world, and all of humanity.

---

[14] Pope Benedict XVI, *Encyclical Letter Deus Caritas Est* [hereafter, *DCE*] (Vatican City: Liberia Editrice Vaticana, 2005), §13.

[15] For a brief study of the Augustinian influence upon Ratzinger's ecclesiology and theology of liturgy, see Cong Quy Joseph Lam, C.Ss.R., *Joseph Ratzinger's Theological Retractions* (Bern, Switzerland: Peter Lang, AG, 2013), 147–211. For a full treatment of the impact of Augustine on Ratzinger's theology, see Lam, *Theologische Verwandtschaft: Augustinus von Hippo und Joseph Ratzinger/Papst Benedikt XVI* (Würzburg: Echter, 2009). Helmet Hoping has also highlighted the notion of sacrifice as gift: "The essence of sacrifice (*Opfer*) is not the violence of the *homo necans*, but rather the gift, even unto the sacrifice of one's own life, as in Jesus' sacrifice on the Cross." *My Body Given for You*, 17. On the development of the notion of sacrifice as gift, see Joachim Negel, *Ambivalentes opfer: Studien zur Symbolik, Dialektik und Aporetik eintes theologischen Fundamentalbegriffs* (Paderborn: Schöningh, 2005); Max ten Hompel, *Das Opfer als Selbsthingabe und seine ideale Verwirklichung im Opfer Christi: Mit Besonderer Berücksichtigung neuerer Kontroversen* (Freiburg: Herder, 1920).

[16] Ratzinger, JRCW11, 15 (JRGS11, 43).

[17] Ratzinger, JRCW11, 15 (JRGS11, 43). Citing the work of Louis Bouyer, Monsignor Robert Sokolowski asserts that "a sacrifice is not a dedication of something profane to God but an entry into and a participation in what God already possesses." See Robert Sokolowski, *Eucharistic Presence: A Study in the Theology of Disclosure* (Washington, DC: The Catholic University of America Press, 1994), 76–79.

[18] Ratzinger, JRCW11,15 (JRGS11, 43–44).

The Augustinian emphasis on love as sacrifice's true meaning is essential to comprehending sacrifice in Ratzinger's liturgical theology.[19] In his development of Augustine's insight, Ratzinger highlights the initial love of God for the person, which brings about a "process of purification and transformation, in which we are not only open for God but also united with one another."[20] Sacrificial love, which is initiated by God in the person of Jesus Christ,[21] enables the Christian to enter into a communion of love with both God and his neighbor.

The cultic sacrifices of the Old Testament are transformed by the sacrifice of Jesus Christ, and subsequently, worship takes on a different meaning. Worship should transform the very being of the person participating in the liturgy. Ratzinger describes this change as the "transformation of our being into the logos, unification with it."[22] The communion with the *Logos* incarnate marks the "new worship," which Christ establishes through his new exodus and by assuming his identity as the new Temple.

## CENTRALITY OF THE EXODUS

A true exodus that begins with Baptism and can be deepened by the Eucharist is one of the foundational notions in Ratzinger's theology of salvation history.[23] Exodus depicts the freedom that awaits Israel if they are faithful

---

[19] On the Augustinian notion of sacrifice in the *City of God*, see Uwe Michael Lang, "Augustine's Conception of Sacrifice in *City of God*, Book X, and the Eucharistic Sacrifice," *Antiphon* 19, no. 1 (2015): 29–51. Lang has a comprehensive list of the theological literature on the theme of sacrifice in Augustinian theology. Also see Basil Studer, "Das Opfer Christi nach Augustins '*De civitate Dei*' X, 5–6," *Studia Anselmiana* 79 (1980): 93–108.

[20] Ratzinger, JRCW11, 552 (JRGS11, 651).

[21] "Die Initiative Gottes hat einen Namen: Jesus Christus—der Gott, der selbst Mensch wird und sich für uns gibt." Ratzinger, JRCW11, 552 (JRGS11, 651).

[22] Ratzinger, JRCW11, 555 (JRGS11, 654).

[23] On the themes from the Exodus narrative throughout Ratzinger's work, see Réal Tremblay, C.Ss.R., "L'Exode,' une idée maîtresse de la pensée théologique du Cardinal Joseph Ratzinger," in *Historia, memoria futuri: mélanges Louis Vereecke (70e anniversaire de naissance)*, ed. Réal Tremblay and Dennis Joseph (Roma: Editiones Academiae Alphonsianae, 1991), 435–461. Also see Réal Tremblay, "L' <<Esodo>> tra prologia ed escatologia," in *Ritrovarsi Donadosi: Alcune idee chiave della teologia di Joseph Ratzinger—Benedetto XVI*, ed. Réal Tremblay (with Stefano Zamboni) (Vatican City: Lateran University Press, 2012), 43–65. In this article Tremblay deepens his previous study of this theme in Ratzinger. See also Seán Corkery, *A Liberation Ecclesiology?: The Quest for Authentic Freedom in Joseph Ratzinger's Theology of the Church* (Bern: Peter Lang, 2015), 163–186.

to the covenant, the law, and worship as outlined carefully by God at Sinai. Ratzinger notes that the Exodus is not achieved "by the particular boldness or industry of Moses, but by a religious event, the true sacrifice, which anticipates an essential ingredient of the Torah."[24] The freedom, which is at the heart of the Exodus, is only an anticipation of the liberation that comes from communion with Jesus Christ. In Ratzinger's estimation, the Exodus of Israel out of Egypt was anticipated by the exodus of Abraham from Ur to travel to Canaan (Gen 12:1).

Moses and Elijah, who are "valid interpreters of the Exodus," appear at the Transfiguration.[25] Insightfully, Ratzinger comments, "The authentic nature of the exodus story thus becomes visible in Elijah: exodus refers neither to a geographical nor to a political way. This path cannot be traced on a geographical or political map. An exodus that does not lead to covenant and does not find its 'land' in living according to the covenant is not a true exodus."[26] An authentic exodus is not limited to a physical journey. Above all, it is a spiritual pilgrimage destined for communion with God.

Embracing the Christian faith is the beginning of an exodus that took place at Baptism, which Ratzinger emphasizes (citing Romans 6) is "death and resurrection."[27] Baptism marks the beginning of our exodus as Christians, whereas the Eucharist deepens our exodus. Both sacraments are instrumental

---

[24] Joseph Ratzinger, *Church, Ecumenism and Politics: New Endeavors in Ecclesiology* [hereafter, *CEP*], trans. Michael J. Miller, et al. (San Francisco: Ignatius Press, 2008), 249–50.

[25] Joseph Ratzinger, *A New Song for the Lord: Faith in Christ and Liturgy Today* [hereafter, *NSL*], trans. Martha M. Matesich (New York: The Crossroad Publishing Company, 1997), 15; *Jesus von Nazareth: Beiträge zur Christologie*, Joseph Ratzinger Gesammelte Schriften 6/2 [hereafter, *JRGS6/2*], ed. Gerhard Ludwig Müller (Freiburg: Herder, 2013), 971–972.

[26] Ratzinger, *NSL*, 15 (*JRGS6/2*, 972). On the use of the Exodus as a theme in liberation theology, see Arthur F. McGovern, S.J., *Liberation Theology and Its Critics: Toward an Assessment* (Eugene, OR: Wipf & Stock, 1989), 62–69. Alluding to the use of the Exodus narrative by certain liberation theologies, Ratzinger argues: "In the case of the radicalized political theologians, on the other hand, the relationship between Old and New Testaments is taken back into the Old; redemption becomes the Exodus, interpreted in a political way, as the secular act of liberation, and thus the Kingdom of God becomes the product of the human act of liberation. In this process, it is not only Christology that totally loses its own features; the Old Testament itself is deprived of its dynamic that points ahead and upward, and it is turned around even in its own direction of movement." Joseph Ratzinger, *A Turning Point for Europe?* trans. Brian McNeil (San Francisco: Ignatius Press, 2010), 77.

[27] Joseph Ratzinger, *Truth and Tolerance* [hereafter, *TT*], trans. Henry Taylor (San Francisco: Ignatius Press, 2004), 87.

in this spiritual pilgrimage insofar as they help the faithful to realize the conversion, which is at the heart of our exodus.[28] The liturgy is simultaneously a preparation for and an anticipation of the ultimate exodus that will come with the eschaton.

Previous theologians used the theory of play as their *point du départ* in defining the liturgy, but Ratzinger finds the theory lacking.[29] In explaining the analogy of play, Ratzinger comments that liturgy, similar to a "game has its own rules, sets up its own world, which is in force from the start of play but then, of course, is suspended at the close of play."[30] Play is also without purpose, and consequently, it brings about a certain form of freedom that temporarily liberates people from their daily work and anxiety. Ratzinger comments that the crucial element missing from the analogy is that play is also a form of anticipation or rehearsal for a later stage in life. Hence, liturgy has by its very nature an eschatological component.

In light of the renewed interest in Sacred Scripture, Ratzinger explains liturgy in light of salvation history, with an emphasis on the notion of sacrifice. Ratzinger, citing St. Augustine's *De Civitate Dei X*, defines sacrifice as the process of transformation whereby the person conforms to God in his *theōsis*, or divinization.[31] Divinization is the other half of what Ratzinger elsewhere describes as the "novel two-sidedness" of the covenant fulfilled by Jesus Christ. On the one hand, there is the "incarnation of God" and on the other hand, the "divinization of man."[32]

---

[28]  Ratzinger, *NSL,* 20 (JRGS6/2, 970): "Now let us put this in plain terms; Christian exodus calls for a conversion which accepts the promise of Christ in its entirety and is prepared to lose its whole life to this promise. Conversion, then, also calls for going beyond self-reliance and for entrusting ourselves to the mystery, the sacrament in the community of the Church, in which God enters my life as agent and frees it from its isolation."

[29]  See Guardini's chapter "The Playfulness of the Liturgy," in *The Spirit of the Liturgy* [hereafter, GSL], trans. Ada Lane (New York: The Crossroad Publishing Company, 1998), 61–72. On Guardini's theory of liturgy as play in contrast with the thought of Ratzinger on the liturgy, see Gunda Brüske, "Spiel oder Anbetung? Romano Guardini und Joseph Ratzinger über den Sinn der Liturgie," 91–110.

[30]  Ratzinger, JRCW11, 5 (JRGS11, 32).

[31]  Ratzinger, JRCW11, 551 (JRGS11, 649). Edward Kilmartin notes that *De Civitate Dei* 10.6: "This is the sacrifice of Christians: the many one body in Christ" is the central concept of sacrifice for Augustine. Kilmartin summarizes this passage as a commentary of Augustine on Romans 12:1–3. See Edward J. Kilmartin, S.J., *The Eucharist in the West: History and Theology*, ed. Robert Daly (Collegeville, MN: The Liturgical Press, 1998).

[32]  Joseph Ratzinger, *Many Religions, One Covenant: Israel, the Church and the World* [hereafter, *MROC*], trans. Graham Harrison (San Francisco: Ignatius Press, 1999), 74; *Zeichen unter den Völkern: Schriften zur Ekklesiologie und Ökumene*, Gesammelte

Salvation history is the unfolding of the relationship between God and humanity.

The human person must ultimately become like God, but he will not be able to do this without God becoming man. The ultimate end of the journey, which began with ancient Israel in their Exodus from Egypt towards the Promised Land, is divinization. When the person's journey towards communion with God is fully realized, then divinization becomes a reality, marking the end of the person's spiritual liberation or exodus. Consequently, the analogy of play applied to the liturgy falls short because it does not engage the ultimate *telos* of our exodus.

One of Ratzinger's main conclusions regarding the narrative of the Exodus is that God desires for Israel to experience the freedom that they enjoyed from the beginning through their worship that has been obscured by the Fall. Given the fact that creation culminated in the time of worship and rest observed on the Sabbath (see Gen 2:1–3), the Fall represents, in part, humanity's rejection of worship and leisure, which must be renewed. The very purpose of creation is the covenant, which involves both "God's gift of himself to man, but also man's response to God."[33] The response of humanity is carried out in love, which Ratzinger underscores is the authentic meaning of worship. In order to make their way towards the divinization, humanity must be liberated from its bondage to sin.

The Israelites would eventually become enslaved not only to the Egyptians but also to other activities that were not directed towards authentic worship. Commenting on the Sabbath, Ratzinger describes the situation:

> [Fallen people] had to be snatched from their obstinate attachment to their own work. God had to begin afresh to make them his very own, and he had to free them from the domination of activity. *Operi Dei nihil praeponatur:* The worship of God, his freedom, and his rest come first. Thus and only thus can the human being truly live.[34]

The Exodus takes on both historical and symbolic significance in the plan of providence to bring humanity back to its proper freedom, which

---

Schriften 8/2 [hereafter, JRGS8/2], ed. Gerhard Ludwig Müller, (Freiburg: Herder, 2010), 1117.

[33] Ratzinger, JRCW11, 14 (JRGS11, 42).

[34] Joseph Ratzinger, *In the Beginning: A Catholic Understanding of Creation and the Fall* [hereafter, *ITB*], trans. Boniface Ramsey, O.P. (Huntington, IN: Our Sunday Visitor, 1990).

it enjoyed from the moment of creation. Ratzinger maintains that the seven-day creation account could be interpreted as a metaphor to highlight the importance of the Sabbath and its relation to the covenant.[35]

In Ratzinger's theology, the Sabbath is the day of the human person's participation in God's freedom because all people share in the freedom of the joy of being children of God.[36] The celebration of the Sabbath is also a form of eschatological anticipation of the ultimate exodus that awaits the faithful. A day of rest and worship is a foretaste of the world to come and a share in the divine life. Ratzinger comments that the Sabbath is "the anticipation of the messianic hour, not only in thoughts and desires but in concrete action."[37] Israel was meant to live in hopeful expectation, which begins with their worship and is realized further in their relationship with one another. As an eschatological foretaste, worship "is an imitation of God himself and therefore a preliminary exercise in the world to come."[38] In contradistinction with the Pagan cults of nature, worship for ancient Israel is not merely "an imitation of the course of the world in miniature."[39] The Exodus restores the true freedom of the Israelites to worship and to participate in the fullness of the moral life flowing forth from their worship.

In his commentary on the significance of the Exodus, Ratzinger highlights his recurring thesis that the Promised Land is only the means to a greater end—worship of God. Simultaneously, in the course of their Exodus, the Israelites will receive the gift of the Law as an inseparable part of their worship. During the Exodus, God desires for Israel to learn that authentic worship (cult) and living a morally upright life are essential parts of the true sacrifice that God desires, which God makes known through the Ten Commandments (Exod 20:1–17) and the covenant on Mount Sinai (Exod 24).[40] God has entered into a covenant with humanity, which is observed through obedience and love.

Worship, law, and ethics are inseparable orders that God has given to humanity to guide them to their proper end in communion with him.[41] The Promised Land is a gift given to Israel by God so that they might live in authentic freedom by observing proper worship. True worship consists

---

[35] Ratzinger, JRCW11, 197 (JRGS11, 247).
[36] Ratzinger, JRCW11, 198 (JRGS11, 247).
[37] Ratzinger, JRCW11, 199 (JRGS11, 247).
[38] Ratzinger, JRCW11, 199 (JRGS11, 249).
[39] Ratzinger, JRCW11, 199 (JRGS11, 249).
[40] Ratzinger, JRCW11, 8 (JRGS11, 36–7).
[41] Ratzinger, JRCW11, 9 (JRGS11, 37).

of living a life governed by the law and embracing morals directed towards God while simultaneously rooting this ethical life in the liturgy.[42] This form of worship is eschatological in that it "gives us a share in heaven's mode of existence, in the world of God, and allows light to fall from the divine world into ours."[43] Given the divine form of liturgy, worship cannot simply be made or constructed. Consequently, Ratzinger uses the example of the false worship of the golden calf, which was noted in the previous chapter, as a concrete representation of the false, self-generated, and self-absorbed cult.[44] This form of false worship symbolizes humanity's rejection of God and his covenant in favor of a false form of autonomy. Idolatry is a form of subordination of *logos* to *ethos*.

The *actio Dei*, emphasized throughout Ratzinger's liturgical theology, is the corrective to this attitude of fallen humanity.[45] Commenting on the essence of liturgy in another work, Ratzinger consistently maintains that "Liturgy is God's work, or it does not exist at all. With this 'first' of God and of his action, which looks for us in earthly signs, the universality of all liturgy and its universal public nature are given; we cannot comprehend them from the category of congregation, but only from the categories of People of God and Body of Christ."[46] Ancient Israel finds its true identity in collectively receiving the form of worship entrusted to them by God and observing it faithfully. Autonomy is antithetical to the covenantal relationship that Israel is called to have with God.

True freedom comes from participating in God's life through

---

[42] Ratzinger, JRCW11, 10 (JRGS11, 38): Ratzinger affirms that "worship and law cannot be completely separated from each other. God has a right to a response from man, to man himself, and where that right of God totally disappears, the order of law among men is dissolved, because there is no cornerstone to keep the whole structure together."

[43] Ratzinger, JRCW11, 10 (JRGS11, 38).

[44] Ratzinger, JRCW11, 12 (JRGS11, 39–40). In Jewish theology, there is an emphasis on the realization of the kingdom of God and a recovery of Eden that parallels the views espoused by Ratzinger. See Jacob Neusner, *Handbook of Rabbinic Theology: Language, System, Structure* (Boston, MA: Brill Academic Publishers, 2002), 559–599. Also see Neusner, "Living under the Yoke of the Kingdom of Heaven," in Jacob Neusner and Bruce Chilton, *Jewish-Christian Debates* (Minneapolis, MN: Fortress Press, 1998).

[45] In a certain sense, the incident involving the golden calf manifests the perennial issue of doubt and mistrust of God that took place with the fall. In lieu of the trusting and loving relationship that should govern humanity's relationship with God, the dominance of *technē* overshadows their relationship. This will also govern their relations with all people. See Ratzinger, *ITB*, 64–71.

[46] Ratzinger, JRCW11, 466 (JRGS11, 555). Chapter three discusses the theme of ecclesiology and its relation to Christology, the liturgy, and eschatology in more detail.

observance of his covenant, which calls for a particular liturgical and ethical form instituted by him. The *ethos* of love commanded by God that comes forth from their worship is the safeguard that Israel receives so that *logos* of their worship does not become meaningless or empty. A self-enclosed *logos* is another form of idolatry insofar as it turns the faithful towards the self completely separated from the love of the other person.

One of the chief characteristics of the New Law and new exodus in Jesus Christ was its universality in contradistinction with the limitation of law and worship for Israel in its covenantal form in the Old Testament, which was directed to a particular people in a limited historical context. Paradoxically, the covenant made between God and humanity is universal, yet it could not be fulfilled universally in its current form under the law.[47] Ratzinger identifies Jesus Christ as the climax of salvation history, who lived under the constraint of the law as a faithful Jew while simultaneously serving as the mediator of a new universal Covenant.[48] The various covenants that are given in the Old Testament with Noah, Abraham, Jacob (Israel), and Moses are interpreted by Ratzinger as part of one Covenant "realized in the plurality of covenants."[49] This understanding offers greater insight into the gift of the New Covenant, which Jesus Christ relates to the Eucharist celebrated at the Last Supper. The covenant of the Last Supper is interpreted by Ratzinger as the counterpart to the Mosaic covenant received on Mount Sinai (Exod 24).[50]

The heart of the new exodus is the celebration of the Eucharist at the Last Supper, which clearly alludes to the formation of a New Covenant. If Christ is really leading a new exodus, then it would be consistent for him to celebrate a new Passover.[51] The words of institution used at the Last Supper, whether found in the Markan (Matt 26:26–29; Mark 14:22–25) or Pauline (Luke 22:14–23; 1 Cor 11:23–26) tradition, point towards the New Covenant, which can only be fully understood by examining the ratification of the Old Covenant at Sinai, which took place with Moses sprinkling blood on the people of Israel in Exodus 24.[52]

---

[47] Ratzinger, *MROC*, 38 (JRGS8/2, 1093).

[48] Ratzinger, *MROC*, 38 (JRGS8/2, 1093).

[49] Ratzinger, *MROC*, 57 (JRGS8/2, 1106).

[50] Ratzinger, *MROC*, 58 (JRGS8/2, 1106).

[51] See Brant Pitre's discussion of the New Passover in his *Jesus and the Last Supper* (Grand Rapids, MI: Eerdmans, 2015), 374–443.

[52] On the theological significance of the ratification of the covenant by sacrifice, see Thomas Joseph White, O.P., *Exodus* (Grand Rapids, MI: Brazos Press, 2016), 208–18. Drawing upon the distinction between the internal and external acts of sacrifice

Commenting on the words of institution, Ratzinger underscores that the words used in reference to the cup in the Markan (what he refers to as the "Markan-Matthean" tradition) and the Pauline (what he refers to as the "Paul-Luke" account) narratives of the Last Supper allude to Exodus 24:

> In Matthew and Mark the words uttered over the chalice are: "This is my blood of the covenant, which is poured out for many." Matthew adds, "for the forgiveness of sins." In Paul and Luke, however, the cup is referred to in these words: "This cup is the new covenant in my blood"; and Luke adds, "which is shed for you." "Covenant" and "blood" stand here in grammatical apposition. In Matthew-Mark the gift of the cup is "the blood," which is further defined as "the blood of the covenant." In Paul-Luke the cup is "the new covenant," which is described as ratified "in my blood." A second difference is that only Luke and Paul speak about the *new* covenant. A third important difference is that only Matthew and Mark gives us the words "for many."[53]

The words of institution from the Markan tradition refer explicitly to the Old Covenant of Mount Sinai (Exod 24) as all four accounts make reference to blood.[54] As Moses sprinkled blood upon the altar at Mount Sinai he proclaimed, "Behold the blood of the covenant which the LORD has made with you in accordance with all these words" (Exod 24:8).[55] In his

---

in the thought of Aquinas (see *ST* II-II, qq. 81–88), White highlights the continuity and fulfillment of Christ's New Covenant in relation to the Sinai covenant: "Atonement-substitution and covenant unity are both recapitulated in the blood of Christ. He atones for our sins by offering a sacrifice of love and obedience on our behalf, making satisfaction for human sin. Instead of becoming a subject to the divine wrath on our behalf (which makes little sense, due to his innocence), he offers the love of charity to God where we have failed to love. The blood of Christ shed in sacrifice for all peoples is in turn the ground of covenantal unity." White, *Exodus*, 213.

[53] Ratzinger, *MROC*, 58–59 (JRGS8/2, 1106–1107).

[54] For a thorough account of the biblical significance of the phrase "blood of the covenant," see Brant Pitre, *Jesus and the Last Supper*, 90–120.

[55] Ratzinger, *MROC*, 58 (JRGS8/2, 1106). The phrase "blood of the covenant" is only found in one other passage of the Old Testament, Zechariah 9:11. Timothy C. Gray, *The Temple in the Gospel of Mark: A Study in Its Narrative Role* (Grand Rapids, MI: Baker Academic, 2010), 160. Commenting upon the use of "blood" in relation to the Eucharist, Ratzinger maintains that blood "also stands for self-giving [*Hingabe*], for a life that poured itself out, so to speak, gives itself away for us and to us. Thus the blood relationship is also involvement in the dynamic of this life, of this 'blood poured out.' Our existence is energized in such a way that life itself should become a 'being

commentary upon the relation between the reference to the Sinai covenant with these words of institution, Ratzinger notes that sacramental communion brings about "an utterly concrete—and corporeal—community with this incarnate human being, Jesus and hence with his divine mystery."[56] This "utterly concrete" community in communion with the incarnate *Logos* is unified by a New Covenant that is a part of the new exodus, which is inseparable from the celebration of the Passover. Scripture scholar Pitre argues that the "*Passover is ordered to the covenant at Mount Sinai. For it is the Passover sacrifice that sets the exodus in motion, and ultimately makes it possible for the twelve tribes to fulfill the goal of offering the covenant sacrifice on Mount Sinai.*"[57] By insisting that the Last Supper as a new Passover inaugurates a new exodus, Pitre is making a bold claim—one that is consistent with Ratzinger's theology of exodus.

At the beginning of this section, it has been maintained that Ratzinger presented the various aspects of an exodus as a liberation that resulted in a covenant, a journey from death into life, or a conversion. In other words, exodus is never limited to liberation from merely physical slavery. Significantly, Pitre highlights the only other Old Testament context for the phrase "blood of the covenant" in Zechariah 9:9–12, 16–17, noting that blood is "described as inaugurating a new exodus, in which the captives of Israel will be 'set free,' not from slavery to Pharaoh, but from the 'waterless Pit'—an image used elsewhere to describe Sheol, the realm of the dead (cf. Pss 28:1; 30:3; 143:7; Isa 38:18; Ezek 31:16; 32:24–30). In other words, this exodus is not just new, it is eschatological."[58] Ratzinger does not make this explicit reference to Zechariah and the relationship between the new Passover and the new exodus, but nevertheless these conclusions are present in his theology in a fragmentary manner.

The clear allusion to the Sinai Covenant in Exodus 24:8 is critical for Ratzinger as this suggests that Jesus is a new Moses forming a new covenantal liturgy for a newly formed people of God.[59] Above all, Ratzinger

---

for others,' as we can see right before our eyes in the pierced heart of Christ." Joseph Ratzinger, *On the Way to Jesus Christ*, trans. Michael J. Miller (San Francisco: Ignatius Press, 2004), 116.

[56] Ratzinger, *MROC*, 60 (JRGS8/2, 1108).

[57] Pitre, *Jesus and the Last Supper*, 415.

[58] Pitre, *Jesus and the Last Supper*, 416.

[59] See Joseph Ratzinger, *Called to Communion* [hereafter, *CTC*], trans. Adrian Walker (San Francisco: Ignatius Press, 1996), 27–29, here, 28; *Zeichen unter den Völkern: Schriften zur Ekklesiologie und Ökumene*, Gesammelte Schriften 8/1 [hereafter, JRGS8/1], ed. Gerhard Ludwig Müller, (Freiburg: Herder, 2010), 230: "[The Last

notes that "the idea of sacrifice unquestionably enters into the Last Supper event through the concept of 'blood of the covenant': the liturgy of the life and death of Jesus Christ is interpreted as a covenantal sacrifice, which adopts the Mosaic first step at a higher level and directs it to its authentic meaning."[60] Just as sacrifice and covenant formed Israel into a covenantal people, the Eucharist as the sacrament of the New Covenant forms the Church into a new Israel that is sent forth to invite all people to enter into an exodus in Christ.

As evidenced above, Ratzinger affirms the continuity between the New Covenant instituted by Jesus as the new Moses at the Last Supper and the Sinai covenant, but he makes the further argument that the Gospel of John and the Letter to the Hebrews go beyond the typical connection that is made between the Last Supper and the Passover to highlight the relationship of the Last Supper to the "cosmic Day of Atonement." Ratzinger claims, "The institution of the Eucharist is to be seen as a cosmic Day of Atonement—an idea also suggested in St. Paul's Letter to the Romans" (3:24).[61] Christ is acting as the high priest that is offering an eternal sacrifice that impacts the life of the Christian beyond the context of cultic

---

Supper] is the making of a covenant and, as such, is the concrete foundation of the new people: the people come into being through its covenant relation to God. We could also say that by his eucharistic action, Jesus draws the disciples into this relationship with God and, therefore, into his mission, which aims to reach 'the many,' the humanity of all places and of all times."

[60] Ratzinger, JRCW11, 212 (JRGS11, 264). Also see Ratzinger, JRCW11, 548 [JRGS11, 647]. These are the only two instances within his collected volume on the liturgy wherein Ratzinger addresses this particular passage from Exodus.

[61] Ratzinger, *MROC*, 63 (JRGS8/2, 1110). Ratzinger notes the "connection between the [high priestly prayer of Jesus] in John 17 and the liturgy of Yom Kippur is convincingly brought out" in "André Feuillet, *Le Sacerdoce du Christ et ses ministres* (Paris: Pierre Téqui, 1972), esp. 39–63." Ratzinger, *MROC*, 63n11. For the impact of Feuillet on Ratzinger, also see Joseph Ratzinger, *Jesus of Nazareth: Holy Week: From the Entrance into Jerusalem to the Resurrection* [hereafter, JN II], trans. Vatican Secretariat of State (San Francisco: Ignatius Press, 2011), 76–82; *Jesus von Nazareth: Beiträge zur Christologie,* Joseph Ratzinger Gesammelte Schriften 6/1 (hereafter, JRGS6/1), ed. Gerhard Ludwig Müller (Freiburg: Herder, 2013), 477–481. Elsewhere, Ratzinger discusses the Passover of Jesus in relationship to the Day of Atonement based on the cosmic symbolism of the liturgical calendar in Ratzinger, JRCW11, 64–65 (JRGS11, 99–100). N. T. Wright contends, "The controlling metaphor [for Christ's sacrificial death anticipated by the Last Supper] that [Jesus] chose for his crucial symbol was not the Day of Atonement, but Passover: the one-off moment of freedom in Israel's past, now to be translated into the one-off moment which would inaugurate Israel's future." N. T. Wright, *Jesus and the Victory of God*, vol. 2, *Christian Origins and the Question of God* (Minneapolis, MN: Fortress Press, 1997), 605.

sacrifice. Ratzinger develops his description of this cosmic act of atonement as he insists that "Christ gives glory to God by sacrificing himself and thus bring human existence within God's own being."[62] Communion with the *Logos* is made possible by Christ's death on the Cross. Ratzinger quotes the Old Testament scholar Hartmut Gese (b. 1929) to relate the Last Supper with the Passover and the Day of Atonement:

> He who is crucified represents God on his throne and unites us with him through the sacrifice of the human blood that is his life. God becomes accessible to us and appears to us in him who is crucified. The reconciliation is effected, not from man's side in a rite of substitionary shedding of blood or giving of life, but from God's.[63]

This interpretation of the Pauline passage (Rom 3:25) emphasizes that the substitionary sacrifice of Jesus Christ alone achieves the communion and reconciliation between God and humanity. Ratzinger further develops the understanding that the Cross alone "provides the Eucharistic liturgy with its reality and contents and lifts it above what is merely ritual and symbolic."[64] The Eucharist re-presents the sacrifice of the Cross drawing the faithful into this sacrifice so that they might make the sacrificial love paradigmatic for their own lives.

Ratzinger links this sacrificial meal to the Exodus as he establishes the Last Supper in relation to the notion of the New Covenant. The previous section has demonstrated that Ratzinger comments explicitly on the relationship between an exodus and a covenant. In addition to the Sinai covenant, Ratzinger notes that the words of Christ at the Last Supper are also a reference to the New Covenant announced by Jeremiah (31:31–34).[65] The institution of the Holy Eucharist is at the heart of Christ's ministerial work as priest, prophet, and king. Jesus makes a covenant with his Father on behalf of the New Israel. It is through communion with Christ's Body and Blood that his disciples become a "people."[66] The Old

---

[62] Ratzinger, JRCW11, 334 (JRGS11, 402).

[63] Hartmut Gese, *Zur biblischen Theologie: Alttestamentliche Vorträge* (Munich: Christian Kaiser, 1977), 105, quoted in Ratzinger, JRCW11, 335 (JRGS11, 402).

[64] Ratzinger, JRCW11, 336 (JRGS11, 404).

[65] Ratzinger, *CTC*, 26 (JRGS8/1, 228). Also see *MROC*, 63–65 (JRGS8/2, 1110–1111). Additionally, Ratzinger interprets the Pauline account of the Last Supper also as a prophetic critique of the self-sufficiency of cultic sacrifices. Ratzinger, JRCW11, 212–213 (JRGS11, 265–266).

[66] Ratzinger, *CTC*, 28–29 (JRGS8/1, 228–30).

Covenant is a particular covenant for the descendants of Abraham based on the principle of inheritance, and it is conditionally dependent on one's observance of the Law. The New Covenant is universal for all peoples based on the spiritual relationship created by sacrament and faith and irrevocably given in and through the life of grace.[67] The New Covenant of the new exodus is accompanied by an exhortation to the New Law of charity (which is embodied by Jesus himself)[68] and ultimately a new form of worship in "spirit and truth" (John 4:24). What characterizes the newness in worship is that it goes beyond mere cultic ritual and transforms the ordinary life of the believer into a form of self-giving love.

In the Matthean-Marcan accounts of the Last Supper, Ratzinger notes the significant use of the phrase "for many" (Matt 26:28; Mark 14:24), which highlights Christ's role as the Suffering Servant and his identity as existing "for" (pro-existence) others. Ratzinger connects the phrase "for many" with the Suffering Servant songs of Deutero-Isaiah: "The prophet says that the Servant of God has borne the sins of many (53:12) and thus has freed them from guilt (53:11)."[69] The New Covenant is based on the sacrificial love of the Suffering Servant who will carry the burden of man. In an article on vicarious representation, Ratzinger comments that the figure of the Suffering Servant represents Israel's own mission and that Israel must subsequently "experience the mystery of vicarious representation as the true center of its historical existence."[70] Israel is called to suffer *for* the sake of others. In the context of the Last Supper, Jesus is giving the Suffering Servant song its definitive meaning in relation to his own mission. The German Scripture scholar Peter Stuhlmacher comments on Jesus's sacrifice "for many," and he also draws upon the parallels to the Suffering Servant song:

> Jesus also takes on this substitutionary suffering of Israel as God's Servant when he gives his life as a ransom for many. In his

---

[67] Ratzinger, *MROC*, 66–67 (JRGS8/2, 1112–1113).

[68] See Ratzinger's comments on Jesus as the New Torah. Ratzinger, *MROC*, 69–71 (JRGS8/2, 1114–1115).

[69] Ratzinger, JRCW11, 213 (JRGS11, 266).

[70] Ratzinger, "Vicarious Representation," trans. Jared Wicks, S.J., in *Letter & Spirit* 7 (2011): 212. Originally published as "Stellvertretung," in *Handbuch theologischer Grundbegriffe*, ed. Heinrich Fries, 2 vols. (Munich: Kösel, 1962–63), 2:566–575 (see *Jesus von Nazareth: Beiträge zur Christologie*, Joseph Ratzinger Gesammelte Schriften 6/2 [hereafter, JRGS6/2], ed. Gerhard Ludwig Müller [Freiburg: Herder, 2013], 911–923).

self-sacrifice, Jesus offers his life vicariously not only for Israel but also for the nations of the world, that is, for all people far from God.[71]

Jesus Christ is presented as a substitutional sacrifice on behalf of the world. Ratzinger argues that Christ "takes up the Suffering Servant theme and interprets in these terms the meaning of his life and death and thereby gives the idea of worship its definitive meaning."[72] Cultic sacrifices are displaced by the vicarious sacrifice of Christ's love poured out on the Cross and anticipated by the Last Supper.

The key to understanding the vicarious nature of Christ's sacrifice is the love and obedience offered by Jesus to the Father, which is symbolized by the outpouring of his blood.[73] In his theological reflections on the life and mission of Jesus of Nazareth, Ratzinger describes this worship at the Last Supper as "new" because it draws humanity into Christ's vicarious sacrifice: "Our participation in Christ's body and blood indicates that his action is 'for many,' for us, and that we are drawn in the 'many' through the sacrament."[74] The sacraments will become the means by which every member of the New Israel can participate in the pro-existence of Jesus Christ.[75]

Jesus's entire life is an existence "for" other people, particularly "the many." Through their participation in the sacraments, Christians are able to share in the sacrificial gift "for" others. The theme of pro-existence will be developed below in the fourth section of this chapter. The former way of worship will be replaced by Jesus, who is the embodiment of the new

---

[71] Peter Stuhlmacher, *Reconciliation, Law, & Righteousness: Essays in Biblical Theology* (Philadelphia, PA: Fortress Press, 1986), 24. Stuhlmacher bases his interpretation of the Marcan "for many" on Isaiah 43:3–4 and 52:13–53:12.

[72] Ratzinger, JRCW11, 214 (JRGS11, 267).

[73] See Thomas Aquinas, *Summa Theologiae* [hereafter, *ST*] III, trans. The Fathers of the English Dominican Province (Westminster, MD: Christian Classics, 1981), q. 48, a. 2. "He properly atones for an offense who offers something which the offended one loves equally, or even more than he detested the offense. But by suffering out of love and obedience, Christ gave more to God than was required to compensate for the offense of the whole human race. First of all, because of the exceeding charity from which He is suffering; secondly, on account of the dignity of His life which He laid down in atonement, for it was the life of One who was God and man; thirdly, on account of the extent of the Passion, and the greatness of the grief endured, as stated above" (*ST* III q. 46, a. 6).

[74] Ratzinger, *JN* II, 134 (JRGS6/1, 519).

[75] See Joseph Ratzinger, *Jesus of Nazareth: Holy Week: From the Entrance into Jerusalem to the Resurrection* [hereafter, *JN* II], trans. Vatican Secretariat of State (San Francisco: Ignatius Press, 2011), 331–332 (JRGS6/1, 395–396).

worship and an exodus himself. Thus, Ratzinger concludes that "the Last Supper is a sacrifice that we receive with thanksgiving, a sacrifice that in our memorial truly enters into our midst."[76] The paschal sacrifice is made ever present in the celebration of the Eucharist.

Turning to the notion of "remembrance" as a hermeneutical key to unlock the relationship between history and the present, Ratzinger notes that it is "a type of making-present: when Israel commemorates salvation history, it receives it as something present, enters into that history, and becomes a participant in its reality."[77] Ratzinger also notes the eschatological characteristic of "remembrance": "It is man's recollection of God's saving acts but, precisely thus, also God's recollection of what is still outstanding: a call of hope and trust in what is yet to come."[78] In summary, drawing upon another Pauline passage: "For as often as you eat this bread and drink the chalice, you proclaim the Lord's death until he comes" (1 Cor 11:26), Ratzinger stresses that this remembrance is a proclamation "that creates reality in the word of remembering and proclaiming."[79]

Ratzinger emphasizes once again that the liturgy is a *logikē latreia* to demonstrate the link between word and sacrament that the notion of proclamation introduces.[80] The words of the liturgy are not simply a remembrance of the past, but they also take upon deeper significance because of the sacrifice of the *Logos*. The Roman Canon makes an explicit reference to the liturgy as *logikē latreia* with the use of the phrase *rationabile obsequium*. Ratzinger comments that the use of the phrase by the Canon "shows an awareness that human words can become true worship and sacrifice only if they are given substance by the life and suffering of him who is himself the Word." The Eucharist is a "true sacrifice," Ratzinger concludes, because

> [it] is the word of the word; in it speaks the one who, as Word, is life. By putting these words into our mouths, letting us pronounce them with him, he permits us and enables us to make the offering with him: his words become our words, his worship our worship, his sacrifice our sacrifice."[81]

---

[76] Ratzinger, JRCW11, 215 (JRGS11, 268).

[77] Ratzinger, JRCW11, 216 (JRGS11, 269).

[78] Ratzinger, JRCW11, 216 (JRGS11, 270).

[79] Ratzinger, JRCW11, 217 (JRGS11, 270).

[80] Ratzinger, JRCW11, 217 (JRGS11, 270). In this passage Ratzinger uses the phrase "rational [or word-like] sacrifice," which is a literal translation of the Greek *logikē latreia*.

[81] Ratzinger, JRCW11, 267 (JRGS11, 324).

The primacy of *logos* reaches its definitive meaning within the Eucharist as Ratzinger maintains that the only authentic or true sacrifice is a reception of the sacrificial gift of Christ's love. The new Israel can enter into the new exodus of Christ because, as Ratzinger repeatedly emphasizes, God has loved us first (1 John 4:10).

Sacrificial love is at the heart of the liturgy and a mark of the true exodus that all people have been made for. This authentic form of sacrifice culminates in the divinization of the believer. Through the gift of grace, the liturgy enables the faithful believer to enter into the life of Christ. Liturgical theologian David Fagerberg describes divinization as "enter[ing] into the life of the Trinity, to be swept up into the energies that flow between the three Persons." Further on, Fagerberg defines the liturgy as "the Trinity's perichoresis kenotically extended to invite our synergistic ascent into deification."[82] Through the celebration of the sacred liturgy, the person enters into Christ's "pro-existence" within the Trinity, and subsequently, he is called to live out a divinized life through a consistent love of neighbor. In the subsequent sections, this chapter will continue to highlight an eschatology in Ratzinger's theology that is made visible through a life of charity that flows forth from the liturgy, which represents the culmination of the exodus that began at Baptism.

## Temple Worship

In light of his emphasis on the continuity between the Old and New Covenant, Ratzinger emphasizes that Christ himself is both the new Temple and the new Lamb. Based upon his reading of the New Testament, Ratzinger insists that the final end of "liturgy and of all priestly ministry is to make the world as a whole a temple and a sacrificial offering for God. This is to bring about the inclusion of the whole world into the Body of Christ, so that God may be all in all" (cf. 1 Cor 15:28)."[83] The crucifixion, which will transform the cultic system of the Old Testament with Christ's establishment of a New Covenant, is anticipated by the Last Supper.

The New Covenant, as explained above in the discussion of the Last Supper in relation to Exodus 24:8, is ratified by Christ's death and Resurrection. The ultimate meaning of the new exodus will only be realized

---

[82] David Fagerberg, "Liturgy and Divinization," in *Called to Be the Children of God: The Catholic Theology of Human Deification*, ed. David Vincent Meconi, S.J., and Carl Olson (San Francisco: Ignatius Press, 2016), 279.

[83] Ratzinger, *CTC*, 127–28.

with Christ assuming the identity of the new Temple as he obediently embraces the call to make a paschal gift of himself to humanity. Ratzinger consistently highlights the theme of Christ himself as the new Temple: "A new worship is being introduced, in a Temple not built by human hands. This Temple is his body, the Risen One, who gathers the peoples and unites them in the sacrament of his body and blood."[84] Developing the themes explained earlier in the discussion of the new exodus, Ratzinger insists that Christ has developed a new form of worship with the Eucharist that is not limited to mere cultic ritual.

In order to understand the newness of the worship brought by Christ, it is necessary to understand the patristic description employed by Ratzinger to the relationship of the Old and New Testaments in three stages as shadow, image, and reality.[85] Typically, the shadow represents a type in the Old Testament that foreshadows an image in the New Testament. Reality represents what will be revealed by the eschaton and fulfills what is anticipated by the image. Ratzinger applies this patristic idea to liturgy.

On the foundational level (the shadow), there is the celebration of the Eucharist at the Last Supper, which is foreshadowed in the Old Testament by the sacrifices of the Temple. The Last Supper and worship are given their ultimate meaning through the Cross and Resurrection of Christ. On the secondary level (image), the celebration of the liturgy developed according to Ratzinger from a synthesis of both synagogue and Temple liturgies.[86]

---

[84] Ratzinger, *JN* II: 21–22 (JRGS6/1, 435–436).

[85] Ratzinger, JRCW11, 32 (JRGS11, 63). St. Ambrose, *On the Death of Sartyrus* (Book II), 109: "For we know that according to the Law there are these three, the shadow, the image or likeness, and the reality; the shadow in the Law, the image in the Gospel, the truth in the judgment. But all is Christ's, and all is in Christ, Whom now we cannot see according to the reality, but we see Him, as it were, in a kind of likeness of future things, of which we have seen the shadow in the Law. So, then, Christ is not the shadow but the likeness of God, not an empty likeness but the reality. And so the Law was by Moses, for the shadow was through man, the likeness was through the Law, the reality through Jesus. For reality cannot proceed from any other source than from reality." Trans. H. de Romestin, E. de Romestin and H. T. F. Duckworth, Nicene and Post-Nicene Fathers, Second Series 10, ed. Philip Schaff and Henry Wace (Buffalo, NY: Christian Literature Publishing Co., 1896), rev. and ed. for New Advent by Kevin Knight, accessed June 20, 2015, http://www.newadvent.org/fathers/34032.htm.

[86] Ratzinger firmly expresses his view regarding the influence of both Hebrew liturgies on the New Covenant in contrast with some modern theologians: "[T]he exclusive model of the liturgy of the New Covenant has been thought to be the synagogue—in strict opposition to the Temple, which is regarded as an expression of the law and therefore as an utterly obsolete 'stage' in religion. The effects of this theory have been disastrous.

In the celebration of the liturgy in the present, Christians become contemporary with the past: "In the Eucharist we are caught up and made contemporary with the Paschal Mystery of Christ, in his passing from the tabernacle of the transitory to the presence and sight of God."[87] The unity with Christ the incarnate *Logos* in the liturgy enables the "today," which unites both the past and the present simultaneously. Ratzinger concludes, "If the essence of the past is not simply a thing of the past but the far-reaching power of what follows in the present, then the future, too, is present in what happens in the liturgy: it ought to be called, in its essence, an anticipation of what is to come."[88]

The liturgy is inherently ("in its essence") eschatological. So finally, there is the level of reality spoken by the Fathers that is unveiled by the *eschaton*.[89] In order to gain insight into the eschatological reality that is anticipated in worship, it is necessary to discuss in detail the shadow of sacrifice and the Temple.

Abraham's would-be sacrifice of Isaac (Gen 22:1–14) and the Passover liturgy (Exod 12) offer insight into sacrificial offerings as shadows of the true sacrificial Lamb. Out of the obedience of faith, Abraham is willing to sacrifice his only son, Isaac, who was promised to him by God. When they reach the place of sacrifice, Isaac asks the question "Where is the lamb?" In reply, Abraham remarks that "God will provide." An angel of the Lord prevents Abraham from carrying out the sacrifice, and God gives Abraham a ram caught in the thicket to be sacrificed. Ratzinger comments that "representative sacrifice [*Vertretungsopfer*] is established by divine command."[90] What is significant is that there is no mere replacement given as in the case of the ram that was sacrificed by Abraham in lieu of Isaac, but Christ the Lamb of God is provided as an authentic representative through whom people can be taken to God.[91]

On the nature of sacrifices, Ratzinger maintains, "All sacrifices are acts

---

Priesthood and sacrifice are no longer intelligible. The comprehensive 'fulfillment' of pre-Christian salvation history and the inner unity of the two Testaments disappear from view. Deeper understanding of the matter is bound to recognize that the Temple, as well as the synagogue, entered into Christian liturgy." Ratzinger, JRCW11, 29 (JRGS11, 59–60).

[87] Ratzinger, JRCW11, 33 (JRGS11, 65).

[88] Ratzinger, JRCW11, 33 (JRGS11, 65).

[89] Ratzinger, JRCW11, 32–34 (JRGS11, 63–66).

[90] Ratzinger, JRCW11, 22 (JRGS11, 51). For Matthew Levering, this would-be sacrifice of Abraham (*Aqedah*) highlights the centrality of sacrifice as the part of the obedience and fidelity that precedes communion. See Levering, *Sacrifice and Community*, 29–49.

[91] Ratzinger, JRCW11, 22 (JRGS11, 51).

of representation, which, from symbols, in this great act of real representation become reality, so that the symbols can be dropped without one iota being lost."[92] Notably, Ratzinger describes the symbolism of these sacrifices without any further explanation or citation. Only when one turns to his lecture at Fontgombault can a person get insight into his understanding of symbolism: "Augustine interprets the Old Testament sacrifices as symbols pointing to this real sacrifice [that unites us in communion with God], and that is why, he says, worship had to be changed, the sign had to give way to the reality."[93] The reality that fulfills the shadow and image of Temple worship and the Eucharistic liturgy is the vocation to charity. This fidelity to the *ethos* of love is a realization of the eschatological love in the present.

The use of representation in relation to sacrifice is a reference to the stress that Ratzinger places upon the sacrifice of Christ on the Cross as a vicarious representation.[94] In Ratzinger's view, "Vicarious representation is a fundamental category of biblical revelation, which however, most likely because it lacks a corresponding philosophical model, plays only a meager role in theology."[95] Jesus will become the ultimate vicarious or representative sacrifice so that Christians will be able to offer ourselves as living sacrifices. Vicarious representation defines one of the primary effects of the Eucharist as a sacrifice in that "Christians live first of all and totally from the Lord's service of representation and at the same time they receive it as the basic law of their own being."[96] The representative and symbolic characteristics of sacrifices in general prepare the way for their true meaning of sacrifice in light of the Eucharist and Christ's sacrifice on the Cross. Subsequently, it is critical to understand the role of the Paschal Lamb in both the Old and New Testaments to understand and to appreciate the symbolism of this sacrifice, which Ratzinger describes above in Augustinian terms, and the centrality of vicarious representation.

---

[92] Ratzinger, *MROC*, 41 (JRGS8/2, 1095).

[93] Ratzinger, JRCW11, 550–51 (JRGS11, 649–50). Here Ratzinger cites Augustine, *De civitate Dei* X, 5: "All the manifold sacrificial precepts that were given by God concerning the services in the tabernacle or the Temple are therefore supposed to refer symbolically to the love of God and neighbor."

[94] For commentary on the use of *Stellvertretung* or "pro-existence" theology throughout the work of Ratzinger, see Christopher Ruddy, "'For the Many,' The Vicarious-Representative Heart of Joseph Ratzinger's Theology," *Theological Studies* 75, no. 3 (2014): 564–84.

[95] Ratzinger, "Vicarious Representation," 209 (JRGS6/2, 911).

[96] Ratzinger, "Vicarious Representation," 213 (JRGS6/2, 916).

The centrality of the Paschal Lamb in the Passover liturgy in Exodus 12 offers insight into the significance of representative sacrifice. Ratzinger summarizes the role of the lamb in the Jewish Passover: "The lamb appears clearly as the ransom through which Israel is delivered from the death of the firstborn. Now this ransom serves also as a reminder."[97] The Passover symbolizes the deliverance intended for every person and for all of creation. This deliverance will take place with the true Paschal Lamb. Ratzinger underscores the use of the phrase "first-born" (Luke 2:7) and the phrase "first-born of all creation" (Col 1:15) in reference to Christ, indicating his role as the Lamb through whom sanctification and redemption of all takes place.[98] The discussion of the sacrificial lamb in the Old Testament sets the stage for Ratzinger's general analysis of cultic sacrifice in the Old Testament. At this point of the discussion, Ratzinger draws upon various texts of the Scriptures to demonstrate the inadequacy and insufficiency of cultic sacrifices. Particularly, among the prophets, God gives a clarion call for something more than the sacrifices of ancient Israel: "For I desire mercy and not sacrifice" (Hos 6:6; see 1 Sam 15:22; also Matt 9:13).[99]

The basis for Ratzinger's emphasis on the Augustinian notion of sacrifice finds its root in the Scripture passage dealt with previously. Temple worship itself is critiqued by the psalmist: "If I were hungry, I would not tell you; for the world and all that is in it is mine. Do I eat the flesh of bulls, or drink the blood of goats? Offer to God a sacrifice of thanksgiving, and pay your vows to the Most High" (Ps 50 [49]:12–14).[100] Ratzinger comments that the true worship, which Yahweh desires from his people, is "love for one's brethren" that "without which external worship becomes an empty, indeed, repulsive farce (cf. Ps 40 [39]:6ff; 50[49]:7ff; 51[50]:16f; Isa 1:11ff.; Jer 6:20; 7:22f.)."[101] In light of the connection between worship and ethics, the cultic sacrifices of ancient Israel are unsatisfactory because

---

[97] Ratzinger, JRCW11, 22 (JRGS11, 52).

[98] Ratzinger, JRCW11, 22 (JRGS11, 52).

[99] Ratzinger, JRCW11, 212 (JRGS11, 265); also cited in Ratzinger, JRCW11, 22–23 (JRGS11, 52–53). Beyond the texts cited by Ratzinger, there are ample texts from the prophets that are critical of the practice of sacrifice without a corresponding interior conversion. See Amos 5:21–27; Hosea 8:13; Isaiah 2:9–19; 7:9; 29:13; Micah 6:6–8; Jeremiah 6:20; 7:21; and Zachariah 7:5. See Yves Congar, *The Mystery of the Temple*, trans. Reginald F. Trevett (London: Burn & Oates, 1962), 54–79 (especially, 56–60).

[100] Quoted in Ratzinger, JRCW11, 23 (JRGS11, 52). Hosea 6:6 as quoted by Matthew's Gospel is a "key element in the redefinition" of sacrifice and the Temple by Jesus in N. T. Wright's commentary on Jesus and the Temple. *Jesus and the Victory of God*, 426.

[101] Ratzinger, JRCW11, 212 (JRGS11, 265).

there is no corresponding love towards God and neighbor. These sacrifices are a shadow of the true image of sacrifice: Jesus Christ, the Paschal Lamb.

There is a sense of inadequacy of cultic sacrifices within the Old Testament. In his reflections in *Jesus of Nazareth*, Ratzinger cites the Letter to the Hebrews to critique cultic sacrifice: "The author [of the Letter to the Hebrews] describes Old Testament worship as a 'shadow' (10:1) and gives this as his reason: 'It is impossible that the blood of bulls and goats should take away sins' (10:4)."[102] Ratzinger draws his readers' attention to the fact that the sacred author of Hebrews quotes Psalm 40:6–8, which highlights obedience to the word of God as a replacement for Temple sacrifices: "Living within and on the basis of God's word had been recognized as the right way to worship God."[103] True worship consists of the person living in accordance with God's word. Ratzinger claims, "The more the person becomes 'word'—or rather: the more his whole existence is directed toward God—the more he accomplishes true worship."[104] As explained earlier, the Pauline notion of *logikē latreia* defines the new or true worship established by Jesus Christ by the Last Supper, the Cross, and the Resurrection. Only in Jesus assuming his identity as both the new Temple *and* the new Paschal Lamb can the true or new worship that God ultimately desires take place because it is in him that every Christian can be transfigured in the new exodus.

The identification of Jesus's Passion and Cross as his exodus is indispensable for understanding Ratzinger's emphasis upon the end of the old Temple. In St. Luke's account of the Transfiguration as discussed above, Moses and Elijah spoke to Jesus about the exodus, which he was going to accomplish in Jerusalem (Luke 9:31). The exodus of Christ is the Cross, which Ratzinger describes as "a departure from this life, a passage through the 'Red Sea' of the Passion, and a transition into glory—a glory, however, that forever bears the mark of Jesus' wounds."[105] It becomes difficult to interpret the Last Supper as anything but a type of Passover meal (albeit a new type), which anticipates the exodus of Christ on the Cross and his entrance into glory following the Resurrection. The insufficiency of cultic sacrifices, as discussed above, is accompanied by the notion of the temporality of the Temple in Jerusalem. First, Jesus prophesizes about the destruction of the Temple (Matt 24:1–2; Mark

---

[102] Ratzinger, *JN* II, 233 (JRGS6/1, 590).
[103] Ratzinger, *JN* II, 233 (JRGS6/1, 591).
[104] Ratzinger, *JN* II, 234 (JRGS6/1, 591).
[105] Ratzinger, *JN* I, 311 (JRGS6/1, 380).

13:1–2). Then he promises to rebuild the Temple in three days following its destruction (John 2:19).

Only a unified life of worship and ethics oriented towards God can deliver Israel from their tendency to form a self-generated cult. The Incarnation marks the beginning of the new exodus that is fulfilled in the Cross and Resurrection. Ratzinger comments decisively:

> In Jesus's self-surrender on the Cross, the Word is united with the entire reality of human life and suffering. There is no longer a replacement cult. Now the vicarious sacrifice [*Stellvertretung*] of Jesus takes up and leads us into the likeness with God, that transformation into love, which is the only true adoration. In virtue of Jesus's Cross and Resurrection, the Eucharist is the meeting point of all the lines that lead from the Old Covenant, indeed, from the whole of man's religious history. Here at last is right worship, ever longed for and yet surpassing our powers: adoration "in spirit and truth." The torn curtain of the Temple is the curtain torn between the world and the countenance of God. In the pierced heart of the Crucified, God's own heart is opened up—here we see who God is and what he is like. Heaven is no longer locked up. God has stepped out of his hiddenness.[106]

Salvation history reaches its culmination as worship reaches its final form in Christian liturgy. The shadow of worship in the Old Testament finds its true image in Christ, who leaves the Eucharist as a perpetual remembrance of his Paschal Mystery. The intersection between past, present, and future meet in the liturgy as the Eucharist symbolically makes the Exodus and Passover of Christ present. The incarnate *Logos,* as both the Paschal Lamb and the new Temple, becomes the sole locus for authentic worship.

The self-giving sacrificial love of Jesus on the Cross has permanently replaced cultic sacrifices. Christian worship is the means by which the Church is able to participate in the new Passover of Christ. The Eucharist allows Christians to participate in the eschatological worship of heaven through sacramental signs.[107] The symbolic gift that is made present in the Eucharist is highlighted for Ratzinger by the word *semel,* "once for all," as it has been used in the Letter to the Hebrews in contradistinction with the

---

[106] Ratzinger, JRCW11, 28 (JRGS11, 58–59).
[107] Ratzinger, JRCW11, 36 (JRGS11, 68).

many sacrifices of ancient Israel.[108] Ratzinger comments that the "exterior act of being crucified is accompanied by an interior act of self-giving."[109] This act of self-gift, which takes place in a particular moment in history, is made present always in the celebration of the liturgy. Consequently, the liturgy enables Christians to enter contemporaneously into Christ's Paschal Mystery.[110] The further purpose of making Christ's sacrificial love available to the faithful new Israel in the present moment is so they might "logicize" their lives by offering their own lives as living sacrifices (Rom 12:1).[111] This commitment to sacrificial love is also an eschatological anticipation of the love.

The eschatological dimension is an integral dynamic of the Eucharist, which Ratzinger claims "has the goal of transforming humanity and the world into the New Heaven and New Earth, into the unity of the risen Body."[112] The new temple, which has not been built by human hands, is present in Christ. At the same time, the construction of the new temple has not reached its completion:

> The great gesture of embrace emanating from the Crucified has not yet reached its goal; it has only just begun. Christian liturgy is liturgy on the way, a liturgy of pilgrimage toward the transfiguration of the world, which will only take place when God is "all in all."[113]

There is an isolation that takes place in light of the Fall that isolates the individual "I" with a false autonomy.

The liturgy presents the true ontology of the person as a person made for another "thou," or communion. Ratzinger describes this adequate anthropology as a "Eucharistic personalism," wherein there is a "drive toward union, the overcoming of the barriers between God and man, between 'I' and 'thou' in the new 'we' of the communion of saints."[114] Every person that the Christian encounters is his potential brother and sister, who can be brought into the communion of Christ. The liturgy enables every Christian to live a moral life *in* Christ by being "taken up into [Jesus's] being 'for' humanity." Ratzinger comments that this moral

---

[108] Ratzinger, JRCW11, 33 (JRGS11, 64).
[109] Ratzinger, JRCW11, 33 (JRGS11, 64).
[110] Ratzinger, JRCW11, 33 (JRGS11, 65).
[111] Ratzinger, JRCW11, 34 (JRGS11, 66).
[112] Ratzinger, JRCW11, 53 (JRGS11, 87).
[113] Ratzinger, JRCW11, 30 (JRGS11, 61).
[114] Ratzinger, JRCW11, 53 (JRGS11, 87).

dimension is simultaneously eschatological as Christians are "incorporated into the great historical process by which the world moves toward the fulfillment of God being 'all in all.'"[115] The new exodus is not meant to be a limited experience for members of the new Israel. This liberation in Jesus Christ is destined for all people, but those who have embarked upon this journey are called to evangelize others so that they, too, might participate in the joys of the new Pasch.

The Resurrection brings the Pasch to its fulfillment as it enables Christians to participate in the new worship of Christ that is not limited to a particular place of worship as Jesus becomes the new Temple. Ratzinger comments, "With his Resurrection, a new way of worshipping God begins, no longer on this or that mountain, but 'in spirit and truth' (John 4:23)."[116] The Resurrection marks the end of the history of salvation as ancient Israel anticipates the "awakening of the dead as the end of history." Ratzinger articulates that they awaited this event "quite literally as the *eschaton*, as the final action of God."[117] Contrary to the expectation that the eschaton will occur at the end of history, belief in the Resurrection, according to Ratzinger, is belief in the "*eschaton in* history" or "in the historicity of God's eschatological action."[118] In light of the new or true worship outlined above, the Christian participates in this eschatological action to the degree that he or she fully participates in the existence of Christ for others. Hence, one can witness the "*eschaton in* history" through love manifested in the lives of the faithful. The celebration of the liturgy extends beyond the rite itself as people make visible its effects through a life marked by charity.

One can only appreciate Ratzinger's statement above when a person understands that the "eschaton is ultimately no one and nothing other than the glorified Christ as the abode of a new humanity: He is the true 'land' of the future, to which all promises lead."[119] The liturgy becomes a true Parousia in light of the Incarnation. In the Prologue of John, the eschaton entered into history as "[T]he Word became flesh and dwelt among us, full of grace and truth; we have beheld his glory, glory as of the only-begotten

---

[115] Ratzinger, JRCW11, 35 (JRGS11, 67).

[116] Ratzinger, *JN* II, 22 (JRGS6/1, 436).

[117] Joseph Ratzinger, *Principles of Catholic Theology: Building Stones for a Fundamental Theology* [hereafter, *PCT*], trans. Sister Mary Frances McCarthy, S.N.D. (San Francisco: Ignatius Press, 1987), 186.

[118] Ratzinger, *PCT*, 187.

[119] Joseph Ratzinger, Dogma and Preaching: Applying Christian Doctrine to a Daily Life [hereafter, DP], trans. Michael J. Miller (San Francisco: Ignatius Press, 2011), 113.

Son from the Father" (v. 14). Scripture scholars, such as Nicholas Perrin, note that John is clearly presenting the incarnate *Logos* as the "glory cloud pitching its tent among the Sinai generation."[120] As the new Temple, Jesus opens up worship universally, so that all people can participate in the glory of God, whereas with the old Temple, as Yves Congar notes, "the layout of various parts of the Temple symbolized this system whereby access became more and more restricted and confined to a smaller number of people."[121] Only in light of the reality of the passing away of the Temple under the Old Covenant can the new worship take place. Ratzinger maintains that "universality is an essential feature of Christian worship. It is the worship of an open heaven. It is never just an event in the life of a community that finds itself in a particular place."[122] The advent of the new Temple that brings about this new worship is symbolized in Ratzinger's theology of liturgy by the pierced heart of Christ (John 19:37).[123] The new exodus is now opened up universally so that all may participate in worship of the new Temple, the *Logos* made flesh.

The Resurrection marks the end of Christ's exodus, in which every Christian is called to participate with every aspect of his life. Ratzinger refers to this participation in the resurrected life of Christ as a "theology of existence":

> [T]he theology of Resurrection gathers all salvation history within itself and concentrates it on its existence-oriented meaning so that, in a very literal sense, it becomes a theology of existence, a theology of *ex-sistere*, of that exodus by which the human individual goes out from himself and through which alone he can find himself. In this movement of ex-sistere, faith and love are

---

[120] Nicholas Perrin, *Jesus the Temple* (Grand Rapids, MI: Baker Academic, 2010), 53.

[121] See Yves Congar, O.P., *The Mystery of the Temple*, 143. Congar continues, "There was the Court of the Gentiles, the Court of the Women open only to Israelites, the Court of Israel entered only by Jews in a state of ritual purity; the terrace reserved for priest and Levites, the Holy Place where the appointed priests fulfilled their ministry, and so were bound by regulations imposing a stricter ritual purity, and finally the Holy of Holies, into which only the High Priest entered and then but once a year, after he had offered a sacrifice both for his own impurities and those of the people. These provisions had their reason and their meaning, they signified the inclusion of the whole people within the person of its true high priest, Christ, who bears us in himself and represents us all before his Father. But they were only temporary." Congar, *The Mystery of the Temple*, 143–44.

[122] Ratzinger, JRCW11, 30 (JRGS11, 61).

[123] Ratzinger, JRCW11, 28–29 (JRGS11, 58). Also see Ratzinger, JRCW11, 270 (JRGS11, 327).

ultimately united—the deepest significance of each is that *Exi*,
that call to transcend and sacrifice the *I* that is the basic law of
history of God's covenant with man and ipso facto, the truly basic
law of all human existence.[124]

The realization of the *eschaton* continues to be made present in history
through the life of grace in the Christian who participates fully in the
celebration and fruits of the liturgy.

The effects of the *eschaton* are made present in a degree analogous
to the Eucharist particularly through the highest form of witness, martyrdom.[125] Ratzinger highlights the fact that martyrdom was perceived as
a real liturgical sacrifice in the ancient Church.[126] Citing a sermon from
Peter Chrysologus (ca. 380–ca. 450), Ratzinger makes the argument that
the Christian in imitation of Jesus has a vocation to be both sacrifice to
God and priest.[127] On the one hand, the Christian has received the call to
become a living sacrifice to God; on the other hand, believers have received
the call to offer up every aspect of daily life to be transformed in light of
Christ's love.

In the celebration of the liturgy itself, nature—as represented by
various material objects such as water, bread, wine, or oil—receives an
outpouring of grace through the Word and is transformed supernaturally.
Analogously, the human person is transformed by grace and exists in the
world as an eschatological sign of God's love. Liturgy, by its very nature,
is directed towards the transformation of the world beyond it. Alluding
to the countless men and women who have embraced the true nature of
sacrifice as divinization, Ratzinger remarks, "The self-transcendence
of the merely liturgical is inscribed in the core of Christian liturgy and
proves its worth again and again in very practical ways in those who live
most profoundly and purely on their participation in the earthly-heavenly
liturgy."[128] The *eschaton* continues to reveal itself through the life of the
faithful people of God, who are heroically struggling to live a life of holiness *in* history.

---

[124] Ratzinger, *PCT*, 189.

[125] See Ratzinger, JRCW11, 346–51 (JRGS11, 414–20).

[126] Ratzinger JRCW11, 34 (JRGS11, 66).

[127] See Peter Chrysologus, *Sermo* 108 (PL 52:499f), quoted in Ratzinger, JRCW11, 555
(JRGS11, 654).

[128] Ratzinger, JRCW11, 579 (JRGS11, 700–01).

## THE *GRUNDGESTALT* OF THE HOLY EUCHARIST[129]

The previous section has shown that the celebration of the Last Supper cannot be fully understood apart from the new exodus, the new Temple, and the centrality of sacrifice understood ultimately as love. In light of this context, it is critical to affirm the primacy of the sacrificial character of the Eucharist as Ratzinger consistently argues that the new worship is marked by the Church's participation with and in the sacrificial prayer of the incarnate *Logos* through the Eucharist. Among German-speaking theologians in the twentieth century, a dispute arose concerning the sacrificial nature of the Eucharist.[130] I will highlight the history of this debate briefly in order to develop the contrast between Romano Guardini and Joseph Ratzinger on the *Grundgestalt*, or basic structure, of the Eucharist and to underscore the significance of Ratzinger's position in arguing for the primacy of sacrifice as the essence of the Eucharist.

Ratzinger is wary of scholars who would remove the notion of sacrifice from the theology of the Eucharist because this would transform the fundamental essence of the sacrament. Ratzinger highlights the work of Stefan Orth, who offers a survey of recent literature dedicated to the theme of sacrifice.[131] Orth sums up his position: "[M]any Catholics themselves today ratify the verdict and the conclusion of Martin Luther, who says that to speak of sacrifice is 'the greatest and most appalling horror' and a 'damnable idolatry'; this is why we want to refrain from all that smacks of sacrifice including the whole Canon, and retain only that which is pure

---

[129] This section has been previously published as part of the article: Ronald Millare, "The Hermeneutic of Continuity and Discontinuity between Romano Guardini and Joseph Ratzinger: The Primacy of Logos," *Nova et Vetera* (English) 18, no. 2 (Spring 2020): 553–563.

[130] See Manfred Hauke, "The 'basic structure' (*Grundgestalt*) of the eucharistic celebration according to Joseph Ratzinger," in *Benedict XVI and the Roman Missal: Proceedings of the Fourth Fota International Liturgical Conference,* ed. Janet Elaine Rutherford and James O'Brien (Dublin: Four Courts Press, 2013), 70–113. I am relying upon Hauke's historical and theological account of this controversy among German speaking theologians to contextualize the position of Ratzinger.

[131] Stefan Orth, "Renaissance des Archaischen? Das neuerliche theologische Interesse am Opfer," *Herder Korrespondenz* 55 (2001): 195–200, cited in Ratzinger, JRCW11, 543 [JRGS11, 642]. Cf. Philip McCosker, "Sacrifice in Recent Catholic Thought: From Pardon to Polarity, and Back Again?" in *Sacrifice and Modern Thought*, ed. Julia Mészaros and Johannes Zachhuber (Oxford: Oxford University Press, 2013), 132–146; Richard Schenk, O.P., "Opfer und Opferkritik aus der Sicht römisch-katholischer Theologie," in *Zur Theorie des Opfers: Ein interdisziplinäres Gespräch*, ed. Richard Schenk (Stuttgart: Fromman-holzbook, 1995), 193–250. McCosker and Schenk offer surveys of recent contemporary literature among Catholic theologians on the notion of sacrifice.

and holy."[132] Orth concludes his summative thoughts by commenting that the Church, following the Second Vatican Council, "led people to think of divine worship chiefly in terms of the feast of the Passover related in the accounts of the Last Supper."[133] In his commentary on Orth's statement, Ratzinger argues that the Passover and sacrifice should be viewed as mutually exclusive notions. Within this section, I will argue that Ratzinger's position presents a nuanced view of the primacy of sacrifice in relation to the Eucharist that is overshadowed by other German theologians of the twentieth century.

Citing the work of Wilhelm Imkamp (b. 1951), the theologian Manfred Hauke has traced the tendency towards proposing the Eucharistic sacrifice as a meal to the theologian Franz Seraph Renz (1860–1916).[134] A student of Renz, Franz Sales Wieland (1877–1957) reaffirmed the theories of Renz and proposed the thesis that the Eucharist was identified only as a meal prior to Irenaeus. Hauke summarizes one thread of the argument for Wieland: "Only after Irenaeus did the thanksgiving sacrifice [*Danksagungsopfer*] become a presentation/offering sacrifice [*Darbringungsopfer*]."[135] This position would draw criticism from theologians such as the Austrian Emil Dorsch S.J. (1867–1934), who presented patristic evidence (prior to Irenaeus) that supported the notion of the Eucharist as a sacrificial offering of Christ's Body and Blood.[136] The discussion revolving around the

---

[132] Orth, "Renaissance des Archaischen," 198. Cited in Ratzinger, JRCW11, 543 (JRGS11, 642).

[133] Orth, "Renaissance des Archaischen," 198. Cited in Ratzinger, JRCW11, 543 (JRGS11, 642).

[134] Wilhelm Imkamp, "Die katholische Theologie in Bayern von der Jahrhundertwende bis zum Ende des Zweiten Weltkrieges," in Walter Brandmüller, ed., *Handbuch der bayerischen Kirchengeschichte* III (St. Ottilien: EOS, 1991), 576–78, cited by Manfred Hauke, "The 'basic structure' (*Grundgestalt*) of the eucharistic celebration according to Joseph Ratzinger," 70. The work of Franz Renz is entitled *Die Geschichte des Messopferbegriffs oder der alte Glaube und die neuen Theorien über das Wesen des unblutigen Opfers*, 2 vols. (Freising: F. P. Datterer, 1901 and 1902). Gerhard Rauschen, *Eucharist and Penance: In the First Six Centuries of the Church* (St. Louis, MO: Herder, 1913), 62–63.

[135] Hauke, "The 'basic structure' (*Grundgestalt*) of the eucharistic celebration according to Joseph Ratzinger," 7.

[136] See Hauke, "The 'basic structure' (*Grundgestalt*) of the eucharistic celebration according to Joseph Ratzinger," 70–71. Also see Rauschen, *Eucharist and Penance*, 74–98. Rauschen provides the history of exchanges between Wieland and Dorsch along with the patristic texts used by Wieland as he makes his claim favoring the meal characteristic of the Eucharist as it was celebrated in the pre-Irenic period. Rauschen rejects Wieland's thesis after his very apt summary of the arguments presented: "Wieland, in particular, has done much towards clearing up the testimony of the early Fathers in

structure of the Mass would find continual interest among the German theologians of the liturgical movement such as Romano Guardini,[137] Joseph Pascher,[138] and Josef Andreas Jungmann, S.J.[139] All of these thinkers have been influential in various ways upon the liturgical theology of Ratzinger, particularly Guardini and Pascher.

Guardini, whose influence upon Ratzinger has been outlined in the previous chapter, maintained that the understanding of the *Grundgestalt* is an essential task of liturgical renewal: "Therefore one of the most important tasks of liturgical education is to reveal as clearly and as vigorously as possible the interior structure of the divine events. So what is the basic structure [*Grundgestalt*] of the Mass? It is that of the meal."[140] Interestingly, the fourth edition of Guardini's work omitted the chapter concerning the *Grundgestalt* of the Mass. In his preface, Guardini explained that he excluded this section from a previous edition because there was a misunderstanding of his thesis that was read as a rejection of the Tridentine doctrine of the Eucharist as a "true and proper sacrifice."[141] Nevertheless, the understanding of the meal as the primary content of the Mass would continue to gain support among other figures who would influence Ratzinger such as Gottlieb Söhngen and Michael Schmaus.[142]

---

regard to the Eucharist. But for very good reasons we cannot follow him in the contention that before the time of Irenaeus the idea of the Christian altar was foreign to the Church, and that in the days of Irenaeus the conception of the Eucharistic sacrifice underwent an essential change" (98).

[137] Romano Guardini, *Besinnung vor der Feier der heiligen Messe*, 2 vols. (Mainz: Matthias Grünewald, 1939).

[138] Joseph Pascher, *Eucharistia: Gestalt und Vollzug* (Münster und Krailling: Aschendorff und Wewel, 1947).

[139] Josef Andreas Jungmann, *Missarum Sollemnia*, 2 vols. (Wein: Herder, 1948). On the impact of this debate on these various German theologians of the liturgical movement, see JRCW11, 299–318 [JRGS11, 359–382]. Also see Hauke, "The 'basic structure' (*Grundgestalt*) of the eucharistic celebration according to Joseph Ratzinger," 74–86.

[140] Guardini, *Besinnung vor der Feier der heiligen Messe*, 72, cited in Hauke, 77.

[141] Guardini, *Besinnung vor der Feier der heiligen Messe*, 14, cited in Hauke, 77–78.

[142] See Hauke, "The 'basic structure' (*Grundgestalt*) of the eucharistic celebration according to Joseph Ratzinger," 79–80. In Söhngen's nuanced development of Guardini, he maintains, "A sacramental sacrifice can have the form [*Gestalt*] of a meal, because a sacramental sacrifice is a sacrifice not in its proper form, but in a different form." *Das sakramentale Wesen des Meßopfers* (Essen: Augustin Wibbelt, 1946), 59, cited in Hauke, "The 'basic structure' (*Grundgestalt*) of the eucharistic celebration according to Joseph Ratzinger," 80. This is a modification of Söhngen's original thesis found in his *Der Wesensaufbau des Mysteriums*, Grenzfragen zwischen Theologie und Philosophie 6 (Bonn: Hanstein, 1938) summarized by Edward Kilmartin: "Christ who suffered,

Despite the impact of these various thinkers upon Ratzinger in other areas of theology, he would maintain the preeminence of sacrifice as the authentic *Grundgestalt* in both the theology and celebration of the Eucharist. The significance of the primacy of sacrifice for our work is that it also communicates the eschatological nature of the liturgy.

In Ratzinger's estimation, the proper relation between dogmatic and liturgical theology is the "central problem of liturgical reform."[143] Ratzinger rejects the thesis that there can be a total separation between dogmatic and liturgical theology. Theology is a symphonic whole with distinct and complementary parts.[144] If there is a constitutive relationship between the *lex orandi* and *lex credendi*, then there must be a way to reconcile these two theological notions. Joseph Pascher introduced the notion of sacrificial symbolism as part of the meal structure of the Eucharist; the distinct offering of bread and wine symbolize the sacrificial offering of Christ's blood.[145]

The thesis of Jungmann had greater significance for Ratzinger because the Austrian theologian argues that the *Grundgestalt* of the Eucharist, beginning in the apostolic period, affirms the prominence of *eucharistia* over the meal aspect.[146] Ratzinger defines the *eucharistia*, as employed by Jungmann, as "the prayer of anamnesis (reminiscence) in the shape of a thanksgiving."[147] Further on, Ratzinger highlights the later research of Jungmann, which argues that Luther's use of the word "supper" (*Abendmahl*) was a "complete innovation in the sixteenth century."[148]

---

the Christus Passus, still bears the marks of his passion and under this formality is present in the liturgical mysteries. This absolute and substantial presence implies the virtual presence of the historical redemptive acts of Christ and grounds the objective presence of the past saving acts which are realized (in their effects) in the individual subject of the liturgical celebrations." Edward J. Kilmartin, S.J., *The Eucharist in the West: History and Theology*, ed. Robert Daly (Collegeville, MN: The Liturgical Press, 1998), 284. On the development of Söhngen's view of sacramental sacrifice, see Kilmartin, 284–291.

[143] Ratzinger, JRCW11, 301 (JRGS11, 361).

[144] Marc Cardinal Ouellet has expressed the need to restore liturgy to its primary place "as the privileged source of trinitarian and ecclesiological doctrine. *Lex orandi, lex credendi, lex theologandi.*" See Ouellet, *Mystery and Sacrament of Love: A Theology of Marriage and the Family for the New Evangelization*, trans. Michelle K. Borras and Adrian J. Walker (Grand Rapids, MI: Eerdmans Publishing Company, 2015), 13.

[145] Ratzinger, JRCW11, 301 (JRGS11, 362).

[146] Jungmann, *Missarum sollemnia*, vol. 1, 327, cited in Ratzinger JRCW11, 301 (JRGS11, 362).

[147] Ratzinger, JRCW11, 301 (JRGS11, 362).

[148] Jungmann, "'Abendmahl' als Name der Eucharistie," in *Zeitschrift für Katholische*

This *eucharistia* thesis of Jungmann, in Ratzinger's view, establishes the necessary unity between liturgical and dogmatic theology.

Based on the words of Jesus Christ used at the Last Supper, Ratzinger cites the work of the German New Testament scholar Heinz Schürmann (1913–1999), among others, and claims that Jesus "actually underwent, in an inward and anticipatory manner, his Death on the Cross."[149] Additionally, the *eucharistia* thesis is connected to Ratzinger's *logos*-centered theology and his trinitarian understanding of both the Cross and the Eucharist.[150] Ratzinger emphasizes the latter point: "The Eucharistic Prayer is an entering into the prayer of Jesus Christ himself; hence it is the Church's entering into the Logos, the Father's Word, into the Logos' self-surrender to the Father, which, in the Cross, has also become the surrender of humanity to him."[151] The *eucharistia* thesis highlights the central role of Ratzinger's emphasis on the notion of the *logikē latreia* in his liturgical theology. The unity between the Church's Eucharist and Christ's self-sacrifice is deepened by the *eucharistia* thesis. This thesis provides the foundational emphasis on the spiritual notion of *logikē latreia* in the life of the Christian, which is ultimately a participation in the sacrificial love of Christ himself. Beyond the unity between liturgical theology and dogmatics, Ratzinger wants to connect the Last Supper of Jesus with the Church's celebration of the Eucharist.

Ratzinger consistently highlights the newness of the Lord's celebration of the Last Supper in relation to the traditional Jewish Passover meal to establish the necessary continuity between Jesus's celebration of the Last Supper and the Eucharist celebrated by the primitive Church. Ratzinger, drawing upon the exegetical work of Heinz Schürmann,[152] contends: "What the Lord is doing is something *new*. It is woven into an old context—that of the Jewish ritual meal—but is clearly recognizable as an independent entity."[153] In a later work, Ratzinger demonstrates commitment to this idea by emphasizing that Jesus is celebrating his "new Passover":

---

*Theologie* 93 (1971): 93, cited in JRCW11, 302 (JRGS11, 362). Ratzinger reiterates this point from Jungmann again in *JN* II, 142 (JRGS6/1, 524).

[149] Ratzinger, JRCW11, 302 (JRGS11, 362).

[150] Ratzinger, JRCW11, 302 (JRGS11, 362).

[151] Ratzinger, JRCW11, 302 (JRGS11, 362–363).

[152] Heinz Schürmann, *Ursprung und Gestalt: Erörterungen und Besinnungen zum Neuen Testament*, Kommentare und Beiträge zum Alten und Neuen Testament 27 (Düsseldorf: Patmos, 1970), 77–99.

[153] Ratzinger, JRCW11, 304 (JRGS11, 365); emphasis added.

One thing emerges clearly from the entire tradition: essentially, [the Last Supper] was not the old Passover but the *new* one, which Jesus accomplished in this context. Even though the meal that Jesus shared with the Twelve was not a Passover meal according to the ritual prescriptions of Judaism, nevertheless, in retrospect, the inner connection of the whole event with Jesus' death and Resurrection stood out clearly. It was Jesus' Passover. And in this sense he both did and did not celebrate the Passover: the old rituals could not be carried out—when their time came, Jesus had already died. But he had given himself, and thus he had truly celebrated the Passover with them. The old was not abolished; it was simply brought to its full meaning.[154]

The key idea is that the Last Supper is the Passover of Jesus himself, which Ratzinger argues is the "full meaning" of the Passover. At this point in his study of the Last Supper, Ratzinger draws upon this Pauline text for an explanation of this new Passover: "Cleanse out the old leaven that you may be new dough, as you really are unleavened. For Christ, our Paschal Lamb, has been sacrificed" (1 Cor 5:7).[155] The identification of Jesus as the

---

[154] Ratzinger, *JN* II, 114 (JRGS6/1, 508). The relationship between the Last Supper and the Passover is a complicated issue that remains debated among Scriptural scholars and theologians. One of the difficulties to work through is reconciling the discrepancy in chronology of the Last Supper according to the Synoptic Gospels with the Johannine account. Many scholars, including Ratzinger, have relied upon the work of Annie Jaubert. See her *The Date of the Last Supper* (New York: Alba House, 1965). The partial solution presented by Ratzinger is the emphasis on the new exodus led by Jesus. This reading coincides incidentally with N. T. Wright's position as he contends the Last Supper "brought Jesus' own kingdom-movement to its climax. It indicated that the new exodus, and all that it meant, was happening *in and through Jesus*." N. T. Wright, *Jesus and the Victory of God*, 557. Similar to Ratzinger's arguments, Wright claims that the Last Supper is a new Passover that can only be fully understood in relation to Temple-action. The Last Supper in Wright's view anticipates the death of Christ symbolically and serves as another sign of the kingdom, which Christ is establishing. Wright concludes, "Passover looked back to the exodus, and on the coming of the kingdom. Jesus intended this meal to symbolize the new exodus, the arrival of the kingdom through his own fate." Wright, *Jesus and the Victory of God*, 559. Also see Wright, 554–559. For the most comprehensive work on the Last Supper, see the previously cited Brant Pitre, *Jesus and the Last Supper*. See his discussion of the various hypotheses on the dating of the Last Supper, *Jesus and the Last Supper*, 251–373.

[155] Ratzinger, *JN* II, 114 (JRGS6/1, 508). Also see Benedict's Homily for Easter Sunday April 12, 2009, where he touches upon this theme of the "new Passover" and Christ as the Paschal Lamb. The relation of the Passover to the Eucharist is also the subject of

Paschal Lamb brings out the essence of the Last Supper as a "real anticipation of the Cross and Resurrection in the Eucharistic gifts."[156] The final conclusion presented by Ratzinger is that the Eucharist is both a meal *and* a sacrifice.

Insofar as the Last Supper presents the new Passover of Christ, it is an anticipation of the Cross and Resurrection. Ratzinger concludes that the notion of the Eucharist as solely a meal is "historically a crass oversimplification."[157] Elsewhere, Ratzinger maintains that the Pasch of Jesus Christ is essential to defining the liturgy. Commenting on *Sacrosanctum Concilium*, Ratzinger maintains that the Pasch "forms the central category of liturgical theology of the Council. All other aspects are comprised in it."[158] Among theologians and exegetes, the post-conciliar emphasis on the notion of the meal as central to the identity of the Eucharist is simply not consonant with the true understanding of the liturgy.

The thesis of the *eucharistia* affirms sacrifice as the authentic *Grundgestalt* of the Eucharist. Ratzinger summarizes the argument in which he develops the proper tension between the Eucharist as a meal *and* a sacrifice: "Thus *eucharistia* is the gift of *communio* in which the Lord becomes our food; it also signifies the self-offering of Jesus Christ, perfecting his trinitarian Yes to the Father by his consent to the Cross and reconciling us all to the Father in this 'sacrifice.'"[159] Ratzinger concludes that there is "no opposition between 'meal' and 'sacrifice'; they belong inseparably together in the new sacrifice of the Lord."[160] Sacrifice is a core doctrine that cannot be separated from the Eucharist. In his lecture at Fontgombault, Ratzinger opines, "The crisis of liturgy has its basis in central notions about man that cannot be overcome by trivializing the liturgy and making it into a simple gathering or merely a fraternal meal."[161] There are elements of both sacrifice and communion in the Eucharist that unfold in their proper order.

Assigning the communal meal aspect primacy or logical priority over

---

a previous homily given on Holy Thursday, April 5, 2007. Also see Joseph Ratzinger, *Behold the Pierced One: An Approach to Spiritual Christology* [hereafter, *BPO*], trans. Graham Harrison (San Francisco: Ignatius Press, 1986), 114–121.

[156] Ratzinger, *JN* II, 115 (JRGS6/1, 505).

[157] Ratzinger, JRCW11, 311 (JRGS11, 374).

[158] Ratzinger, JRCW11, 578 (JRGS11, 700).

[159] Ratzinger, JRCW11, 311 (JRGS11, 374).

[160] Ratzinger, JRCW11, 311 (JRGS11, 374).

[161] Ratzinger, JRCW11, 550 (JRGS11, 648). Significantly, John Paul II shares the sentiments of Ratzinger: "At times one encounters an extremely reductive understanding of the Eucharistic mystery. Stripped of its sacrificial meaning, it is celebrated as if it were simply a fraternal banquet." *Ecclesia de Eucharistia*, §10.

the Eucharist as a sacrifice places the proverbial cart before the horse. Sacrifice and meal are never mutually exclusive in the Eucharist. In an interview concerning change and permanence in the sacred liturgy, Ratzinger, drawing from the example of the entire history of ancient religions, notes that "sacrifice and meal are inseparably united. The sacrifice facilitates *communio* with the divinity, and men receive back the divinity's gift in and from the sacrifice."[162] Similar to John Paul's position in *Ecclesia de Eucharistia*, Ratzinger maintains that the relationship between sacrifice and communion is evident not only in the Church's theology of the Eucharist but also in the practice of various ancient religions. At the same time, Ratzinger is presenting a different conception of sacrifice that transcends mere cultic notions of sacrifice in light of the self-giving love of Jesus Christ. Sacrifice takes on new meaning in light of salvation history and Ratzinger's keen interest in highlighting the centrality of the covenant.

In order to relate the liturgy and eschatology to one another, it is critical to establish the notion of sacrifice as the *Grundgestalt* of the Eucharist. The emphasis upon the Eucharist as a meal, over and above the Eucharist as a sacrifice, contributes to the development of an immanentized view of the liturgy and eschatology. The next section demonstrates how Ratzinger stresses the understanding of sacrifice as self-giving love in his theology of liturgy. Hence, the emphasis upon the vertical communion between God and humanity that is part and parcel of the sacrificial character of the Eucharist does not preclude the horizontal communion, which is expressed fully by a life of charity. Every member of the faithful is called to enter into the "pro-existence" of Jesus as a mark of his participation in the sacrificial prayer and life of Christ.

## Pro-Existence

Ratzinger's theology of sacrifice culminates in the faithful participating in Jesus's sacrificial love by entering into his own pro-existence.[163] Commenting upon the use of "for" in all four accounts of the Last Supper, Ratzinger strongly insists, "[The word 'for'] may be considered the key not only to the Last Supper accounts, but to the figure of Jesus overall. His entire being is expressed by the word 'pro-existence'—he is there, not for himself, but for others." Ratzinger continues, "This is not merely a dimension of

---

[162] Ratzinger, JRCW11, 529 (JRGS11, 625–626).

[163] On the theme of pro-existence, see Heinz Schürmann, "Pro-Existenz" als Christologischer Grundbegriff" *Analecta Cracoviensia* XVII (1985): 345–371.

his existence, but its innermost essence and its entirety. His very being is a 'being for.' If we are able to grasp this, then we have truly come close to the mystery of Jesus, and we have understood what discipleship is."[164] Understanding the significance of "pro-existence" is essential for comprehending the authentic meaning of sacrifice, understanding and the true terminus of the exodus in the selfless life and love of the *Logos* incarnate, and for unpacking the significance of Ratzinger's spiritual Christology.[165]

Regarding spiritual Christology,[166] Ratzinger offers some insight into the meaning of this term with this commentary on the Lukan account of the Transfiguration. Ratzinger's insights are found within his brief outline of the filial thesis of his Christology: "Thus Luke suggests that the whole of Christology—our speaking of Christ—is nothing other than the interpretation of his prayer: the entire person of Jesus is contained in his prayer."[167] Spiritual Christology is an understanding first of Jesus's identity as a Son of the Father that is manifested by the manner in which he addresses and prays to the Father.[168] Furthermore, spiritual Christology is concerned with the notions of communion and participation as they identify the life

---

[164] Ratzinger, *JN* II, 134 (JRGS6/1, 519). For an analysis of the principle of "for" (*Für*) as a central concept in Ratzinger's Christology, see Anna Elisabeth Meiers, *Eschatos Adam: Zentrale Aspekte der Christologie bei Joseph Ratzinger/Benedikt XVI* (Regensburg: Friedrich Pustet, 2019), 210–221. She will examine this principle in light of the larger theme of the *Stellvertretung* in Ratzinger's Christology.

[165] Christopher Ruddy argues that pro-existence is the one word that summarizes Ratzinger's Christology and soteriology. See his article, "'For the Many,'" 570–73, here 570. Ruddy's article has been insightful in our own appreciation of Ratzinger's use of the notion of *Stellvertretung* for ecclesiology in addition to Christology.

[166] McGregor maintains, "Ratzinger's spiritual Christology is composed of three elements: seven Christological theses, a theology of the heart, and a Eucharistic spirituality. All three elements are to be found in *Behold the Pierced One*. The theses delineate his spiritual Christology" (Peter John McGregor, *Heart to Heart: The Spiritual Christology of Joseph Ratzinger* [Eugene, OR: Pickwick Publications, 2016], xi). Further on McGregor adds, "An analysis of these seven [christological] theses reveals that four of them—the filial, soteriological, dogmatic, and volitional—constitute the content of Ratzinger's spiritual Christology. The remaining personal, ecclesial, and hermeneutical theses are methodological" (*Heart to Heart*, xii). Also see the brief discussion of these Christological theses in Christoph Cardinal Schönborn, O.P., "Zu den Quellen des christologischen Denkens im Werk von Joseph Ratzinger," in *Zur Mitte der Theologie im Werk von Joseph Ratzinger/Benedikt XVI* ed. Michael Heim and Justinus C. Pech (Regensburg: Friedrich Pustet, 2013), 104–108. Schönborn highlights our participation in the prayer of Christ as the center of Christology: "Die Christologie wird im Gebet geboren, nirgendwo sonst" (108).

[167] Ratzinger, *BPO*, 20 (JRGS6/2, 697).

[168] See Ratzinger, *BPO*, 15–22 (JRGS6/2, 693–698).

of the Christian with the filial life of Christ.[169] In Ratzinger's spiritual Christology it is important to begin with the communion between Jesus's two natures and the insight that this offers for our communion with him. Ultimately, the goal of communion with Christ is the participation of the Baptized in Christ's identity as a Son of the Father and in his selfless love *for* others.

Ratzinger's spiritual Christology is clearly an attempt at unifying the emphasis on the division between Jesus's human and divine natures within contemporary theology and an effort to overcome the dichotomy between the historical Jesus and the divine Son of God.[170] In his preface for the work *Behold the Pierced One*, Ratzinger acknowledges his own interest in spiritual Christology, which began as he was preparing a talk for a Congress on the Sacred Heart of Jesus at Toulouse in 1981.[171] Upon reading the texts from the Third Council of Constantinople from AD 681, Ratzinger concludes that the Council's ultimate goal was "the achievement of a spiritual Christology." Further, Ratzinger contends "it was only from this point of view that the classical formulas of Chalcedon appear in the proper perspective."[172] Spiritual Christology offers a clear insight into the distinction between Jesus's two natures, while at the same time uniting the two natures. One cannot understand spiritual Christology, which connects humanity and Christ, without a clear articulation of the unity

---

[169] See Ratzinger's comments on the dimension of God's Fatherhood whereby we become children of God only by participating in communion with Jesus's humanity and hence his Sonship. Ratzinger, *JN* I, 138–39 (JRGS6/1, 245–246).

[170] Ratzinger, *IC*, 194 (JRGS4, 183): "For the time being, let us note that alongside the union of the God of faith and the God of the philosophers, which we recognized in the first article as the basic assumption and structural form of the Christian faith, a second, no less decisive alliance appears, namely, that of the *logos* and *sarx*, of word and flesh, of faith and history. The historical man Jesus is the Son of God, and the Son of God is the man Jesus. God comes to pass for man through men, nay, even more concretely, through *the* man in whom the quintessence of humanity appears and who for that very reason is at the same time God himself" (emphasis in the original; both in the English and the German).

[171] For the text of the talk that Ratzinger offered in Toulouse for the Congress on the Sacred Heart of Jesus in 1981, see Ratzinger, *BPO*, 47–69 (JRGS6/2, 72–690). All of the texts given at this Congress have been published as *Towards a Civilization of Love: A Symposium on the Scriptural and Theological Foundations of the Devotion to the Heart of Jesus* (San Francisco: Ignatius Press, 1985). Throughout his works, Ratzinger praises the development of Christology, which the formula of Chalcedon represents. See Ratzinger, *DP*, 119; 122.

[172] Ratzinger, *BPO*, 9. On the significance of the Christology of the Third Council of Constantinople as an interpretation of the teaching of the Council of Chalcedon, see Meiers, *Eschatos Adam*, 170–180.

that exists between Jesus's human and divine natures. Christology cannot be isolated from other doctrines, particularly the liturgy. Consequently, a focus on Christology, in light of Chalcedon and Constantinople III, is critical for comprehending Ratzinger's theology of liturgy.[173]

In his preface for *A New Song for the Lord*, which has been cited previously in the introduction, Ratzinger contends, "Only a close connection with Christology can make possible a productive development of the theology and practice of liturgy."[174] The freedom of divinization, which is the goal of the new exodus, can only be found in Jesus Christ. This freedom is a result of the union of the two natures of Jesus Christ. As a result of the hypostatic union and the *communicatio idiomatum*, "the greatest possible change has taken place in the human person, the only change which meets his desire: he has become divine."[175] In light of this divinization, Ratzinger concludes that the faithful can "describe that prayer which enters into the praying of Jesus and becomes the prayer of Jesus in the Body of Christ as freedom's laboratory."[176] The human person as an individual "I" is able to enter into the prayer of Jesus, but this would not be possible without the Incarnation.

Ratzinger maintains that the neo-Chalcedonian theology articulated

---

[173] On the influence of the Council of Constantinople III and the theology of Maximus the Confessor in Ratzinger's understanding of Chalcedonian Christology, see Meiers, *Eschatos Adam*, 170–180.

[174] Ratzinger, preface to *NSL*, x. Ratzinger articulates a similar sentiment on another occasion: "In order to grasp the spiritual content of the Eucharist, we therefore have to understand the spiritual tension of the [God-man]: only in spiritual Christology will the spirituality of the Sacrament also open up. On account of its overwhelming interest in [ontology] and history, Western theology has somewhat neglected this point of view, even though in reality it represents precisely the link between the various parts of theology as likewise between theological reflection and the concrete spiritual realization of Christianity." Joseph Ratzinger, *Pilgrim Fellowship of Faith: The Church as Communion* [hereafter, PFF], ed. Stephan Otto Horn and Vinzenz Pfnür, trans. Henry Taylor (San Francisco: Ignatius Press, 2005), 79–80 (JRGS8/1, 324). Also see Ratzinger, *BPO*, 90 (JRGS8/1, 324).

[175] Ratzinger, *BPO*, 42 (JRGS6/2, 715).

[176] Ratzinger, *BPO*, 42 (JRGS6/2, 715). McGregor convincingly argues that human freedom is the ultimate end of Ratzinger's spiritual Christology. See McGregor, *Heart to Heart*, 242–278. Significantly, he highlights a passage from St. Maximus the Confessor, who identifies the human person as "the laboratory in which everything is concentrated and in itself naturally mediates between the extremities of each division [of being]." Maximus, *Ambiguum* 41 (PG 91:1305 A–B), quoted in McGregor, *Heart to Heart*, 242. On the relationship between freedom, nature, and Christology in Maximian theology, see Demetrios Harper, *The Analogy of Love: St. Maximus the Confessor and the Foundations of Ethics* (Yonkers, NY: St. Vladimir's Seminary Press, 2019), 137–202.

by the Third Council of Constantinople (AD 680–681) deepened the Church's understanding of the union of Jesus's two natures as it "teaches that the unity of God and man in Christ involves no amputation or reduction in any way of human nature."[177] Further, the Third Council of Constantinople "abolishes all dualism or parallelism of the two natures, such as had always seemed necessary in order to safeguard Jesus' human freedom."[178] The latter theological insight is a critical contribution as it distinguishes between the two wills of Jesus and affirms the freedom by which the two wills become united. In light of this development, Ratzinger argues, "This free unity—a form of unity created by love—is higher and more interior than a merely natural unity. It corresponds to the highest unity there is, namely trinitarian unity."[179] Jesus freely submits his human will to the divine will.

In the work of Maximus the Confessor, there is an emphasis on the significance of the human will of the *Logos* as he "so humbles himself that

---

[177] Ratzinger, *BPO*, 38 (JRGS6/2, 712). Elsewhere, Ratzinger comments on the significance of the Third Council of Constantinople and the Second Council of Nicaea (AD 787): "Most of the time the Christological models of the first half of our century went no further than Chalcedon, but Chalcedon is only completely understood when we read it in conjunction with later councils." Ratzinger, *NSL*, 8. On the significance of the Christology articulated by the Council of Constantinople III and the related theology of St. Maximus the Confessor, see Aaron Riches, *Ecce Homo: On the Divine Unity of Christ* (Grand Rapids, MI: Eerdmans Publishing, 2016), 128–152; Edward T. Oakes, S.J., *Infinity Dwindled to Infancy: A Catholic and Evangelical Christology*, 153–168; Christoph Cardinal Schönborn, *God Sent His Son: A Contemporary Christology*, trans. Henry Taylor (San Francisco: Ignatius Press, 2010), 198–206; Andrew Louth, *Maximus the Confessor* (New York: Routledge, 2006), 48–62; Cardinal Christoph Schönborn, *God's Human Face: The Christ Icon*, trans. Lothar Krauth (San Francisco: Ignatius Press, 1994), 102–133; Hans Urs von Balthasar, *Cosmic Liturgy: The Universe According to Maximus the Confessor*, trans. Brian E. Daley, S.J. (San Francisco: Ignatius Press, 2003), 207–275; Meiers, *Eschatos Adam*, 174–178; and Demetrio Bathrellos, *The Byzantine Christ: Person, Nature, and Will in the Christology of Saint Maximus the Confessor* (Oxford: Oxford University Press, 2004), 34–59, 99–174.

[178] Ratzinger, *BPO*, 38 (JRGS6/2, 712).

[179] Ratzinger, *BPO*, 39 (JRGS6/2, 712). Ratzinger elaborates on Constantinople III's use of the Trinitarian doctrine for the sake of Christology: "The highest unity there is—the unity of God—is not a unity of something inseparable and indistinguishable; rather, it is a unity in the mode of communion—the unity that love creates and love is. In this fashion, the Logos takes the being of the man Jesus into his own being and talks about it with his own 'I': 'I have come down from heaven, not to do my own will, but the will of him who sent me' (Jn 6:38). It is in the obedience of the Son, in the unity of both these wills in the one assent to the will of the Father, that the communion between human and divine being is consummated." Ratzinger, *BPO*, 92 (JRGS8/1, 326).

he adopts a man's will as his own and addresses the Father with the I of this human being; he transfers his own I to this man and thus transforms human speech into the eternal Word, into his blessed 'Yes, Father.'"[180] This is critical for the human person, who has been made along with the cosmos to be divinized by God. The human person must be able to do this freely if he is truly going to realize his spiritual exodus successfully.

The Christological heresy that dominates Ratzinger's concerns is Nestorianism. Ratzinger claims "we are fighting windmills when we still rail against an assumed monophysitic danger today" when the true threat is a "one-sided separation Christology (Nestorianism) in which, when one reflects on the humanity of Christ, his divinity largely disappears, the unity of his person is dissolved, and reconstructions of the merely human Jesus dominate, which reflect more the ideas of our times than the true figure of the Lord."[181] This has obvious consequences for eschatology and liturgy.

---

[180] Ratzinger, *BPO*, 41 (JRGS6/2, 714). Elsewhere, Ratzinger notes this quality of Christ citing Maximus once again: "[T]he exterior act of being crucified is accompanied by an interior act of self-giving (the Body is 'given up for you'). 'No one takes [my life] from me,' says the Lord in St. John's Gospel, 'but I lay it down of my own accord' (10:18). This act of giving is in no way just a spiritual occurrence. It is a spiritual act that takes up the bodily into itself, that embraces the whole man; indeed, it is at the same time an act of the Son. As St. Maximus the Confessor showed so splendidly, the obedience of Jesus' human will is inserted into the everlasting Yes of the Son to the Father." Ratzinger, JRCW11, 33 (JRGS11, 64).

[181] Ratzinger, *NSL*, 10. Further on, Ratzinger continues to articulate the same concern: "It is not monophysitism that threatens Christianity but a new Arianism, or, to put it more mildly, at least a quite pronounced new Nestorianism to which, incidentally, with a kind of inner logic, a new iconoclasm corresponds" (24). Ratzinger alludes to the concern of monophysitism among the faithful in the writings of J. A. Jungmann, Karl Adam, F. X. Arnold, and Karl Rahner. Rahner describes the Church in the pre-Vatican II period as struggling with a "crypto-monophysitism." Karl Rahner, S.J., *Theological Investigations*, vol. 1, *God, Christ, Mary, and Grace*, trans. Cornelius Ernst, O.P. (Baltimore, MD: Helicon, 1961), 185–200. In the latter part of his life, Rahner maintains if "it is possible to be an orthodox Nestorian or an orthodox Monophysite . . . I would prefer to be an orthodox Nestorian." Karl Rahner S.J., *Karl Rahner in Dialogue: Conversation and Interviews, 1965–1982*, ed. Paul Imhof and Hubert Biallowons (New York: The Crossroad Publishing Company, 1986), 126–27, quoted in *Ecce Homo*, 9–15, here 9. Riches argues that Rahner "sought to emphasize the *inconfusus, immutabilis* side of the Chalcedonian formulation against the *indivisus, inseparabilis* pole of unity in order to free the finitude of the humanity of Christ from the divine unity of the Logos and so give a more authentic account of Jesus's true humanity" (14). Similar to the concerns of Ratzinger, Thomas Joseph White maintains in his exceptional work on Christology "that there exists a tendency in modern Christology that is of a decidedly Nestorian character, and that this tendency derives from the mature Christological

In eschatology, too much emphasis will be placed on the horizontal relationship of charity, overshadowing the vertical dynamic. Subsequently, various theologies of hope and political theologies have focused on the full realization of the kingdom of God here on earth. Within the liturgy, the human aspects will be emphasized to the point of reducing the liturgy to the caprice of humanity. This is a common theme in Ratzinger, which Aaron Riches summarizes aptly:

> According to Ratzinger, the contemporary Liturgy suffers on account of a dualism in Christology, a discretely disassociated anthropology that presumes it is possible to imitate the "human" Jesus apart from the "divinity" of the Son of God. Under this condition, the Liturgy becomes increasingly focused on "our" humanity (the self-evident "given" of our nature). The Liturgy is thus inclined to become a "self-enclosed" parody of *latria*, a parody that fails to doxologically open in *metanoia* to the divine horizon of the filial-union Jesus gives to the world in giving himself (i.e., his own personhood). In this way, the contemporary form of the Liturgy is posited as betraying a Nestorian disassociation of humanity and divinity in Christ. Attempting to discretely follow the "pure" humanity of Jesus, the Liturgy loses the Person of the Son and in so doing loses the personal pattern of humanity's divine *sequela*.[182]

Consequently, Ratzinger stresses that the liturgy is above all the *opus Dei*. In

---

thinking of Karl Rahner." Further on, White explains that in his Nestorian Christology, Rahner "locates the ontological union of God and man in Christ in the same place where Nestorianism typically locates it: uniquely in the spiritual operations of the man Jesus, particularly as they are conformed by the divine indwelling to the mystery of God himself." Thomas Joseph White, O.P., *The Incarnate Lord: A Thomistic Study in Christology* (Washington, DC: The Catholic University of America Press, 2015), 76. For the full context of these remarks and an overview of the Nestorian character of many modern Christologies in tension with the Christology of Aquinas, see White, *The Incarnate Lord*, 75–125.

[182] Aaron Riches, "After Chalcedon: The Oneness of Christ and the Dyolethelite Mediation of His Theandric Unity," *Modern Theology* 24, no. 2 (April 2008): 208. Riches's article has been very insightful in highlighting Ratzinger's concerns regarding a prevailing Nestorianism in contemporary theology. My comments in this section draw from Riches's scholarship, which is unique in underscoring the significance of this Christological issue for the theology of liturgy and other contemporary issues in theology. I am grateful to Tracey Rowland for directing me towards the scholarship of Riches.

the realm of eschatology, he becomes critical of theologies that focus solely on political or human solutions to the challenge of injustices. The larger concern for the theology of liturgy and eschatology is a result of the "Nestorian disassociation." The liturgy makes visible the invisible communion between the natural and the supernatural, the human and the divine, history and ontology, body and soul, nature and grace, creation and eschatology. Only an understanding of Jesus Christ in light of the full wisdom of the Church, especially in light of the Councils of Chalcedon and Constantinople III, can aid us in understanding these circles of communion.

Ratzinger emphasizes the Christology of Chalcedon and its completion with Constantinople III to insist upon his foundational thesis that Jesus Christ is the person through whom every Christian can enter into a *dia-logos* with God. For Ratzinger, Jesus is the incarnate *Logos*, who comes "from someone else" and "to someone else."[183] Jesus Christ, the Son, eternally proceeds from the Father, and he is made flesh by the Spirit in the womb of the Blessed Virgin Mary so that he can be given to the world. Eternity and time meet one another in the Incarnation through Mary's *fiat* (Luke 1:38).

In the Johannine account of Jesus's public ministry, Christ's sense of his mission *from* the Father is clear: "I have come down from heaven, not to do my own will, but the will of him who sent me" (John 6:38). In Ratzinger's analysis of this passage from the Gospel of John, he makes clear that there is an intimate *communio* between the human will of Jesus and the divine will of the *Logos*. According to Ratzinger, drawing upon the insight of St. Maximus the Confessor, "There are not two 'I's in him, but only one. The Logos speaks in the I-form of the human will and mind of Jesus; it has become his I, has become adopted into his I, because the human will is completely one with the will of the Logos."[184] This complete subordination of Jesus's human "I" to the divine "Thou" is the model for every human person who desires to embrace what it means to become a Christian.

The union between Jesus's two natures, coupled with his insistence upon the primacy of the *logos*, is the key to understanding Ratzinger's Eucharistic mysticism:

> The mysticism of identity, in which the Logos and the inner dimension of man blend together, is transcended by a Christological mysticism: the Logos, who is the Son, makes us son in the

---

[183] Ratzinger, *IC*, 189 (JRGS4, 180).
[184] Ratzinger, *BPO*, 39 (JRGS6/2, 712–713).

sacramental fellowship in which we are living. And if we become sacrifices, if we ourselves become conformed to the Logos, then this is not a process confined to the spirit, which leaves the body behind it as something distanced from God. The Logos himself has become a body and gives himself to us in his Body. That is why we are being urged to present our bodies as a form of worship consistent with the Logos, that is to say, to be drawn into the fellowship of love with God in our entire bodily existence, in bodily fellowship with Christ.[185]

Just as there is a union between the two natures of Jesus Christ, there should be a union between each member of the faithful and Jesus Christ. Through the sacraments we become one with Christ, which means that we become united with all people in communion with him. Elsewhere, Benedict XVI describes this sacramental mysticism as "social in character, for in sacramental communion I become one with the Lord, like all other communicants. . . . Union with Christ is also union with all those to whom he gives himself."[186] Communion with Jesus Christ is not simply a spiritual process, but it should impact the life of the person such that they become a living sacrifice that lives in communion with other people. Ratzinger is describing the Christological *ethos* that is characterized by sacrificial love that every person is called to, but it is necessary to examine the foundational *logos* of this *ethos* that originates with Ratzinger's early Christology.

In the area of Christology, Ratzinger tries to unite two different perspectives that will be foundational for defining the significance of *logos* in his Christology: the theology of the Incarnation and the theology of the Cross. Ratzinger notes that the former "sprang from Greek thought and became dominant in the Catholic tradition of East and West," whereas the latter "based itself on St. Paul and the earliest forms of Christian belief and made a decisive breakthrough in the thinking of the Reformers."[187] The two different tendencies within Christology has caused a rift in thought that ultimately separates Christology from soteriology.

The theology of the Incarnation, Ratzinger contends, is focused on the question of ontology as it "centers around the fact that here a man *is* God and that, accordingly at the same time God is man." Further, Ratzinger

---

[185] Ratzinger, JRCW11, 350–351 (JRGS11, 419).
[186] Benedict, *DCE*, §1.
[187] Ratzinger, *IC*, 229 (JRGS4, 213).

maintains that this theology "tends toward a static, optimistic view."[188] In contradistinction with this view, the theology of the Cross in Ratzinger's perspective "leads rather to a dynamic, topical, anti-world interpretation of Christianity, which understands Christianity only as a discontinuously but constantly appearing breach in the self-confidence and self-assurance of man of his institutions, including the Church."[189] In a certain sense there is a fundamental gap between these two theological approaches that cannot be overcome, yet Ratzinger is able to see the potential beginning with the theology of Incarnation that can only be fulfilled by the theology of the Cross. The unity between these two theologies, Ratzinger argues, is discovered when we realize the "*being* of Christ ('Incarnation' theology!) is *actualitas*, stepping beyond oneself, the exodus of going out from self; it is not a being that rests in itself, but the act of being sent, of being son, of serving. Conversely, this 'doing' is not just 'doing' but 'being'. . . . This being is exodus, transformation."[190] It is not difficult to see a formulation of one of his fundamental theses, the primacy of *logos* over *ethos*, as the influence in this Christological thesis.

The *logos* of the Christ is not static but ordered towards relation. Specifically, the *logos* of Christ is ordered towards an *ethos* of love, which is the true realization of sacrifice. Ratzinger defines Christian sacrifice as "nothing other than the exodus of the 'for' that abandons itself, a process perfected in the man who is all exodus, all self-surpassing love."[191] Ratzinger continues, "The fundamental principle of the sacrifice is not destruction but love. And even this principle only belongs to the sacrifice to the extent that love breaks down, opens up, crucifies, tears—as the form that love takes in a world characterized by death and self-seeking."[192] Jesus Christ is a living embodiment of the exodus of love in which all Christians are called to participate because the human person is only fully realized through self-giving.

While relationship is not an essential part of who human persons are, as it is with the Divine Persons of the Trinity, the faithful are nevertheless called to participate in the Son's existence "for" the other.[193] In light

---

188 Ratzinger, *IC*, 229 (JRGS4, 213).

189 Ratzinger, *IC*, 229–30 (JRGS4, 213).

190 Ratzinger, *IC*, 230 (JRGS4, 214).

191 Ratzinger, *IC*, 289 (JRGS4, 264).

192 Ratzinger, *IC*, 289 (JRGS4, 264).

193 Ratzinger maintains, "Person is the pure relation of being related, nothing else. Relationship is not something extra added to the person, as it is with us; it only exists at all as relatedness." *IC*, 289 (JRGS4, 264). Also see Ratzinger, *Joseph Ratzinger* in

of Scripture's characterization of Christ as the last Adam or "the second Adam," Ratzinger makes the claim that Christ is the "true fulfillment of the idea of the human person, in which the direction of meaning of this being comes fully to light for the first time." Subsequently, Ratzinger insists that if this is the case, then "the Christological concept of person is an indication for theology of how person is to be understood as such."[194] Ratzinger outlines two major steps in what he describes as the "hominization" of the human person.

The first step of "hominization" occurred with the creation of the human person as he "crossed by the step from animal to *logos*." But this first step was only completed in Ratzinger's estimation "when the *Logos* itself, the whole creative meaning, and man merge into each other."[195] The Incarnation marks the final step in the "hominization" in Ratzinger's view: "[M]an is most fully man, indeed *the* true man, who is most unlimited, who not only has contact with the infinite—the Infinite Being!—but is one with him: Jesus Christ. In him 'hominization' has truly reached its goal."[196] The bold claim of Ratzinger is that the *logos* of the human person can only be fully realized by the Incarnation of the *Logos*. Communion with Jesus Christ redefines our identity; consequently, divinization marks the end of our exodus of love because communion with Christ enables the human person to enter into the dynamic of existing "for" others.

As was demonstrated in the first section of this chapter, the human person fully becomes himself by entering into the self-giving love of the incarnate *Logos*, which begins with Baptism and is deepened within the celebration of the Eucharist. In Baptism, Christians enter into the filial relationship with God the Father as we become "sons in the Son": "[W]e ourselves are destined to be sons, to enter into the Son's relationship with God and so to be transported into the unity of the Spirit with the Father. Being baptized would thus be the call to share in Jesus' relationship with

---

Communio, vol. 2, *Anthropology and Culture*, 107–11, here 108: "In God, person means relation. Relation, being related, is not something superadded to the person, but it *is* the person itself. In its nature the person exists only *as* relation. Put more concretely, the first person does not generate in the sense that the act of generating a son is added to the already complete person, but the person *is* the deed of generating, of giving itself, of streaming itself forth. The person is identical with this act of self-donation."

[194] Ratzinger, *Joseph Ratzinger in Communio,* vol. 2, *Anthropology and Culture,* trans. Stephen Wentworth Arndt, eds. David L. Schindler and Nicholas J. Healy (Grand Rapids, MI: Eerdmans Publishing, 2013), 114. For further discussion of Christ as the "last Adam," see Ratzinger, *IC*, 234–43 (JRGS4, 217–25).

[195] Ratzinger, *IC*, 235 (JRGS4, 218).

[196] Ratzinger, *IC*, 235 (JRGS4, 218).

God."[197] One of the key concepts in Ratzinger's spiritual Christology is participation of the baptized in the divine filiation of Christ.

Baptism marks the beginning of the Christian's exodus as Ratzinger claims that in Baptism "we lose ourselves as a separate, independent 'I' and find ourselves again in a new 'I.' It is the sacrament of death and—by that fact, but also *only* by that fact—the sacrament of resurrection."[198] The new resurrected life in Christ precludes isolation or autonomy as life in communion with others becomes synonymous with being a Christian: "[B]eing a Christian means being like the Son, becoming a son; that is, not standing on one's own and in oneself, but living completely open in the 'from' and 'toward.'" [199] The Incarnation and the Cross fully reveal that the new identity that the Christian receives with Baptism is a life defined by the preposition "for."[200]

Jesus fully revealed the full meaning of living a life "for" others as he became a vicarious sacrifice upon the Cross at Calvary, but at the same time he modeled for Christians the life that they are called to have as a result of their communion with him. The liturgy, Ratzinger claims, is not limited merely to the "mere *actio liturgica*"; it is meant to be "the 'logicizing' of my existence, my interior contemporaneity with the self-giving of Christ. His self-giving is meant to become mine, so that I become contemporary with the Pasch of Christ and assimilated unto God."[201] The Cross reveals that Christians are made for a sacrificial life that is marked by selfless love. The anthropological implication of the Cross is that Christ gives of himself so that we might participate in his sacrifice and also give of ourselves in love.

The Eucharist is a participation in the Pasch that enables the faithful to participate and become "contemporary with the Pasch of Christ and assimilated unto God." Commenting upon the sacrificial nature of the Eucharist, Ratzinger maintains, "God gives that we may give. This is the essence of the Eucharistic sacrifice, of the sacrifice of Jesus Christ; from the earliest times, the Roman Canon has expressed it thus: '*De tuis donic*

---

[197] Ratzinger, *PCT*, 32.

[198] Ratzinger, *PCT*, 33.

[199] Ratzinger, *IC*, 187 (JRGS4, 178).

[200] Ratzinger, *IC*, 251 (JRGS4, 232): "Because Christian faith demands the individual but wants him for the whole and not for himself, the real basic law of Christian existence is expressed in the preposition 'for.'" Also see Ratzinger, *IC*, 234 (JRGS 4, 218): "Man is finally intended for *the* other, the truly other, for God; he is all the more himself the more he is with the *entirely* Other, with God.

[201] Ratzinger, JRCW11, 34 (JRGS11, 66).

*ac datis offerimus tibi'*—'from your gifts and offering we offer you.'"[202] Jesus Christ gives of himself, so that his followers may give through a life "for" others.

Christians have received a new "I" in Christ within Baptism that lives not only in communion with the divine "You" or "Thou" but in the new "we" of the Church. The Holy Eucharist deepens this communion begun at Baptism: "[T]he Eucharist is not aimed primarily at the individual. Eucharistic personalism is a drive toward union, the overcoming of the barriers between God and man, between 'I' and 'thou' in the new 'we' of the communion of saints."[203] The call to a life of "pro-existence" is a fulfillment of the Eucharistic personalism described by Ratzinger. The human person is called to live a life "for" others. In view of the reality of the communion that the faithful received with Baptism, which is deepened by the Eucharist, Christians are called to live in communion with other people. The liturgy compels each member of the Body of Christ to strive for unity and communion, which presupposes a life directed towards "the other" in love.

## SUMMARY AND CONCLUSION

In light of the focus of this chapter on the centrality of sacrifice and Ratzinger's spiritual Christology, the emphasis on the primacy of *logos* in the previous chapter comes to full fruition in the person of Jesus Christ. Christ's death on the Cross and his triumph over it through the Resurrection is his own exodus, which he inaugurated at the Last Supper. Christians begin their journey on this new exodus by entering into communion with the incarnate *Logos*, beginning at Baptism.

---

[202] Ratzinger, JRCW11, 264 (JRGS11, 321).

[203] Ratzinger, JRCW11, 53 (JRGS11, 87). Elsewhere, Ratzinger develops this notion of the "I-thou" and "we" relationship that is introduced by Christology: "In my judgment Christology has a further significance for the understanding of the concept of 'person' in its theological sense. It adds the idea of 'we' to the idea of 'I' and 'you.' Christ, whom Scripture calls the final Adam, that is, the definitive human being, appears in the testimonies of faith as the all-encompassing space in which the 'we' of human beings gathers on the way to the Father. He is not only an example that is followed, but he is the integrating space in which the 'we' of human beings gathers itself towards the 'you' of God. . . . On *both* sides there is neither the pure 'I,' nor the pure 'you,' but on both sides the 'I' is integrated into the greater 'we.' Precisely this final point, namely, that not even God can be seen as the pure and simple 'I' toward which the human person tends, is a fundamental aspect of the theological concept of the person." Ratzinger, *Joseph Ratzinger in Communio*, vol. 2, *Anthropology and Culture*, 117.

The identity of Jesus as the new Temple and new Lamb is critical to understanding Ratzinger's theology of liturgy and maintaining the primacy of sacrifice as the *Grundgestalt* of the Holy Eucharist. The understanding of the Mass primarily as a sacrifice enables Ratzinger to develop the moral implications of the Eucharist.[204] Sacrifice, which is fully manifested by love for another, is a visible manifestation of a life oriented towards the eschaton. The "pro-existence" of Christ becomes incarnate in the life of the believer through his commitment to worship as a *logikē latreia*.

Consonant with Johannine theology, Ratzinger emphasizes the destruction of the old Temple along with the establishment of Jesus's body as the new Temple so he can develop his insistence that Jesus is instituting a new worship.[205] This new form of worship is characterized by its universality, a transformed view of sacrifice as charity, and its stress upon the *logos*. The establishment of Jesus Christ, the incarnate *Logos*, as the new temple deserving of our complete worship is critical to comprehending the full significance of this new worship. Communion with the *Logos* enables Christians to participate in his sacrificial form of life, which is why it is critical for Ratzinger to maintain the primacy of sacrifice with respect to the Eucharist.

The Eucharist celebrated at the Last Supper is fundamentally a sacrifice that leads to a communion as symbolized by the meal aspect. Sacrifice precedes the Eucharist as a meal, but sacrifice and meal are not mutually exclusive for Ratzinger. This chapter demonstrates that the Last Supper provides the "dogmatic content" (*Gehalt*) for the Eucharist, but the form

---

[204] Cf: Thomas P. Rausch, S.J., *Pope Benedict XVI: An Introduction to His Theological Vision* (New York: Paulist Press, 2009), 137: "Though Benedict's encyclical *Sacramentum Caritatis* develops the social implications of the Eucharist more than his earlier writings do, his approach risks a one-sided emphasis on Eucharist as including us in something already accomplished in Christ's sacrifice." This reading of Ratzinger does not hold up when one considers the fact that the emphasis upon the sacrificial character of the liturgy can only be fully understood coupled with the vocation of the person to enter into the sacrificial love of the incarnate *Logos*. In contrast with Rausch's view, see Ratzinger, *IC*, 251–54 (JRGS4, 232–234). Already in one of his earlier works, Ratzinger makes explicit the social implications of worship.

[205] In Ratzinger's understanding of the relationship between Jesus and the Temple, there is a strong resonance with Johannine theology, as he begins the second part of *Jesus of Nazareth* with Jesus's entrance into Jerusalem and the cleansing of the Temple. See Ratzinger, *JN* II, 1–23 (JRGS6/1, 421–437). On the Johannine theology of Jesus as the new Temple, see P. W. L. Walker, *Jesus and the Holy City: New Testament Perspectives on Jerusalem* (Grand Rapids, MI: Eerdmans Publishing, 1996), 161–200; Nicholas Perrin, *Jesus the Temple*, 50–55.

(*Gestalt*) of the liturgy develops over time in Ratzinger's theology. In light of Ratzinger's theology of the new Exodus and new Temple, the Eucharist must first and foremost be a sacrifice. The meal aspect of the Eucharist emphasizes the theme of communion, which each member of the Body of Christ has with one another because of their communion with the incarnate *Logos* in the Eucharist. The Eucharist gives the faithful access to participate in Christ's existence "for" others.

The Christological theme of Christ's "pro-existence" is necessary to comprehend Ratzinger's theology of liturgy and eschatology. The vicarious representation of Christ on the Cross is paradigmatic for every Christian who participates in the liturgy. The sacrifice of Jesus is to be made present in the life of every Christian through a life of self-giving love. The eschaton continues to occur *in* history through the celebration of the liturgy and in a lesser but analogous degree within the transformed life of the Christians who truly worship in accord with the *Logos*. Thus, sacrifice is ultimately directed at developing the communion that is the Church. For this reason, this study of Ratzinger's spiritual Christology and his emphasis on the theme of sacrifice leads to the engagement with his Eucharistic ecclesiology in the next chapter.

CHAPTER 3

# Eucharistic *Communio* in a *Logos*-centric Key

GOD HIMSELF IS A COMMUNION of divine persons and through the incarnate *Logos*, he has formed the Church as both the "sign and instrument" of this communion in the world to offer a message of authentic hope.[1] The primacy of *logos* in Ratzinger's thought leads him to develop his ecclesiology not simply in terms of communion or even Eucharistic communion, but specifically with reference to the *Logos*. Thus, he states that the Church "came into existence because someone lived and suffered his word; by reason of his death, his word is understood as word par excellence, as the meaning of all being, as logos."[2] Therefore, a key contribution of Ratzinger's ecclesiology is the way in which he connects the notion of *communio* with the triune God, sacrifice (specifically the Eucharistic sacrifice), and *logos*.[3] In view of the pri-

---

[1] *LG*, §1. Unless otherwise noted, translations of conciliar documents come from Norman P. Tanner, ed., *Decrees of the Ecumenical Councils*, 2 vols. (Washington, DC: Sheed & Ward and Georgetown University Press, 1990).

[2] Joseph Ratzinger, *Principles of Catholic Theology: Building Stones for a Fundamental Theology* [hereafter, *PCT*], trans. Sister Mary Frances McCarthy, S.N.D. (San Francisco: Ignatius Press, 1987), 26.

[3] See Joseph Ratzinger, *Behold the Pierced One: An Approach to Spiritual Christology* [hereafter, *BPO*], trans. Graham Harrison (San Francisco: Ignatius Press, 1986), 88–100; *Jesus von Nazareth: Beiträge zur Christologie*, Joseph Ratzinger Gesammelte Schriften 6/2 [hereafter, *JRGS6/2*], ed. Gerhard Ludwig Müller (Freiburg: Herder, 2013), 322–332; here, 88 (*JRGS6/2*, 322): "We are now in a position to say that [communio ecclesiology's] source lies in Christology: the incarnate Son is the 'communion' between God and men. Being a Christian is in reality nothing other than sharing in the mystery of the Incarnation, or as St. Paul puts it: the Church, insofar as she is the Church, is the 'Body of Christ' (i.e., a participation on the part of men in that communion between man and God which is the Incarnation of the Word). Once this has been

macy of *logos*, this chapter will demonstrate the close relationship between liturgy and eschatology in light of ecclesial *communio*. Both the identity and mission of *communio* are realized by the Eucharist, which also anticipates the full *communio* that will only come about with the eschaton.

The notion of *communio* serves as a fundamental theme in the *logos*-centric theology of Ratzinger that unifies his theology of liturgy with his eschatology. First, this chapter examines the personalist influence, particularly from the thought of Martin Buber and Henri de Lubac, upon Ratzinger's thought. Ratzinger constantly makes reference to the need for the "I" of the individual person to enter into a communion with the eternal "Thou" by uniting himself through a communion with the "I" of Jesus Christ.[4] This communion with Christ makes every member

---

grasped, it is clear that there can be no separation of Church and Eucharist, sacramental communion and community fellowship." Also see Joseph Ratzinger, *Pilgrim Fellowship of Faith: The Church as Communion* [hereafter, PFF], ed. Stephan Otto Horn and Vinzenz Pfnür, trans. Henry Taylor (San Francisco: Ignatius Press, 2005), 127; *Zeichen unter den Völkern: Schriften zur Ekklesiologie und Ökumene*, Gesammelte Schriften 8/1 [hereafter, JRGS8/1], ed. Gerhard Ludwig Müller, (Freiburg: Herder, 2010), 576.

4   Ratzinger explicitly acknowledges that "Henri de Lubac has shown that the 'I' of the Christian professions of faith is not the isolated ego of the individual person; rather, it is the collective 'I' of the Church. When I say, 'I believe,' then this means precisely that I am going beyond the limits of my private subjectivity so as to enter into the collective subject of the Church and, in her, to enter into the knowledge that transcends the ages and the limits of time. The act of faith is always an act of becoming a participant in a totality; it is an act of *communio*, a willingness to be incorporated into the communion of witnesses, so that we with them and in them may touch the untouchable, hear the inaudible, and see the invisible." Joseph Ratzinger, "Handing on Faith and the Sources of the Faith," in *Handing on the Faith in an Age of Disbelief*, trans. Michael J. Miller (San Francisco: Ignatius Press, 2006), 27–28. Ratzinger cites de Lubac's *Geheimnis aus dem wir leben*, trans. Karlheinz Bergner and Hans Urs von Balthasar (Einsiedeln: Johannes, 1967), 68. Also see Ratzinger, *PCT*, 22–25; Joseph Ratzinger, *Church, Ecumenism and Politics: New Endeavors in Ecclesiology* [hereafter, CEP], trans. Michael J. Miller, et al. (San Francisco: Ignatius Press, 2008), 36–42; *Zeichen unter den Völkern: Schriften zur Ekklesiologie und Ökumene*, Gesammelte Schriften 8/1 [hereafter, JRGS8/1], ed. Gerhard Ludwig Müller, (Freiburg: Herder, 2010), 660–666. There are also strong parallels between these passages and the following from *Lumen Fidei*: "Faith is not simply an individual decision which takes place in the depths of the believer's heart, nor a completely private relationship between the 'I' of the believer and the divine 'Thou,' between an autonomous subject and God. By its very nature, faith is open to the 'We' of the Church; it always takes place within her communion. . . . We can respond [in the baptismal liturgy] in the singular—'I believe'—only because we are part of a greater fellowship, only because we also say 'We believe.' This openness to the ecclesial 'We' reflects the openness of God's own love, which is not only a relationship between the Father and Son, between an 'I' and a 'Thou,' but is also, in the Spirit, a 'We,' a

of the faithful a part of the Body of the *Logos*, which is the Church herself (a collective "I" or "we"). Second, Ratzinger's way of grounding ecclesiology in the Eucharistic and liturgical self-offering of the incarnate *Logos*, in whose "I" the entire Church has communion, underscores once more the primacy of the *logos* of *communio* over the primacy of *ethos* that has been promoted in the post-conciliar period. Finally, this chapter connects the above points about a *logos*-centric ecclesiology and liturgy with Ratzinger's eschatology, specifically with his contribution to debates over the theology of hope.[5] Ratzinger's theology of hope depends upon the primacy of the Eucharistic *Logos* as the true source of hope for the world, by contrast to views of hope espoused by Metz and Moltmann that depend upon worldly action.

The previous chapter focused on the centrality of sacrifice as the culmination of Christ's exodus, which highlighted and explicated further by honing in on Ratzinger's presentation of Christ as the new Temple and the new Lamb. Furthermore, the significance of pro-existence was established as the heart of Ratzinger's spiritual Christology. The dominant leitmotif of sacrifice in the previous chapter finds its complement in the theme of *communio* in this chapter.[6] The notion of *communio* has gained much prominence in ecclesiology following the Second Vatican Council and after the reaffirmation of this ecclesial identity by the 1985 Synod.[7]

In light of the ecclesiology espoused at the Second Vatican Council, Avery Cardinal Dulles, S.J., defines the Church "as [a] sacrament that brings about spiritual communion among human beings and between them and God. This communion preeminently includes the members of the Church."[8] In his ecclesiology, Ratzinger emphasizes the eschatological identity and mission of the Church as a sacrament of unity that exists to

---

communion of persons" (§39).

[5]  For an excellent introduction to the theme of hope in the writings of Ratzinger/Benedict XVI, see Tracey Rowland, "Variations on the Theme of Christian Hope in the Works of Joseph Ratzinger/Pope Benedict," in *The Culture of the Incarnation*, (Steubenville, OH: Emmaus Academic, 2017), 69–87.

[6]  On the close relationship between sacrifice and communion in the Eucharist, see J. M. R. Tillard, O.P, *The Eucharist: Pasch of God's People*, trans. Dennis L. Wienk (Staten Island, NY: Alba House, 1967), 121–27.

[7]  Ratzinger maintains that "this *communio* ecclesiology actually became the centerpiece of Vatican II's teaching on the Church, the new and yet thoroughly primordial thing that this recent Council wanted to give us." Ratzinger, *CEP*, 17 (JRGS8/1, 262).

[8]  Avery Cardinal Dulles, "Trends in Ecclesiology," in *Called to Holiness and Communion: Vatican II on the Church*, ed. Steven Boguslawski, O.P., and Robert Fastiggi (Scranton, PA: University of Scranton Press, 2009), 2.

draw the world into communion with the incarnate *Logos*. The Church's celebration of the sacred liturgy anticipates the full experience of what it means to belong to a communion that will be fully revealed only in the eschaton.

## THE *LOGOS* OF *COMMUNIO*

One of the hallmarks of twentieth-century theology was a shift towards personalism, which impacted Ratzinger's approach to the notion of *logos* not simply as a static concept such as "reason" or "meaning."[9] The *Logos* is above all a divine Person with whom the faithful are called to enter into communion, so that as a united People of God they can participate in his sacrificial love. The Jewish personalist philosopher Martin Buber influenced Ratzinger's personalist approach in his theology. Buber's work *I and Thou (Ich und Du)* was "a spiritual experience [for Ratzinger] that left an essential mark."[10] Unfortunately, Ratzinger does not elaborate in detail

---

[9]  Many theologians of the twentieth century will be influenced by personalism. Avery Cardinal Dulles describes Ratzinger as "a personalist in philosophy." Dulles, *The Church and Society: The Laurence J. McGinley Lectures, 1988–2007* (New York: Fordham University Press, 2008), 480. Personalism includes a diverse group of thinkers including Max Scheler, Charles Peguy, Jacques Maritain, Gabriel Marcel, Peter Wüst, Dietrich von Hildebrand, Theodor Haecker, Armando Carlini, Michele Federico Sciacca, and Carlo Arata. See Kenneth Schmitz, *The Texture of Being: Essays in First Philosophy*, ed., Paul O'Herron (Washington DC: CUA Press, 2020), 133–134n4. Collins asserts that Ratzinger's method might be better termed a "dialogical" theology rather than a "personalist" theology. The person of Jesus Christ is the center of Ratzinger's thought. Specifically, the emphasis is on the individual persons in communion with him, who allow them to share in his *dia-logos* with the Father in the Holy Spirit. Christopher S. Collins, *The Word Made Love: The Dialogical Theology of Joseph Ratzinger/Benedict XVI* (Collegeville, MN: Liturgical Press, 2013), 18–19. We have established that Ratzinger describes this union between the "I" and "thou" in the "we" of the communion of saints as "eucharistic personalism."

[10]  Emery de Gaál, *The Theology of Pope Benedict XVI: The Christocentric Shift* (New York: Macmillan Palgrave, 2010), 28. Elsewhere, de Gaál maintains "reading Romano Guardini's book *The Lord* and Martin Buber's classic *I and Thou*, [Ratzinger] discovered in Jesus Christ a relational God." Emery de Gaál, *O Lord, I Seek Your Countenance: Explorations and Discoveries in Pope Benedict XVI's Theology* (Steubenville, OH: Emmaus Academic, 2018), 140. In his last interview with the journalist Peter Seewald, the pope emeritus acknowledges: "I revered Martin Buber very much. For one thing he was the great representative of personalism, the I-Thou principle permeates his entire philosophy. Of course I have also read his complete works. He was a bit fashionable at that time. He had newly translated the Holy Scriptures together with Rosenzweig. His personalistic viewpoint and his philosophy, which was nourished by the Bible, were made fully concrete in his Hasidic tales. This Jewish piety, completely uninhibited in faith

on the specific impact that Buber had upon him; yet there are throughout his writings echoes of Buber, who argued that the remedy against the alienation and loneliness of the twentieth century could only be remedied by individuals (the "I") returning to communion with "the Eternal Thou."[11]

and simultaneously always standing in the centre of the concerns of this time, his mode of having faith in today's world, his whole person—all this fascinates me." *Last Testament: In His Own Words*, trans. Jacob Philips (New York: Bloomsbury, 2016), 99. It is also noteworthy that Romano Guardini, a major influence upon Ratzinger's thought, collaborated with Buber in the 1920s. See Robert Krieg, ed., *Romano Guardini: Proclaiming the Sacred in the Modern World* (Chicago, IL: Liturgical Training Press, 1995), 7, 201. Robert Royal, *A Deeper Vision: The Catholic Tradition in the Twentieth Century* (San Francisco: Ignatius Press, 2015), 136–37: "[Guardini's] first major book, *Vom Geist der Liturgie* (*On the Spirit of the Liturgy*) appeared in 1918, when he was only thirty-three, and attracted wide attention not only among Catholics but even among established non-Christians like Martin Buber (the Jewish Philosopher and author of *I-Thou*), who subsequently invited Guardini to participate in a regular Jewish-Christian dialogue in Frankfurt. Buber's personalism deepened Guardini's own, and the two of them remained friends for the rest of their lives". In addition to Buber, Ratzinger was also influenced by the personalist philosopher Dietrich von Hildebrand (1889–1977) and Ferdinand Ebner (1882–1931). See Rowland, *Benedict XVI: A Guide for the Perplexed* (New York: T & T Clark, 2010), 22–23; de Gaál, *The Theology of Pope Benedict XVI*, 43. For a focused study on the affinity between Buber and Ratzinger, see Markus Rutsche, *Die Relationalität Gottes bei Martin Buber und Joseph Ratzinger* (München: Grin, 2007). Rutsche's work is brief, but he highlights the theme of relationality in Ratzinger's theology and the kinship of this theme with Buber's thought. In addition to Buber and Ebner, Ratzinger was influenced by the personalist thought of the moral theologian Theodor Steinbüchel (1888–1949). During his seminary studies in Freising, Ratzinger describes Theodor Steinbüchel's *Der Umbruch des Denkens* [The Revolution of Thought] as a "key book." According to Ratzinger, Steinbüchel "recounted with great verve the revolutionary shift from the dominance of neo-Kantianism to the personalistic phase." *Salt of the Earth: The Church at the End of the Millennium*, trans. Adrian Walker (San Francisco: Ignatius Press, 1997), 60. On the significance of engaging the thought of Steinbüchel for Ratzinger, see Elio Guerriero, *Benedict XVI: His Life and Thought*, trans. William J. Melcher (San Francisco: Ignatius Press, 2018), 64–68; de Gaál, *The Theology of Pope Benedict XVI*, 25–27; and Joseph Ratzinger, *Milestones: Memoirs 1927–1977* [hereafter, *MM*], trans. Erasmo Leiva-Merikakis (San Francisco: Ignatius Press, 1998), 43. For an overview of Ratzinger's formation in personalist thought and the development of his own personalist theology, see Andrzej Proniewski, "Joseph Ratzinger's Philosophical Theology of the Person," *Rocznik Teologii Katolickiej* 17 (2018): 219–236.

[11] Tamra Wright, "Self, Other, Text, God," in *The Cambridge Companion to Modern Jewish Philosophy*, ed. Michael L. Morgan and Peter Eli Gordon (New York: Cambridge University Press, 2007), 102–21. Cited by Collins, *The Word Made Love*, 13. On the influence of personalistic themes from the writings of Buber, Ebner, and Marcel which have resonance in Ratzinger, see *Dialogische Unsterblichkeit: eine Untersuchung*

The subjective shift of modernity continues to assume an autonomous "I" without reference to the "Thou." Throughout his writings, by contrast, Ratzinger draws upon the "I-Thou" model of Buber and other personalist thinkers to develop a theology that consistently relies upon *communio* as the paradigm for the "I-Thou" relationship.[12] Christ is the incarnate *Logos*, who enables the "I" of the individual person to enter into a relationship of *communio* with God the Father (the eternal "Thou") in the Spirit. The Church becomes a "we," which every individual "I" participates in as a result of his *communio* with the "Thou."

The Church, which is a sacrament of the Body of Christ, is both a "sign and instrument" of this *communio*.[13] The *communio* of the Church is expressed fully in the celebration of the liturgy that anticipates the

---

*zu Joseph Ratzingers Eschatologie und Theologie* (Leipzig: St. Benno-Verlag, 1986), 182–86. Also see Nachtwei, "Auf der Suche nach einer Antwort auf die Fragen des heutigen Menschen," in *Hoffnung auf Vollendung: Zur Eschatologie von Joseph Ratzinger*, ed. Gerhard Nachtwei (Regensburg: Friedrich Pustet, 2015), 24–26. Nachtwei cites Ratzinger affirming the influence of Buber and Ebner on the dialogical conception of the person by the Second Vatican Council in *Gaudium et Spes*, no. 12. See Joseph Ratzinger, "Kommentar zum ersten Kapitel des ersten Teils der Pastoralkonstitution über die Kirche in der Welt von heute: Gaudium et spes,'" in *Zur Lehre des Zweiten Vatikanischen Konzils*, Gesammelte Schriften 7/2, ed. Gerhard Ludwig Müller (Freiburg: Herder, 2012), 805. The personalist influence upon Ratzinger via the writings of Søren Kierkegaard, Ferdinand Ebner, Martin Buber, and Theodor Stienbüchel has been noted by his then-prefect in the Freising seminary, Alfred Läpple. See his *Benedikt XVI. Und seine Wurzeln: Was den Studenten Joseph Ratzinger prägte* (Augsburg: St. Ulrich Verlag, 2006), 152. Also see Hansjürgen Verweyen, *Joseph Ratzinger—Benedikt XVI: Die Entwicklung seines Denkens* (Darmstadt: Primus Verlag, 2007), 29; 108–109 and Proniewski, "Joseph Ratzinger's Philosophical Theology of the Person."

[12] See Rowland, *Benedict XVI*, 14–15, de Gaál, *The Theology of Pope Benedict XVI*, 27–28, Collins, *The Word Made Love*, 13–16. The approach of Ratzinger surpasses the personalism of thinkers like Buber in his emphasis of the mediation of the "I-Thou" relationship through the Church. The Church is the body of Christ that enables the individual "I" to share in the life of the eternal "Thou" through the life of grace given in the sacraments. "We encounter him [Jesus Christ] as a living Person only in the foretaste of his presence which is called 'Church.' At this point we begin to see how it may be possible to purify and accept the inheritance of Asia. The latter is correct in refusing to see individual identity as an encapsulated 'I' over against a similarly encapsulated 'Thou' of God, ignoring the existence of other 'I's which are themselves related individually and separately to this divine Thou. Here we see the limitation of the kind of personalism which was developed between the Wars by Ebner, Buber, Rosenzweig, E. Brunner, Steinbüchel and others." Joseph Ratzinger, *The Feast of Faith: Approaches to a Theology of Liturgy*, trans. Graham Harrison (San Francisco: Ignatius Press, 1986), 28–29.

[13] *LG*, §1.

*communio* that will be unveiled with the eschaton.[14] The autonomy of an individual "I" is overcome through communion with the eternal "Thou" in the Eucharist. The newly formed "we" is the relationship that all of humanity is destined for in the eschaton.

The human person is called to enter into a relationship with God, who is an eternal "we," who enables the human person to enter into the dynamic of relationship with other people. Further, Ratzinger elaborates, "Christ, the one, is here the 'we' into which Love, namely the Holy Spirit, gathers us and which means simultaneously being bound to each other and being directed toward the common 'you' of the one Father."[15] Ratzinger contends that humans are "most profoundly human when they step out of themselves and become capable of addressing God on familiar terms."[16] From *the beginning*, the human person has been given this capacity for God (*capax Dei*) in his nature. The "I" has become alienated as a result of a departure from this fundamental relationship between God and the human person. Consequently, Ratzinger develops his spiritual Christology to emphasize the human person's call to participate in this "we" communion by becoming a "son in the Son" through Baptism.

---

[14] In his explanation of the origin and purpose of the theological journal *Communio*, Ratzinger writes, "*Communio* must be first understood theologically. Only then can one draw implications for a sacramental notion of *communio*, and only after that for an ecclesiological notion. *Communio* is a communion of the body and blood of Christ (e.g., 1 Cor 10:16)." Ratzinger, "*Communio*: A Program," in *Joseph Ratzinger in Communio*, vol. 1, *The Unity of the Church*, trans. Stephen Wentworth Arndt, eds. David L. Schindler and Nicholas J. Healy (Grand Rapids, MI: Eerdmans Publishing, 2010), 128; Joseph Ratzinger, *Zur Lehre des Zweiten Vatikanischen Konzils: Formulierung—Vermittlung—Deutung*, Joseph Ratzinger Gesammelte Schriften 7/2 (hereafter, JRGS7/2), ed. Gerhard Ludwig Müller (Freiburg: Herder. 2012), 1117.

[15] See *Joseph Ratzinger in Communio*, vol. 2, *Anthropology and Culture*, trans. Stephen Wentworth Arndt, eds. David L. Schindler and Nicholas J. Healy (Grand Rapids, MI: Eerdmans Publishing, 2013), 116–118, here 117. On Ratzinger's pneumatology, see his "The Holy Spirit as Communio: Concerning the Relationship of Pneumatology and Spirituality in Augustine," in *Joseph Ratzinger in Communio*, vol. 2, 168–83. Ratzinger notes the challenge in speaking about the Holy Spirit: "There is a certain difficulty in speaking about the Holy Spirit, even a certain danger. He withdraws from us into mystery even more than Christ. It is quite possible that this topic has sparked only idle speculation and that human life is being based upon self-made fantasies rather than reality" (168). For Ratzinger's teaching on the Holy Spirit, see *IC*, 331–37; "Alcune forme bibliche ed ecclesiali di 'Presenza' dello Spirito nella storia," in *Spirito Santo e storia*, ed. L. Sartori (Rome: Ave, 1977), 51–64; and Ratzinger, *PFF*, 176–208.

[16] Joseph Ratzinger, *In the Beginning: A Catholic Understanding of Creation and the Fall* [hereafter, *ITB*], trans. Boniface Ramsey, O.P. (Huntington, IN: Our Sunday Visitor, 1990), 48.

In Ratzinger's view, the act of faith or belief enables the human person to enter into a familial relationship of *communio* with the Trinity: "[B]elief in the Trinity is *communio*; to believe in the Trinity means to become *communio*. Historically, this means that the 'I' of the credo-formulas is a collective 'I,' the 'I' of the believing Church, to which the individual 'I' belongs as it believes."[17] *Communio*, or the relationship between the human "I" and the divine "Thou," is fundamental for the very being of the human person. He is able to achieve this union by participating in the larger "I" of the Church. Ratzinger insists that faith "introduces us into the dynamic circle of Trinitarian love that not only unites subject and object but even brings individual subjects together without depriving them of their individuality."[18] The individual "I" is only realized fully in the *communio* of the Church's faith in the Most Blessed Trinity. The Christian doctrine of the Trinity reveals the fundamental *communio* anthropology, which is manifested fully in the person and life of Jesus Christ.

By its very nature, Christianity precludes any isolation or autonomy because the God that it worships is a communion of divine Persons, entering into communion with the incarnate *Logos* is essential for salvation, and the Church exists as a sign and instrument of this communion. In essence, Christianity is about participation or *communio*. The Christian participates in the divine filiation of the Son so that he can share in the life of *communio* with the Blessed Trinity. Ratzinger reiterates this point clearly throughout his writings: "To become a Christian means to become incorporated in the Son, in Christ, so that we become 'sons in the Son.'"[19] The Incarnation allows the human person to be able to share in the gift of adopted filiation with God the Father.

---

[17] Ratzinger, *PCT*, 23.

[18] Ratzinger, *PCT*, 26. Faith has a dialogic structure according to Ratzinger: "Man comes to deal with God in coming to deal with his fellowmen. Faith is fundamentally centered on 'You' and 'We'; only via this double clamp does it link man with God. The corollary of this is that by the inner structure of faith our relationship to God and our fellowship with man cannot be separated from each other; the relationship to God, to the 'You,' and to the 'We' are intertwined; they do not stand alongside each other." Joseph Ratzinger, *Introduction to Christianity* [hereafter, *IC*], trans. J. R. Foster (San Francisco: Ignatius Press, 2004), 93–94; Joseph Ratzinger, *Einführung in das Christentum: Bekenntnis—Taufe—Nachfolge*, Joseph Ratzinger Gesammelte Shriften 4, [hereafter, JRGS4] ed. Gerhard Ludwig Müller (Freiburg: Herder, 2014), 99–100.

[19] Joseph Ratzinger, *The Meaning of Christian Brotherhood* [hereafter, *MCB*], trans. W. A. Glen-Doeple, 2nd ed. (San Francisco: Ignatius Press, 1993), 539; *Zeichen unter den Völkern: Schriften zur Ekklesiologie und Ökumene*, Gesammelte Schriften 8/1 [hereafter, JRGS8/1], ed. Gerhard Ludwig Müller, (Freiburg: Herder, 2010), 74.

The "I" of the human person is able to enter into an intimate relationship with the "Eternal Thou" because it participates in the "I" of the Son through grace. The natural need for *communio* can only be fulfilled by the supernatural end of the human person becoming a "son with the Son." This emphasis on divine filiation in Ratzinger's Christology directs him towards his emphasis on a *communio* ecclesiology: "[B]eing a Christian means becoming a son with the Son and thus, precisely by reason of one's belief in God, being incorporated also into the communion of saints, the Body of Christ."[20] An act of faith is never an isolated act. The "I," which professes belief, is part of the larger "I" of the living Body of Christ.[21]

The Fall commences with the person's alienation from God and from his fellow people, which will bring about the need for the isolated "I" to have a means to return to communion with the eternal "Thou." Adam and Eve chose to be "like God" without him (Gen 3:1–5). Ratzinger points

---

[20] Ratzinger, *PCT*, 39. On the significance of *communio* in Ratzinger's theology, see Maximilian Heinrich Heim, O. Cist., *Joseph Ratzinger: Life in the Church and Living Theology*, trans. Michael J. Miller (San Francisco: Ignatius Press, 2007), 286–30. *Communio* ecclesiology is a broad term with different nuances and interpretations. See Dennis M. Doyle, *Communion Ecclesiology* (Maryknoll, NY: Orbis Books, 2000). It is significant to note that some of these ecclesiologies differ fundamentally in their interpretation of *communio*. Avery Cardinal Dulles outlines two different tendencies. Dulles characterizes one tendency in one of these ecclesiologies as "particularist" because it prioritizes the local church, whereas the other tendency is termed "universalist" because it begins with the global church. In their interpretation of *communio*, the universalists "understand it as meaning participation in the divine life, achieved through the objective means of grace, notably the sacraments," whereas the particularists understand the term as "directly signifying a fellowship of love and intimacy. This local communion, in which the members know one another and interact, orients its members toward communion with God and with all other human beings, without restriction." Notably, for our own purposes, Dulles characterizes Leonardo Boff and Jean-Marie Tillard as particularists (Tillard is specifically described as a moderate particularist), and he refers to Henri de Lubac and Joseph Ratzinger as moderate universalists. Most theologians have characteristics of both tendencies. See Avery Cardinal Dulles, S.J., *Church and Society*, 129–41, here, 135.

[21] "[T]he Christian is not alone in his search for God and Christ; rather, he knows that he is supported by the comprehensive 'I' of the Church, which makes him a contemporary of Jesus Christ and thereby conveys God into time and him into eternity." Joseph Ratzinger, *Dogma and Preaching: Applying Christian Doctrine to a Daily Life* [hereafter, *DP*], trans. Michael J. Miller (San Francisco: Ignatius Press, 2011), 44. The individual "I" is taken up into the communal "I" of the body of Christ. "[T]o become one with Christ means to lose one's 'oneself,' to cease to regard one's own ego as an absolute. . . . The ethic of Christ is essentially an ethic of the body of Christ." Ratzinger, *MCB*, 55 (JRGS8/1,76).

out the irony and absurdity of this choice: "[Adam and Eve] do not make themselves gods, which in fact they cannot do, but rather caricatures, pseudo-gods, slaves of their own abilities, which then drag them down."[22] Original Sin begins with the primordial human couple rejecting their nature (*logos*). The redemption of humanity lies in the recovery of their authentic *logos* in the Son.

The Church is Christ's instrument of salvation that has been entrusted with the mission of restoring people back into communion with Christ and other people. God has intended for the Church to serve as the "sign and instrument" of the *communio* for all of creation from the beginning. *Communio* can never be the effort of the human person alone.[23] This type of communion is offered fully in the Eucharist, which is celebrated by the Church. Ratzinger affirms the unity between the Eucharist and the Church: "The Church is *communio*; she is God's communing with humanity in Christ and hence the communing of people with one another—and, in consequence, sacrament, sign, instrument of salvation. The Church is the celebration of the Eucharist; the Eucharist is the Church; they do not simply stand side by side; they are one and the same."[24] The Eucharist is a sacrament of Christ, and in light of the identification between the Church and the Eucharist, the Church is the universal sacrament of communion which the sacraments point towards.[25] Through the Eucharist, Christ "builds up the Church as His body, and through His body that rises again he unites us with the triune God and with each other."[26] The Eucharist is an outward sign of the authentic *logos* of the human person that Christ realizes, so that the human person can enter into communion with the Trinity and other people.

Thus, a recurrent theme in Joseph Ratzinger's writings is that the *communio* ecclesiology of the Church "in its inmost nature" is Eucharistic.[27]

---

[22] Ratzinger, *ITB*, 71. The individual human "I" is incomprehensible apart from the Divine "Thou," which underscores the absurdity of the Fall. Ratzinger, *DP*, 81.

[23] According to Ratzinger, the human person needs "a communion that goes beyond that of the collective; a unity that reaches deep into the heart of man and endures even into death." Ratzinger, *PCT*, 53.

[24] "The Eucharist is the *sacramentum Christi* and, because the Church is *Eucharistia*, she is therefore also *sacramentum*—the sacrament to which all the other sacraments are ordered." Ratzinger, *PCT*, 53.

[25] Ratzinger, *PCT*, 53.

[26] Ratzinger, *PFF*, 131 (JRGS8/1, 579).

[27] Ratzinger, *PFF*, 131 (JRGS8/1, 579). See Ratzinger, *CEP*, 17–20 (JRGS8/1, 262–266); Ratzinger *PCT*, 252–254. This thesis of the Church as a eucharistic *communio* shapes Ratzinger's *Called to Communion*. For the background and development of Ratzinger's

Such Eucharistic ecclesiology finds its origins in the writings of Henri de Lubac, S.J.,[28] and many Orthodox theologians.[29] Ratzinger maintains that

---

*communio* ecclesiology, see Aidan Nichols, O.P., *The Thought of Benedict XVI: An Introduction to the Theology of Joseph Ratzinger* (New York, NY: Burn & Oates, 2005), 136–139; D. Vincent Twomey, S.V.D., *Pope Benedict XVI: The Conscience of Our Age—A Theological Portrait* (San Francisco: Ignatius Press, 2007), 58; Tracey Rowland, *Ratzinger's Faith: The Theology of Pope Benedict XVI* (Oxford: Oxford University Press, 2008), 84–104.

[28] "Above all, more than anyone else, the great French theologian Henri de Lubac in his magnificent and learned studies made it clear that in the beginning the term *'corpus mysticum'* referred to the Eucharist. For St. Paul and the Fathers of the Church the idea of the Church as the Body of Christ was inseparably connected with the concept of the Eucharist in which the Lord is bodily present and which He gives us His Body as food. This is how a *eucharistic ecclesiology* came into existence" (emphasis added). Joseph Cardinal Ratzinger, "The Ecclesiology of Vatican II," no. 2, *EWTN*, accessed November 7, 2015, https://www.ewtn.com/catholicism/library/ecclesiology-of-vatican-ii-2069. This address given by Cardinal Ratzinger at the opening of the Pastoral Congress of the Diocese of Aversa (Italy) is an updated version of his lecture "Ecclesiology of Vatican II" found in Ratzinger, *CEP*, 13–35 (JRGS8/1, 258–282). Joseph Cardinal Ratzinger makes the bold assertion that the Second Vatican Council's ecclesiology was moving in the direction of Father Henri de Lubac's understanding of eucharistic ecclesiology. See Ratzinger, *PCT*, 50. In the estimation of Aidan Nichols, O.P., "[H]e [Ratzinger] is, along with Henri de Lubac, one of the first Catholic thinkers to adopt a full-scale, systematically elaborated, 'eucharistic ecclesiology.'" *The Thought of Benedict XVI*, 47–48. For de Lubac's development of eucharistic ecclesiology, see Henri de Lubac, S.J., *Corpus Mysticum: The Eucharist and the Church in the Middle Ages*, ed. Laurence Paul Hemming and Susan Frank Parsons, trans. Gemma Simmonds, CJ, Richard Price, and Christopher Stephens (Notre Dame, IN: University of Notre Dame Press, 2006).

[29] Among the Eastern Orthodox Theologians advocating a eucharistic ecclesiology, the most prominent were: Nikolai Afanas'ev (1893–1966), Alexander Schmemann, and John Zizioulas. See Nichols, *The Thought of Benedict XVI*, 137–138. Ratzinger notes that Afanas'ev "writes about a eucharistic ecclesiology strictly conceived as located in the local Church, as long ago as 1943." See also Ludwig Freiherr von Hertling, "Communio und Primat—Kirche und Papsttum in der christlichen Antike," *Una Sancta* 17 (1962): 91–125. Ratzinger contrasts this work with Afanas'ev as a work that conceived of a communion ecclesiology "in a wholly Catholic sense." Ratzinger acknowledges that this article was a "key text" for him. Ratzinger, *PFF*, 131n3. Also see Ratzinger's comments differentiating the ecclesiological views of the Eastern Orthodox and the West in Ratzinger, *PCT*, 292–94. On Afanas'ev, see Aidan Nichols, O.P., *Theology in the Russian Diaspora: Church, Fathers, Eucharist in Nikolai Afanas'ev, 1893–1966* (Cambridge: Cambridge University Press, 2008); Peter Plank, *Die Eucharistieversammlung als Kirche: Zur Entstehung und Entwicklung der euchristischen Ekklesiologie Nikolaj Afanasjevs (1893–1966)*, Das östliche Christentum, Neue Folge 31 (Würzburg: Augustinus, 1980). Also see Paul McPartlan, *The Eucharist Makes the Church: Henri de Lubac and John Zizioulas in Dialogue* (Edinburgh: T & T Clark, 1993). Zizioulas is critical of

the Eucharist anchors the ecclesiological concept of *communio* in its proper meaning, uniting "talk about the Church with talk about God and with living with God's help and living with God."[30] The Eucharist ensures that *communio* is directed towards the vertical relationship between the human person and God and the horizontal relationship between one human person and another person. The vertical and horizontal relationships are not mutually exclusive.[31]

The Holy Eucharist and the Church are bound up with one another in Ratzinger's estimation: "The Eucharist is the *sacramentum Christi* and, because the Church is *Eucharistia*, she is therefore also *sacramentum*—the sacrament to which all the other sacraments are ordered."[32] The Church is the visible realization of our communion with God, the ultimate

---

the eucharistic ecclesiology of Afanas'ev because of two basic errors. On the one hand, Afanas'ev considers the parish a complete and universal ("catholic") Church. On the other hand, he prioritizes the local Church ("in its parochial or even episcopal form") over the universal Church. See John D. Zizioulas, *Being as Communion: Studies in Personhood and Church*, (Crestwood, NY: St. Vladimir's Seminary Press, 1985), 23–26; 132–33. Also see Zizioulas's contrast of Afanas'ev with the views of other Orthodox theologians such as Schmemann and Meyendorff on the question of primacy. John D. Zizioulas, "Recent Discussions on Primacy in Orthodox Theology," in *The One and the Many: Studies on God, Man, the Church, and the World Today*, ed. Gregory Edwards, (Alhambra, CA: Sebastian Press, 2010), 274–87, especially 280–83. For insight into Zizioulas's understanding of the relationship between the Eucharist and the Church, see his *The Eucharistic Communion and the World*, ed. Luke Ben Tallon (New York: T & T Clark, 2011), 99–111. On the significance of the shared eucharistic ecclesiology for ecumenical relations, see Aidan Nichols, O.P., *Rome and the Eastern Churches: A Study in Schism*, rev. ed. (San Francisco: Ignatius Press, 2010), 359–64. Also see Helmut Hoping, *My Body Given for You: History and Theology of the Eucharist*, trans. Michael J. Miller (San Francisco: Ignatius Press, 2019), 380–409.

[30] Ratzinger, *PFF*, 132 (JRGS8/1, 580).

[31] The unity between the vertical and horizontal relationships wrought by the Incarnation is central to Ratzinger's theology in the estimation of Menke. Karl-Heinz Menke, *Der Leitgedanke Joseph Ratzingers: Die Verschränkung von vertikaler und horizontaler Inkarnation* (Paderborn: Schöningh, 2008), 45. Menke explores this theme as a hermeneutical key to understanding Ratzinger's theology.

[32] Ratzinger, *PCT*, 53. Ratzinger also characterizes this communion brought about by the Eucharist as the "eucharistic meal of brotherhood" and as a "sacrament of brotherhood." See Ratzinger, *MCB*, 38–40 (JRGS8/1, 64–66); 68–74 (JRGS8/1, 84–89); emphasis added. Ratzinger stresses the sacramental character of the Church as the Body of Christ is characteristic of the Augustinian influence upon his ecclesiology. See his dissertation published in *Volk und Haus Gottes in Augustins Lehre von der Kirche: Die Dissertation und weiter Studien zu Augustinus und zur Theologie der Kirchenväter* [hereafter, JRGS1], Gesammelte Schriften 1, ed. Gerhard Ludwig Müller (Freiburg im Breisgau: Herder, 2011), 288–92.

vocation of all of God's people. The Holy Eucharist prefigures this union and simultaneously achieves it for those living in a state of grace. Consequently, Ratzinger will maintain that the institution of the Holy Eucharist by Christ at the Last Supper marks the conception of the Church.

Joseph Ratzinger, in defining Eucharistic ecclesiology, argues that the Last Supper, insofar as it parallels the covenant of Mount Sinai, could mark the moment when the Church was founded.[33] As the blood of animals sprinkled by Moses at Sinai (Exod 24:8) ratified the Old Covenant with Israel, Christ at the Last Supper ratifies the New Covenant with the gift of his own Body and Blood in perfect obedience and love.[34] This essential part of living the New Covenant for the Church enables Ratzinger to say that the "Church is, in essence a Mass (sent out: 'missa'), a service of God, and therefore a service of humanity and a service for the transformation of the world."[35] The Holy Sacrifice of the Mass enables the Church to enjoy an original dynamic of self-sacrificial love that she does not find anywhere else. This sacrifice of love that is achieved through union with God in Jesus Christ is ordered towards unity within the Church.

The communion brought about by the Holy Eucharist is an anticipation of the unity that the Church is ordered to with the eschaton and hence why Ratzinger stresses the Church's sacramental identity. In the celebration of the liturgy, the Church encounters both multiplicity and unity.[36] In his thoughts on the Holy Eucharist as the source of ecclesial unity, Ratzinger re-echoes St. Ignatius of Antioch, the Doctor of Unity. In his *Letter to the Magnesians*, St. Ignatius writes, "Be one . . . one supplication, one mind, one hope, in love and in joy undefiled. . . . Therefore, run together as into one temple of God, as to one altar, as to one Jesus Christ who came forth from one Father, and is with and has gone to one."[37] Jesus Christ in the Blessed Sacrament is the source of unity for the Church.

---

[33] Ratzinger, *CEP*, 17 (JRGS8/1, 262). Incidentally, the Russian Orthodox theologian Nikolai Afanas'ev espouses the thesis that the Church was instituted in embryonic form at the Last Supper but actualized at Pentecost. See Aidan Nichols, *Theology in the Russian Diaspora,* 107. For a further treatment of the Last Supper in relation to the covenants throughout salvation history, particularly the Mosaic covenant at Mount Sinai, see Ratzinger, *MROC*, 63–71 (JRGS8/2, 1110–1115).

[34] See the previous discussion of the relation between the Last Supper and the Sinai covenant in chapter two.

[35] Ratzinger, "Ecclesiology of Vatican II," no. 2.

[36] Ratzinger, "Ecclesiology of Vatican II," no. 2.

[37] *Smyrnaeans* 7:1–2, quoted in Pope Benedict XVI, General Audience, March 14, 2007, found in *The Fathers,* vol. 1, Wednesday *General Audiences from March 7, 2007– February 27, 2008* (Huntington, IN: Our Sunday Visitor, 2008), 17.

Ratzinger affirms the view of Ignatius: "Christ is everywhere whole. . . . At the same time Christ is everywhere only one, so I can possess the one Lord only in the unity that He is, in the unity of all those who are also His Body and who through the Eucharist must evermore become it."[38] The Holy Eucharist guarantees the unity of the Church and assures her solid foundation; therefore, the celebration of the Eucharist makes the Church of Christ present in "all legitimate local communities of the faithful."[39] In the words of St. Ignatius of Antioch, "Where Jesus Christ is, there is the Catholic Church."[40] The Holy Eucharist truly makes the Church,[41] who she is in her unique identity, set apart from other ecclesial communities. Consistent with his thesis regarding the primacy of *logos*, Ratzinger insists, "Church cannot be made but only received, that is to say, received from a source where she already exists and really exists: from the sacramental communion of his Body as it makes its way through history."[42] *Ethos* or praxis cannot bring about a unity that is received from the Lord through the celebration of the Eucharist.

In order to distinguish his Eucharistic ecclesiology from the view of Orthodox theologians such as Nikolai Afanas'ev, Ratzinger maintains that in addition to being "whole everywhere," Christ is "also only one everywhere, and therefore I can have the one Lord only in the unity that he himself is, in the unity with the others who are *also* his Body and are supposed to become it ever anew in the Eucharist."[43] The *logos* of *communio*, which is defined by the Eucharist, can only be fully appreciated by embracing both unity and catholicity. The shortcoming of Afanas'ev's ecclesiology is that he tries to develop an ecclesiology that is defined by a self-sufficient unity, which is why he logically favors the autonomy of local churches.

The use of "breaking of the bread" by St. Luke in the Acts of the Apostles to describe the Eucharist establishes it as a fundamental pillar of the Church's daily life and highlights the Eucharist's role in defining the mission (*ethos*) of the Church. After receiving the gift of the Holy Spirit at Pentecost, the Church was devoted to the "apostles' teaching and fellowship [communion—*koinonia*], to the breaking of the bread and to the prayers" (Acts 2:42). The use of the phrase the "breaking of the

---

[38] Ratzinger, "Ecclesiology of Vatican II," no. 2.

[39] *LG*, §26.

[40] *Smyrnaeans* 8:2, quoted by Pope Benedict XVI, *The Fathers*, 17.

[41] *CCC* §1396.

[42] Ratzinger, *CEP*, 20 (JRGS8/1, 265).

[43] Ratzinger, *CEP*, 20 (JRGS8/1, 265).

bread" expresses the social requirement of the Eucharist, which should direct someone towards a complete giving of self.[44] The transformation, which changed bread into the Body of Christ, is meant to inform the way of life for each and every Christian. In the words of institution, Christ said, "This is my body which is given for you" (Luke 22:19). This means the breaking of bread that takes place in the Eucharist should involve the transformation of every aspect of a person's life into Christ's life for the world. The full significance of the words of institution employed by Christ at the Last Supper means the person is "existing-for-others."[45] The Eucharistic ecclesiology of Ratzinger lays a foundation for his understanding of the Pauline notion of *logikē latreia* and the *ethos* of love, which the book will develop in the next chapter.

The *logos* of *communio* directs every Christian to an *ethos* of self-love in imitation of Jesus Christ. Ratzinger concludes, "The goal of eucharistic communion is a total recasting of a person's life, breaking up a man's whole 'I' and creating a new 'We.'"[46] This communion with Christ enables the person to enter into union with everyone in relationship with Christ: "Communion with Christ is of necessity a communication with all those who are his: it means that I myself become part of this new 'bread' which he creates by transubstantiating all earthly reality."[47] Through the Incarnation, Jesus Christ is the means by which every person has access to the divine Trinitarian *communio*. This *communio* fellowship is made visible in the Church, particularly in her celebration of the liturgy. Commenting upon Pauline ecclesiology, Ratzinger contends: "Being a Christian in reality is nothing other than sharing in the mystery of the Incarnation, or as St. Paul puts it: the Church, insofar as she is the Church, is the Body of Christ. . . . [T]here can be no separation of Church and Eucharist, sacramental communion and community fellowship."[48] Liturgy is intended to be the external expression of the authentic *logos* of *communio* developed in theological anthropology, Christology, ecclesiology, and eschatology.

The call to communion finds its fulfilment in the eschaton with the general resurrection of the dead when the elect are united as members of the one Body of Christ in worship. Communion for the individual

---

[44] Joseph Ratzinger, *Called to Communion* [hereafter, *CTC*], trans. Adrian Walker (San Francisco: Ignatius Press, 1996), 43 (JRGS8/1, 239).

[45] Joseph Ratzinger, *God Is Near Us: The Eucharist, The Heart of Life*, ed. Stephan Otto Horn and Vinzenz Pfnür, trans. Henry Taylor (San Francisco: Ignatius Press, 2003), 79.

[46] Ratzinger, *BPO*, 89 (JRGS8/1, 323).

[47] Ratzinger, *BPO*, 89 (JRGS8/1, 323).

[48] Ratzinger, *BPO*, 89 (JRGS8/1, 322).

Christian begins with the sacrament of Baptism, and it is deepened in the Holy Eucharist. The eschatological *communio* is anticipated already in the unity of the Church here on earth, which is gathered together as one Body of Christ in the celebration of the sacred liturgy. The relationship between Eucharistic ecclesiology and *communio* (both the earthly and the eschatological) becomes clearer as the origin and meaning of *corpus Christi mysticum* is discussed below.

The development of ecclesiology in the twentieth century owes much in part to the work of Henri de Lubac in highlighting the patristic notion relating the Eucharist and the Church, which deepened Ratzinger's understanding of ecclesiology. His work *Corpus mysticum* offered profound insights into the understanding of the notion of the Church as the Body of Christ (*Corpus Christi*). The German theologian Rudolf Voderholzer summarizes well de Lubac's thesis: "The True Body of Christ, Corpus Christi *verum*, is the Church, while Corpus Christi *mysticum* is the Eucharist. In the early medieval period, there was a stronger emphasis on the Real Presence of Christ in the Eucharist, and the adjectives were switched."[49] Consequently, the Church was characterized as the mystical (*mysticum*) Body of Christ and the Eucharist was characterized as the true (*verum*) Body of Christ. The recovery of the identity of the Church as the true Body of Christ is a major theme in ecclesiology articulated by the Second Vatican Council's Constitution on the Church, *Lumen Gentium*. The articulation of this motif in contemporary theology finds its roots in part in the scholarship of de Lubac.[50] The image of the Body of Christ is a concrete symbol of the Church's call to be a *communio* in the world reflecting the communion of the Trinity and anticipating the eschatological communion that awaits the pilgrim Church. The Holy Eucharist literally *makes* the Church into a living communion, which is, first and foremost, the Body of Christ.

---

[49] Rudolf Voderholzer, *Meet Henri de Lubac: His Life and Work*, trans. Michael J. Miller (San Francisco: Ignatius Press, 2008), 54. For an overview of the theological debate in the medieval period relating to the Real Presence, see Jaroslav Pelikan, *The Christian Tradition: A History of the Development of Doctrine—The Growth of Medieval Theology (600–1300)* (Chicago, IL: University of Chicago Press, 1978), 184–204; Lawrence Feingold, *The Eucharist: Mystery of Presence, Sacrifice, and Communion* (Steubenville, OH: Emmaus Academic, 2018), 233–258.

[50] De Lubac is presenting insights into this theme of ecclesiology from patristic and scholastic scholarship. The close relationship between the Church and the Eucharist is certainly not unique to contemporary theology. On the organic link between ecclesiology and the Eucharist in St. Thomas, see Gilles Emery, O.P., *Trinity, Church, and the Human Person: Thomistic Essays* (Naples, FL: Sapientia Press, 2007), 156–72.

In *Lumen Gentium*, the Body of Christ is the preeminent identity of the Church, which precedes the Church as the People of God, and this theological framework will direct Ratzinger's understanding of the centrality of *communio* in defining the Church.[51] Many subsequent articulations of post-conciliar ecclesiology have focused on the term "People of God." This phrase was used eighty times in various conciliar documents (especially *Lumen Gentium*).[52] According to de Lubac, the use of the phrase "people of God" was meant to "complete the analogy of the Body of Christ."[53] The intent in the use of the phrase was to highlight the continuity and fulfillment between the two covenants of Sacred Scripture. In other words, the limited election of Israel as the people of God on Mount Sinai finds its fulfillment in the universality of the New Covenant of Christ, promised at the Last Supper and ratified on Calvary.[54] The "people of God" explicitly refers to Israel in the Old Testament, while the concept of the "body of Christ" refers to the Church (the New Israel) in the New Testament.[55]

The notion of the Church as "sacrament" is a key term that has been significant for ecclesiology in modern theology. In the Second Vatican Council, Ratzinger claims that the word "sacrament" was first used in reference to the Church in a proposed schema presented in March 1963 for the document that became known in its final form as *Lumen Gentium*,

---

[51] The image of the Church as the Body of Christ complements the notion of the Church as the Temple of the Holy Spirit. These images precede the third image of the Church as the People of God in *Lumen Gentium*. However, it is not unusual to find theologies of the Church which begin with or emphasize the Church as People of God first and foremost. On the theological implications of beginning with the Church as the Body of Christ before emphasizing the image of the People of God, see Benoît-Dominique de La Soujeole, O.P., *Introduction to the Mystery of the Church*, trans. Michael J. Miller (Washington, DC: The Catholic University of America Press, 2014), 61–63.

[52] It was also used in the Decree on Missionary Activity (*Ad Gentes*), the Decree on the Ministry and Life of Priests (*Optatam Totius*), and the Pastoral Constitution on the Church in the Modern World (*Gaudium et Spes*). See Heim, *Joseph Ratzinger*, 9.

[53] Henri de Lubac, interview by Angelo Scola, *De Lubac: A Theologian Speaks* (Los Angeles: Twin Circle Publishing, 1985), 8, quoted in Heim, *Joseph Ratzinger*, 79. For a brief description of the similarities of and the differences between the images of the Church as the Body of Christ and the People of God, see Dulles, *Models of the Church* (New York: Doubleday Books, 1987) 53.

[54] See Ratzinger, *MROC*, 47–77 (JRGS8/2, 1099–1119).

[55] Joseph Ratzinger, *The Ratzinger Report: An Interview with Vittorio Messori*, trans. Salvator Attanasio and Graham Harrison (San Francisco: Ignatius Press, 1985), 47. Cardinal Dulles offers a similar distinction relating the People of God to the covenant under the Old Law and the Body of Christ to the uniqueness of the New Covenant. See Dulles, *Models of the Church*, 54.

the Dogmatic Constitution on the Church.[56] Ratzinger laments that in the years following the Council, "the concept of Church as a sacrament is not yet deeply entrenched either in the consciousness of the Church or in theology."[57] The argument that Ratzinger puts forth to support his critique is that this identity of the Church as sacrament is "mutually complementary and explanatory" to the more popular expression used in reference to the Church, "people of God"; subsequently, Ratzinger insists that "only against the background provided by the concept 'sacrament' can the concept of 'people of God' becoming meaningful."[58] The identity of the Church as "sacrament" enables the true *logos* of the Church to shine forth, whereas the notion of the "people of God" can easily subject the Church to emphasize a worldly or political *ethos* without the guidance of a sacramental *logos*.[59] As a sacramental "sign," the Church "becomes what it

---

[56] Ratzinger, *PCT*, 44: "The word [*sacramentum*] had not appeared in the first draft of the Theological Commission, which had been prepared by Sebastian Tromp, S.J., the principal author of Pius XII's encyclical on the Mystical Body. Nor had it occurred in the first alternative draft offered by the Belgian theologian Gérard Philips on November 22, 1962. Toward the end of 1962, Philips revised his text and distributed it in photocopies. On March 6, 1963, the Commission accepted as the basis of further discussion this revision, which contained the words that survived all further alterations: *Cum vero Ecclesia sit in Christo signum et instrumentum seu veluti sacramentum intimae totius generis humani unitatis eiusque in Deum unionis.*" The text approved by the commission would appear in a slightly altered form as *Lumen Gentium*, [hereafter, LG], §1. The word *sacramentum* is used in two other instances by the Council. Drawing from St. Cyprian of Carthage, the Church is described as "the visible sacrament of this saving unity" (*sacramentum visibile huius salutiferae unitatis*) in LG §9. The Church is also referred to as having been constituted by Christ as the "universal sacrament of salvation" (*universal salutis sacramentum*) in LG §48. On the developments of the various drafts of the Dogmatic Constitution *Lumen Gentium*, see Heim, *Joseph Ratzinger*, 29–38.

[57] Ratzinger, *PCT*, 45.

[58] Ratzinger, *PCT*, 45.

[59] Ratzinger observes that the notion of the People of God "was very soon being understood on the basis of the way 'people' is used in political language generally; in the realm of liberation theology it was according the Marxist usage of 'people' as opposed to the ruling classes; and in general it was widely understood in the sense of the rule of the people, which was supposedly at last going to be applied to the Church." Ratzinger, *PFF*, 127 (JRGS8/1, 576). Arthur McGovern notes that the focus on the Church as the "people of God" is critical for Leonardo Boff's understanding of the church embodied by base communities. The priority of *ethos* in Boff's ecclesiology is evident in his characterization of the marks of the church embodied by base communities: "a unity of equals in community, a holiness that shows itself in militant commitment to liberation, an apostolicity that ministers to those in most need, and a catholicity that struggles in

is by pointing beyond itself; as a sign it does not rest in itself but is always on the way to something else."[60]

An overemphasis has been placed on the concept of "people," such that the Church is reduced from a mystery to a sociological body. This has resulted in using the phrase in an ideological manner antithetical to the hierarchical and sacramental aspects of the Church.[61] Ratzinger stresses

---

behalf of a universal cause of liberation." Arthur F. McGovern, S.J., *Liberation Theology and Its Critics: Toward an Assessment* (Eugene, OR: Wipf & Stock, 1989), 216–17. Boff insists, "There is a fundamental equality in the church. All are people of God. All share in Christ, directly and without mediation. Therefore all share in the services of teaching, sanctifying, and organizing the community." Leonardo Boff, *Church: Charism and Power: Liberation Theology and the Institutional Church* (New York: The Crossroad Publishing Company, 1985), 59. In addition to subordinating *logos* to *ethos*, we can make the argument that Boff's understanding of the *logos* of the Church has been influenced by Afanas'ev's focus on priority of the local church. Dulles comments upon the impact of Afanas'ev on liberation theologians citing the example of Boff, who "maintained that the Church is not constituted hierarchically from above; it 'reinvents' itself from below, by the action of believers at the 'base.' Some European Catholics, following a similar logic, hold that any local community has from Christ, who is present in it, the power to constitute itself as a church and to produce its own Eucharist." Dulles, *Church and Society*, 450. This erroneous notion is alluded to by the Congregation of the Doctrine of the Faith in its Letter to the Bishops, *Some Aspects of the Church Understood as Communion*: "The Church, some say, would arise 'from the base.' These and other similar errors do not take sufficiently into account that it is precisely the Eucharist that renders all self-sufficiency on the part of the particular Churches impossible" (§11).

[60] Ratzinger, *PCT*, 47. Elsewhere, Ratzinger comments upon the sacramental character of the Church: "A Church that sees itself sacramentally understands that it partakes of the meaning of a sign, whose responsibility it is to point beyond itself. If the Church is a 'sacrament,' a sign of God's presence among men, then it does not exist for its own sake. Its responsibility becomes a responsibility of pointing beyond itself. It is like a window which best fulfills its function by allowing one to see greater things through it." Joseph Ratzinger, *Theological Highlights of Vatican II*, trans. Henry Traub, S.J., Gerard C. Thormann, and Werner Barzel (Mahwah, NJ: Paulist Press, 2009), 78–9 (Joseph Ratzinger, *Zur Lehre des Zweiten Vatikanischen Konzils,* Gesammelte Schriften 7/1, ed. Gerhard Ludwig Müller [Freiburg im Bresigau: Herder, 2012] [hearafter, JRGS7/1], 377).

[61] Ratzinger, *CEP*, 21 [JRGS8/1, 267]. The problematic usage of this phrase was highlighted by the 1985 synod on the Second Vatican Council. In an initial report at the synod of 1985, Cardinal Danneels comments, "Above all, the concept of the Church as People of God has been defined in an ideological manner and detached from complementary concepts in the Council: body of Christ and temple of the Holy Spirit." *Synode Extraordinaire: Célébration de Vatican II* (Paris: Cerf, 1986), 34, quoted by Avery Cardinal Dulles, S.J., "The Reception of Vatican II at the Extraordinary Synod of 1985" in *The Reception of Vatican II*, ed. Giuseppe Alberigo, Jean-Pierre Jossua, and Joseph A. Komonchak, trans. Matthew J. O'Connell (Washington, DC: The Catholic

the complementarity that exists between the two images and maintains that one could define the Church as *"People of God resulting from the Body of Christ."*[62] Once again Ratzinger underscores the identity of the People of God as an image that preserves the unity between the two covenants, whereas the Body of Christ is a new formulation given to the Church beginning with the Last Supper symbolic of the new identity that the Church receives from the Holy Eucharist.[63] This Eucharistic identity of the Church enables theologians of the twentieth century and the Second Vatican Council to speak of the Church as a sacrament.

As a sacrament, the Church is a sign that anticipates and realizes the eschatological *communio*. The Eucharistic ecclesiology developed by de Lubac allows for a greater emphasis on the Church's sacramental identity. The ecclesiology of Ratzinger is Christocentric, insofar as communion with Christ forms the basis for the *communio* of the Church. In Ratzinger's Christocentric ecclesiology, the influence of personalist thought becomes evident with his emphasis on the communion of the individual "I" via the sacraments with the Eternal "Thou." Sacramental *communio* here below is a foretaste of the eschatological *communio* that will be fully realized with the communion of saints. We have also established that *communio* is the *logos* for the Church. This *logos* of the Church is derived from her communion with Christ in the Eucharist; consequently, there is an intrinsic relationship between liturgy and ecclesiology.

---

University of America Press, 1987), 352. The pros and cons of the usage of this phrase were also addressed by the International Theological Commission's document "Select Themes of Ecclesiology on the Occasion of the Eighth Anniversary of the Closing of the Second Vatican Council," in *International Theological Commission: Texts and Documents 1969–1985*, ed. Michael Sharkey (San Francisco: Ignatius Press, 1989), 271–273. The contrast between the two different approaches, one favoring the use of the "People of God" versus another employing "Body of Christ" in reference to the Church, was beginning in the early part of the 1940s and in Ratzinger's view, "defined the discussion [about ecclesiology] of the [Second Vatican] Council." Joseph Ratzinger, *Fundamental Speeches from Five Decades*, [hereafter, *FSFD*], ed. Florian Schuller, trans. Michael J. Miller, J. R. Foster, and Adrian Walker (San Francisco: Ignatius Press, 2012), 119.

62  Ratzinger, *FSFD*, 122. Ratzinger has already espoused this view in his dissertation that the Church is the People of God only through the Body of Christ: "Kirche ist Volk Gottes nur im und durch den Leib Christi." *Volk und Haus Gottes* in Ratzinger, *Volk und Haus Gottes in Augustins Lehre von der Kirche: Die Dissertation und weiter Studien zu Augustinus und zur Theologie der Kirchenväter* [hereafter, JRGS1], Gesammelte Schriften 1, ed. Gerhard Ludwig Müller (Freiburg im Breisgau: Herder, 2011), 52.

63  Ratzinger, *FSFD*, 122.

## ECCLESIOLOGY AND LITURGY

The order of the dogmatic constitutions of the Second Vatican Council demonstrates the preeminence of Christocentrism and the primacy of *logos* that is foundational for Ratzinger's theology. The Constitution on the Liturgy, *Sacrosanctum Concilium*, was issued prior to the Constitution on the Church, *Lumen Gentium*. On the logical ordering of this sequence Ratzinger comments, "There were practical reasons for the fact that [*Sacrosanctum Concilium*] was the first [Constitution issued by the Second Vatican Council]."[64] But the most important rationale for this order in Ratzinger's estimation was "worship, adoration, comes first. And thus God does. . . . [*Lumen Gentium*] should be seen as being inwardly bracketed together with it. The Church derives from adoration, from the task of glorifying God. Ecclesiology, of its nature, has to do with liturgy."[65] The subsequent Constitutions of the Second Vatican Council continue to build upon the logic that governs the issuance of *Sacrosanctum Concilium* prior to *Lumen Gentium*.[66] Ratzinger continues, "[T]he third Constitu-

---

[64] Ratzinger, *PFF*, 126 (JRGS8/1, 575).

[65] Ratzinger, *PFF*, 126 (JRGS8/1, 575). Elsewhere Ratzinger addresses the significance of the Council beginning with the Constitution on the liturgy and the implications of this document for ecclesiology: "The decision to begin with the liturgy schema was not merely a technically correct move. Its significance went far deeper. This decision was a profession of faith in which is truly central to the Church—the ever renewed marriage of the Church with the Lord, actualized in the eucharistic mystery where the Church, participating in the sacrifice of Jesus Christ, fulfills its innermost mission, the adoration of the triune God. . . . The text implied an entire ecclesiology and thus anticipated (in a degree that cannot be too highly appreciated) the main theme of the entire Council—its teaching on the Church." Ratzinger, *Theological Highlights of Vatican II*, 31 (JRGS7/1, 306).

[66] Although the liturgy is the *theologia prima*, an argument can be made for the overall theological priority of *Lumen Gentium* above *Sacrosanctum Concilium*. See Christian D. Washburn, "The Theological Priority of *Lumen Gentium* and *Dei Verbum* for the Interpretation of the Second Vatican Council," *The Thomist* 78 (2014): 107–34. Washburn maintains that *Lumen Gentium* and *Dei Verbum* maintain a priority over *Sacrosanctum Concilium* and *Gaudium et Spes*. Cf. Massimo Faggioli, "Sacrosanctum Concilium and the Meaning of Vatican II," *Theological Studies* 71 (2010): 437–452. "The definition of *Sacrosanctum Concilium* as 'le parent pauvre de l'herméneutique conciliaire' (the forgotten element in the hermeneutics of Vatican II) is correct because, as we have seen, its hermeneutical function has been consistently downplayed. The dire need for a hermeneutics of Vatican II once again centered on *Sacrosanctum Concilium* is justified on the basis of a chronologically rooted relationship between the liturgical constitution—the first document approved at the council—and Vatican II as such. The necessity of and opportunity for a hermeneutics of the council based on *Sacrosanctum Concilium* becomes clear if we take into account that it opens the way for a new balance

tion talks about the Word of God, which calls the Church together and is at all times renewing her. The fourth Constitution shows how the glory of God presents itself in an ethos, how the light we have received from God is carried out into the world, how only thus can God be fully glorified."[67]

The first three Constitutions present the *logos* of communion with God as the ultimate goal of human nature, whereas *Gaudium et Spes* presents the *ethos* of presenting this *logos* to the world. In the post-conciliar period, the original purpose of *Sacrosanctum Concilium* has been overlooked:

> It seems to me that most of the problems in the concrete implementation of the liturgical reform are connected with the fact that the [Second Vatican] Council's approach starting with the Pasch was not kept in mind sufficiently; people stuck too much to merely practical matters and thereby ran the risk of losing sight of the center. It seems to me, therefore, essential to take up this approach again as the guiding norm of renewal and to deepen further what was necessarily only suggested by the Council. Pasch means the inseparability of Cross and Resurrection, as it is portrayed especially in the Gospel of John.[68]

As has been previously discussed, within the post-conciliar period, the norm has been to subordinate the authentic *logos* of the liturgy to *ethos*. Consequently, the true essence of the liturgy has become obscured. The priority is to assert the Paschal Mystery as the definitive form of the liturgy's *logos*.

The emphasis on *ethos* first and foremost has overshadowed the role of the liturgy in the worship of God. The primacy of the adoration of God has become displaced by an attitude that led "many liturgical experts [to rush] into considerations about how we can shape the liturgy in a more

---

between the 'clash of ecclesiologies' at the council, and the gravitational center of the Church of Vatican II: Scripture and the Eucharist." Faggioli, "Sacrosanctum Concilium and the Meaning of Vatican II," 450.

[67] Ratzinger, *PFF*, 126 (JRGS8/1, 575).

[68] Joseph Ratzinger, *Theology of the Liturgy: The Sacramental Foundation of Christian Existence* [hereafter, JRCW11], ed. Michael J. Miller, trans. John Saward, Kenneth Baker, S.J., Henry Taylor, et al., Collected Works 11 (San Francisco: Ignatius Press, 2014), 579; *Theologie der Liturgie: Die sakramentale Begründung christlicher Existenz* [hereafter, JRGS11], Gesammelte Schriften 11, ed. Gerhard Ludwig Müller (Freiburg im Breisgau: Herder, 2008), 701.

attractive way, to communicate better, so as to get more and more people actively involved."[69] Consequently, Ratzinger concludes that these experts "have apparently quite lost sight of the fact that the liturgy is actually 'done' for God and not for ourselves."[70] The liturgy, characterized as the *opus Dei*, properly frames the relationship between God and humanity.

The theme that unites the four major constitutions of Vatican II is characterized by a Christocentrism (or *Logos-centrism*) that is foundational for addressing the relationship between God and every human person. In this focus on God's primacy, the understanding of the Church as the Body of Christ is critical for the ecclesiology outlined by the Council. The theologian Massimo Faggioli highlights what he perceives as a certain discontinuity between the Constitution on the Liturgy and the Constitution on the Church: "It is clear that, although there is a unity of the *ecclesiologies* of Vatican II, there is a difference between the eucharistic ecclesiology of *Sacrosanctum Concilium* and the ecclesiology of *Lumen Gentium*."[71] Expanding on this claim, he quotes from a work of Antonio Acerbi: "In *Lumen Gentium* there is no systematic discussion of the ecclesiological role of the Eucharist."[72] Despite the claims made by Faggioli and Acerbi, however, there is a close unity between liturgy and ecclesiology that is evident in the discussion above concerning the Church's identity as a *communio* that reflects the communion of the Trinity and the preeminence of the Church as the Body of Christ. On this understanding, it becomes difficult *not* to see the continuity between the Constitutions highlighted by Ratzinger. It was the ecclesiology of the Church as the Body of Christ that guided the early members of the liturgical movement. As far as both Constitutions are concerned, there is a consistency in the use of the image of the Church as the Body of Christ.

*Sacrosanctum Concilium* makes clear the role of the entire Body of Christ in the liturgy: "Furthermore, the mystical body of Jesus Christ, the head and its members, is together giving complete and definitive public

---

[69] Ratzinger, *PFF*, 126 (JRGS8/1, 575). For an example of the subordination of *logos* to *ethos* illustrated by the use of the principles of the American Liturgical Movement, which led to substantial changes in the celebration of the liturgy and church architecture prior to the Second Vatican Council, see Thomas Buffer, "The American Liturgical Movement, Social Justice and Architectural Change," *Antiphon* 20, no. 3 (2016): 241–67.

[70] Ratzinger, *PFF*, 126 (JRGS8/1, 575–76).

[71] Massimo Faggioli, *True Reform: Liturgy and Ecclesiology in 'Sacrosanctum Concilium'* (Collegeville, MN: Liturgical Press, 2012), 71.

[72] Antonio Acerbi, *Due ecclesiologie. Ecclesiologia giuridica ed ecclesiologia di comunione nella Lumen gentium* (Bologna: EDB, 1975), 505, quoted in Faggioli, *True Reform*, 71.

expression to its worship. This is why all liturgical celebrations, inasmuch it is the work of Christ the priest and his body, which is the Church, is above all an activity of worship."[73] This liturgy, which is carried out by the Body of Christ on earth, is an anticipation and realization of the worship of the eschatological Church.[74] *Lumen Gentium* clearly claims that the identity of the Church as both the kingdom of Christ and the Body of Christ is made visible in the Holy Eucharist: "Through the sacrament of the eucharistic bread, there is represented and produced the unity of the faithful, who make up one body in Christ."[75] The unity of the Church as the Body is an eschatological sign of the communion that awaits the elect, which we established in the first section of this chapter by insisting upon the understanding of *communio* as the *logos* of the Church. The Constitution on the Church emphasizes the Eucharistic ecclesiology, which is allegedly absent: "When we really participate in the body of the Lord through the breaking of the bread, we are raised up to communion with him and among ourselves."[76] There is a consistent ecclesiology in both constitutions that reflects the development already present above in the liturgical movement.

The renewed interest in the notion of the Body of Christ in ecclesiology, which would later impact the liturgical movement, began in the nineteenth century with Johann Adam Möhler (1796–1838) and the Tübingen school of theology. The predominant ecclesiological model, under the influence of St. Robert Bellarmine (1542–1621), was an institutionalist one.[77] Möhler's view stressed a more organic approach,

---

[73] *SC*, §7. In his lecture on the theology of liturgy at Fontgombault, Ratzinger cites this text from *Sacrosanctum Concilium* to define liturgy. Hence Ratzinger is highlighting the ecclesiology of the Body of Christ as a key to understanding liturgy.

[74] Cf. *Sacrosanctum Concilium*, in Norman P. Tanner, ed., *Decrees of the Ecumenical Councils*, 2 vols. (Washington, DC: Sheed & Ward and Georgetown University Press, 1990), §8.

[75] *LG*, §7.

[76] *LG*, §7.

[77] For an overview of the institutional model, see Dulles, *Models of the Church*, 34–46. The particular contribution of Bellarmine to this model is an emphasis on the external features that characterize the "one and true Church," which Dulles summarizes as "profession of the true faith, communion in the sacraments, and submission to legitimate pastors [in particular, the Supreme Roman Pontiff]" (16). This ecclesiological definition of Bellarmine, as cited by Dulles, is found in Robert Bellarmine, *De controversiis*, tom. 2, liber 3, *De ecclesia militante*, cap. 2, "*De definition Ecclesiae*," vol. 2 (Naples: Giuliano, 1857), 75. On the ecclesiology of Bellarmine, see John Hardon, S.J., "Robert Bellarmine's Concept of the Church," in *Studies in Medieval Culture*, vol. 2, ed. J. Sommerfeldt (Kalamazoo, MI: Western Michigan Press, 1966), 120–27.

emphasizing the analogue of the human body with its various organs as a fitting model for how the Church operates: "It has an inbuilt vital principle thanks to which it can grow, repair itself, and adapt itself to changing needs."[78] The Church, as the supernatural Body of Christ, is guided and renewed by the Holy Spirit as its internal, divine, life-giving principle. Möhler's teaching on the Church is one of the key insights from the nineteenth century that would influence the liturgical movement.[79]

One of the main figures in the early history of the liturgical movement is the Belgian monk Lambert Beauduin, OSB (1873–1960). Beauduin is well known for reechoing Pope St. Pius X's call for the need for the active participation of all people in the liturgy.[80] During the celebration of the

---

[78] Dulles, *Models of the Church*, 50. In the midst of the proceedings of the Second Vatican Council, Ratzinger offered a paper in 1963 commenting on various themes in the current ecclesiological discussions beginning with the historical background of Pope Pius XII's encyclical *Mystici Corporis*. He highlights the two ecclesiological trends, which were developed by the nineteenth century leading to the early part of the twentieth century. On the one hand, we have the aforementioned institutional model, which Ratzinger traces back to Bellarmine and the *Roman Catechism*. The latter source, Ratzinger notes, retains much of Augustine's ecclesiological insight. On the other hand, we have the new organic interpretation, which Ratzinger attributes to Möhler (*Die Einheit in der Kirche*, 1825) and Pilgram (*Physiologie der Kirche*, 1860). In the period following the First World War, the latter model began to dominate the theological conversation as new editions of the work of Möhler and Pilgram were printed. The recovery of this patristic insight received official magisterial support in the encyclical of Pope Pius XII. Ratzinger, *FSFD*, 112–119.

[79] According to R. W. Franklin, "[Mohler's] teaching that the mystery of the incarnation is reflected in both the Eucharist and the church became the fundamental theological contribution of the nineteenth century to the liturgical movement." "Response: Humanism and Transcendence in the Nineteenth Century Liturgical Movement," *Worship* 59, no. 4 (1985): 348. For a general history of the impact that nineteenth-century theology had on the history of the Liturgical movement, see Thomas F. O'Meara, O.P., "The Origins of the Liturgical Movement and German Romanticism," *Worship* 59, no. 4 (1985): 326–342.

[80] See Lambert Beauduin, O.S.B., *Liturgy the Life of the Church*, 3rd ed., trans. Virgil Michel, O.S.B. (Farnborough, Hampshire: St. Michael's Abbey Press, 2002). Beauduin underscores the preeminence of active participation in the Church's mission: *"Active participation* in the liturgical life of the Church is a capital factor in the supernatural life of the Christian.... Let us change the routine and monotonous assistance at acts of worship into an *active and intelligent participation*; let us teach the faithful to pray and confess these truths in a body: and the liturgy thus practiced will insensibly arouse a slumbering faith and give new efficacy, both in prayer and action" (19, 21). Beauduin highlights active participation as one of the main aims of the liturgical movement: "[T]he members of the Liturgical Movement desire to contribute with all their strength to the attainment of the following aims: The active participation of the Christian people in the holy Sacrifice of the

community Mass in a Benedictine monastery, Beauduin contemplated the notion of the Church as the Body of Christ. He came to the conclusion that the Holy Eucharist was the source of life for the Church.[81] In order for the Church to be what she is, the "sign and instrument" of God's communion with humanity, she celebrates the liturgy. The Eucharist is the divine wellspring for her life in the world, which unites each person to Christ and subsequently to one another. The linkage between the Body of Christ ecclesiology and the liturgy is essential for laying the foundation of the sacramental *logos*.

The realization of communion within the Eucharist compels each Christian to be an active and living member of the body engaged in an *ethos* of self-giving love. The ultimate aim of the liturgical movement, the fullest form of participation, was to bring divinization into greater focus.[82] To emphasize reform as *the* goal of the liturgical movement does a great disservice to the fundamental purpose of the full realization of the person's freedom in the divine life. The recurring emphasis on active participation (*participatio actuosa*) in *Sacrosanctum Concilium* is complemented by the call of the Church, which is the mission to draw others into the *communio* of the Church. This is an anticipation and realization of

---

Mass by means of understanding and following the liturgical rites and texts" (52).

[81] Paul McPartlan, S.J., "Liturgy, Church and Society," *Studia Liturgica* 34 (2004): 147–64. According to McPartlan (158–159): "Beauduin's sudden insight at community Mass was that if the Church is the body of Christ, then it lives in and from the Eucharist. Thus did the idea of the body of Christ begin to become concrete. The linkage of Church and Eucharist is, of course, fundamental to Eucharistic ecclesiology, and de Lubac's *Corpus Mysticum* massively consolidated that linkage. The major conceptional step that was still needed was to say that if the Church lives from the Eucharist, then the Church should be patterned as a network of Eucharistic communities, as the *Catechism of the Catholic Church* now teaches: 'The Church,' it says, 'is the People that God gathers in the whole world. She exists in local communities and is made real as a liturgical, above all a Eucharistic, assembly' (no. 752)."

[82] One of the members of the early liturgical movement in the United States, the Benedictine Godfrey Diekmann, made the claim that divinization was one of the major themes of the liturgical movement that was overlooked in discussions relating to the liturgy following the Second Vatican Council. Robert Barron, *The Strangest Way: Walking the Christian Path* (Maryknoll, NY: Orbis Press, 2002), 29. Among his many notable contributions to the liturgy, Godfrey Diekmann served as a *peritus* for the Second Vatican Council, he was a consultor for the preparatory commission to the committee that drafted *Sacrosanctum Concilium*, and he was a founding member of the International Committee on English in the Liturgy (ICEL). See Robert L. Tuzik, ed., *How Firm a Foundation: Leaders of the Liturgical Movement* (Chicago, IL: Liturgy Training Publications, 1990), 245–54.

the eschatological end of the communion of saints (*communio sanctorum*).

The significance of this section was to develop further the relationship between the liturgy and ecclesiology. With the eschaton, the unity of the Church will be fully realized. In the meantime, the Church is an instrument of the call to *communio* here below. One of the well-established scholastic axioms is "action follows being" (*agere sequiter esse*), which is why this section has emphasized the order of the Second Vatican Documents defining *logos* through the liturgy (*Sacrosanctum Concilium*), revelation (*Dei Verbum*), and ecclesiology (*Lumen Gentium*) prior to the *ethos* of engaging the modern world (*Gaudium et Spes*). *Communio* is the very being or essence (the *logos*) of the Church. Consequently, the Church has a mission to proclaim the true saving hope, which is Jesus, the incarnate *Logos*, so that other people may be able to enter into communion with him.

## HOPE AND ESCHATOLOGY

As the liturgy reorients the worshippers to the eschaton, the eschatological pilgrimage within the liturgy is not mutually exclusive with loving the people of God here below. The proper understanding of the relationship between the liturgy and eschatology allows for the virtues of hope and charity to realize their full potential. This section will contrast the theology of hope developed by Ratzinger under the influence of Josef Pieper with the theology of hope developed by Johann Baptist Metz and Jürgen Moltmann. Ratzinger emphasizes the realization of eschatological hope as the fruition of the liturgy "according to the *logos*" that is manifested fully in a love for neighbor. Despite the critiques of Ratzinger's ecclesiology that claim he focuses on the person's vertical relationship with God, there is clearly an emphasis on the horizontal mission of charity (*ethos*) that proceeds from the love of God expressed fully in the liturgy (*logos*).[83]

---

[83] See Philip A. Franco, "The Communion Ecclesiology of Joseph Ratzinger: Implications for the Church of the Future," in *The Annual Publication of the College Theology Society* vol. 51, *Vatican II: Forty Years Later*, ed. William Madges (Maryknoll, NY: Orbis Books, 2005), 3–25. "[I]t seems fair to suggest that the most obvious criticism of Ratzinger's work is his overemphasis of the vertical aspect of communion to the detriment of the horizontal. Ratzinger's ecclesiology puts precious little emphasis on the horizontal bonds of human community and therefore has little to say in terms of social justice and other issues of human solidarity." (15) This is a serious misreading of the ecclesiology of Ratzinger. This work has already demonstrated that the vertical communion deepens the call to horizontal communion. Pope Benedict XVI, Encyclical Letter *Deus Caritas Est* [hereafter, DCE] (Vatican City: Liberia Editrice Vaticana, 2005), §14: "A Eucharist which does not pass over into the concrete practice of love is intrinsically

The primacy of *logos* over *ethos* and the subordination of *logos* to *ethos* are the two fundamental positions that orient the two contrasting theologies of hope of Ratzinger and Pieper on the one hand and Metz and Moltmann on the other hand. In chapter one, the Guardinian influence of the primacy of the *logos* in Ratzinger has been established. For Metz, the *logos* is never merely static thought. He asserts that the *logos* of Christology "is nourished by a praxis: the praxis of discipleship. It expresses a knowledge that is essentially practical."[84] Hence, Metz emphasizes the primacy of praxis as a central tenet within theology, and thus theology is essentially a political theology, which Metz defines as a practical fundamental theology: "The faith of Christians is a praxis in history and society that understands itself as a solidaristic hope in the God of Jesus as the God of the living and the dead, who calls all to be subjects in God's presence."[85] In Metz's view, Christians demonstrate their commitment to what he describes as a "thoroughly apocalyptically expectant praxis of discipleship" through their struggle throughout history as "subjects in solidarity with one another."[86] Hope is realized as an imminent expectation through a dedication to a political praxis that struggles to bring temporal injustices to an end.[87]

Moltmann characterizes the Church's eschatological mission in terms of a realized hope in history and for the world: "[The] 'Church for the world' can mean nothing else but 'Church for the kingdom of God' and the renewing of the world."[88] Moltmann continues to explain the eschatological commitment of the Church: "[T]o put it concretely, the Church takes up the society with which it lives—into its own horizon of expectation of the eschatological fulfilment of justice, life, humanity and sociability, and communicates in its own decisions in history its openness and readiness for this future and its elasticity towards it."[89] The imminent fulfillment of eschatological hope is a unifying theme for the political theology of Metz and Moltmann's theology of hope. *Logos* is subordinated to

---

fragmented." Chapter four examines the Church's mission of charity in more detail.

[84] Johann Baptist Metz, *Faith in History and Society: Toward a Practical Fundamental Theology*, trans. J. Matthew Ashley (New York: The Crossroad Publishing Company, 2013), 62.

[85] Metz, *Faith in History and Society*, 81.

[86] Metz, *Faith in History and Society*, 81.

[87] Metz, *Faith in History and Society*, 81–84. Metz explains further the various characteristics of his practical fundamental theology.

[88] Jürgen Moltmann, *Theology of Hope*, trans. James W. Leitch (London: SCM Press, 2002), 328.

[89] Moltmann, *Theology of Hope*, 328.

an immediate *ethos*. Ratzinger summarizes the effect that this subordination has had on the development of eschatology:

> Eschatology, the expectation of the world to come, is no longer seen within the theology of creation but, rather, replaces creation: the real world worth living in is yet to be created, namely, by man himself, contrary to what he finds already in place. This also means, then, that the *pragma* of human word is no longer situated within the *Logos* of the creation that has taken place but, rather, abolishes the *Logos*. Man himself is the eschatological creator, whom *Logos* does not precede but only follows: in the beginning is not "the Word" but "the deed."[90]

The primacy of *ethos* will redefine the meaning of hope. In light of the theology of Metz and Moltmann, it becomes difficult to conceive of hope as a supernatural virtue. Hope is reduced to the work of transforming society through justice. Liberation for the oppressed and the suffering is the authentic realization of the hope envisioned by Metz and Moltmann. Ratzinger will be critical of this instantiation of hope because it reduces the kingdom of God to the consummation of human political activity.[91] Ratzinger is emphatic that "eschatology is not necessarily bound to any particular philosophy of history but only to ontology."[92] In Ratzinger's view, eschatology has a Christocentric nature, which will lead to a theology of hope in contradistinction with Metz and Moltmann: "The absorption of eschatology into Christology, which occurred in principle with the decision to believe in Christ, means that it was also absorbed into the concept of God and that the apocalyptic pattern of the theology of history retreated into the background."[93] Rooted and centered in Christ, the eschaton cannot fully come to fruition *in* history through the sole efforts of the human person. The imminent realization of the eschaton in the present moment takes place within the sacred liturgy and within the life of the believer in response to grace. What will differentiate Metz

---

[90] Ratzinger, *DP*, 380.

[91] See Joseph Ratzinger, *Eschatology: Death and Eternal Life*, ed. Aidan Nichols, O.P., trans. Michael Waldstein, 2nd ed. (Washington, DC: The Catholic University of America Press, 2007), 57–60; *Auferstehung und ewiges Leben: Beiträge zur Eschatologie und zur Theologie der Hoffnung* [hereafter, JRGS10], Gesammelte Schriften 10, ed. Gerhard Ludwig Müller (Freiburg: Herder, 2012), 83–86.

[92] Ratzinger, *CEP*, 232 (JRGS10, 405).

[93] Ratzinger, *CEP*, 233 (JRGS10, 405–406).

and Moltmann's theology of hope from the views espoused by Pieper[94] and Ratzinger will be their preference of a natural and imminent hope, whereas the latter will adhere to a view of hope that is supernatural and sacramental.[95] The contrast of the theology of hope found in Moltmann and Metz will highlight the unity between liturgy and eschatology within Ratzinger's theology.

Ratzinger develops a liturgical theology with an eschatological view that seeks the eschaton above, yet at the same time he redirects the faithful to an authentic love of neighbor here on earth. Ratzinger's theology of hope results in a mission of charity that creates a delicate balance between love of God and neighbor. Eschatology and liturgy taken up together can

---

[94] Josef Pieper maintains that hope is a virtue only and insofar as it is theological or supernatural: "[W]hile justice, prudence, or courage may very well be natural virtues of natural man, hope is a virtue *only* when it is a *theological* virtue; hope becomes a virtue precisely through that which renders it a theological, supernatural virtue." Josef Pieper, *The End of Time: A Meditation on the Philosophy of History*, trans. Michael Bullock (San Francisco: Ignatius Press, 1999), 146–147; emphasis in the original. Elsewhere Pieper emphasizes hope as a supernatural virtue: "When we say, then, that hope is a virtue only when it is a theological virtue, we mean that hope is a steadfast turning toward the true fulfillment of man's nature, that is, toward good, only when it has its source in the reality of grace in man and is directed toward supernatural happiness in God." *On Hope*, trans. Mary F. McCarthy (San Francisco: Ignatius Press, 1986), 26. On the philosophy of hope in Pieper, see Bernard N. Schumacher, *A Philosophy of Hope: Josef Pieper and the Contemporary Debate on Hope*, trans. D. C. Schindler (New York: Fordham University Press, 2003), 203–253.

[95] A similar parallel is present in the different perspectives of hope in the work of Ernst Bloch and Gabriel Marcel. Paul O'Callaghan describes Marcel's notion of hope as "directed toward a transcendent Divinity," whereas Bloch's conception of hope as one "that fully involves the material world." Paul O'Callaghan, *Christ Our Hope: An Introduction to Eschatology*, (Washington, DC: The Catholic University of America Press, 2011), 7–8. Also see O'Callaghan, "Hope and Freedom in Gabriel Marcel and Ernst Bloch," *Irish Theological Quarterly* 55 (1989): 213–239. The work of Bloch will be very influential on the thought of Moltmann. See O'Callaghan, *Christ Our Hope*, 13–14. Also see Schwarz, *Eschatology* (Grand Rapids, MI: Eerdmans, 2000), 142–143; 222–224. Ratzinger describes the significant impact of Marxist influence during his time in Tübingen that was introduced via the thought of Bloch and Moltmann: "While until now Bultmann's theology and Heidegger's philosophy had determined the frame of reference for thinking, almost overnight the existentialist model collapsed and was replaced by the Marxist. Ernst Bloch was now teaching in Tübingen and made Heidegger contemptible for being petty bourgeois. At about the same time as I arrived, Jürgen Moltmann came to the Faculty for Lutheran Theology. In his fascinating book *A Theology of Hope*, Moltmann gives a wholly new and different conception of theology from Bloch's perspective." Ratzinger, *MM*, 136. For a brief and critical analysis of Bloch from a perspective sympathetic to the view of Marcel, see Josef Pieper, *Hope and History*, trans. David Kipp (San Francisco: Ignatius Press, 1994), 73–93.

guide social ethics to their proper end without lapsing into an immanentism. The key to unite these two disciplines within theology is to root them in Christ, who is fully God and fully man.

Ratzinger argues that authentic Christian exodus is characterized by "imitation of the whole and undivided Christ," which means one cannot simply reduce the imitation of Christ to following the human or historical Jesus.[96] Within contemporary theology there is an emphasis on either the human nature of Christ or the divine nature of Christ at the expense of the unity between the two natures, which leads to two different Christologies with differing tendencies: a Christology that places heavy emphasis upon Christ's human nature (a neo-Arianism or neo-Nestorianism) or a Christology that stresses Christ's divine nature (a neo-monophysitism).

The Spanish theologian Candido Pozo identifies the positions of two groups of theologians who responded to the problem of preparation for the Parousia as "incarnationists" and "eschatologists."[97] What both groups share in common is the emphasis on the necessity of preparing for the Parousia. According to Pozo, eschatologism is "characterized by its insistence on the interior and invisible nature of this process of construction. The Christian will work to create a better world. . . . But this positive contribution is not externally perceptible."[98] The Christian seeks the kingdom of God, but this work for the kingdom is not outwardly visible. Incarnationism "will accentuate the connectedness between the invisible and visible, by virtue of which the invisible preparation of the Kingdom necessarily has a repercussion on the ever growing development of humanity."[99] The emphasis in the latter view is the work of the Christian who concretely contributes to the building up of the kingdom of God in *this* world. As representatives of these differing theological views in the period following the Second Vatican Council, Pozo highlights von Balthasar among the eschatologists and Metz among the incarnationists.[100]

---

[96] Joseph Ratzinger, *A New Song for the Lord: Faith in Christ and Liturgy Today* [hereafter, *NSL*], trans. Martha M. Matesich (New York: The Crossroad Publishing Company, 1997), 6.

[97] See Candido Pozo, S.J., *Theology of the Beyond*, trans. Mark A. Pilon (New York: Alba House, 2009), 97–130. According to Pozo, he draws upon the insight of Léopold Malevez, S.J. (1900–1973) for the distinctions between eschatologism and incarnationism. See Léopold Malevez, "Deux théologies catholiques de l'histoire," *Bijdragen* 10 (1949): 225–240. Also see José Luis Illanes, *Christianismo, historia, mundo* (Pamplona: Eunsa, 1973).

[98] Pozo, *Theology of the Beyond*, 100.

[99] Pozo, *Theology of the Beyond*, 101.

[100] See Pozo, *Theology of the Beyond*, 110–113. In an earlier stage of the controversy, Pozo

Although Ratzinger would certainly trend towards the position of the "eschatologists," his view could be described as a *via media* between the eschatologists and incarnationists. Ratzinger's view is sacramental in that it embraces both the work of God and the role of the human person in the building of the kingdom, always giving priority to the work of God. In company with the eschatologists, there is certainly an emphasis on the primacy of the *actio Dei* or *logos* over the work of the person (*ethos* or praxis), but at the same time the grace received from the encounter with Jesus in the liturgy transforms the person here *and* now. The full realization of the kingdom will only be achieved in the eschaton, yet simultaneously the gift of grace enables the Christian to proclaim the kingdom of God in word and deed. There is a prudence that Ratzinger embraces to distinguish human progress from the divine growth of the kingdom. Ultimately, Ratzinger demonstrates that the kingdom of God is realized by the human person cooperating fully with grace, which is consistent with his theology of hope that emphasizes this virtue as a supernatural gift calling for a human response.

The theological virtue of hope is clearly grounded in trusting God's initiative for the good of humanity and the world. The *Catechism of the Catholic Church* defines hope as the theological virtue "by which we desire the kingdom of heaven and eternal life as our happiness, placing our trust in Christ's promises and relying not on our own strength, but on the help of the grace of the Holy Spirit."[101] The realization of hope will never solely be the consummation of the efforts of the faithful within the Church and society working towards justice and liberation for the poor and oppressed. When the foundation for hope proceeds from a primacy of *ethos* or praxis rather than a primacy of *logos*, then it is easy to develop a caricature of hope that does not come close to its supernatural end. A true theology of hope must always begin and end with Christ as its authentic *Logos*.

The Christological interpretation of the eschaton advocated by Ratzinger becomes clearer in contrast with the emerging theology of hope and political theology of Moltmann and Metz. Ratzinger contends that Moltmann's vision "put[s] Christianity into practice by transforming the world, using the criterion of hope."[102] The mission of the kingdom of God is placed solely in the hands of the human person. Moltmann's theology

---

claims eschatologism is represented by Louis Bouyer, Jean Daniélou, and Yves Congar. He lists M. I. Montuclard, D. Dubarle, G. Thils, and B. Solages among the representatives of the incarnationalist view. Pozo, *Theology of the Beyond*, 99–100.

[101] *CCC* §1817.

[102] Ratzinger, *Eschatology*, 58 (JRGS10, 84).

of hope would give birth to various forms of liberation theology, political theology, black theology, and the theology of revolution.[103] Despite the

---

[103] Ratzinger, *Eschatology*, 58 (JRGS10, 84). On the influence of the political theology of Metz upon the development of liberation theology, see Elizabeth Schüssler Fiorenza, "Political Theology: An Historical Analysis," *Theological Digest* 25:4 (1997): 317–34. On liberation theology, see Clodovis Boff, *Theology and Praxis: Epistemological Foundations*, trans. Robert R. Barr (Eugene, OR: Wipf & Stock, 2009); Gustavo Gutiérrez, *A Theology of Liberation: History, Politics, and Salvation*, trans. Sister Caridad Inda and John Eagleson (Maryknoll, NY: Orbis Books, 1988); Arthur F. McGovern, S.J., *Liberation Theology and Its Critics: Toward an Assessment* (Eugene, OR: Wipf & Stock, 1989); and Tracey Rowland, "Liberation Theology and the Papacy of Francis," in *Catholic Theology* (New York: Bloomsbury T & T Clark, 2017), 167–203. Liberation theology is a collective description for a movement within theology that begins with praxis. It is noteworthy that Gustavo Gutiérrez would acknowledge a shift from his previous position affirming the primacy of praxis in the new introduction of the revised edition of his work: "The ultimate norms of judgment [in theology] come from the revealed truth that we accept by faith and not from praxis itself." *A Theology of Liberation*, xxxiv. Elsewhere Gutiérrez affirms this point in describing the general task of theology: "The role of theology is not in fact to forge an ideology that would justify social and political positions already taken but rather to help believers let themselves be judged by the Word of the Lord. Theology cannot therefore give up the critical function of faith vis-á-vis every historical realization. I begin from the conviction that the theological task is a vocation that arises and is exercised in the heart of the ecclesial community. Indeed, its starting point is the gift of faith in which we welcome the truth of the Word of God, and its contributions are at the service of the evangelizing mission of the church." Gustavo Gutiérrez and Gerhard Cardinal Müller, *On the Side of the Poor: The Theology of Liberation*, trans. Robert A. Krieg and James B. Nickoloff (New York: Orbis, 2015), 1. The Argentinian theologian Juan C. Scannone outlines four currents within liberation theology, which start from (1) "the pastoral praxis of the church," (2) "the praxis of revolutionary groups," (3) "historical praxis," or (4) "the praxis of the peoples of Latin America." McGovern, *Liberation Theology and Its Critics*, xvi–xviii. Many of the bishops in Latin America would represent the first current. The early writings of Hugo Assman are associated with the second current. Gustavo Gutiérrez and the Boffs would be representative of the third current. Finally, Scannone and fellow Argentinian Lucio Gera would be associated with the fourth current. Incidentally, Scannone will have an influence upon the thought of Pope Francis. Scannone was a seminary professor of the then Jorge Bergoglio when he was in formation with the Society of Jesus. See Juan C. Scannone, "El papa Francisco y la teología del pueblo," *Razón y Fe* 1395 (2014): 31–50; Scannone, *La teología del pueblo: Raíces teológicals del papa Francisco* (maliaño: Editorial Sal Terrae, 2017); Rafael Luciani, *Pope Francis and the Theology of the People*, trans. Phillip Berryman (Maryknoll, NY: Orbis Books, 2017); Massimo Borghesi, *The Mind of Pope Francis: Jorge Bergoglio's Intellectual Journey*, trans. Barry Hudock, (Collegeville, MN: Liturgical Press Academic, 2017), 44–55. For a comprehensive view on the background of Pope Francis's social thought, see Thomas R. Rourke, *The Roots of Pope Francis's Social and Political Thought: From Argentina to the Vatican* (Lanham, MD: Rowan & Littlefield, 2016).

merits of certain theologies of liberation,[104] Ratzinger raises two objections concerning particular theologies of liberation: (1) the reduction of eschatology to political utopianism overshadows authentic Christian

---

[104] In an interview concerning liberation theology, the then Prefect for the Congregation of the Doctrine of Faith, Gerhard Cardinal Müller, notes: "It is necessary to distinguish between a correct version of liberation theology and an incorrect one. In my opinion, good theology has God and His love as its starting point and is about the freedom and glory of God's children. Therefore, Christian theology deals with the God-given gift of salvation. Marxist anthropology is quite different from Christian anthropology because it regards man as deprived of freedom and dignity. Communism is about the dictatorship of the proletariat; good theology, on the contrary, is about love and freedom. Both communism and neo-liberal capitalism deny the transcendent dimension of human existence, restricting their action to the material sphere of human life. Capitalism and communism are two sides of the same coin. On the contrary, true liberation theology draws upon the Bible, the Fathers of the Church and the teaching of Vatican Council II to build up God's kingdom." "Liberation Theology Interview with Archbishop Gerhard Ludwig Müller," interview by Wlodzimeir Redzioch, October 1, 2013, *Inside the Vatican*, accessed August 28, 2016, http://insidethevatican.com/uncategorized/liberation-theology-interview-archbishop-gerhard-ludwig-muller. Also see Gustavo Gutiérrez and Gerhard Cardinal Müller, *On the Side of the Poor*. Both contributors offer more nuances to the meaning of liberation theology. Müller concludes: "The methodological claim of liberation theology, with its transforming praxis, is nothing other than a new formulation of the originating event of theology in general. First comes discipleship to Christ, and from this discipleship comes a formulation of the confession that actually concerns Jesus." *On the Side of the Poor*, 82. With limited development of the claim, Müller argues that "we can understand liberation theology on the whole to be a socially applied *nouvelle théologie*, as formulated by Henri de Lubac, or, also to be a theology of grace, as developed by Karl Rahner, now applied to history and society" (81). The relationship between grace and nature is the fundamental context for understanding liberation theology. Müller does not explain which theologies of liberation have been formed by the theology of de Lubac versus the theologies developed in light of Rahner in this work. See Rowland, *Catholic Theology*, 189–191. Elsewhere, Müller notes that the liberation theology of Gustavo Gutiérrez as a "*nouvelle théologie* oriented to the social*," which would link the thought of Gutiérrez with the theology of de Lubac. Gerhard Cardinal Müller (with Father Carlos Granados), *The Cardinal Müller Report: An Exclusive Interview on the State of the Church*, trans. Richard Goodyear (San Francisco: Ignatius Press, 2017), 28. One of the prominent voices in liberation theology, Juan Luis Segundo, notes that "[Leopold] Malevez anticipated what Karl Rahner, from a more speculative point of view, baptized with a term that had wide currency and acceptance: *the supernatural existential*. This term said, in reality, the same thing expressed by Malevez, although it gave it more explicitly the universal dimensions that corresponded to it. Although the intimate relationship with God and with heaven may not belong to *human nature*, no real human existence developed on a purely natural plane. From the beginning of humanity, God's grace placed all persons on the path toward the intimate relationship with him and with celestial life." Juan

hope, and (2) this type of politics is ordered to the false end of transforming human nature and the world.[105]

The kingdom of God cannot be achieved by the efforts of the human person alone, especially politics. Ratzinger is emphatic that "the Kingdom of God is not a *political* norm of political activity, but it is a *moral* norm of that activity. . . . The issue of a politics that will be genuinely responsible in Christian terms belongs to moral theology, not eschatology."[106] Politics finds its proper cue from ethics and not the eschaton. The danger of an immanentized hope is that it leads to a skewed vision of anthropology and eschatology, which ultimately threatens the human person and the proper mission of the Church. Consequently, Ratzinger claims, "The setting asunder of eschatology and politics is one of the fundamental tasks of Christian theology."[107] What does Ratzinger propose as an alternative solution to this false marriage between eschatology and politics under the guise of hope? Ratzinger finds the answer in one of the key themes of the New Testament: divine filiation.

In contrast with the dead-end pursuits of anthropocentric or technocratic progress, Jesus Christ presents each person with authentic freedom because he alone can offer redemption.[108] This freedom can be realized in the lives of those who have responded fully to the life of grace. Ratzinger insists that "[The Kingdom of God] is found in those persons whom the finger of God has touched and who have allowed themselves to be made God's sons and daughters."[109] This transformation of men and women into sons and daughters of God requires their free will but cannot take place without the initiative and gift of God's grace in Baptism. In the sacraments, a person is able to become a "son with the

---

Luis Segundo, S.J., *Theology and the Church: A Response to Cardinal Ratzinger and a Warning to the Whole Church,* trans. John W. Diercksmeier (Minneapolis, MN: Winston Press, 1985), 76. Later in this work, Segundo summarize his position: "[T]here can be no liberation theology without the full understanding of the Council of Orange about the supernatural beginning of faith in its widest sense, reaffirmed by the Second Vatican Council, which adopted, with different words, the supernatural existential of Karl Rahner." *Theology and the Church,* 154.

[105] Ratzinger, *Eschatology,* 59 (JRGS10, 5). Chapter four examines these themes again in more detail through its study of Pope Benedict XVI's *Spe Salvi.*

[106] Ratzinger, *Eschatology,* 59 (JRGS10, 86).

[107] Ratzinger, *Eschatology,* 59 (JRGS10, 86).

[108] See Pope Francis, *Laudato Sí* (Vatican City: Libreria Editrice Vaticana, 2015), §§106–114.

[109] Ratzinger, *Eschatology,* 62 (JRGS10, 88).

Son."[110] Communion with Christ defines Ratzinger's theology of hope, and his emphasis on the influence of the sacraments upon the ontology of the human person will place his thought at critical odds with Moltmann and Metz, as they have a different understanding of the role of the *logos* in relation to *ethos* or praxis.

Hope is not simply one aspect of eschatology or a unique tract within theology according to the perspective of Moltmann. Eschatology defines theology completely, whereas hope fully expresses the true understanding of eschatology. Pozo maintains the view that Moltmann's paradigmatic work on this topic, *Theology of Hope*, "intends to represent the concentration of the whole of theology in the notion of hope."[111] Christianity is synonymous with eschatology in the writings of Moltmann: "The eschatological is not one element *of* Christianity, but it is the medium of Christian faith as such, the key in which everything in it is set, the glow that suffuses everything here in the dawn of an expected new day."[112] Theology's *point de départ* is eschatological hope, which impacts all of theology in Moltmann's estimation. He presents hope as "the foundation and the mainspring of theological thinking."[113] What has hindered the full development of eschatological hope in theology has been the Hellenization of Christianity.[114] Moltmann reframes the orientation of eschatology in light of what he claims is the authentic biblical view whereby God makes promises throughout salvation history in contradistinction with Christianity's appropriation of the Greek notion of *logos*: "The real language of Christian eschatology, however, is not the Greek *logos*, but the *promise* which has stamped the language, the hope and the experience of Israel."[115] Hope in God's promises has been the guiding lodestar for the faith of the people of Israel, which remains for Christians. Consequently, Moltmann claims that hope has a primacy over and above the virtue of faith. The

---

[110] Ratzinger, *PCT*, 39: "Being a Christian means becoming a son with the Son and thus, precisely by reason of one's belief in God, being incorporated also in the communion of saints, the Body of Christ."

[111] Pozo, *Theology of the Beyond*, 40. Moltmann himself maintains, "[E]schatology means the doctrine of the Christian hope, which embraces both the object hoped for and also the hope inspired by it. From first to last, and not merely in the epilogue, Christianity is eschatology, is hope, forward looking and forward moving, and therefore also revolutionizing and transforming the present." Moltmann, *Theology of Hope*, 16.

[112] Moltmann, *Theology of Hope*, 16.

[113] Moltmann, *Theology of Hope*, 19.

[114] Moltmann describes this underlying issue as "acute Hellenization of Christianity" or "acute Christianizing of Hellenism," *Theology of Hope*, 157.

[115] Moltmann, *Theology of Hope*, 40–41.

latter maintains a priority, but the certainty and confidence of hope is the ultimate end.[116] The promises made by God in the Old Covenant receive their full relevance only in light of the Resurrection of the Christ.

The promise of the Resurrection provides hope for a transformation of the world within history. The future always offers hope for the present moment, and this is further confirmed by Christ. Metz maintains, "Christian hope is meaningful only when the world can be changed by him in whom this hope hopes, and is thus open to that for which this hope hopes; when it is full of all kinds of possibilities (possible for God) and open to the resurrection of the dead."[117] The focus for Moltmann, with the Resurrection of Christ and the promise of the resurrection of the dead, is the hope that in the future God will transform the present world.[118] Moltmann maintains that Christians do not place their hope in the person of Jesus Christ *per se* as much as they hope in the promise of what God can and will do: "Our hope in the promises of God, however, is not hope in God himself or in God as such, but it hopes that his future faithfulness will bring it also the fullness of what has been promised."[119] Hope looks towards the fulfillment of a reality greater than the present moment. Moltmann emphasizes the importance of the future action that God will bring about, lest Christians slip into a form of passive hope *in* God. This narrow view of hope is perhaps ironically derived from the traditional understanding of Christ's presence within the sacraments.

In his attempt to contribute to the dehellenization of Christianity, Moltmann objects to the understanding of eschatology that favors

---

[116] "[I]n the Christian life faith has the priority, but hope the primacy." Moltmann, *Theology of Hope*, 20. Moltmann reiterates this point later in his work: "Faith in Jesus as the Christ is not the end of hope, but it is the confidence in which we hope (Heb. 11.1). Faith in Christ is the prior of the two, but in this faith hope has the primacy" (229).

[117] Moltmann, *Theology of Hope*, 92.

[118] "The Christian hope for the future comes of observing a specific, unique event—that of the resurrection and appearing of Jesus Christ. The hopeful theological mind, however, can observe this event only in seeking to span the future horizon projected by this event." Moltmann, *Theology of Hope*, 194.

[119] See Moltmann, *Theology of Hope*, 119: "To be sure, it can be said that our hope is hope in the coming of the faithfulness of God, that is expects the promised future from the coming of God himself and not apart from him. . . . Hope, where it holds to the promises, hopes that the coming of God will bring it also 'this and that'—namely, his redeeming and restoring lordship in all things. It does not merely hope personally 'in him,' but has also substantial hopes of his lordship, his peace and his righteousness on earth. Otherwise hope itself could unobtrusively change into a kind of fulfilment and there would be nothing more in which our hopes could be fulfilled."

realization of the eschaton via the liturgy because the fulfillment of the eschaton is in the future and never in the present. Moltmann critiques the view that closely relates the liturgy and eschaton because in light of such a view, "History thus loses its eschatological direction."[120] Subsequently, Moltmann claims, "In place of the eschatological 'not yet' (*noch nicht*) we have a cultic 'now only' (*nur noch*), and this becomes the key-signature of history *post Christum*."[121] The anticipation of the eschaton within the liturgy introduces a dichotomy in Moltmann's view with how eschatology should be understood. A sacramental eschatology (what Moltmann terms a "presentative theology") displaces an eschaton that is realized here in this world. This introduces a dualistic approach that separates the world from a remote kingdom.[122] Moltmann appropriates Paul's critique of the Hellenistic ecstasy in the church of Corinth as a corrective to what he views as a Hellenistic-influenced theology.

The so-called "presentative eschatology," which has developed as a result of Hellenism, is corrected by Paul's "*eschatologia crucis*" that is the foundation for a "truly futurist eschatology."[123] Moltmann uses this interpretation of Paul, drawing upon the scholarship of Ernst Käsemann (1906–1988), to outline a different understanding of the sacraments in contradistinction with his "presentative eschatology": "The baptized are dead with Christ, if they are baptized into his death. But they are not already risen with him and translated into heaven in the perfect tense of the cultus. They attain participation in the resurrection of Christ by new obedience, which unfolds itself in the realm of the hope of resurrection."[124] Participating in the death of Christ is separated from the share in the hope of the resurrection. The latter becomes a future reality that can never take place within the liturgy, but it can take place only by the person's obedience to God here on earth. The grace of the resurrection is reduced to a promissory note that is fulfilled only if the person demonstrates fidelity to Christ in his daily life. Freed from what Moltmann views as a narrow-sighted eschatology, Christian discipleship (termed "creative discipleship") "cannot consist in adaptation to, or preservation of, the existing social and judicial orders. . . . [It] sets things right and puts them in order."[125] As a result of the promise of hope, the Christian can work on

---

[120] Moltmann, *Theology of Hope*, 159.
[121] Moltmann, *Theology of Hope*, 159.
[122] Moltmann, *Theology of Hope*, 159.
[123] Moltmann, *Theology of Hope*, 160.
[124] Moltmann, *Theology of Hope*, 161.
[125] Moltmann, *Theology of Hope*, 334–35.

his own to restore justice within history. It is not difficult to see how a theology of hope is within close reach of a political theology.

Similar to Moltmann, Johann Baptist Metz asserts that hope has a primary place within theology. Metz opines: "The intention and task of any Christian theology may be defined as 'an apology for hope.'"[126] Citing 1 Peter 3:15, Metz defines hope in terms of the historical and societal present. In a manner similar to Moltmann, Metz articulates hope in a manner that does not affirm hope as a supernatural or theological virtue. The focus of hope is the natural struggle to alleviate oppression and suffering in this world *vis-à-vis* a political theology. The driving factor for Metz's political theology is his concern in addressing the challenge of theodicy.[127] In particular, contemporary theology's point of departure is "after Auschwitz," which Metz describes as "accept[ing] the fact that concrete history, and the theological experience of non-identity connected with it, have broken into theology's logos."[128] Human suffering has forever marked the human condition such that theology must be political and affirm the primacy of praxis or *ethos*. The authentic remembrance of human suffering necessitates this transformation of theology.

In Metz's view, theology can no longer affirm the primacy of *logos* lest it remain mere academic abstraction. Theology by its very nature, Metz argues, is both mystical and political: "Theology remains bound to a praxis of faith that is dually constituted as mystical-political. In this sense

---

[126] Metz, *Faith in History and Society*, 23.

[127] See Johann Baptist Metz, *A Passion for God: The Mystical-Political Dimension of Christianity*, trans. J. Matthew Ashley (New York: Paulist Press, 1998), 54–71.

[128] Metz, *A Passion for God*, 25. Elsewhere Metz explains the significance of "after Auschwitz" as a foundation for his theology: "[Auschwitz] signals a horror for which I have found neither a place nor a language in theology, a horror which bursts all the familiar ontological and metaphysical certainties in our talk about God and restricts theology to using those 'weak' concepts and categories of thought that are sensitive to the situation—in the style of a new, secondary nominalist, as it were." Metz, "God: Against the Myth of the Eternity of Time," in *The End of Time? The Provocation of Talking About God: Proceedings of a Meeting of Joseph Cardinal Ratzinger, Johannes Baptist Metz, Jürgen Moltmann, and Eveline Goodman-Thau*, ed. Tierno Tainier Peters, and Claus Urban (New York: Paulist Press, 2004), 27–28. Also see Metz, "Theology in the New Paradigm," in *An Eerdmans Reader in Contemporary Political Theology*, ed. William T. Cavanaugh, Jeffrey W. Bailey, and Craig Hovey (Grand Rapids, MI: Eerdmans Publishing, 2012), 322–323; originally published as Johann Baptist Metz, "Theology in the New Paradigm: Political Theology," in *Paradigm Change in Theology*, ed. Hans Küng (New York: Crossroad, 1989). Metz rejects any discussion of metaphysics or ontology in favor of a narrow view of history and memory. See Metz, "Theology in the New Paradigm," 41–43.

fundamental theology must allow itself to be systematically interrupted by such a praxis."[129] Consistent with his assertion concerning the primacy of praxis (*ethos*) for theology, Metz claims that theology "cannot be a pure 'book theology' or nothing but a 'guild theology'—precisely for the sake of its claim to provide foundations. It must take up new experiences and new praxes to keep it from becoming the reproduction of concepts of earlier experiences and earlier praxes."[130] History dictates the direction of theology for Metz and Moltmann. Consequently, the emphasis is on a practical theology that moves beyond mere theory. Metz maintains this position clearly: "A practical fundamental theology opposes the undialectical subordination of praxis to theory and ideas. It insists on the intelligible force of praxis itself, understood in terms of a 'theory-praxis' dialectic. In this respect, it does theology under the 'primacy of praxis.'"[131] As a praxis, theology has the role of ensuring that the individual person's identity as a subject is ensured and stands at the forefront of history. The praxis of a Christian always has an ethically defined meaning: (1) it critiques all forms of violence or hate, (2) it can never come forth from the ruling social totality, and (3) it cannot ignore the call to suffer in solidarity.[132] The preeminence of social praxis dictates that theology must be political, which means that Christians preserve their identity as subjects.[133]

The central idea within Metz's political theology is the role of memory, what he describes as the "dangerous memory" of Jesus Christ.[134] The

---

[129] Metz, *Faith in History and Society*, 30.

[130] Metz, *Faith in History and Society*, 30.

[131] Metz, *Faith in History and Society*, 61.

[132] Metz, *Faith in History and Society*, 66–67.

[133] Metz argues: "[The idea of God] is also political in itself: it is political as an idea that expresses as an option: opting for a state of affairs in which all people are able to be subjects and ought to become subjects. It follows from this that Christian memory's freedom over and against the existing situation consists not just in the fact that it imagines a fictitious counterworld (the way art does, for example). Rather, it appeals to the history of human beings as subjects in God's presence and tries to compel Christians to respond to the practical demands that this history makes. Their praxis ought to give some inkling of the fact that all persons are called to be subjects in the presence of God." Metz, *Faith in History and Society*, 76.

[134] See Metz, *Faith in History and Society*, 87–113; 169–185. Bruce T. Morrill underscores the importance of this concept in Metz's theology: "Through critical theory's assessment of the threatened situation of the world and its negative dialectics of suffering in history Metz constructs the hermeneutical key for unlocking the powerful message of Christianity from the modern manacles of privatized religion and institutional power structures. Metz interprets the gospel as the 'dangerous memory' of Jesus Christ, the *memoria Jesu Christi*. The importance of this insight for Metz cannot be understated,

fundamental mission for the Church and her political theology is to serve as a witness to this dangerous memory. Metz describes the "dangerous" character of this memory of Jesus Christ (*memoria Jesu Christi*), which "holds a particular anticipation of the future as a future for the hopeless, the shattered and oppressed." What makes it dangerous and liberating is that it "badgers the present and calls into question, since it does not remember just any open future, but precisely this future, and because it compels believers to be in a continual state of transformation in order to take this future into account."[135] The Church gives a public witness to the dangerous memory of the liberation that has been realized by the Cross and Resurrection of Jesus Christ. This memory of suffering is "an anticipatory remembering; it holds the anticipation of a specific future for humankind as a future for the suffering, for those without hope, for the oppressed, the disabled, and the useless of this earth."[136]

Theology is developed from the history of suffering that is made consciously present through memory in opposition to the traditional concerns of metaphysics that revolve around the question of being. Metz contends that the "*a priori* of suffering is what orients theology's claim to truth when, as a political theology, it incorporates the historical, social, and cultural situation in its talk about God."[137] The remembrance of how other people have suffered and the perception of their suffering in the present moment is a concrete way in which the Church is called to remember God. Christians act from the *a priori* of suffering and transform history and politics to assist those who suffer.[138]

Similar to the futuristic eschatology of Moltmann, Metz favors an apocalyptic eschatology[139]: "Following Christ is not something that can

---

for he considers it basic and 'central' to his entire theological project." *Anamnesis as Dangerous Memory: Political and Liturgical Theology in Dialogue* (Collegeville, MN: The Liturgical Press, 2000), 31.

[135] Metz, *Faith in History and Society*, 89.

[136] Metz, *Faith in History and Society*, 112.

[137] Metz, "God: Against the Myth of the Eternity of Time," in *The End of Time?*, 42.

[138] Metz, *Faith in History and Society*, 113: "What the memory of suffering brings into political life, on the other hand, is a new moral imagination with regard to others' suffering, which should bear fruit in an excessive, uncalculated partiality for the weak and the voiceless. But this is the way the Christian *memoria passionis* can become a ferment for that new political life for which we are searching, so that we might have a human future."

[139] See Metz, *Faith in History and Society*, 81–82. "An important theological statement (which encompasses all other assertions about God, for example, about God's being as creator) corresponds to this theological primacy of apocalyptic eschatology: God is God of the living and of the dead, God of universal justice and of the resurrection of the dead" (82).

be lived without the idea of the Parousia, without looking forward to the second coming. . . . What corresponds to following Christ is an existence based absolutely on hope: a life with an apocalyptic goal."[140] The disciple of Christ must live in the present moment with an expectation of an imminent fulfilment of the apocalypse. Jesus's call to the Apostles, which is re-echoed to each of his followers, "Follow me!" cannot be separated from the prayer "Come, Lord Jesus!"[141] Political theology is inseparable from the apocalypse. The resurrection of the dead is concretely a hope for a revolution of political action in favor of those who have suffered injustices, both the living and the dead.[142]

The anamnestic approach favored by Metz naturally includes solidarity for the Church to the future and to the past. Metz defines solidarity as "a category of assistance, of supporting and encouraging the subject in the face of that which threatens him or her most acutely and in the face of his or her suffering."[143] Apathy or indifference to the plight of the other is not an option for a true follower of Jesus. The uniquely Christian aspect of solidarity is that it remembers those who have died, as it should motivate and guide political actions to remedy injustices that have led to the suffering and death of other people.

Both Moltmann and Metz share in the rejection of ontology in favor of a history that is oriented by the future apocalypse. A fundamental idea that also unites their theologies is a subordination of *logos* to *ethos* or praxis. This theology of hope or political theology is realized imminently. Ratzinger engages the theology of Moltmann and Metz and attempts to reorient their thought, maintaining the unity between history and ontology and affirming the primacy of the *logos*. Consequently, Ratzinger affirms the liturgy as the *prima theologia*, which is a perspective that is necessary to understand eschatology properly.

## RATZINGER'S *LOGOS*-CENTRIC HOPE

Joseph Ratzinger critiques both Moltmann's theology of hope and Metz's political theology.[144] He treats them together because of the influence that

---

[140] Johann Baptist Metz, *Followers of Christ: The Religious Life and the Church*, trans. Thomas Linton (Mahwah, NJ: Paulist Press, 1978), 75–76, quoted in Morrill, *Anamnesis as Dangerous Memory*, 40.

[141] Metz, *Faith in History and Society*, 163.

[142] Metz, *Faith in History and Society*, 84.

[143] Metz, *Faith in History and Society*, 209.

[144] Ratzinger outlines the development and basic influences upon Metz's theology and

Moltmann had on the thought of Metz,[145] and the criticism of both think-ers remains the same. The eschatological vision of Moltmann and Metz obfuscates the proper end of the kingdom of God. The kingdom is realized in part through the transformation of the world, but Moltmann and Metz offer an interpretation that views this change solely via the efforts of the polis. Ratzinger clearly argues on the other hand that

> the realization of God's Kingdom is not itself a political process. To misconceive it as such is to falsify both politics and theology. The inevitable result is the rise of false messianic movements which of their very nature and from the inner logic of messianic claims finish up in totalitarianism.[146]

---

subsequent political or liberation theologies that originate from the same ideologi-cal sources, which he contends "is fusing more and more with neo-Marxist ideas and, thereby, becoming increasingly narrow; this movement is distancing itself ever more rapidly from its starting points. Its initial approach was found in the theology of the world that J. B. Metz developed by fusing Karl Rahner's interpretation of Thomism in terms of transcendental philosophy with the interpretations of the world inspired by Luther and elaborated by Friedrich Gogarten. In its encounter with Ernst Bloch, this theology of the world turned, first, into the theology of hope and, then, with logical con-sistency into political theology. Today this trend has developed far beyond the teachings of its founders into a general reform pragmatism having various currents; more and more it has come to be a movement without any big names." *DP*, 380–381. Also see *MM*, 135–138. Ratzinger notes that during his work as a lecturer in Tübingen he witnessed the displacement of existentialism with Marxist thought within the faculty of theology among thinkers such as Moltmann. Ratzinger argues that "the destruction of theology that was now occurring (through its politicization as conceived by Marxist messianism) was incomparably more radical precisely because it took biblical hope as its basis but inverted it by keeping the religious ardor but eliminating God and replacing him with the political activity of man." *MM*, 137. For an insightful overview of the history of political theology and its close relationship with liberation theology, see John Milbank, *Theology & Social Theory: Beyond Secular Reason* (Malden, MA: Blackwell Publishing, 2006), 230–256. Milbank's summary and analysis highlights the drawbacks of theo-logical proposals such as that of Metz's theology of the world in its embrace of Marxism and secularism: "Marxism here proves to be precisely that consoling doctrine which can appear to suggest that the aims of Christian ethics and of Christian socialism can be achieved, indeed *must be* achieved, through the apparently alien workings of secular-ization and politicization. The temporal dialectic which draws justice out of injustice, legitimates the theological dialectic which discovers salvation in human independence from God" (247).

[145] Metz affirms the close affinity that his political theology has with the eschatology of Moltmann while at the same time differentiating his work in their understanding of praxis. See Metz, *Faith in History and Society*, 65.

[146] Ratzinger, *Eschatology*, 58 (JRGS10, 85). Ratzinger expresses similar concerns

Ratzinger's first objection is that both thinkers obscure the true nature of hope. A transcendent and supernatural hope is displaced by the natural "hope" in a political utopia. The second objection concerns the nature of politics. Ratzinger contends that within political theology the "mystery of God is invoked in order to justify political irrationalism, and so is reduced to being a pseudo-mystery. The transformation of human nature, and the world with it, is possible only as a miracle of grace."[147] The primacy of a theology of liturgy for Ratzinger enables him to maintain a balance in his own explication of hope and eschatology that are not present in the viewpoints espoused by Moltmann and Metz. The underlying or foundational issue is ontological and has to do with how nature relates to grace (and history to ontology). In the sacramental ontology of Ratzinger, the natural order is fulfilled in the supernatural world of grace. At the same time, the sanctified human person is called to bring about the realization of hope within the world, but he or she must first seek hope from what is above.

Hope's role in Ratzinger's theology is properly situated because of the tension that he maintains between eschatology and liturgy. This relationship, as this work has consistently established, is derived from the central role of Jesus Christ in Ratzinger's theology. The foundational doctrine that Jesus Christ is a divine Person with a fully human nature and fully divine nature, which was firmly defined by the Council of Chalcedon, remains the crystal clear interpretive key for Ratzinger.[148] Emery de Gaál summa-

---

elsewhere: "[T]he destruction of theology that was now occurring (through its politicization as conceived by Marxist messianism) was incomparably more radical precisely because it took biblical hope as its basis but inverted it by keeping the religious ardor but eliminating God and replacing him with the political activity of man. Hope remains, but the party takes the place of God, and, along with the party, a totalitarianism that practices an atheistic sort of adoration ready to sacrifice all humanness to its false god." Ratzinger, *MM*, 137.

[147] Ratzinger, *Eschatology*, 59 (JRGS10, 85).

[148] Ratzinger notes the significance of Chaledonian Christology: "I encountered [Jesus] initially, not in literature or philosophy, but in the faith of the Church. This means that from the beginning I knew him, not as a great figure of the past (like Plato or Thomas Aquinas), but as someone who is alive and at work today, someone whom people can encounter today. It means, above all, that I have come to know him within the history of the faith that has its origin in him and according to the vision of the faith that received its most enduring formulation at the Council of Chalcedon. In my view, Chalcedon represents the boldest and most sublime simplification of the complex and many-layered data of tradition to a single central fact that is the basis of everything else: Son of God, possessed of the same nature as God *and* of the same nature as we have. In contrast to the many other approaches that have been attempted in the course of

rizes the consistent argument for Christology as the underlying issue of all theological controversies: "Primarily, the question is one of Jesus Christ's divinity and the Incarnation's relationship to the praxis of faith. Invariably, the foundational understanding of faith and discipleship becomes one-sided and confusing as the believer follows only the human Jesus and no longer also the divine Christ."[149] When one separates the two natures of Christ and favors an understanding of Jesus in his human nature, de Gaál notes, "One thereby reduces faith to an imitation (if not a mimicry) of a human exemplar. Christ's divinity is not addressed and is perhaps even downright negated."[150] The Christocentric theology of Ratzinger underscores the cause of the gap between the theology of hope as it will be articulated later by Moltmann and Metz and the understanding of hope developed by Ratzinger. Quoting Konrad Weiß, Josef Pieper summarizes the false versions of hope: "All attempts to construct a ready-made image of the future of historical man are burdened by the grave discrepancy that 'it is not humanity that is the goal of the Incarnation.'"[151] The attempt to humanize Christ at the expense of his divinity has led to a narrow-sighted political theology and what Ratzinger refers to above as the "emasculation of hope." When hope is no longer rooted in a proper understanding of who Jesus Christ is, it is inevitably recreated in the image of the whims and temporal desires of the human person. Josef Pieper lays a foundation that will implicitly and explicitly influence Ratzinger.[152]

In order to understand the virtue of hope, Pieper begins his analysis by highlighting the human person's anthropological condition as a "viator," or pilgrim, "on the way." He maintains that "to be a *viator* means to be making progress towards eternal happiness; to have encompassed this goal, to be a *comprehensor*, means to possess beatitude."[153] Consequently, the human person travels as a pilgrim this side of heaven seeking fulfilment, which he cannot fully realize on earth. The only answer to the

---

history, Chalcedon interpreted Jesus theologically. I regard this as the only interpretation that can do justice to the whole range of tradition and sustain the full impact of the phenomenon itself. All other interpretations become too narrow at some point; every other conception embraces only one part of the reality and excludes another. Here and here alone does the whole of the reality disclose itself." Ratzinger, *DP*, 122.

[149] De Gaál, *The Theology of Pope Benedict XVI*, 3.
[150] De Gaál, *The Theology of Pope Benedict XVI*, 3.
[151] Pieper, *Hope and History*, 113.
[152] For the influence of Pieper's *Hope and History (Hoffnung und Geschichte)* on Ratzinger, see JRGS10, 412–428.
[153] Pieper, *On Hope*, 12.

tension experienced by every person as a result of what Pieper describes as the "not-yet-existing-being" of his existence is hope.[154]

Hope is the proper virtue for the *viator* who desires the proper reality of his existence to come into being. Hope is a theological virtue whereby the human person realizes his human nature in its supernatural end. Theological virtues in Pieper's estimate are the "utmost degree of supernatural potentiality for being" because they are "grounded in a real, grace-filled participation in the divine nature, which comes to man through Christ (2 Pet 1:4)."[155]

One of the major problems with political theology, whereby politics displaces theological virtue, is highlighted by this understanding of theological virtue. As it has been shown in Ratzinger's critique of Moltmann and Metz, eschatological politics gains a status of "pseudo-mystery," claiming for itself what only grace can bring about in human nature. Implicitly, this position of Moltmann and Metz is a rejection of the primacy of the *logos*, as they claim that a person can realize what hope promises through our own human efforts, as opposed to the traditional position that salvation is something that is received from God as a grace. What unites Ratzinger's position in Christology, liturgy, eschatology, and ecclesiology is a rejection of the modern notion of "makeability" that is characteristic of the modern *logos*. Corkery comments that this attitude of "makeability" characterizes the "second phase of modernity (the phase of so-called 'technical rationality') that inflated human capability and suggested that the hoped-for future was ours to shape."[156]

When hope is conceived of only as a natural virtue, then it can easily slip into human ideologies that ironically threaten the freedom and dignity of the person that it sets out to defend. The displacement of hope as a supernatural or theological virtue to solely a natural virtue has obscured the proper final destination for the *viator*. Similarly, in his analysis of the caricature of hope presented by Bloch and Marx, Ratzinger describes their understanding of hope as the "product of human activity." Hope is limited

---

[154] See Pieper, *On Hope*, 20–21.

[155] Pieper, *On Hope*, 25.

[156] James Corkery, S.J., *Joseph Ratzinger's Theological Ideas: Wise Cautions and Legitimate Hopes* (Mahwah, NJ: Paulist Press, 2009), 53. On this notion of "makeability," Corkery maintains that Ratzinger has been influenced by Hans Freyer. See Freyer, *Theorie des gegenwärtigen Zeitalters* (Stuttgart: Deutsche Verlags-Anstalt, 1955), 15–31. For an overview of this theme of "makeability" (*Machbarkeit*) throughout the writings of Ratzinger, see Ralph Weimann, *Dogma und Fortschritt bei Joseph Ratzinger* (Paderborn: Schöningh, 2012), 65–78.

to the natural plane alone as Ratzinger explicates the view of Bloch: "What one cannot do oneself is very consciously excluded. One could not hope for what one cannot control; there are directives only for what we ourselves can bring about."[157] Hope is reduced to what the human person is able to bring about through his own autonomous efforts. Writing as the Supreme Pontiff Benedict XVI, Ratzinger will provide the proper supernatural perspective to define hope in light of God's image rather than the continual work to recast it through an anthropocentric lens.

In his second encyclical, *Spe Salvi*, Pope Benedict XVI outlines the Christian understanding of the virtue of hope in opposition to the narrow and short-sighted view of "human" (merely material) progress.[158] This magisterial teaching is an explicit attempt to redirect some of the misperceptions of the theology of hope and political theology of Moltmann and Metz. The various aspects of true hope will receive their full development in light of the Church's social doctrine in *Caritas in Veritate*. The message of hope offered by Christianity is "performative" and not simply "informative."[159] Hope can bring about true change in the life of the person and it is at the heart of the Church's mission to proclaim this authentic hope that has redeemed and formed her.

While various thinkers of the nineteenth century have promoted progress as man's true "hope," Christian hope brings about a change in the very depths of the person that transcends merely material goods. One of the main problems of modern politics was described, as we have previously quoted, by Eric Voegelin as an "immanentization of the eschaton." Based on a secular humanism, modern politics promises a false freedom allegedly fulfilled by material progress. Pope Benedict describes this as

[p]rogress toward the better, toward the definitively good world, no longer comes simply from science but from politics—from a

---

[157] Ratzinger, JRGS10, 416.

[158] For an overview of the various themes in *Spe Salvi*, see Josef Kreiml, "Die Enzyklika Papst Benedikt XVI. Über die christliche Hoffnung: "Spe salvi" als reife Frucht eines langen Denkweges," in *Hoffnung auf Vollendung: Zur Eschatologie von Joseph Ratzinger*, ed. Gerhard Nachtwei (Regensburg: Friedrich Pustet, 2015), 259–82. Kreiml argues that *Spe Salvi* is consistent with themes that Ratzinger has engaged in an essay that Ratzinger wrote entitled, "Die Zukunft des Heils" in 1975 (See JRGS10, 489–509). This essay was originally published in Ulrich Hommes and Joseph Ratzinger, *Das Heil des Menschen. Innerweltlich-Christlich* (Munich: Kösel Verlag, 1975), 31–63.

[159] Pope Benedict XVI, Encyclical Letter *Spe Salvi* [hereafter, SS] (Vatican City: Liberia Editrice Vaticana, 2007), §22.

scientifically-conceived politics that recognizes the structure of history and society and thus points out the road towards revolution, towards all-encompassing change.[160]

The fundamental problem of modern politics is that it makes an eschatological promise which it cannot possibly fulfill because of the fallen nature of the human person. The human person can only be truly fulfilled in a transcendent communion with God in the true kingdom, which is not of this world (John 18:36).

Throughout *Spe Salvi*, Pope Benedict emphasizes the solidarity offered through the message of salvation, which underlies his position of articulating the reality of the Church's identity and mission in light of the call to *communio*. Henri de Lubac has demonstrated that "salvation has always been considered a 'social reality'" according to the wisdom of the Church Fathers.[161] An authentic Christian vision of hope has been displaced by a false secular "hope."[162] Christians have forgotten that they are pilgrims or "strangers and sojourners" who will find their home in the real kingdom of God. As Pope Benedict points out, "While we must always be committed to the improvement of the world, tomorrow's better world cannot be the proper and sufficient content of our hope."[163] Hope is directed towards a transcendent kingdom, which can be made present "wherever [Christ] is loved and wherever his love reaches us." Love alone, Benedict continues, assists each person to find a "life that is 'truly' life."[164] Atheist humanism, which has dominated the culture of the nineteenth and twentieth centuries, has led to an individualized conception of faith focused solely on one's own salvation. In God's absence in this type of culture, "man himself is now called to establish justice."[165] A world with such a materialist and immanent view is without any transcendent hope. The autonomous isolationism threatens the human person's dignity, which is to be respected at all times. Only authentic hope, which brings about true communion and solidarity, can assist the human person in overcoming the alienation which is wrought by such a secularized culture.

Material progress alone will never be sufficient to bring about hope or salvation. Progress, particularly among the sciences and technology,

---

[160] *SS*, §20.

[161] *SS*, §14.

[162] See *SS*, §30.

[163] *SS*, §39.

[164] *SS*, §31.

[165] *SS*, §42.

must be guided by moral norms to ensure the protection of the dignity of each and every person. Benedict prophetically warns, "Science can contribute greatly to making the world and mankind more human. Yet it can also destroy mankind and the world unless it is steered by forces that lie outside it."[166] Hence, science must be guarded by the principle "It is not science that redeems man: man is redeemed by love."[167] The love which has brought about redemption is a living person with whom we are called to enter into communion; hence, "Life in its true sense is not something we have exclusively in or from ourselves: it is a relationship."[168] Above all, life, in its full sense, is a relationship with Christ. Recognition of the person's transcendent vocation and dignity enables a person truly to *live*. Once again, Benedict reiterates his insistence upon the Christian's call to participate in the "pro-existence" of Christ: "Being in communion with Jesus Christ draws us into his 'being for all'; it makes it our own way of being. He commits us to live for others, but only through communion with him does it become possible truly to be there for others, for the whole."[169] Communion with Christ allows the human person to realize his or her full call to be in relation with others.

Vertical communion leads to a stronger sense of horizontal communion, as Benedict notes: "Love of God leads to participation in the justice and generosity of God toward others."[170] Authentic love directs the human person to solidarity and communion with others. Communion is meant to frame each person's way of life. Individualistic autonomy is contrary to the call to communion that each person is meant to answer: "[N]o man is an island, entire of itself. Our lives are involved with one another, through innumerable interactions that are linked together. No one lives alone. No one sins alone. No one is saved alone."[171] Benedict's emphasis on self-giving communion as the end for the human person coupled with

---

[166] *SS*, §25.

[167] *SS*, §26.

[168] *SS*, §27.

[169] *SS*, §28.

[170] *SS*, §28.

[171] *SS*, §48. Elsewhere, Ratzinger asserts, "The doctrine of the body of Christ simply formulates with that final consistency that Christology makes possible a truth which ·was quite predictable on the basis of anthropology alone. Every human being exists in himself and outside himself: everyone exists simultaneously in other people. What happens in one individual has an effect upon the whole of humanity, and what happens in humanity happens in the individual. 'The Body of Christ' means that all human beings are one organism, the destiny of the whole the proper destiny of each." *Eschatology*, 190 (JRGS10, 195).

his argument against modernity's faith in materialistic progress is ultimately rooted in his liturgical theology. The eschatological unity sought by humanity is anticipated and realized already in the liturgy. Unity was a defining theme for the Fathers of the Church in Ratzinger's estimation, which is why Ratzinger has placed so much emphasis on sacramental *communio* as the *logos* of the Church, as we established in our first section of this chapter.

In order to underscore the patristic emphasis upon unity for the Church, it is necessary to turn briefly to Ratzinger's *The Unity of the Nations*.[172] Ratzinger contends, "Unity was not just one among other themes here but rather the leitmotiv of the whole."[173] Salvation history is directed towards Jesus Christ overcoming the disunity wrought by sin. Christ radically transforms humanity through his Incarnation. The human nature of Jesus Christ served as "the divine fishing rod that caught the [humanity] of all people and was now pulling it in" so that everyone "would be brought into the unity of the body of Christ, the God-man, and out of the fatal division that characterized the isolation known as sin."[174] What was divided as a result of the sin of Adam is overcome by Jesus Christ, the new Adam. At the heart of the Gospel, "Jesus Christ introduced a new dynamic into humanity, the dynamic of the passage out of a being that was divided into many individual parts and into the unity of Jesus Christ, the unity of God."[175] In contrast with the artificial unity sought by an eschatologically driven politics, unity is brought about by and in Jesus Christ through his Church.

The Church is a sign and instrument of the unity as it is an incarnation of "humanity's movement towards the unity of God."[176] The Fathers referring to the Church as the "body of Christ" affirms the view that the Church is this movement towards unity, which begins with the sacraments:

---

[172] Twomey comments that Ratzinger is developing insights that Ratzinger first proposed in his dissertation in this work on the Fathers. Twomey, *Pope Benedict XVI*, 72. This work appears in Ratzinger's collected works in the same volume as his dissertation on Augustine, which supports the claim of Twomey. See *Die Einheit der Nationen: Eine Vision der Kirchenväter* in JRGS1, 555–607.

[173] Joseph Ratzinger, *The Unity of the Nations: A Vision of the Church Fathers*, trans. Boniface Ramsey (Washington, DC: The Catholic University of America Press, 2015), 24 (JRGS1, 567).

[174] Ratzinger, *The Unity of the Nations*, 26–27 (JRGS1, 568).

[175] Ratzinger, *The Unity of the Nations*, 28 (JRGS1, 568).

[176] Ratzinger, *The Unity of the Nations*, 28 (JRGS1, 568).

> The unheard-of new thing toward which history aimed was the drawing in of humankind into the unity of God, which began the life and suffering of the Lord. The unfolding of this beginning into the concrete history of individual human beings occurred, then, in the celebration of the Eucharist that was built on the foundation of Baptism. Here, at the Lord's table, what happened was that human beings, in eating Christ's body, themselves became Christ's body and were assimilated into the body of the New Adam.[177]

The liturgy brought about an authentic unity for Christians beginning in Baptism and culminating in the Eucharist. The unity brought about by the sacraments is directed towards communion with all people. Transcendent hope is realized concretely in the daily life of the Christian as he passes "from the primacy of the individual ego to the unity of the members of the body of Christ."[178] On the one hand, the Eucharist is an eschatological anticipation and foretaste of unity. On the other hand, the Eucharist compels the Christian to work towards unity, which it realizes through the communion that occurs among those transformed by Christ.[179] The Church will never be able to realize fully this unity on her own or without affirming the primacy for the love of God. In light of Augustinian theology, Ratzinger affirms that the Church as the "city of God" exists as a "sacramental-eschatological entity, which lives in this world as a sign of the coming world."[180] The Church exists in the world to bring about unity in Christ that will be actualized with the eschaton. Simultaneously, the liturgy allows the Church to anticipate an imminent eschaton. Upon this foundational understanding of the relationship between liturgy and eschatology, Ratzinger affirms the primacy of the liturgy as a *logikē latreia*. This understanding of liturgy demonstrates that the hope is truly "performative" and not simply "informative."[181]

---

[177] Ratzinger, *The Unity of the Nations*, 29–30 (JRGS1, 569).

[178] Ratzinger, *The Unity of the Nations*, 31 (JRGS1, 570).

[179] Ratzinger, JRCW11, 370 (JRGS11, 441–42): "The goal of the Eucharist is the transformation of those who receive it in authentic communion with his [Christ's] transformation. And so the goal is unity, that we, instead of being separated individuals who live alongside or in conflict with one another, might become, with Christ and in him, one organism of self-giving and might live unto the resurrection and the new world."

[180] Ratzinger, *The Unity of the Nations*, 113 (JRGS1, 606).

[181] See *SS*, §§1–3.

This chapter contrasted two different views of hope, which are the consequences of understanding the relationship of liturgy and eschatology and its relationship to ecclesiology from differing viewpoints. In the view of Ratzinger and Pieper, the Eucharist, eschatology, and ecclesiology are inseparable, whereas for Metz and Moltmann, the liturgy has no significant role in the understanding of eschatology, hope, ecclesiology, or the theology of politics. The frequent caricature of Ratzinger's view is that his understanding of hope and eschatology precludes or ignores the concern that the Church should have for people who are less fortunate. It becomes clearer that nothing could be further from the truth because Ratzinger emphasizes the primacy of the vertical relationship between humanity and God as the foundation for a stronger horizontal communion between one person and other people. The Church receives her *logos* from the Eucharist, which in turn leads the Church to consistently engage in an *ethos* that proclaims this hope in both word and deed. Relating the liturgy and eschatology is essential for Ratzinger to continue to make the case for a sacramental eschatology.

## SUMMARY AND CONCLUSION

In a speech entitled "The Nature and Limits of the Church," Ratzinger defines the Church concisely as the *"People of God resulting from the Body of Christ."*[182] The priority of the Church as the Body of Christ or as a Eucharistic *communio* is a fundamental theme in his ecclesiology. The Eucharist forms the Church into this *communio* with and for Christ; consequently, it has been argued in this chapter that the *logos* of the Church is *communio*. The biblical image of the people of God reminds the Church of the gift of unity that she has received from Christ in the New Covenant.

In another sense, *communio* is the *ethos* that defines the Church's mission. Ratzinger describes this call to *communio* that begins with the Eucharist: "Whenever I am united with Christ, I am also united with my neighbor, and this unity does not end at the communion rail; rather, it is just beginning there."[183] The eschatological mission to work for the unity of the Church can only be properly understood by giving primacy to the *logos*, which, in relation to ecclesiology, defines the Church by the identity

---

[182] Ratzinger, *FSFD*, 122. Originally published as "Wesen und Grenzend der Kirche, in *Studien und Berichte der Katholischen Akademie in Bayern*, vol. 24, *Das Zweite Vatikanische Konzil*, ed. K. Forster (Würzburg: Echter-Verlag, 1963), 47–68.

[183] Ratzinger, JRCW11, 363 (JRGS11, 433).

she has received from the Eucharist. The *logos* of the Church was emphasized in the first part of this chapter, whereas in the latter part of this chapter, the *ethos* as it is understood by Ratzinger was introduced. The ecclesiological visions of Metz/Moltmann and Ratzinger have the same goal of establishing unity, but their approaches are fundamentally different because they approach the dynamic between *logos* and *ethos* in opposite ways.

The liturgy reveals that the Church's true nature and her call to sacrifice is communion, which is the Body of Christ. The eschatological mission of the Church is to strive for unity at all times and at all places until at the eschaton God gives his Church the gift of full unity. At present, the unity of the Church is rooted in the mystery of the Holy Eucharist, which both realizes and anticipates communion with God and neighbor. The *ethos* of the Church, which is consistent with her identity (*logos*), can be defined as the *sacramentum caritatis*.

# CHAPTER 4

# *Logikē Latreia* and an *Ethos* of Charity

ONE OF THE ESSENTIAL ELEMENTS in the definition of the sacraments is that they were instituted by Christ as *signs*. Thomas Aquinas contends that a sacrament is a sign of the past (e.g., the Passion of Christ), an indication of what is effected in the present through Christ's Passion (grace), and a "foretelling of future glory."[1] Aquinas refers to the Eucharist as "the sign of supreme charity" because it nourishes the unity of the communicants with Christ and thereby builds the Church in charity.[2] Extending the argument set forth in the previous chapter that the Eucharist, as a sacrament of communion, forms the *logos* of the Church, this chapter demonstrates that Ratzinger emphasizes with Aquinas that the Eucharist forms the identity and mission of the Church as a sacrament of charity. The *ethos* of charity flows forth from Eucharistic worship understood as *logikē latreia*.

Throughout this book, it has been emphasized that *logos* precedes *ethos* in Ratzinger's theology. So, this chapter will first insist upon the close relationship between the *logos* of communion and the *ethos* of self-giving love that flows from this *logos*. Second, it will be argued that one of Ratzinger's central claims is that the Pauline notion of the *logikē latreia* ("worship according to the *logos*"), found in Romans 12:1, is "the most appropriate way of expressing the essential form of the Christian liturgy."[3] Third,

---

[1]  Thomas Aquinas, *Summa Theologiae* [hereafter, ST] III, trans. The Fathers of the English Dominican Province (Westminster, MD: Christian Classics, 1981), q. 60, a. 3.

[2]  *ST* III, q. 75, a. 1: "Unde hoc sacramentum est maximae caritatis signum, et nostrae spei sublevamentum, ex tam familiari coniunctione Christi ad nos." On the Eucharist and its relationship to charity in Aquinas, see Matthew Levering, *Sacrifice and Community: Jewish Offering and Christian Eucharist* (Malden, MA: Blackwell Publishing, 2005), 95–114.

[3]  Joseph Ratzinger, *Theology of the Liturgy: The Sacramental Foundation of Christian Existence* [hereafter, JRCW11], ed. Michael J. Miller, trans. John Saward, Kenneth

the virtue of charity is a manifestation of the eschatological life that is the norm for the Christian. Charity is the *ethos* that flows from the sacramental *logos*, and this is the consistent teaching found in Benedict XVI's writings.[4]

The previous chapter demonstrated that the Eucharist provides the *logos* for the Church and eschatology in Ratzinger's theology. The present chapter emphasizes that this sacramentalized view of the eschaton does not preclude the call to service *in* the world. Christians have an obligation and a duty to bring the joys of the kingdom to everyone in this world. The Italian theologian Livio Melina expresses the Eucharistic roots of Christian action succinctly: "If Christian action is called to participate in God's dynamism of love that has entered history, it finds its secret source and its efficacy in the Eucharist, the permanent actualization of Christ's paschal self-giving."[5] An *ethos* of charity springs forth from the *logos* of communion. Melina maintains that the Eucharist is "the hidden seed of the kingdom that is to come, the dynamic energy that lets us participate

---

Baker, S.J., Henry Taylor, et al., Collected Works 11 (San Francisco: Ignatius Press, 2014), 30; *Theologie der Liturgie: Die sakramentale Begründung christlicher Existenz* [hereafter, JRGS11], Gesammelte Schriften 11, ed. Gerhard Ludwig Müller (Freiburg im Breisgau: Herder, 2008), 61.

4  Twomey maintains, "Love of God and love of neighbor: that is the secret of Pope Benedict XVI, and that will be the core of his universal teaching." Twomey recorded these words several months before Benedict published his first encyclical, *Deus Caritas Est*. See D. Vincent Twomey, S.V.D., *Pope Benedict XVI: The Conscience of Our Age—A Theological Portrait* (San Francisco: Ignatius Press, 2007), 17. According to Alfred Läpple, Ratzinger's prefect for his studies during his time in the seminary in Freising, Ratzinger's first significant work as a seminarian was a German translation of Aquinas's disputed questions on charity, *De Caritate*. G. Valente and P. Azzaro, "Aquel nuevo comienzo que floreció entre los escombros," *30 Días* XXXIV (enero-febrero 2006), 54, cited in Blanco Sarto, *La Teología de Joseph Ratzinger: Una Introducción* (Madrid: Ediciones Palabra, 2011), 189. In his dissertation, Ratzinger develops his understanding of the Church's mission of charity, which flows forth from her unity. See his *Volk und Haus Gottes* in Ratzinger, *Volk und Haus Gottes in Augustins Lehre von der Kirche: Die Dissertation und weiter Studien zu Augustinus und zur Theologie der Kirchenväter* [hereafter, JRGS1], Gesammelte Schriften 1, ed. Gerhard Ludwig Müller (Freiburg im Breisgau: Herder, 2011), 207–32; 273–97. Ratzinger addresses the question of charity in relation to Augustine's response to the Donatist controversy. He also relates the Eucharist to charity and ethics in light of the wisdom from other Church Fathers, such as Saints Hillary, John Chrysostom, and Cyril of Alexandria.

5  Livio Melina, *The Epiphany of Love: Towards a Theological Understanding of Christian Action*, trans. Susan Dawson and Stephan Kampowski (Grand Rapids, MI: Eerdmans Publishing, 2010), 133.

in Jesus' charity."[6] Melina's insights highlight what James Corkery notes are two key features of Ratzinger's theological work: (1) The essential paschal pattern of authentic Christian existence, and (2) love as the essence of Christianity.[7] The identity and mission of the Church come forth directly from Jesus's mission of charity and his identity as the communion between God and humanity. The Church's commitment to this mission of charity is part of her eschatological calling to draw all things into communion with God by participating in the life and sacrificial love of the incarnate *Logos*.

## COMMUNION AND MISSION

Communion is the fundamental aspect of the Church's being (*logos*), and she has received the call to extend this reality into the world to help overcome the fallen tendency of humanity towards autonomy and alienation from God. Pope Benedict XVI affirms, "'Communion' is truly the Good News, the remedy given to us by the Lord to fight the loneliness that threatens everyone today, the precious gift that makes us feel welcomed and beloved by God, in the unity of his People gathered in the name of the Trinity; it is the light that makes the Church shine forth like a beacon raised among the peoples."[8] The full realization of the human person's social nature, inherent in the call to communion, will be realized within

---

[6]   Melina, *The Epiphany of Love*, 133.

[7]   See James Corkery, S.J., *Joseph Ratzinger's Theological Ideas: Wise Cautions and Legitimate Hopes* (Mahwah, NJ: Paulist Press, 2009), 33–36. As we have already established, Corkery has a good grasp of the fundamental theological ideas of Ratzinger, but we cannot always consistently agree with his assessments, which seem to be editorial in nature rather than deep critical analyses. In his commentary on love as a main facial feature of Ratzinger's theological corpus, Corkery notes, "I sometimes detect a certain 'spiritualising' in Ratzinger—and in his preferred antecedents Augustine and Bonaventure (especially the latter)—that suggest a disdain for actual history and for human natural capacities." *Joseph Ratzinger's Theological Ideas*, 35. Corkery offers little development beyond further comments about the "'spiritualising,' anti-rational, anti-intellectual direction of Bonaventure's theology," which is reflected in Ratzinger's thought when he espouses the view that "simple believers need protection from the power of intellectuals." *Joseph Ratzinger's Theological Ideas*, 35–36. No citation of any primary text of Ratzinger is given by Corkery. There are certainly helpful introductory insights into Ratzinger's theology, but the text is filled with editorial critiques that do not truly engage Ratzinger's arguments.

[8]   Pope Benedict XVI, General Audience, March 29, 2006, in *The Apostles and Their Co-Workers. Wednesday General Audiences from March 15, 2006–February 14, 2007* (Huntington, IN: Our Sunday Visitor, 2007), 22.

the eschaton; nevertheless, the Church has the eschatological mission to bring others into this pilgrimage in communion with God here on earth.

The Second Vatican Council emphasized that the foundation for the missionary nature of the Church is the Trinitarian mission itself.[9] Within the communion of the Trinity there are two missions: the Son is sent by the Father while the Holy Spirit is "sent by the Father in the name of the Son."[10] All three Persons of the Trinity are involved in the "mission" *ad extra* in the economy (*oikonomia*) of love. God's innermost life, as *communio*, reveals the purpose of his mission or economy.[11] Since it is only in communion with Christ that the Church participates in this Trinitarian *communio*, the Church must also be understood in light of Christ's pro-existence. One of the unique contributions to Ratzinger's ecclesiology is that he applies his understanding of Christ's vicarious representation to the mission of the Church:

> The deepest essence of the Church is to be together, with Christ, the *totus Christus*, head and members. If the essence of Christ's mission is vicarious representation, then [the Church] has no other essence itself. Its essence is simply this "standing-for.". . . Because the Church is essentially not-for-itself, but is instead for-the-others; because its essence is never closed-off against the other, but is an open entity [*eine offene Größe*], it must therefore burst forth [*treiben*] in mission. Mission is the visible manifestation of that "for," which belongs to the essence of the Church.[12]

Analogous to Christ, the Church has proceeded "from" the communion with Trinity, so subsequently her mission is to live "for" the world.

The main purpose of all missionary activity is simply to reveal the love of God made visible in the person of Jesus Christ.[13] The Incarnation unveils that God desires a *communio* with all of humanity. In the words of the Second Vatican Council's Dogmatic Constitution on Divine

---

[9] Pope John Paul II, Encyclical Letter *Redemptoris Missio* (Vatican City: Libreria Editrice Vaticana, 1990) §1.

[10] *CCC* §263.

[11] See *CCC* §236.

[12] Joseph Ratzinger, *Zeichen unter den Völkern: Schriften zur Ekklesiologie und Ökumene*, Gesammelte Schriften 8/1 [hereafter, JRGS8/1], ed. Gerhard Ludwig Müller, (Freiburg: Herder, 2010), 216. English trans. from Christopher Ruddy, "'For the Many,' The Vicarious-Representative Heart of Joseph Ratzinger's Theology," *Theological Studies* 75, no. 3 (2014): 574.

[13] *Redemptoris Missio*, §2.

Revelation: "In His goodness and wisdom God chose to reveal Himself and to make known to us the hidden purpose of His will (see Eph 1:9) by which through Christ, the Word made flesh, man might in the Holy Spirit have access to the Father and to come to share in the divine nature."[14] This is why St. John Paul II affirms that "the Church is missionary by *her very nature*."[15]

The Church, as the universal sacrament of salvation, is a *sign* of the *communio* accomplished in the redemption of Jesus Christ. At the same time, the Church is the *instrument* through which that *communio* is accomplished. The foundation of the Church as the new People of God is brought about by Christ when he adopted those "who believe in him into the community of his own self (of his 'Body'). He achieved this by transforming his death into an act of prayer, an act of love, and thus by making himself communicable."[16] The Church's mission can only be understood when the Church is viewed as the subject of the faith in Jesus Christ. Ratzinger's spiritual Christology deepens the unity between Christ and the Church, such that his ecclesiology cannot be fully understood apart from his Christology.

Two narratives in Johannine theology, the washing of the disciples' feet and the high priestly prayer, illuminate Ratzinger's analysis of the dynamic shared between communion and mission. In the narrative of Jesus's washing of the feet (John 13), Ratzinger underscores the patristic notions of *sacramentum* and *exemplum* to explain the significance of the washing of the feet.[17] The *sacramentum* refers to the "entire mystery of Christ" whereby he "draws close to us, enters us through His Spirit, and transforms us. But precisely because this *sacramentum* truly 'cleanses' us, renewing us from within, it also unleashes a dynamic of new life."[18] The new life is the participation of the Christian in the self-giving love of *Logos*, whose sacrificial love we are able to participate in. The mystery of communion defines the newness of life and the new commandment to love as Christ has loved (John

---

14   Unless otherwise noted, translations of conciliar documents come from Norman P. Tanner, ed., *Decrees of the Ecumenical Councils*, 2 vols. (Washington, DC: Sheed & Ward and Georgetown University Press, 1990).

15   *Redemptoris Missio*, §5; emphasis added.

16   Joseph Ratzinger, *Behold the Pierced One: An Approach to Spiritual Christology* [hereafter, *BPO*], trans. Graham Harrison (San Francisco: Ignatius Press, 1986), 30; *Jesus von Nazareth: Beiträge zur Christologie*, Joseph Ratzinger Gesammelte Schriften 6/2 [hereafter, JRGS6/2], ed. Gerhard Ludwig Müller (Freiburg: Herder, 2013), 704.

17   Joseph Ratzinger, *Jesus of Nazareth: Holy Week: From the Entrance into Jerusalem to the Resurrection* [hereafter, *JN* II], trans. Vatican Secretariat of State (San Francisco: Ignatius Press, 2011), 62–65; *Jesus von Nazareth: Beiträge zur Christologie*, Joseph Ratzinger Gesammelte Schriften 6/1 [hereafter, JRGS6/1], ed. Gerhard Ludwig Müller (Freiburg: Herder, 2013), 465–468.

18   Ratzinger, *JN* II, 62 (JRGS6/1, 466).

13:34). Ratzinger argues that the "newness can come only from the gift of being-*with* and being-*in* Christ."[19] The *logos* of *communio* is emphasized as a pro-existence for the Church. Consequently, the *sacramentum* or the *logos* of the Church "becomes an *exemplum*, an example, while always remaining a gift. To be a Christian is primarily a gift, which then unfolds in the dynamic of living and acting in and around the gift."[20] The mission of the Church, which consists of drawing others into this dynamism of "being-*with*" and "being-*in*" communion with Christ, becomes even clearer in Jesus's high priestly prayer.

In his attempt to draw out the relationship between the high priestly prayer of Jesus and the ritual of the Day of the Atonement, Ratzinger describes Jesus's prayer as *logikē latreia*. Ratzinger elaborates, "Admittedly, this 'word' that supplants the sacrificial offering is no ordinary word. To begin with, it is no mere human speech, but rather the word of him who is '*the* Word,' and so it draws all human words into God's inner dialogue, into his reason and his love."[21] As was mentioned in chapter two, Ratzinger emphasizes the decisive break embodied by Jesus's new form of worship from the cultic sacrifices of the Temple. The previous discussion of sacrifice, new temple, and new worship enables one to appreciate that Ratzinger interprets Jesus as praying for the Church to be able to embrace her pro-existence in Christ. Jesus's prayer for the sanctification of the Church in the truth (John 17:17, 19) includes the dynamic of being set apart (consecrated) and entering into the dynamic of existing "for."[22] What appear to be opposite poles of being apart and being "for" are illustrated for Ratzinger by insight into John's Gospel that he receives from the scholarship of Bultmann:

> The holiness that Jesus received from the Father is his "being for the world," or "being for his own." His holiness is "no static difference in substance from the world, but is something Jesus achieves only by completing the stand he has made for God and against the world. But this completion means sacrifice. In the sacrifice he is, in the manner of God, so *against* the world that he is at the same time *for* it."[23]

---

[19] Ratzinger, *JN* II, 64 (JRGS6/1, 467).

[20] Ratzinger, *JN* II, 65 (JRGS6/1, 468).

[21] Ratzinger, *JN* II, 80 (JRGS6/1, 479–480).

[22] Ratzinger, *JN* II, 86 (JRGS6/1, 484).

[23] Ratzinger, *JN* II, 88 (JRGS6/1, 485); emphasis in the original. Ratzinger cites Rudolf Bultmann, *The Gospel of John: A Commentary*, trans. G. R. Beasley-Murray (Oxford:

The tension between being "set apart" and being "for" is overcome as Christ the high priest offers himself as the vicarious representative in a sacrifice that is made present in every Eucharist. It has been explained in the previous chapter that the Eucharist makes the Church, so it can be concluded with Ratzinger that in light of her communion, the Church's mission is to work for unity "that can come into existence only from God and through Christ and yet is so concrete in its appearance that in it we are able to see God's power at work."[24] Consistent with his argument that the *logos* has primacy over *ethos*, the mission of the Church as "being sent" like Christ must be understood in Ratzinger's view as sacramental. Ratzinger contends that the sacramental mission of the Church is "not self-generating, nor is it something man-made, but it is a matter of being incorporated into the 'Word that existed from the beginning' (cf. 1 Jn 1:1), into the communion of witnesses called forth by the Spirit."[25] The high priestly prayer of Christ ultimately emphasizes the Church's participation in the pro-existence of Christ and the priority of the Spirit that brings about communion of others with the Church. The Church can embrace the simultaneous call to communion and mission because Christ himself has fulfilled the sacrifice that transcends space and time by offering his *logos* to the Father to make atonement between God and humanity.

The Church's identity as a *communio* is inseparable from her call to mission. St. John Paul II has emphasized the unity between the nature of the Church as a *communio* and mission in his Apostolic Exhortation *Christifideles Laici*: "Communion and mission are profoundly connected with each other, they interpenetrate and mutually imply each other, to the point that *communion represents both the source and the fruit of mission: communion gives rise to mission and mission is accomplished in communion.*"[26] Just as the Apostles were instructed to gather the leftover fragments from the miraculous multiplication of loaves, so the Church has been entrusted by Christ with the mission to unite and reunite all into the *communio* found in the Church and embodied by the Holy Eucharist (John 6:12). God wills for all people to be saved, and this can only be accomplished through their *communio* with Christ the Redeemer (1 Tim 2:3–4).

The goal of *communio* explicitly highlights mission as an integral

---

Blackwell, 1971), 511.
[24] Ratzinger, *JN* II, 96 (JRGS6/1, 492).
[25] Ratzinger, *JN* II, 98 (JRGS6/1, 493).
[26] Pope John Paul II, Apostolic Exhortation *Christifidelis Laici* (Vatican City: Libreria Editrice Vaticana, 1988), §32.

part of the Church's life. In the words of the Second Vatican Council: "[The Church] has been set up by Christ as a *communion* of life, love and truth; by him too it is taken up as the instrument of salvation for all, and sent on a *mission* to the whole world as the light of the world and the salt of the earth."[27] One of the central purposes of mission is to draw people into "fraternal communion" (Acts 4:32). *Communio* has been a primary responsibility of the Church from the beginning. This communion of the pilgrim Church here on earth anticipates the full realization of the *communio sanctorum* in the eschaton.

Ratzinger articulates the causal relationship between the Eucharist and the Church, wherein Christ has an obvious chronological and ontological priority that makes a vertical and horizontal communion a reality.[28] In view of the Church's Eucharistic identity, Benedict contends that for the Church, "Communion always and inseparably has both a vertical and a horizontal sense: it is communion with God and communion with our brothers and sisters. Both dimensions mysteriously converge in the gift of the Eucharist."[29] The ontology of the Church as a communion compels her simultaneously always to be a mission. The Church must continually widen her horizontal communion with others so that other individuals may participate in this vertical communion with God. The liturgy prepares for this eschatological future in the present as it realizes the goal of communion through the Eucharist.

The liturgy brings about the eschatological unity, which is part of

---

[27] *Lumen Gentium*, §9; emphasis added.

[28] "The Church 'draws her life from the Eucharist.' Since the Eucharist makes present Christ's redeeming sacrifice, we must start by acknowledging that 'there is a causal influence of the Eucharist at the Church's very origins.' The Eucharist is Christ who gives himself to us and continually builds us up as his body. Hence, in the striking interplay between the Eucharist which builds up the Church, and the Church herself which 'makes' the Eucharist, the primary causality is expressed in the first formula: the Church is able to celebrate and adore the mystery of Christ present in the Eucharist precisely because Christ first gave himself to her in the sacrifice of the Cross. The Church's ability to 'make' the Eucharist is completely rooted in Christ's self-gift to her. Here we can see more clearly the meaning of St. John's words: 'he first loved us' (*1 Jn* 4:19). We too, at every celebration of the Eucharist, confess the primacy of Christ's gift. The causal influence of the Eucharist at the Church's origins definitively discloses both the chronological and ontological priority of the fact that it was Christ who loved us 'first.' For all eternity he remains the one who loves us first." Pope Benedict XVI, *Post-synodal Apostolic Exhortation Sacramentum caritatis* [hereafter, SCa] (Vatican City: Libreria Editrice Vaticana, 2007), §14. Also see Joseph Ratzinger, *Called to Communion* [hereafter, *CTC*], trans. Adrian Walker (San Francisco: Ignatius Press, 1996), 82.

[29] *SCa*, §76.

the Christian mission; simultaneously, the work remains incomplete. Ratzinger describes Christian liturgy as a "liturgy on the way, a liturgy of pilgrimage toward the transfiguration of the world, which will only take place when God is 'all in all.'"[30] The realization of God becoming "all in all" is achieved in part within every Eucharistic celebration. At the same time, Christians who work to bring about this reality are mindful that only Jesus Christ can bring this to fruition beginning with the Eucharist.

The Eucharist has an eschatological dynamism with the "goal of transforming humanity and the world in the New Heaven and New Earth, into the unity of the risen Body."[31] The call to mission that has been entrusted to every Christian with the reception of Baptism is developed by and consummated in the Eucharist, which is both the source and fulfillment of mission. Through the Eucharist, Christians are able to become a "Eucharist and thereby themselves a 'heart' and 'love' for the Church."[32] A person living in true communion with Jesus Christ cannot live in alienation from his neighbor. The Christian drawing from the wellspring of the liturgy is compelled in particular to love the least of his brothers and sisters among the poor and unwanted.[33]

Every member of the Body of Christ is drawn into the pro-existence of Christ. Hence, the liturgy as a *logikē latreia* is the heart of Ratzinger's theology of liturgy that represents the full implication of the primacy of the *logos* for the liturgy and the *ethos* of charity that flows forth from this liturgical *logos*. In the section that follows, it is critical to view the liturgy as a *logikē latreia* for the realization of the eschatological identity and mission of the Church, which is to unite all things in Christ's sacrificial love.

## LITURGY AS *LOGIKĒ LATREIA*

Hope is never individualistic for the Christian as it is always directed towards the good of others. Benedict XVI emphatically opines, "Our hope is always essentially also hope for others; only thus is it truly hope for me too. As Christians we should never limit ourselves to asking: how can I save myself? We should also ask: what can I do in order that others may be saved and that for them too the star of hope may rise?"[34] The Church, as

---

[30] Ratzinger, JRCW11, 30 (JRGS11, 61).

[31] Ratzinger, JRCW11, 53 (JRGS11, 87).

[32] Ratzinger, JRCW11, 354 (JRGS11, 423).

[33] See *CCC* §1397, emphasis in the original: "*The Eucharist commits us to the poor.*"

[34] Pope Benedict XVI, Encyclical Letter *Spe Salvi* [hereafter, SS] (Vatican City: Liberia Editrice Vaticana, 2007), §48.

was illustrated in the previous section, has a mission to bring about unity in Christ, which she carries out primarily through the liturgy. Ratzinger claims the "basic law of Christianity" is the "Easter law of the Pasch, or passage."[35] The Christian's identity has been recast in Christ such that he always lives "for" another person. Consequently, the liturgy is described by Ratzinger above all as a *logikē latreia*; subsequently, the self-giving of Christians becomes identical with Christ's own sacrifice.[36] The human person enters into communion with hope incarnate, the *Logos* made flesh, and this transforms his existence. Subsequently, the person presents this *logos* to others.

The notion of sacrifice developed previously in chapter two becomes clearer in light of the *logos*. The conception of the Eucharist as a *logikē latreia* found in Romans 12:1 is one of the most often cited passages in Ratzinger's liturgical theology. Much of his writing implicitly or explicitly makes the case that this Pauline concept is, as already cited in the introduction, "the most appropriate way of expressing the essential form of Christian liturgy."[37] An overview of the Pauline scholarship on this passage from Romans will establish why this passage serves as a *point de départ* for Ratzinger's theology of liturgy.

Paul begins his discussion of the Christian moral life in Romans with the following introduction in chapter 12:

> I [urge] you therefore, brethren, by the mercies of God, to present your bodies as a living sacrifice, holy and acceptable to God, which is your spiritual worship [*tēn logikēn latreian*]. Do not be conformed to this world but be transformed by the renewal of your mind, [so] that you may [discern] what is the will of God, what is good and acceptable and perfect. (Rom 12:1–2)

The rhetorical opening indicates the following chapters are an exhortation or *paranesis* as St. Paul begins with the phrase "I urge" or "I appeal"

---

[35] Joseph Ratzinger, *The Unity of the Nations: A Vision of the Church Fathers*, trans. Boniface Ramsey (Washington, DC: The Catholic University of America Press, 2015), 31 (JRGS1, 570).

[36] See Ratzinger, JRCW11, 34 (JRGS11, 66).

[37] Ratzinger, JRCW11, 30; *Auferstehung und ewiges Leben: Beiträge zur Eschatologie und zur Theologie der Hoffnung* [hereafter, JRGS10], Gesammelte Schriften 10, ed. Gerhard Ludwig Müller (Freiburg: Herder, 2012), 60. Ratzinger renders this Greek phrase literally as "*des logosgemäßen Gottesdienstes*" ("divine worship according to the Logos").

[*parakalō*].[38] Among scriptural scholars, there is agreement that these verses are the introduction for the subsequent chapters dealing with the Christian moral life.[39]

The sacrificial language used in verse one is a clear contrast between sacrifice in the ancient world and the new form of sacrifice offered according to the *logos*. Once again, there is consensus among exegetes that this notion of sacrifice is a reference to the sacrificial language employed by ancient Greek religion.[40] In contradistinction with ancient Greek or Jewish sacrifices, the Romans are being urged collectively to offer their bodies as a "living sacrifice, holy and acceptable to God" in lieu of a sacrificial offering of a single animal or person. The Scripture scholar Robert Jewett comments that the phrase "acceptable to God," which is used rarely in the Septuagint, is "employed elsewhere by Paul to depict actions consistent with the divine will (Rom 14:18; Phil 4:18 cf. 'acceptable to the Lord' in Col 3:20)."[41] Sacrifice is transformed by Christ to refer to the everyday life of the Christian, which must be guided by the *logos*. This form of Christian worship is in contrast with all irrational forms of cultic worship that involve sacrifices of dead animals.[42] What is simply rendered as "which is your spiritual worship" is much more nuanced in its meaning.

On January 7, 2009, Pope Benedict noted that the phrase translated in English from St. Paul's letter as "which is your spiritual worship" (*tēn logikēn latreían*) is challenging to translate according to various exegetes. Benedict notes that the Vulgate translates the Pauline phrase as *"rationabile obsequium."* Significantly, the Roman Canon uses the word *"rationabile."*[43] New Testament commentator Brendan Byrne, S.J., high-

---

38  Opening with the words "I urge" or "I appeal" is typical of a Pauline exhortation. Paul will use this phrase throughout his writings as he does in Rom 15:30; 16:17; 1 Cor 1:10; 4:16; 2 Cor 2:8; 10:1; Phil 4:2; Phlm 10. See also Eph 4:1; 1 Tim 2:1. Joseph A. Fitzmyer, S.J., *Romans* (New York: Doubleday, 1993), 639.

39  Robert Jewett, *Romans: A Commentary* (Minneapolis, MN: Fortress Press, 2007), 724.

40  Jewett, *Romans*, 727.

41  Jewett, *Romans*, 729.

42  See Jewett, *Romans*, 730–31; Fitzmyer, *Romans*, 650, and Erik Peterson, *Der Brief an die Römer* (Würzburg: Echter, 1997), 332.

43  Pope Benedict XVI, General Audience, January 7, 2009, Paul VI Audience Hall, found in *Saint Paul*, trans. *L'Osservatore Romano* (San Francisco: Ignatius Press, 2009), 106. The prayer of the Roman Canon, which is a reference to this Pauline passage according to Benedict, in its fuller context is "Quam oblationem tu, Deus, in omnibus, quaesumus, benedictam, adscriptam, ratam, rationabilem acceptabilemque facere digneris." *Missale romanum ex decreto Sacrosancti oecumenici Concilii vaticani II instauratum, auctoritate Pauli PP. VI promulgatum, Ioannis Pauli PP. II cura recognitum*, typis vaticanis (Città

lights two distinct meanings of the adjective *logikos* (often rendered in English as "spiritual") based upon Greco-Roman philosophy and literature. On the one hand, the word can mean "spiritual," which he notes is emphasized as "inward" that is "opposed to the external, physical or material." On the other hand, the word can mean "rational" referring to "that which is distinctive of humans as rational, reflective beings."[44] The theological interpretation that is favored by Ratzinger is the latter.

As explained previously, Benedict XVI highlights the way in which verses in the Old Testament underscore the insufficiency of animal sacrifices such as Psalm 50[49]:12–14: "If I were hungry, I would not tell you; for the world and all that is in it is mine. Do I eat the flesh of bulls, or drink the blood of goats? Offer to God a sacrifice of thanksgiving." And in the subsequent psalm, Benedict notes the reiteration of this theme: "You take no delight in sacrifice; were I to give a burnt offering, you would not be pleased. The sacrifice acceptable to God is a broken spirit; a broken and contrite heart, O God, you will not despise" (Ps 50 [51]:16–17).[45] The Psalmist stresses the inadequacies of the sacrifices being offered by Israel because they lack the contrition of the heart.

Sacrifice has both an external *and* internal component. For a sacrifice to be true, there is a need for a fulfillment of both aspects. Benedict comments, "There is a spiritualization, a moralization of worship: worship becomes only something of the heart, of the mind. But [if] it lacks the body, it lacks the community."[46] There is a need for sacrificial worship, but animal sacrifices in themselves are inadequate when they are not accompanied by a spirit of contrition or repentance. Citing the prophet Daniel (3:15–17) in addition to the previously quoted psalms, Benedict concludes

---

del Vaticano: Libreria Editrice Vaticana, 2002), 574.

[44] Brendan Byrne, S.J., *Sacra Pagina: Romans*, ed. Daniel J. Harrington, S.J. (Collegeville, MN: Liturgical Press, 2007), 365–66. Byrne notes that the understanding of *logikos* as "rational" is highlighted by the Stoics: cf. Epictetus, *Discourses 1.16.20–21; 2.9.2; Philo, Spec. 1.277*). Bryne, *Romans*, 366. Translating the Greek as "rational" is preferable in Byrne's view as it accords with the subsequent verse, which emphasizes the renewal of the mind and discernment. Hence, Byrne renders this portion of verse 1 as "the worship you owe as rational beings." For more on the understanding of the *logikos* in Hellenistic thought, see Raymond Corriveau, C.Ss.R., *The Liturgy of Life: A Study of the Ethical Thought of St. Paul in His Letters to the Early Christian Communities* (Bruxelles: Desclée de Brouwer, 1970), 159–161. Corriveau cites the use of *logikos* in the thought of other Stoics such as Seneca and Epictetus, some of the Neo-Pythagoreans, and the Hermetic writers.

[45] Benedict XVI, *Saint Paul*, 107.

[46] Benedict XVI, *Saint Paul*, 107.

that the Old Testament is directing the faithful towards a renewed sacrifice "in a synthesis that was not yet foreseeable, that could not yet be conceived of."[47] There is a longing for true worship that could not be fulfilled under the Old Covenant.

The meaning of Christ's sacrifice sheds full light on the authentic meaning of *logikos*, which is expressed by the celebration of the liturgy. Once again in his papal audience on this Pauline passage from Romans, Benedict alludes to one of his major Christological themes, the idea of vicarious representation or substitution:

> The sacrificed animals were meant to replace the human being, the gift of self, but they could not. In his gift of himself to the Father and to us, Jesus Christ is not a substitute but truly bears within him the human being, our sins and our desire; he really represents us, he takes us upon himself. In communion with Christ, realized in faith and in the sacraments, despite all our inadequacies, we truly become a living sacrifice: "true worship" is achieved.[48]

The sacrifice of Jesus Christ on the Cross is made present in the Holy Eucharist, and Christians can unite themselves with him on the altar. Hence, Benedict concludes this is why the Church prays for the offering that the faithful participate in during the liturgy to become "*rationabile*" according to the Roman Canon. Christians must conscientiously make the choice to enter into communion with the sacrifice of Christ during the liturgy and beyond it in everyday life. The liturgical life (the "living sacrifice") is a witness of the eschatological life that comes forth from communion with Christ in verse two of Romans 12.

The eschatological significance of this Pauline passage becomes clear with these words from verse two: "Do not be conformed to this world."[49] Living in a manner that is "acceptable" to God is an eschatological sign that stands in contrast with a life that does not conform to the truth and love of the *Logos*. The Scripture scholar Joseph Fitzmyer claims the transformation or metamorphosis which takes place in the Christian's way of thinking "is brought about by the indwelling Spirit of God that 'leads'

---

[47] Benedict XVI, *Saint Paul*, 107.

[48] Benedict XVI, *Saint Paul*, 108.

[49] Craig C. Hill, "Romans," in *The Pauline Epistles, The Oxford Bible Commentary*, ed. John Muddiman and John Barton (Oxford: Oxford University Press, 2010), 84.

those incorporated into Christ through faith and baptism and makes them 'children of God' (8:12–14; cf. Col 3:10; Eph 4:23; Titus 3:5)."[50] Worship is transformed by the *Logos* incarnate, and each individual is called to a transfiguration by grace of divinization that begins with the sacraments. The Christian becomes a living sacrifice with the gift of the Spirit that Paul emphasizes in Romans 8 and beyond.[51] Verse two complements the previous verse insofar as verse 1 concerns the transformation of the body and verse two concerns the metamorphosis of the interior mind.[52] This transformation is a realization of the eschatological in the present time and not a change in an age to come. This Pauline insight is critical for comprehending Ratzinger's proleptic understanding of the liturgy in relation to the eschaton.

Among the Fathers of the Church, Augustine's theological commentary in *De civitate Dei* (10.6) on this Pauline passage is essential to understanding Ratzinger's appropriation of *logikos*.[53] Ratzinger's explicit citation of Augustine regarding this excerpt from Romans has been

---

[50] Fitzmyer, *Romans*, 641.

[51] "The Spirit which has been given us is an inward principle of new life given by God (Rom 8:9–11; 5:5; cf. 1 Thess 4:8). Received into the Christian by faith (Gal 3:2, 14) and baptism (1 Cor 6:11; cf. Rom 6:4) it dwells in him (Rom 8:9, 16). The Spirit, which is the Spirit of Christ (Rom 8:9) is for the Christians as for Christ himself, the principle of resurrection (Rom 8:11) of sanctification (Rom 15:16) and of moral conduct (Rom 8:4–9:13). It is this Spirit, this life, which is manifested in the 'living sacrifice' of the Christian life." Corriveau, *The Liturgy of Life*, 170. On the notion of spiritual sacrifice as it relates to the sacrifice of Christ and the sacrament of the Eucharist, see Colman E. O'Neill, O.P., *Sacramental Realism: A General Theory of the Sacraments* (Chicago: Midwest Theological Forum, 1998), 80–115. On the theme of transformation and conformity to the image of Christ in Romans 12:1–2 and throughout the Pauline corpus, see James G. Samra, *Being Conformed to Christ in Community: A Study of Maturity, Maturation and the Local Church in the Undisputed Pauline Epistles* (New York: T & T Clark, 2006), 95–111.

[52] See Jeremy Driscoll, "Worship in the Spirit of Logos: Romans 12:1–2 and the Source and Summit of Christian Life," *Letter and Spirit* 5 (2009): 87–89. "Following the line of thought that he also pursues in his other writings, Paul [in verse 2] speaks of the renewal of our minds, our inner nature, completing the sense of the offering of *bodies* mentioned in Romans 12:1, and following neatly upon all that [is] implied by Paul's use of the word *logikos*. Both mind and body are involved in the sacrifice, in the worship." Driscoll, "Worship in the Spirit of Logos," 88.

[53] The quotations below from *De Civitate Dei* will come from Augustine, *The City of God: Books VIII-XVI*, trans. Gerald G. Walsh, S.J., and Mother Grace Monahan, O.S.U., The Fathers of the Church 14 (Washington, DC: The Catholic University of America Press, 1963), 125–127.

established previously in chapter two.[54] Augustine writes about the true nature of sacrifice, which in the original meaning of *sacrificium*, is something divine "even though it is done or offered by a person."[55] With the Apostle Paul, Augustine affirms that the body can become a living sacrifice when a person turns away from sin to live a life of virtue. Augustine comments explicitly that "true sacrifices are works of mercy done to ourselves or our neighbor and directed to God."[56] Uwe Michael Lang comments, "Not every good work or work of mercy or act of renunciation is a sacrifice; rather, it is its purpose of finality that makes it a sacrifice."[57] This is an important distinction to make, and it highlights the proper internal disposition that must be present for external acts to become true sacrifices. Consequently, Augustine maintains that the "communion of saints is offered as a universal sacrifice to God through [Jesus Christ] the High Priest."[58]

The Augustinian theme of unity becomes the final end for those who participate as the many members of the one Body presenting themselves as the good, acceptable, and perfect sacrifice in Jesus Christ. Finally, Augustine concludes that the sacrifice of the Church as the one Body of Christ "continues to [be] celebrate[d] in the sacrament of the altar, in which it is clear to the Church that she herself is offered in the very offering she makes to God."[59] In light of this contextualization, one may better understand Ratzinger's frequent use of these Pauline verses in presenting the Christian notion of worship. In two brief verses, the themes of the true nature of sacrifice, the relationship between worship and the eschaton, and the primacy of the *logos* are highlighted.[60] The subsequent part of

---

[54] See Ratzinger, JRCW11, 34–36 (JRGS11, 65–67); Ratzinger, JRCW11, 550–56 (JRGS11, 649–655). Ratzinger's first critical engagement with the notion of sacrifice in Augustine's *De Civitate Dei* occurs in his dissertation on Augustine. See Ratzinger, JRGS1, 264–297.

[55] Augustine, *De Civitate Dei* 10.6 (Walsh and Monahan, 125).

[56] Augustine, *De Civitate Dei* 10.6 (Walsh and Monahan, 126).

[57] Uwe Michael Lang, "Augustine's Conception of Sacrifice in City of God, Book X, and the Eucharistic Sacrifice," *Antiphon* 19, no. 1 (2015): 38. In his dissertation, Ratzinger comments that the characteristic of mercy is necessary for the sacrifice to bring about a conformity of the human person with God [*Gottförmigkeit des Menschen*]. See Ratzinger, JRGS1, 272–73.

[58] Augustine, *De Civitate Dei* 10.6 (Walsh and Monahan, 127).

[59] Augustine, *De Civitate Dei* 10.6 (Walsh and Monahan, 127).

[60] Robert Daly claims that these two verses "are surely among the most important verses in the Pauline corpus, for they present in brief span, as no other text does, the Pauline theology of Christian life." *Christian Sacrifice: The Judaeo-Christian Background Before Origen* (Washington, DC: The Catholic University of America, 1978), 243.

this chapter will validate Benedict's explicit referral to this Augustinian notion of sacrifice as love, which is an anticipation and realization of the communion that will only come to full fruition in the eschaton.

The Greek notion of *logos* finds its definitive meaning in Christ and in the liturgy of the Church. Christology, ecclesiology, theological anthropology, moral theology, liturgy, and eschatology all converge on the significance of one phrase that represents a transition from the conception of sacrifice for ancient Israel towards the definitive notion of sacrifice in light of the *Logos* incarnate, which Ratzinger develops:

> The sacrifice is the "word," the word of prayer, which goes up from man to God, embodying the whole of man's existence and enabling him to become "word," (*logos*) in himself. It is man, conforming himself to *logos* and becoming *logos* through faith, who is the true sacrifice, the true glory of God in the world. Israel's experience of suffering during the Exile and the Hellenistic period first brought the word of prayer into prominence as the equivalent of exterior sacrifice. Now, through the word *logos*, the whole philosophy of *logos* in the Greek world is incorporated in the concept.[61]

The Hellenistic notion of *logos* finds its authentic meaning in worship and the subsequent transformation of the believer as a result of his entrance into union with the *Logos*.

The sacrifice of the *logos* is only able to find its full meaning in the sacrifice of the Word on the Cross. Ratzinger contends, "In Jesus' self-surrender on the Cross, the Word is united with the entire reality of human life and suffering. There is no longer a replacement cult." Jesus becomes the substitutional offering, and hence the notion of sacrifice for the Christian is transformed. Ratzinger continues, "Now the vicarious sacrifice [*Stellvertretung*] of Jesus takes us up and leads us into that likeness with God, that transformation into love, which is the only true adoration."[62] The crucifixion transforms the notion of sacrifice such that all are called to participate in the self-giving love of Christ on a daily basis. True sacrifice becomes living like God.

The cultic notion of sacrifice, which the Pauline notion makes explicit, is an integral part of the Christian witness. Christianity, via the

---

[61] Ratzinger, JRCW 11, 27 (JRGS 11, 57).
[62] Ratzinger, JRCW 11, 28 (JRGS 11, 58).

Fathers of the Church, simultaneously transforms the notion of sacrifice that goes beyond the animal sacrifices of the Old Testament and the Hellenistic idea concerning the sacrifice of the logos such that the Eucharist or "prayer" is the "equivalent of sacrifice."[63] Worship is no longer limited to mere external rites or gestures because of the mysterious participation and communion that is brought about by the *Logos* becoming flesh.

Worship and sacrifice are transformed by the *Logos*, such that the believer is called to enter into the sacrifice of the incarnate *Logos*. In contradistinction with sacrifice under the Old Covenant, the essence of sacrifice is forever transformed by the *Logos*: "[T]rue sacrifice to God is that of man's inmost being, which is itself transformed into worship. The word is the sacrifice; the sacrifice must be wordlike (*logikon*), but the word meant here is of course the "word" in which the whole of man's spirit sums up and expresses itself."[64] Christians are called to participate in the sacrifice of Christ, which brings about a renewal of the person's identity and life in and through the *logos*. Elsewhere Ratzinger articulates, reiterating what has been cited above, the manner in which the worship through and in the *logos* impacts the Christian:

> Divine worship means that we ourselves become wordlike [*logoshaft*], that we conform ourselves to the creative Intellect. But again it is clear that we cannot do this on our own, and so everything seems to end again in futility—until the Logos, the True One, the Son comes, is made flesh, and draws us up to himself in the exodus of the Cross. This true sacrifice that turns us all into sacrifice, in other words, unites us with God and causes us to become godlike, is indeed fixed and founded on an historical event but does not lie behind us as a thing of the past but, rather, becomes contemporary with and accessible to us in the community of the believing, praying Church, in its sacrament: this is what "sacrifice of the Mass" means.[65]

---

[63] Ratzinger, JRCW11, 27–8 (JRGS11, 57–8): "[The Fathers of the Church] saw the Eucharist as essentially *oratio*, sacrifice in the Word, and in this way they also showed how Christian worship stood in relation to the spiritual struggle of antiquity, to its quest for man's true path and for his encounter with God. The Fathers call the Eucharist simply 'prayer,' that is, the sacrifice of the Word, but in so doing, they go beyond the Greek idea of the sacrifice of the *logos* and provide an answer to the question left open by Old Testament theology, which made prayer the equivalent of sacrifice."

[64] Ratzinger, JRCW11, 349 (JRGS11, 418).

[65] Ratzinger, JRCW11, 555 (JRGS11, 654).

Ratzinger emphasizes that it is Christ, the true *Logos*, who draws the faithful into his sacrifice. Through the liturgy, Christ is able to "logify" the communicant who fully participates in eschatological hope of the liturgy.[66] Christ fulfills the hope of Christians, whereas Metz and Moltmann, as was established in the previous chapter, seem to favor the idea of hope as being realized first by Christians.

At the same time, Ratzinger holds in common with Metz and Moltmann the notion that hope can be realized now, but what differentiates their theologies is the manner in which this hope is brought about in the present: "[Eschatological hope] is inseparable from the experience of the presence of the final reality in the eucharistic feast. What this means is that the Christian hope is not some news item about tomorrow or the day after tomorrow. We might put it this way: hope is now personalized."[67] Hope cannot be separated from the celebration of the Eucharist, for in the liturgy, the faithful encounter the "hope [that] is now personalized." Ratzinger articulates the fulfillment of hope through the liturgy first and foremost and a subsequent transformation wrought by the Eucharist in the life of the believer.

As stated above Ratzinger maintains the view that every celebration of the Eucharist is a Parousia. Ratzinger clearly upholds that "[t]he Parousia is the highest intensification and fulfilment of the Liturgy. And the Liturgy is Parousia, a Parousia-like event taking place in our midst."[68] The eschaton is liturgical, and the liturgy is eschatological. Further on, Ratzinger argues, "Every Eucharist is Parousia, the Lord's coming, and yet the Eucharist is even more truly the tensed yearning that he would reveal his hidden Glory."[69] The Eucharist does not fully realize the eschaton. As a "tensed yearning," the liturgy compels the Church to prepare for the coming of the Lord. Hope transforms the Church in the present as the "motif of the Parousia becomes the obligation to live the Liturgy as a feast of hope-filled presence directed towards Christ, the universal ruler. . . . In the Liturgy the Church should, as it were, in following him, prepare

---

[66] Ratzinger, JRCW11, 350 (JRGS11, 418): "We ask that the Logos, Christ, who *is* the true sacrifice, may himself draw us into his act of sacrifice, may 'logify' us, make us 'more consistent with the word,' 'more truly rational,' so that his sacrifice may become ours and may be accepted by God as ours, may be able to be accounted as ours."

[67] Joseph Ratzinger, *Eschatology: Death and Eternal Life*, ed. Aidan Nichols, O.P., trans. Michael Waldstein, 2nd ed. (Washington, DC: The Catholic University of America Press, 2007), 8 (JRGS10, 44).

[68] Ratzinger, *Eschatology*, 203 (JRGS10, 206).

[69] Ratzinger, *Eschatology*, 203 (JRGS10, 207).

for him a dwelling in the world."[70] Hope is the *actio Dei*, but the human person has the freedom and responsibility to embrace the transformative grace that comes from the *Logos* via the sacraments.

The gift of grace allows Christ to enter into the world again through what Ratzinger, drawing upon the insights of St. Bernard of Clairvaux, describes as an *"adventus medius."*[71] This *adventus medius* (or "middle coming") unfolds in different ways as when "[t]he Lord comes through his word; he comes in the sacraments, especially in the most Holy Eucharist; he comes into my life through words or events."[72] The Church, as an incarnation of the kingdom of Christ, brings about this *adventus medius* through both word and sacrament. The Church is the means by which Christ bestows his grace upon the faithful so that they can enter into the dynamic of his life and love, so the fruits of the Parousia of Christ can become present through the divinized life of the person who is transformed by his communion with the *Logos*.

In light of the true nature of sacrifice, the Christian should become completely changed by his communion with Christ. This transformation

---

[70] Ratzinger, *Eschatology*, 204 (JRGS10, 207).

[71] See Matthew J. Ramage, "Benedict XVI, Catholic Doctrine and the Problem of an Imminent *Parousia*," *Josephinum Journal of Theology* 21, no. 1 (2014): 20–22; Ramage, *Jesus Interpreted: Benedict XVI, Bart Ehrman, and the Historical Truth of the Gospels* (Washington, DC: The Catholic University of America Press, 2017), 224–226. Ratzinger cites a text from one of the sermons of St. Bernard of Clairvaux that is found in the office of readings for the Wednesday in the First Week of Advent: "We have come to know a threefold coming of the Lord. The third coming takes place between the other two [*adventus medius*] . . . His first coming was in the flesh and in weakness, this intermediary coming is in the spirit and in power, the last coming will be in glory and majesty" (*In Adventu Domini*, serm. III, 4; V, I; *PL* 183, 45 A; 50 C–D). Ratzinger comments that Bernard develops his understanding of the *adventus medius*, a term which was unknown prior to Bernard's commentary, upon John 14:23: "If a man loves me, he will keep my word, and my Father will love him, and we will come to him and make our home with him." See Ratzinger, *JN* II, 290-92 [JRGS6/1, 633–634]. Also see Weimer, "Die Baugesetze der Geschichtstheologie Joseph Ratzingers," in *Hoffnung auf Vollendung: Zur Eschatologie von Joseph Ratzinger,* ed. Gerhard Nachtwei (Regensburg: Friedrich Pustet, 2015), 56–57. Weimer briefly introduces the notion of *adventus medius* in Ratzinger's theology of history. Weimer underscores Ratzinger's research on Bonaventure, who outlines two principal moments when Christ is revealed in this *adventus medius* within the Church: (1) *adventus Christi in mentem revelatio* and (2) *adventus in carnem auctoritas*. See Joseph Ratzinger, *Offenbarungverständnis und Geschichtstheologie Bonaventuras: Habilitationsschrift und Bonaventura-Studien*, Joseph Ratzinger Gessamalte Schriften, 2 (hereafter, JRGS2), ed. Gerhard Ludwig Müller (Freiburg: Herder, 2009), 219–21; and Ratzinger, JRGS2, 754–57.

[72] Ratzinger, *JN* II, 291 (JRGS6/1, 633).

is made visible in the life of Christians, which is why Paul urges the Romans to offer their bodies as a form of worship according to the *Logos*. The Christian's life must become a Eucharist.[73] The paschal sacrifice of Christ must be fully realized in the manner in which the believer lives in the world. The liturgy anticipates and realizes the eschaton in the worship within the Church, which in turn must become the manner in which a Christian shapes his or her life here and now.

The misperception of eschatology is that its focus should only be on the world that transcends our current existence. However, Ratzinger maintains, "Christian eschatology does not sidestep the shared tasks of the world, shifting the focus of human concern to the beyond, or making us retreat into a private salvation for individual souls."[74] In Ratzinger's estimation, "The starting point of Christian eschatology is precisely commitment to the common justice guaranteed in the One who sacrificed his life for the justice of mankind at large and thus brought it justification.[75] The unity wrought by Jesus Christ in Ratzinger's Christology and ecclesiology enables him to maintain the position that authentic eschatology does not withdraw from the needs of the world. Ratzinger is able to sustain this view because he has developed an eschatology rooted in the liturgy.[76]

---

[73] Ratzinger, JRCW11, 353 (JRGS11, 421–22): "The Eucharist, if it continued to exist over against us, would be relegated to the status of a thing, and the true Christian plane of existence would not be attained at all. Conversely, a Christian life that did not involve being drawn into the Pasch of the Lord, that was not itself becoming a Eucharist, would remain locked in the moralism of our activity and would thus again fail to live up to the new liturgy that has been founded by the Cross."

[74] Ratzinger, *Eschatology*, 100 (JRGS10, 119).

[75] Ratzinger, *Eschatology*, 100 (JRGS10, 119). Pope St. John Paul II expresses a similar sentiment: "A significant consequence of the eschatological tension inherent in the Eucharist is also the fact that it spurs us on our journey through history and plants a seed of living hope in our daily commitment to the work before us. Certainly the Christian vision leads to the expectation of 'new heavens' and 'a new earth' (Rev 21:1), but this increases, rather than lessens, *our sense of responsibility for the world today*." Pope John Paul II, Encyclical Letter *Ecclesia de Eucharistia* (Vatican City: Libreria Editrice Vaticana, 2003), §20.

[76] Jonathan Martin Ciraulo describes Ratzinger's method as governed by an "essentially ecclesiological hermeneutic that is then rendered liturgically. The church is, for Benedict [XVI], *the* hermeneutical lens for interpreting Scripture." "Sacramentally Regulated Eschatology in Hans Urs von Balthasar and Pope Benedict XVI," *Pro Ecclesia* 24, no. 2 (Spring 2015), 232. We maintain that it is a Christological hermeneutic that is rendered liturgically that then serves as the foundation and interpretive key for Ratzinger's theology. Joseph Ratzinger, *Church, Ecumenism and Politics: New Endeavors in Ecclesiology* [hereafter, CEP], trans. Michael J. Miller, et al. (San Francisco: Ignatius Press, 2008),

This chapter has focused on the significance of the Pauline *logikē latreia*, for this notion underscores the unity between the liturgy and eschatology for Ratzinger. The ultimate end of the Eucharist is the transformation of the individual members of the faithful, who are called to live an eschatological life by a commitment to charity in this world. Once again, the final section returns to the Christological theme of "pro-existence" that is the mission of each person, which is deepened and strengthened by Christ through the liturgy. This chapter concentrates on the relationship between the Eucharist and charity, which demonstrates the dynamic that Ratzinger has espoused regarding the *logos* of communion and its *ethos* of charity.

## *Sacramentum caritatis*

In the previous chapter, it has been demonstrated that the full manifestation of hope occurs in the transfigured life of the Christian through his communion with Christ in the liturgy. The virtue of charity surpasses the virtue of hope insofar as it actualizes the person's final end, communion with God (cf. *ST* II–II, q. 23, a. 6, ad 3). For Thomas Aquinas, the Holy Eucharist is the "sacrament of charity" as it is the "sacrament of Christ's Passion according as a person is made perfect in union with Christ."[77] The communion that hope longs for charity makes present. The Eucharist is the primary source for charity.

The understanding of the Eucharist as the "sacrament of charity" is a theme in the papal writings of Benedict XVI. For Aquinas, the Eucharist is simultaneously a sign of the past, present, and future. As a sign of the past, the Eucharist commemorates the Pasch of Jesus Christ. The Eucharist brings about the communion or unity of the Church. Finally, the sacrament is a sign of the future in that it "foreshadows the Divine fruition."[78] Ratzinger, as we have demonstrated earlier, expresses a similar notion regarding the liturgy as he affirms the patristic imagery of shadow, image, and reality.[79] For Aquinas and Ratzinger, the Eucharist has a close

---

27 (JRGS8/1, 273–274): "Even if we speak about the People of God, Christology must remain the center of the teaching about the Church, and, consequently, the Church must be thought of essentially in terms of the sacraments of baptism, Eucharist, and holy orders. We are the People of God by virtue of the crucified and risen Body of Christ and in no other way."

77  *ST III*, q. 73, a. 6, ad 3.

78  *ST III*, q. 73, a. 4.

79  See Ratzinger, JRCW11, 32 (JRGS11, 63).

relationship with the eschaton. As with the Passion of the Lord, Aquinas affirms that the Eucharist "bestows on us the power of coming unto glory."[80] As was mentioned at the beginning of this chapter, the virtue of charity is a manifestation of the eschatological life that is the norm for the Christian; charity is the *ethos* that flows from the sacramental *logos*. Charity is directed ultimately towards God, and furthermore, charity finds its fulfillment in a love of neighbor. Charity for one's neighbor is directed ultimately towards the further end of unity.

The ultimate reality (*res*) of the sacrament of the Eucharist is the participation in the communion with the Mystical Body of Christ wrought by grace and charity.[81] Contemporary theologian Daria Spezzano comments on the Thomistic understanding of the *res* of the Eucharist:

> The *res* of the Eucharist is thus ultimately the deiformity of the Church, because the participation of all of the members in the Trinitarian communion brings about its unity. Christ, through the Holy Spirit, is the principle of unity in the Church because as head he is the author of grace to the members of his body, bestowing on them through the instrumentality of his Passion a deifying share in his own perfect charity and wisdom, which takes the form of this communion.[82]

Through the grace which comes forth from the Eucharist, the Christian can grow in charity and subsequently in participation in the deified life within the Mystical Body of Christ. The human person has been created for a dialogical existence that can only be realized through charity nourished by Christ in the Eucharist. The human person is not called to a solitary existence. The eschaton is by its very nature communal. The communal or dialogical existence begins with the sacraments as a

---

[80] *ST III*, q. 79, a. 2, ad 1.

[81] Cf. *ST*, III, a. 80, a. 4.

[82] Daria Spezzano, *The Glory of God's Grace: Deification According to St. Thomas Aquinas* (Ave Maria, FL: Sapientia Press, 2015), 325–26. Spezzano's text has been very helpful in my own understanding of deification within the work of St. Thomas. Also see Daniel A. Keating, "Justification, Sanctification and Divinization in Thomas Aquinas," in *Aquinas on Doctrine: A Critical Introduction*, ed. Thomas G. Weinandy, Daniel A. Keating, and John P. Yocum (New York: T & T Clark, 2004), 139–158, and A. N. Williams, *The Ground of Union: Deification in Aquinas and Palamas* (Oxford: Oxford University Press, 1999).

Christian becomes a "son with the Son," which allows him to enter into communal and fraternal relationship with other Christians.[83]

The eschatological nature of the Eucharist is realized through commitment to the Church's mission of charity and the life of grace, which proceed from the communion within the Mystical Body of Christ. The ecclesiologist J. M. R. Tillard, commenting on the doctrine of the Eucharist in Aquinas, affirms this assertion: "The confident march toward the Parousia of the Lord is accomplished then only in the Church, and the personal hope of the Christian is increased only proportionally to his most living participation in the mystery of the Mystical Body."[84] Participation in the love of God and the Church's mission of charity is a concrete actualization of the eschaton anticipated by the celebration of the liturgy. The proper relationship between the Eucharist and eschatology redirects the world to its proper end in the loving communion with God and all his saints. In his papal writings, Benedict XVI is able to develop the implications of the relationship between the liturgy and eschatology in the love that the person is called to have for both God and neighbor, which has been nourished by the sacramental *Logos*.[85]

One of the constant themes in the Regensburg Lecture, highlighted in the first chapters, comes from Emperor Manuel II: "Not to act reasonably, not to act with *logos*, is contrary to the nature of God." Faith without reason has resulted in violence, which is opposed to the nature of the *logos*. Reason without faith has resulted in the reduction of knowledge to what can be apprehended via the senses. Benedict's first encyclical, *Deus Caritas Est*, was written in part to address this "world where the name of God is sometimes associated with vengeance or even a duty of hatred and violence."[86] The *Logos* is a person, whom Christians are called to love above

---

[83] Ratzinger, *Eschatology*, 159 (JRGS10, 169): "[T]he Christian idea of immortality is fellowship with other human beings. Man is not engaged in a solitary dialogue with God. He does not enter an eternity with God which belongs to him alone. The Christian dialogue with God is mediated by other human beings in a history where God speaks with men. It is expressed in the 'We' form proper to the children of God. It takes place, therefore, within the 'body of Christ,' in that communion with the Son which makes it possible for us to call God 'Father.' One can take part in this dialogue only by becoming a son with the Son, and this must mean in turn becoming one with all those others who seek the Father."

[84] J. M. R. Tillard, O.P., *The Eucharist: Pasch of God's People,* trans. Dennis L. Wienk (Staten Island, NY: Alba House, 1967), 275.

[85] See Pope Benedict XVI, *Encyclical Letter Deus Caritas Est* [hereafter, *DCE*] (Vatican City: Liberia Editrice Vaticana, 2005), §13.

[86] *DCE*, §1.

all. Communion with the incarnate *Logos* in the Eucharist is the fundamental experience for the individual Christian, which draws him into God's love. Benedict affirms the personal nature of the Christian faith: "Being Christian is not the result of an ethical choice or a lofty idea, but the encounter with an event, a person, which gives life a new horizon and a decisive direction."[87] The intimate communion with the *Logos* enables the Christian to enter into an authentic relationship of selfless love with his neighbor.

The unity and mutual dependence of the command to love both God and neighbor form a major theme in the first encyclical. The affirmation of God as both *agape* and *Logos* will be a foundational theme in Benedict's final encyclical, *Caritas in Veritate*. The stress placed on this unity between the two great commandments in *Deus Caritas Est* and the relationship between the truth and love in *Caritas in Veritate* will lead Benedict to highlight the mission of the Church and vocation of every Christian to an *ethos* of self-giving love. As a fulfillment of an authentic theology of hope, Benedict affirms charity as the greatest fruit, which comes forth from the liturgy.

Benedict begins *Deus Caritas Est* by reflecting upon love's true nature and examining the tension between love as *eros* and love as *agape*.[88] The key insight for Benedict into the dynamism between *eros* and *agape* is that

---

[87] *DCE*, §1. In an interesting parallel, Ratzinger notes that Romano Guardini taught seminarians of his generation that "the essence of Christianity is not an idea, not a system of thought, not a plan of action. The essence of Christianity is a Person: Jesus Christ himself." Joseph Ratzinger, "Guardini on Christ in our Century," *Crisis Magazine 14* (June 1996): 15.

[88] It is beyond the scope of our present inquiry to address in detail Benedict's examination of this tension between love as *eros* and love as *agape*. For an assessment of Benedict's thought on this theme, see D. C. Schindler, "The Redemption of *Eros:* Philosophical Reflections on Benedict XVI's First Encyclical," *Communio* 33, no. 3 (Fall 2006): 375–399; Rodney Howsare, "Why Being with Love? *Eros, Agape,* and the Problem of Secularism," *Communio* 33, no. 3 (Fall 2006): 423–448; Antonio Prieto, "*Eros* and *Agape:* The Unique Dynamics of Love" in in *The Way of Love: Reflections on Pope Benedict XVI's Encyclical Deus Caritas* Est, ed. Livio Melina and Carl A. Anderson (San Francisco: Ignatius Press, 2006), 212–226. The relationship between these two types of love was a concern of the Lutheran theologian Anders Nygren's work, *Eros und Agape: Gestaltwandlungen der christlichen Liebe,* 2 vols. (Gütersloh: Bertelsmann, 1930, 1937). For a summary and critique of Nygren's work, see Josef Pieper, *About Love,* trans. Richard and Clara Winston (Chicago: Franciscan Herald Press, 1974), 59–66; Henri de Lubac, S.J., *Theological Fragments,* trans. Rebecca Howell Balinski (San Francisco: Ignatius Press, 1989), 85–89.

they form one unity of love.[89] This unison of the seemingly incompatible loves is evident in the love that God has for man. The Sacred Scriptures (i.e., Hosea, the Song of Songs, Ezekiel, Jeremiah, etc.) emphasize analogously that God has an *eros* for man, which is also totally *agape*.[90] God, who is the "Logos, primordial reason," is "at the same time a lover with all the passion of a true love."[91] Created in the image of God, the human person is called to enter into a loving communion with other people.

The starting point of *Deus Caritas Est* is John the Apostle's affirmation that "God is love."[92] Contrary to the project of dehellenization, which is critiqued in the Regensburg Lecture, Benedict affirms Christianity's baptism of the Greek notion of *logos*: "The ancient world had dimly perceived that man's real food—what truly nourishes him as man—is ultimately the *Logos*, eternal wisdom: this same *Logos* now truly becomes food for us—as love."[93] It is clear that Pope Benedict was speaking of the Holy Eucharist, which allows the Christian to enter into the "very dynamic of [Christ's] self-giving."[94] The *Logos* is not simply a word or meaning, it is fully defined by love.[95] Consequently, there can be no opposition between love of God

---

[89] "This brings us back to the central theme of the unity (or otherwise) of love and hence the necessity of holding together the erotic or physical dimension—the one for which love is also the fulfillment of need/desire—and the ecstatic or agapic dimension, for which love is identified with oblation. The pope cuts through this dispute by giving an authoritative and masterly answer: love is one. *Eros* and *agape* cannot be set against each other." Angelo Scola, "The Unity of Love and the Face of Man: An Invitation to Read *Deus Caritas Est*," *Communio* 33 (Fall 2006), 326.

[90] *DCE*, §10. According to Pope Benedict XVI, Pseudo-Dionysius the Areopagite calls God both *eros* and *agape*. *DCE*, §9. See *The Divine Names* (IV, 12–14: PG 3:709–713).

[91] *DCE*, §10.

[92] 1 John 4:8; *DCE*, §12.

[93] *DCE*, §13.

[94] In his second encyclical, Benedict expresses this sentiment in a similar way: "Being in communion with Jesus Christ draws us into his 'being for all'; it makes it our own way of being. He commits us to live for others, but only through communion with him does it become possible truly to be there for others, for the whole." *SS*, §28.

[95] In Benedict's writings it is not difficult to hear a resonance with the thought of von Balthasar: "If the fundamental word of this Logos were not love—and, indeed, absolute (un-conditional) and therefore utterly free love, because it is a word that reveals God— then the Christian Logos would have to stand as one of a series with the logoi of other religious wisdom teachings." Hans Urs von Balthasar, *Love Alone is Credible*, trans. D. C. Schindler (San Francisco: Ignatius Press, 2008), 55. On the affinity of Benedict with von Balthasar based on some of the themes developed in *Deus Caritas Est*, see Karl-Heinz Menke, "Die theologischen Quellen der Enzyklika "Deus caritas est," in *Joseph Ratzinger: ein theologisches Profil*, ed. Peter Hofmann (Paderborn: Ferdinand Schöningh, 2008), 50–56.

and love of neighbor. Benedict makes the claim already stated at the beginning of this work: "A Eucharist which does not pass over into the concrete practice of love is intrinsically fragmented."[96] This is one of the boldest statements by Benedict because it implies that the Eucharist is not complete without charity. This is consistent with his Augustinian theology of sacrifice, which highlights the external and internal nature of sacrifice. What is unique is that Benedict is ultimately arguing that the offering of the Eucharist is bound up with a concrete work of charity towards neighbor.

The unity that is brought about by Christ in the Eucharist is, by its nature, oriented towards charity, which is why he can describe the lack of concrete acts of charity as "intrinsically fragmented." St. John Chrysostom exhorts the faithful to find Christ among the altars, among those less fortunate after being nourished by Christ, in a homily on Second Corinthians:

> But you honor indeed this altar, because it receives Christ's body; but him that is himself the body of Christ you treat with [scorn], and when perishing, [you neglect him]. This altar may you everywhere see lying, both in [the streets] and in market places, and may sacrifice upon it every hour; for on this too is sacrifice performed.[97]

Both Chrysostom and Benedict share the view that the sacrifice that Christians have participated in through the celebration of the Eucharist extends into daily life in our encounter with other people. The definition of worship is expanded to include the love practiced beyond the celebration of the liturgy. There is an intrinsic unity between faith, worship, and *ethos*.[98] The constant refrain in the theology of Benedict is that how Christians live their lives should be an external expression of their spiritual worship (cf. Rom 12:2).

The unity between the commandment to love God and to love neighbor is guided by the insight of John in his First Letter. Commenting on the *First Letter of John*, Benedict highlights this point: "The unbreakable bond between love of God and love of neighbor is emphasized. One is so closely

---

[96] *DCE*, §14.

[97] John Chrysostom, "Homily 20 on Second Corinthians," *New Advent*, accessed December 1, 2016, http://www.newadvent.org/fathers/220220.htm.

[98] "Faith, worship, and *ethos* are interwoven as a single reality which takes shape in our encounter with God's *agape*." *DCE*, §14. On the development of Benedict's focus on our participation in the Eucharistic love of the incarnate *Logos*, see Nicola Reali, "Participating in His Gift: The Eucharist," in *The Way of Love*, 240–49.

connected to the other that to say we love God becomes a lie if we are closed to our neighbor or hate him altogether."[99] God's love has become visible for humanity above all in Christ, and he continues to manifest himself in "his Word, in the sacraments, and especially in the Eucharist."[100] The purpose of God loving each person is that every individual might in turn love his neighbor because God has "first loved us" (1 John 4:19).

Full communion or solidarity with other people presupposes communion with God. It is only in communion with God that the Christian is able to "love even the person whom [he does] not like or even know."[101] The *Logos* of God has been revealed as a *communio*. Subsequently, every Christian works to draw others to this *communio*, which they are able to do through loving selflessly as God "first loved us." The initial living and intimate encounter with the incarnate *Logos* are fundamental for the Christian to be able to love his neighbor. Once again Benedict is developing the notion that the human person receives from God in order that he might be able to give. Without an active receptivity on the part of the human person, he will not be able to enter into the dynamic of self-giving love of the *Logos*.

Giving presupposes that one has received the gift of communion with God in Christ. Benedict continues to highlight the tension between the unity of the two loves: "If I have no contact whatsoever with God in my life, then I cannot see in the other anything more than the other, and I am incapable of seeing in him the image of God."[102] The Christian's communion with the incarnate *Logos* enables him to recognize the *logoi* of God reflected in his neighbor. The love of neighbor is a concrete and practical realization of the Christian's love for God.

Benedict places emphasis on the example of St. Teresa of Calcutta because she "constantly renewed [her] capacity for love of neighbor from [her] encounter with the Eucharistic Lord, and conversely this encounter acquired its realism and depth in [her] service to others."[103] Teresa's love for the incarnate *Logos* in the Blessed Sacrament enabled her to love Christ in others. *Logos* comes to full fruition in the life of the Christian only in concrete acts of love. The Kantian self-limitation of reason narrows the true understanding of *logos*; consequently, the understanding of love must be reconnected to truth.

---

99 *DCE*, §16.
100 *DCE*, §17.
101 *DCE*, §18.
102 *DCE*, §18.
103 *DCE*, §18.

In his last encyclical, *Caritas in Veritate*, Benedict once again affirms the full revelation of the *Logos* as a person: "In Christ, *charity in truth* becomes the Face of his Person, a vocation for us to love our brothers and sisters in the truth of his plan. Indeed, he himself is the Truth (cf. Jn 14:6)."[104] In his final encyclical the pope emeritus wants to reorient the Church's social doctrine to its true heart, charity.[105] To safeguard charity from being reduced to sentimentality or feeling, it must be closely linked to the truth (*logos*). Truth cannot be fully understood without charity and vice versa. Benedict maintains, "*Only in truth does charity shine forth*, only in truth can charity be authentically lived. Truth is the light that gives meaning and value to charity."[106] The separation between the two has resulted in an impoverished presentation of the Gospel because God is both the Word (*Logos*) *and* Love (*agape*) simultaneously.

In a cultural milieu dominated by relativism, Benedict contends that "practicing charity in truth helps people to understand that adhering to the values of Christianity is not merely useful but essential for building a good society and for true integral human development."[107] Love must be rooted in the *logos* so it does not degenerate into mere social service. Truth guides charity insofar as it leads to a view of the person that does not reduce him to a means but remains inalienably an end. The essential link between truth and charity preserves authentic human development, which Christianity seeks to serve. The link between truth and charity has been fully revealed through the Incarnation of the *Logos* in Jesus Christ. Understood in light of the Person of Christ, every human person is made to be a gift to another.

The Church's teaching on the authentic development of the human person prescinds from an understanding of the human person as gift. Because love is self-gift, Benedict states: "*the whole Church, in all her being and acting—when she proclaims, when she celebrates, when she performs*

---

[104] Benedict XVI, Encyclical Letter *Caritas in Veritate* [hereafter, *CIV*] (Vatican City: Libreria Editrice Vaticana, 2009), 1; emphasis in the original. Elsewhere, Ratzinger maintains, "This is the real innovation of Christianity: The Logos, the truth in person, is also the atonement, the transforming forgiveness that is above and beyond our capability and incapability." Joseph Ratzinger, *On Conscience* (San Francisco: Ignatius Press, 2006), 40.

[105] *CIV*, §2. In contemporary theology, the tendency has been to focus on justice to the exclusion of charity. Charity is a necessary complement to justice. See *DCE*, §§26–29. Also see Carl Anderson, "Justice and Charity in *Deus Caritas Est*," in *The Way of Love*, 341–351.

[106] *CIV*, §3; emphasis in the original.

[107] *CIV*, §4.

*works of charity—is engaged in promoting integral human development.*"[108] The being and mission of authentic charity coincides with the promotion of integral development. Development devoid of love ceases to promote the good of the human person. Benedict underscores the importance of defining integral human development with the transcendent as its ultimate end:

> Development requires a transcendent vision of the person, it needs God: without him, development is either denied, or entrusted exclusively to man, who falls into the trap of thinking he can bring about his own salvation, and ends up promoting a dehumanized form of development.[109]

Without a transcendent view of the person, materialism subordinates the good of the person for some selfish end. In practice, an immanent or materialist anthropology leads to an inhuman economy, whereby profit becomes the sole end at the expense of the dignity of the person. People are reduced to consumers or a mere means to financial gain. Consequently, Benedict maintains that the *"primary capital to be safeguarded and valued"* is *"the human person in his or her integrity."*[110] Once a society fails to recognize God as the *Logos*, the individuals under the influence of this type of secular culture are unable to appreciate the *logoi* reflected in every individual person. A cultural *logos*, rooted in individualism and materialism, leads in practice to an *ethos* marked by utility and not by gift or love.

No economic, social, or political structure is sufficient to address the needs of integral development. Only an *ethos* of gratuitousness can fully address the whole human person. Benedict defines this *ethos*, "Gratuitousness is present in our lives in many different forms, which often go unrecognized because of a purely consumerist and utilitarian view of life.

---

[108] *CIV*, §11; emphasis in the original.

[109] *CIV*, §11, John Paul II also emphasizes this point: "If one does not acknowledge transcendent truth, then the force of power takes over, and each person tends to make full use of the means at his disposal in order to impose his own interests or his own opinion, with no regard for the rights of others. People are then respected only to the extent that they can be exploited for selfish ends. Thus, the root of modern totalitarianism is to be found in the denial of the transcendent dignity of the human person who, as the visible image of the invisible God, is therefore by his very nature the subject of rights which no one may violate." Pope John Paul II, Encyclical Letter *Centesimus Annus* (Vatican City: Libreria Editrice Vaticana, 1991), §45.

[110] *CIV*, §25; emphasis in the original.

The human being is made for gift, which expresses and makes present his transcendent dimension."[111] The person in modern culture tends to fail in recognizing this transcendence because, according to the pope emeritus, he is erroneously convinced that "he is the sole author of himself, his life and society."[112] The person no longer views his very being as a gift because of the reigning materialist anthropology and individualistic autonomy. The tragic result of this false anthropology has "led him to confuse happiness and salvation with immanent forms of material prosperity and social action."[113] Development is reduced solely to what the person can do here on earth, as if this were his or her ultimate kingdom.

Apart from a sacramental worldview, there is an emphasis on progress and development narrowly conceived under the influence of Marx, among other thinkers. Ratzinger critiques Marxism and theologies influenced by it because they are rooted in the subordination of *logos* to *ethos*, which results in a false notion of development and freedom: "As a form of materialism, [Marxism] necessarily rejects the primacy of the Logos; in the beginning was not reason, but rather the unreasonable; reason, being a product of the development of the irrational, is itself ultimately something irrational."[114] The truth cannot be subject to something that is man-made because Ratzinger concludes that this "means in reality there is no truth."[115] When *logos* is subordinate to *ethos*, the view that human reason can construct the truth becomes established, which ironically leads to its own destruction.

When men and women seek to build these utopias on earth, they end up undermining the freedoms and lives of others to achieve their selfish ends. The remedy to this selfish autonomy is a selfless communion or solidarity among all people, guided by a principle of gratuitousness, which will lead to full development. The source and summit of the call of each individual to a vocation of self-gift, and of the whole body of Christ to embrace a life of gratuitousness, is the Holy Eucharist. The Eucharist

---

[111] *CIV*, §34.

[112] *CIV*, §34.

[113] *CIV*, §34.

[114] Ratzinger, *CEP*, 151–52.

[115] See Ratzinger, *CEP*, 151–52: "This means that things, being unreasonable, have no truth; instead, truth is something that only man can determine; it is something man-made, and that means in reality that there is no truth. There are only human constructs, and this necessarily implies the partisan character of reason, which recognizes in advance the compelling force of historical development, runs ahead of it, and thus elevates the compulsion to the status of freedom."

provides an *ethos of love* that serves as a remedy for the mechanized *ethos* of the selfish utilitarian autonomous culture. In order to understand the meaning and significance of the person's being as gift and his ultimate vocation to participate in the movement of giver and gift, there is a need for a recovery of the unity between love and the truth. This unity has been made visible in the sacrament of the Eucharist.

Christ, the incarnate *Logos*, has first loved every human person so that each person may in turn love everyone else. In his post-synodal Apostolic Exhortation *Sacramentum Caritatis*, Benedict XVI affirms the intrinsic unity between truth and charity, which was discussed above in his encyclical *Caritas in Veritate*: "In the sacrament of the Eucharist, Jesus shows us in particular the *truth about love* that is the very essence of God."[116] Love, in its true nature, gives completely to the other person without demanding anything in return. Jesus demonstrates that the authentic self-gift expressed in the Eucharist is the root of the gratuitousness, which involves the total giving of one's self.[117] The Eucharist is the sacramental means through which every human person is able to enter into the *dia-logos* of Trinitarian love. Benedict maintains that the life of the Blessed Trinity "encounters us and is sacramentally shared with us" in the celebration of the Holy Eucharist.[118] The manifestation of God's love in the Eucharist is intended for the further transformation of the world. In part III of *Sacramentum Caritatis*, Benedict outlines the full meaning of a Eucharistic *ethos* in the life of every Christian.

The life of charity, rooted in a Eucharistic *ethos*, marks the full development of a theology of hope. Benedict begins part III of his apostolic exhortation by reiterating the Pauline theme of the "new and definitive worship of God" as the *logikē latreia*.[119] The clarion call of St. Paul for all

---

[116] *SCa*, §2.

[117] "In the Eucharist Jesus does not give us a 'thing,' but himself; he offers his own body and pours out his own blood. He thus gives us the totality of his life and reveals the ultimate origin of this love." *SCa*, §7.

[118] *SCa*, §8.

[119] *SCa*, §70. The phrase "new worship," which is used by Benedict XVI in this third part of *Sacramentum Caritatis* is also used repeatedly in the second part of *Jesus of Nazareth: Holy Week: From the Entrance into Jerusalem to the Resurrection*. For a treatment of this theme in his earlier works, see Ratzinger's discussion of new worship (*Der neue Kult*) in his dissertation, *Volk und Haus Gottes* in JRGS1, 264–317. Also see a lecture given by Ratzinger in Salzburg in 1958, "Christus, die Kirche und der neue Kult," in JRGS8/1, 157–68. For a brief commentary on this theme in Ratzinger, see Cong Quy Joseph Lam, C.Ss.R., *Joseph Ratzinger's Theological Retractions* (Bern, Switzerland: Peter Lang, AG, 2013), 181–85.

Christians to present their bodies as "a living sacrifice, holy and accept-able to God" (Rom 12:1) "emphasizes the concrete human reality of a worship which is anything but disincarnate."[120] The *Logos* transformed human nature through the Incarnation, which is continually manifested in sacramental worship; consequently, all of human reality is supposed to be transfigured by God's grace. Benedict concludes, "There is noth-ing authentically human—our thoughts and affections, our words and deeds—that does not find in the sacrament of the Eucharist *the form* it needs to be lived to the full."[121] True worship extends beyond the bound-aries of the celebration of liturgy. Every day in the life of the Christian is meant to be an external manifestation of the gift of love, which has been received in the Eucharist. According to Benedict, St. Ignatius of Antioch describes Christians as "those living in accordance with the Lord's Day" (*Iuxta dominicam viventes*).[122] Christians are called to live a life of self-giving love at every moment with God and others.

The Holy Eucharist reveals that there is a reciprocal relationship between the vertical communion with God and the horizontal commu-nion with neighbor insofar as both are realized fully in love.[123] The unity of the commandment to love God and neighbor, affirmed by Benedict in *Deus Caritas Est*, is reiterated in this document as both communions con-verge in the Holy Eucharist. Communion with God is the underlying root and source for a fruitful communion with neighbor. Hence, *communio* is the fundamental *logos* for the Christian because this is the type of love that has been revealed by God as Father, Son, and Holy Spirit.

The *logikē latreia* brings about a transformation in the life of the Christian that does not allow him to remain isolated or selfish. Benedict emphasizes, "Worship pleasing to God can never be a purely private mat-ter, without consequences for our relationships with others: it demands a public witness to our faith."[124] As a result of the close connection between worship and ethics, the Christian seeks to transform the public square by exercising his prophetic role in defending the common good by promoting the dignity and sanctity of all human life, marriage, and the family.

The Holy Eucharist brings about communion for every Christian with both God and neighbor. Subsequently, by its very nature communion

---

[120] *SCa*, §70.

[121] *SCa*, §71; emphasis added.

[122] *SCa*, §72.

[123] "Communion always and inseparably has both a vertical and horizontal sense: it is com-munion with God and communion with our brothers and sisters." *SCa*, §76.

[124] *SCa*, §83.

gives rise to mission. Christians are sent on mission to invite others to the communion that they enjoy through the love of the incarnate *Logos*. According to Benedict, "The love that we celebrate in the sacrament [of the Eucharist] is not something we can keep to ourselves. By its very nature it demands to be shared with all."[125] As the Body of Christ, the Church is a sign of God's inner trinitarian *communio*. At the same time, the Church is also an instrument that works to bring about and deepen this *communio*. This is why Benedict affirms that "[t]ruly, nothing is more beautiful than to know Christ and to make him known to others."[126] The Eucharist draws every member of the faithful into the mission of Christ, for whom the *communio* of every person with his Father in the Spirit is the purpose of his redemptive love. In his efforts to accentuate the "intrinsic relationship between the Eucharist and mission," Benedict hopes that "[t]he more ardent the love for the Eucharist in the hearts of the Christian people, the more clearly will they recognize the goal of all mission: *to bring Christ to others*."[127] Jesus Christ is not an abstract teaching or dogma; he is a living person whom Christians can bring to life through their words and deeds. In particular, a concrete manifestation of the love of Christ is made visible in one's love for another person.

In the Holy Eucharist, Christ has given himself completely for others. Benedict comments: "Each celebration of the Eucharist makes sacramentally present the gift that the crucified Lord made of his life, for us and for the whole world."[128] This demonstration of love's full meaning is meant to be reflected in the love of every Christian through his service of charity toward his neighbor. Benedict emphasizes that Christians, through the celebration of the Eucharist, must become ever more conscious that the sacrifice of Christ is for all, and that "the Eucharist thus compels all who believe in him to become 'bread that is broken' for others, and to work for the building of a more just and fraternal world."[129] The salvation offered by Christ is never for a group of individual "Is." Salvation is a gift intended for the "we" of the Body of Christ.[130] Communion with Christ deepens

---

[125] *SCa*, §84.

[126] *SCa*, §84.

[127] *SCa*, §86.

[128] *SCa*, §88.

[129] *SCa*, §88.

[130] Drawing upon the insights of de Lubac, Benedict affirms the social nature of salvation. See *SS*, §§13–15. De Lubac's emphasis on the Church as sacrament and the social nature of the Church has been a consistent theme in the thought of Ratzinger. See Joseph Ratzinger, *Principles of Catholic Theology: Building Stones for a Fundamental*

one's communion with other people, even those whom one does not like or even know.

A Eucharistic *ethos* enables a person to love all and to work ceaselessly for the world's transformation in Christ's love. Benedict notes, "The mystery of the Eucharist inspires and impels us to work courageously within our world to bring about the renewal of relationships which has its inexhaustible source in God's gift."[131] The faithful must work to reduce the material hunger and poverty which plagues the world, particularly in developing nations. The transformation of *ethos* presupposes the underlying *logos* of love that Christ fully revealed on the Cross, which the Eucharist sacramentally re-presents to the world.

## Summary and Conclusion

The liturgy has implications for how Christians imitate Christ's sacrificial love in this world and fulfill our call in the mission of drawing others into communion with the incarnate *Logos*. The Eucharist never removes Christians from the concerns and cares of this world; a more authentic communion with Christ deepens one's communion and love with one's neighbor. Ratzinger's understanding of the relationship between the liturgy and eschatology reorients the mission of each individual as a member of the Church so that every person becomes a true witness to both hope and charity. The life of every Christian should be an extension of the love that he has encountered through Christ's love in the liturgy.

The Holy Eucharist provides the framework for the *logos* of love that

---

*Theology* [hereafter, PCT], trans. Sister Mary Frances McCarthy, S.N.D. (San Francisco: Ignatius Press, 1987), 48–55; see Joseph Ratzinger, *On the Way to Jesus Christ*, trans. Michael J. Miller (San Francisco: Ignatius Press, 2004), 117–120. Ratzinger first read de Lubac's book *Catholicism* in 1949; he describes reading this work as a "key reading event." Ratzinger continues to explain the impact of de Lubac's work: "[*Catholicism*] gave me not only a new and deeper connection with the thought of the Fathers but also a new way of looking at theology and faith as such. Faith had here become an interior contemplation and, precisely by thinking with the Fathers, a present reality. . . . De Lubac was leading his readers out of a narrowly individualistic and moralistic mode of faith and into the freedom of an essentially social faith, conceived and lived as a *we*—a faith that, precisely as such and according to its nature, was also hope, affecting history as a whole, and not only the promise of a private blissfulness to individuals." Joseph Ratzinger, *Milestones: Memoirs 1927–1977* [hereafter, *MM*], trans. Erasmo Leiva-Merikakis (San Francisco: Ignatius Press, 1998), 98. De Lubac has clearly had a lasting impact on the thought of Ratzinger.

[131] *SCa*, §91.

is ordered to establishing communion among all people, which is the heart of the Church's mission. In *Deus Caritas Est* and *Sacramentum Caritatis*, Benedict XVI describes the manifestation of this *logos* as a concrete Eucharistic *ethos* that allows the life of the Christian to become a constant and daily "living sacrifice" offered in accord with the *logos*. Thus, the fruition of Christian charity flowing from the liturgical life of the Christian is the full *actuosa participatio*. At the same time, the primacy of *logos* establishes what Benedict argues for in *Caritas in Veritate*: a need for truth to safeguard the true meaning of charity. A proper understanding of the relationship between the liturgy and eschatology enables Ratzinger to develop a theology of hope that reaches its fulfilment Eucharistically in the life of charity. A life characterized by charity is the authentic *logikē latreia* to which every Christian is called to in Christ. A life transformed by the Eucharist is both an anticipation and realization of the eschaton, as Pope St. John Paul II declared:

> Proclaiming the death of the Lord "until he comes" (1 Cor 11:26) entails that all who take part in the Eucharist be committed to changing their lives and making them in a certain way completely "Eucharistic." It is this fruit of a transfigured existence and a commitment to transforming the world in accordance with the Gospel which splendidly illustrates the eschatological tension inherent in the celebration of the Eucharist and in the Christian life as a whole: "Come, Lord Jesus!" (Rev 22:20).[132]

Chapter three established the Eucharistic identity of the Church, which is defined by the Church's *logos* of *communio*. In chapter four, it has been argued that the Church's Eucharistic mission is defined by the liturgy as a *logikē latreia* and an *ethos* of hope-filled charity. It is now necessary to demonstrate in our next chapter how the orientation of the faith towards the incarnate and eschatological *Logos* is made visible through worship offered *ad orientem* and liturgy that manifests a *logos*-centric beauty.

---

[132] John Paul II, *Ecclesia de Eucharistia*, §20.

CHAPTER 5

# The *Logos*-Centric Beauty of Heavenly Worship

THIS BOOK HAS FOCUSED on the *lex credendi* and the *lex vivendi*, and now the final part of this work revolves around the *lex orandi*. In the celebration of the liturgy, there has long been an understanding among members of the Church that they are participating in the worship of heaven. The Church invokes the presence of the angels in the threefold *Sanctus* in the liturgy. Commenting upon this prayer, which is based on the text in the Liturgy of St. Mark, the German theologian Erik Peterson (1890–1960) remarks that "the Church should join in with its version of the angels' Sanctus cry [which] is dictated by the very nature of its liturgy." Peterson concludes, "This means that the Church's worship is not that of a human religious society whose liturgy is tied to a temple. Rather, it is a worship that permeates the entire cosmos, in which sun, moon, and all the stars take part."[1]

With Peterson, Ratzinger emphasizes the eschatological and cosmic nature of the liturgy, which is the *logos* that the Church has received.[2]

---

[1]  Erik Peterson, *Theological Tractates*, ed. and trans. Michal J. Hollerich (Stanford, CA: Stanford University Press, 2011), 121. Also see Geoffrey Wainwright, *Eucharist and Eschatology* (New York: Oxford University Press, 1981), 117–118.

[2]  It is demonstrated throughout this chapter that Peterson influenced Ratzinger's emphasis on worship *ad orientem*. See Erik Peterson, *Frühkirche, Judentum und Gnosis* (Freiburg im Breisgau: Herder, 1959), 1–14 and 15–35. For Ratzinger's reliance upon Peterson's scholarship to argue in favor of a restoration and superiority of the eastern orientation during the celebration of the liturgy, see his "On the Question of the Orientation of the Celebration," in J*Theology of the Liturgy: The Sacramental Foundation of Christian Existence* [hereafter, JRCW11], ed. Michael J. Miller, trans. John Saward, Kenneth Baker, S.J., Henry Taylor, et al., Collected Works 11 (San Francisco: Ignatius Press, 2014), 389; *Theologie der Liturgie: Die sakramentale Begründung christlicher*

This chapter explores the implications of the primacy and role of the *logos* as it influences Ratzinger's thought on the orientation of the celebration of the sacred liturgy, the human person's vocation to become a *homo adorans*, and the centrality of beauty as a defining characteristic of the liturgy. These three topics are related because each of them, for Ratzinger, belongs to the way in which the *logos*-centric liturgy should orient the Church eschatologically.

First, the rationale for Ratzinger's repeated insistence upon worship *ad orientem* is explained, which is meant to highlight the inherently eschatological nature of the liturgy and the person's fundamental orientation towards a life in communion with the incarnate *Logos*. Second, Jesus Christ literally embodies the type of person that every believer should become by grace, which is first and foremost a *homo adorans*. In light of his call to become a true *homo adorans*, I will insist that the various bodily gestures used during the liturgy (i.e., kneeling, sitting, or standing) are a form of discipline (*askēsis*) to prepare the person for participation in the eschaton and for his encounter with the *Logos* in the Resurrection. Finally, the "way of beauty" (the *via pulchritudinis*), worship *ad orientem,* and the asceticism of the body serve as concrete expressions of an eschatological liturgy and further support that *logos* has a primacy above *ethos*.

The liturgy is not something made, but it has a *logos* that has been received and that should be made clear through the way in which the liturgy is celebrated. To portray Ratzinger as simply a traditionalist or an aesthete is to misunderstand his interest in underscoring the eschatological and cosmic nature of the liturgy.[3] Ratzinger's goal is to restore

---

*Existenz* [hereafter, JRGS11], Gesammelte Schriften 11, ed. Gerhard Ludwig Müller (Freiburg im Breisgau: Herder, 2008), 464–465. On the influence of Peterson upon Ratzinger's theology, see Siegfried Wiedenhofer, *Die Theologie Joseph Ratzingers/ Benedikts XVI: Ein Blick auf das Ganz*, Ratzinger-Studien 10 (Regensburg: Frie drich Pustet, 2016), 96–98. Peterson will be very significant for Ratzinger in other areas of thought, particularly his critique of political theology, as it has been espoused by Metz and other thinkers. See Peterson, *Theological Tractates*, 68–105. Peterson critiques political theology as it was articulated at the beginning of the twentieth century by Carl Schmitt in his book published in 1922, *Politische Theologie*. See Emery de Gaál, *The Theology of Pope Benedict XVI: The Christocentric Shift* (New York: Macmillan Palgrave, 2010), 148–56.. Also see Benedict XVI, *Last Testament: In His Own Words*, trans. Jacob Philips (New York: Bloomsbury, 2016), 149.

3   For example, see Thomas P. Rausch, S.J., *Pope Benedict XVI: An Introduction to His Theological Vision* (New York: Paulist Press, 2009), 136–138 (here, 137): "[Ratzinger's] stress on the Eucharist as sacrifice and prayer rather than meal—thus his preference for a more formal, priest-centered liturgy with the congregation kneeling—his concern

balance where it has been lost so that the liturgy is seen as the work of the people fully participating in the work and worship of God.

The relationship of the liturgy to its historical past and its eschato-logical future can only be understood if one views the theology of liturgy as a "symbolic theology," which Ratzinger maintains "connects us to what is present but hidden."[4] Ratzinger's contention that liturgical theology revolves around the significance of eschatological and cosmological sym-bolism is consistent with the main thesis of this book concerning the primacy of the *logos*. When one grasps the symbolic nature of his theology of liturgy, then a person understands the eschaton as the definitive *logos* of the liturgy that fulfills the Church's identity and mission as a *communio*.

## CONVERSI AD DOMINUM

The emphasis on the unity of Jesus's two natures achieves the harmony that is critical for understanding the proper relationship between the lit-urgy and eschatology. In liturgical practice, there has been an emphasis on the human aspect of the liturgy to the point of overshadowing the divine and the transcendent aspect. The stress upon the liturgy as solely the work of the people, to the point that it is reduced to a form of *ethos* that has a priority over *logos*, has led to Ratzinger's refrain that the liturgy is first and foremost an *opus Dei*. This context sheds light on Ratzinger's position on liturgy *ad orientem*, which can only be understood in light of the relation-ship of liturgy to eschatology and the cosmos.

The discussion concerning liturgical orientation is actually a relatively minor detail in Ratzinger's theology of the liturgy, which he was using to drive home an even more significant argument that the celebration of the liturgy has traditionally been imbued with eschatological and cosmic sym-bolism. Ratzinger countenanced the omission of this theme, which argues for worship *ad orientem*, from the volume of his collected works dedicated to the liturgy, which he points out is only nine out of two hundred pages in the *Spirit of the Liturgy*.[5]

---

to emphasize the differences between the ordained and the non-ordained, as well as his views on facing east, inclusive language, creativity, dancing—all suggest a much more traditional approach to liturgy." Rausch makes uncritical generalizations about Ratzinger's theology throughout his work. This conclusion reduces Ratzinger's arguments to subjective preferences based on his inclination towards a "much more tra-ditional approach."

4   JRCW11, 36 (JRGS11, 68).
5   Benedict XVI, JRCW11, xvi (JRGS11, 7): "Given this distortion, I thought for a while

Many critical reviews of Ratzinger's work focus on this issue as if it were the central theme of his work.[6] Consequently, these critics miss the

---

about omitting this chapter [on the orientation of liturgical prayer]—nine pages out of a total of two hundred—so that finally a discussion could begin about the essential things in the book about which I had been and am concerned."

[6] See Pierre-Marie Gy, O.P., "Cardinal Ratzinger's *The Spirit of the Liturgy*: Is It Faithful to the Council or in Reaction to It?," *Antiphon* 11, no. 1 (2007): 90–96. Cf. Ratzinger's response in, "*The Spirit of the Liturgy* or Fidelity to the Council: Response to Father Gy," *Antiphon* 11.1 (2007): 98–102. "None of my critics has yet told me why this very simple idea—the Cross, the Crucified, and the Christ who returns as the focal point of the liturgy—is false. Instead, they try to bog me down in archeological debates, the outcome of which is in the end not very important for the liturgical question as such" (101). The main interest of Ratzinger is primarily to define various facets of the liturgy: "the cosmic dimension of the liturgy, the place of the Christian liturgy in the history of religions and the whole basic problematic of human existence that appears through it; the relationship between Israel and the Church in the historical path of the liturgy; the different ways of the Christian liturgy and the relation between cult and culture" (102). It is noteworthy that Father Pierre-Marie Gy, O.P. (1922–2004), was formed by the liturgical movement. In particular, he was influenced by Dom Bernard Botte, O.S.B., and Josef A. Jungmann, S.J. Gy played a significant role in the development of various new liturgical books and he served as a consultor for the preparatory committee that was responsible for drafting *Sacrosanctum Concilium*. See, Anselm J. Gribbin, O. Praem., "Sed Contra: Pierre-Marie Gy's Critique of Cardinal Ratzinger's *The Spirit of the Liturgy*," in *Pope Benedict XVI: Understanding Recent Liturgical Developments* (United Kingdom: Gracewing, 2011), 46–67, here 46; and Anscar J. Chupungco, O.S.B., "The Vision of the Constitution on the Liturgy," in *T & T Clark Companion to Liturgy*, ed. Alcuin Reid (New York: Bloomsbury, 2016), 263–65. In addition to Gy, Ratzinger's position on *ad orientem* receives critique from Pere Farnés, "An Important Work on Liturgy That Ought to Be Read in Its Proper Context," *Antiphon* 20, no. 2 (2016): 78–90. Originally published as "Una Obra Importante Sobre Liturgia Que Debe Leerse en su Verdadero Contexto," *Phase* 42 (2002): 55–76. Farnés acknowledges that the practice of celebrating the liturgy *ad orientem* may have been a practice of the early Church, but he rejects both a restoration of celebrating the liturgy in this manner along with Ratzinger's compromise to place a cross on the altar because it prevents the people from focusing on the primary sign of the consecrated host and wine. Farnés, "An Important Work on Liturgy That Ought to Be Read in Its Proper Context," 78–87. Cf. Joseph Ratzinger, "Cardinal Joseph Ratzinger's Answer to Pere Farnés," in *Antiphon* 20, no. 2 (2016): 90–95. Originally published as "Respuesta del Cardenal Joseph Ratzinger a Pere Farnés," *Phase* 42 (2002): 509–14. Also see Ratzinger's response to criticisms from Olivier Bauer in JRCW 11, 570–71. Originally published as "Réponse à la Lettre Ouverte d'Olivier Bauer," in Revue de Théologie et de Philosophie 135 (2003): 253–56. Cf. Olivier Bauer, "Lettre Ouverte à propos de *L'Esprit de La Liturgie*, Ouvrage du Cardinal Joseph Ratzinger," in *Revue de Théologie et de Philosophie* 135 (2003): 241–51. In both his response to Gy and Bauer, he cites the aforementioned work by Uwe Michael Lang, *Turning towards the Lord,* and an article of Albert Gerhards,

major theological insight of Ratzinger's theology of liturgy. The importance of this self-described detail is clarified by the larger context or purpose, which Ratzinger outlines as one of the three concentric circles in his theology of liturgy: "[T]he cosmic character of the liturgy, which represents more than the coming together of a more or less large circle of people: the liturgy is celebrated in the expanse of the cosmos, encompassing creation and history at the same time."[7] Ratzinger continues, "This was what the orientation of prayer meant: that the Redeemer to whom we pray is also the Creator and, thus, the liturgy also always contains a love for creation and a responsibility for it."[8] The unfolding of history and the created order moves towards its ultimate end in Jesus Christ, the living eschaton. Ratzinger wants the cosmic and eschatological reality of the liturgy to be plainly evident in each and every external aspect of the liturgical celebration, which includes the celebration of the liturgy *ad orientem*.

In Ratzinger's estimation, prayer towards the east (*ad orientem*) is an ancient tradition of the early Church.[9] The celebration of the liturgy *ad*

---

"*Versus orientem—versus populum:* Zum gegenwärtigen Diskussionsstand einer alten Streitfrage," *Theologische Revue* 98 (2002): 15–22. In his response to Farnés he only mentions the work of Gerhards: "Gerhards shows in this article how the great tradition of '*versus orientem*' is very widespread and that it actually covers much more than the early Church, as might be inferred from Fr. Farnés's book review. It also shows Gerhards's deep understanding of the theological foundations of the issues and proposes different possibilities for contemporary practice. This article is an important step forward because it finally breaks the hitherto seemingly united front of liturgists who were going along with the crowd and presenting "*versus populum*" as the only legitimate possibility after the [Second Vatican] Council, as Fr. Farnés also does." "Cardinal Joseph Ratzinger's Answer to Pere Farnés," 94. Cf. Alfred Häussling, "Der Geist der Liturgie: Zu Joseph Ratzingers gleichnamiger Publikation," *Archiv für Liturgiewissenschaft* 43–44.3 (2001/02): 362–95; Reiner Kaczynski, "Angriff an die Liturgiekonstitution? Anmerkungen zu einer neuen Übersetzer-Instruktion," *Stimmen der Zeit* 219 (2001): 651–68; Ratzinger, "Die organische Entwicklung der Liturgie," *Forum katholische Theologie* 21, no. 1 (2005): 36–39. Ratzinger, "Um die Erneuerung der Liturgie: Antwort auf Reiner Kaczynski," *Stimmen der Zeit* 219 (2001): 837–43.

7  JRCW11, xvii (JRGS11, 8).

8  JRCW11, xvii (JRGS11, 8).

9  The view that *ad orientem* dates back to the liturgical practice of the Early Church is certainly not without its critics. For example, see Robin M. Jenson, "Recovering Ancient Ecclesiology: The Place of the Altar and the Orientation of Prayer in the Early Latin Church," *Worship* 89, no. 2 (March 2015): 99–124; Otto Nussbaum, *Der Standort des Liturgen am christlichen Altar vor dem Jahre 1000*, 2 vols. (Bonn: Peter Hanstein, 1965); and Theodor Klauser, *A Short History of the Western Liturgy* (Oxford: Oxford University Press, 1965). Nussbaum and Klauser maintain the view that it was not uncommon for the liturgy to be celebrated *versus populum*. Klaus Gamber takes

*orientem* is preferred by Ratzinger, as has been stated previously, because of the cosmological and eschatological symbolism of this orientation. This is a claim Ratzinger makes repeatedly in various works:

> For the true location and the true context of the eucharistic celebration is the whole cosmos. "Facing east" makes this cosmic celebration of the Eucharist present through liturgical gesture. Because of the rising of the sun, the east—*oriens*—was naturally both a symbol of the Resurrection (and to that extent it was not merely a christological statement but also a reminder of the Father's power and the influence of the Holy Spirit) and a presentation of the hope of the Parousia. Where priest and people together face the same way, what we have is a cosmic orientation and also an interpretation of the Eucharist in terms of Resurrection and trinitarian theology. Hence it is also an interpretation in terms of parousia, a theology of hope, in which every Mass is an approach to the return of Christ.[10]

---

up the view in favor of worship *ad orientem* responding to the works of Nussbaum and Klauser. See his *The Reform of the Roman Liturgy: Its Problems and Background*, trans. Klaus D. Grimm (Fort Collins, CO: Roman Catholic Books, 1993), 77–89; 137–179. The article of Robin Jensen cited above critiques the scholarship of Gamber and subsequent works, which build their own research upon his views. The notable work of recent scholarship, which is subject to Jensen's criticisms, is Uwe M. Lang, *Turning towards the Lord: Orientation in Liturgical Prayer*. This small book is esteemed highly by Ratzinger. See JRCW11, xvi (JRGS11, 7). The other recent source cited by Benedict, which supports the thesis concerning liturgy *ad orientem*, is Stefan Heid, "Gebetshaltung und Ostung in der frühchristlichen Zeit," *Rivista di Archeologia Christiana* 72 (2006): 347–404. Heid's work contains some of the most relevant research on this topic, but Jensen seems to be unaware of this particular article. The latest work of Heid offers a comprehensive treatment of this debate, engaging the thought of Nussbaum, Klauser, Lang, and Gamber. See his *Altar und Kirche: Prinzipien christlicher Liturgie* (Regensburg: Schnell & Steiner, 2019), 435–464. Heid's work is essential reading to engage this ongoing debate. Also see Baldovin, *Reforming the Liturgy*, 105–113. In a very honest assessment, Baldovin notes, "First, it seems to me that historical honesty requires us to admit that the idea that the early liturgy was habitually celebrated *versus populum* was mistaken (as least as far as prayer was concerned—only traditionalist extremists want the Word to be proclaimed in the old-fashioned manner). Second, it must also be admitted that the priest can 'hijack' the liturgy and that the celebration can seem to be purely horizontal. Third, we need to acknowledge that it has never been forbidden to celebrate the liturgy with the priest facing the liturgical east—even in the *Missal of Paul VI*" (112).

[10] JRCW11, 389 (JRGS11, 464). Here Ratzinger cites Everett A. Diederich, S.J., "The Unfolding Presence of Christ in the Celebration of the Mass," *Communio* 5, no. 4 (1978):

The symbolic significance of the traditional eastward liturgical orientation is multivalent for Ratzinger.

The eastern direction, which coincides with the direction in which the sun rises, is a symbol simultaneously of the Lord's Resurrection and the hope of the Lord's Second Coming. Worship *ad orientem* is cosmological, Christological, and eschatological. The unified orientation of the people with the priest celebrant in the same direction also underscores the unity of the Body of Christ in worship of the Father, through the Son, in the Holy Spirit. Drawing upon the insight of Erik Peterson, Ratzinger claims that the early Church maintained the centrality of this cosmological and eschatological symbolism of the eastward orientation during prayer by placing a cross on the eastern wall of homes where Christians gathered.[11] The eschatological significance of this eastward orientation during prayer was eventually displaced by a focus on the cross as a concrete reminder of the Lord's Passion and death.[12] The eastern orientation and Christological form of prayer coincide with one another and underscore the eschatological hope, which once characterized the Temple in the Old Covenant.

Jesus Christ is the living temple towards whom Christians focus their prayer because he is the pinnacle in which humanity is able to encounter God.[13] The psalmist explains the cosmological significance of facing in

---

326–43. Ratzinger is critical of Diederich's view that the orientation of the celebrant *ad orientem* during the liturgy was facing the altar toward the holy of holies. Ratzinger elaborates, "The eastward-facing position of the celebrant in the old Mass was never intended as a celebration toward the holy of holies, nor can it really be described as 'facing the altar.' In fact, it would be contrary to all theological reason, since the Lord is present in the Eucharistic Gifts during the Mass in the same way as he is in the Gifts of the tabernacle that come from the Mass. Thus the Eucharist would be celebrated 'from' the Host 'to' the Host, which is plainly meaningless. There is only one inner direction of the Eucharist, namely, from Christ in the Holy Spirit to the Father." JRCW11, 388 (JRGS11, 463–64). One of the major influences upon Ratzinger's position on *ad orientem*, the French theologian Louis Bouyer (1913–2004), describes the symbolism of eastern orientation as an "eschatological expectation of primitive Christianity: the expectation that is of a last day, the lasting day of eternity, in which the Christus victor would appear as the rising sun which will never set." Louis Bouyer, *Liturgy and Architecture* (Notre Dame, IN: University of Notre Dame Press, 1967), 29.

[11] Erik Peterson, *Frühkirche, Judentum und Gnosis* (Freiburg: Herder, 1959), 1–14; 15–35.

[12] JRCW11, 389 (JRGS11, 464–465).

[13] According to the theologian Fr. Thomas Weinandy, "The old temple with its priesthood therefore becomes redundant for the covenant, and the priesthood it represents has been fulfilled by Jesus enacting the new covenant. Jesus is now the living priest and victim of the new living temple of the new covenant in whom all of mankind has

the same direction as the rising sun: "[The sun] comes forth like a bridegroom leaving his chamber. . . . Its rising is from the end of the heavens, and its circuit to the end of them" (Psalm 19[18]:5–6).[14] Ratzinger maintains that this psalm was interpreted as symbolic of Christ, "who is the living Word, the eternal Logos, and thus the true light of history, who came forth in Bethlehem from the bridal chamber of the Virgin Mother and now pours his light on all the world. The east supersedes the Jerusalem Temple as a symbol."[15] Praying towards the east is symbolic of the celebration of the Incarnation of the eternal *Logos* and at the same time an anticipation of the return of Christ. Aquinas affirms the tradition of praying towards the east in light of Christological, cosmological, and eschatological symbolism:

> There is a certain fittingness in adoring towards the east [*adoramus versus orientem*]. First, because the divine majesty is indicated by the movement of the heavens which is from the east. Secondly, because Paradise was situated in the east according to Genesis 2:8 of the Septuagint, we thus signify our desire [through the orientation of our prayer] to return to Paradise. Thirdly, on account of Christ who is "the light of the world" and called "the Orient" [*Oriens*] in Zechariah 6:12, who ascends above the heaven of heavens to the east [*ad orientem*] (Psalm 67:34), and who is expected to come from the east, according to Matthew 24:27: "As lightning comes out from the east, and appears even into the west, so shall also the coming of the son of man be."[16]

According to the wisdom of Aquinas, praying towards the east is a fitting symbol for Christian worship. The east becomes symbolic of the New Temple or New Jerusalem, embodied by Christ himself.

The presence of Christ in the liturgy is symbolized in part by the altar,

---

admittance to the heavenly sanctuary where his Father dwells. Thus, unlike the old temple with its restricting curtain, Jesus, the new temple, provides open and unencumbered entrée to God." Thomas G. Weinandy, OFM, CAP, *Jesus Becoming Jesus: A Theological Interpretation of the Synoptic Gospels* (Washington, DC: The Catholic University of America Press, 2018), 385.

[14] JRCW11, 41 (JRGS11, 73).

[15] JRCW11, 41 (JRGS11, 73).

[16] Thomas Aquinas, *Summa Theologiae* [hereafter, *ST*] III, trans. The Fathers of the English Dominican Province (Westminster, MD: Christian Classics, 1981), q. 84, a. 3, ad 3.

which serves as an entryway to the eschaton. Ratzinger maintains that "the altar signifies the entry of him who is the Orient into the assembled community and the going out of the community from the prison of this world through the curtain now torn open, a participation in the Pasch, the 'passing over' from the world to God, that Christ has opened up."[17] The altar symbolizes the unity between the worship of the Church, which continues its pilgrimage here on earth with the communion of the saints in heaven. The exodus of Jesus Christ opens up a new center of worship, which was foreshadowed by the Temple.

Under the Old Covenant, the faithful Jews who gathered in the synagogue fixed their attention towards Jerusalem. In light of the New Covenant wrought by Jesus Christ, Christians are able to look east towards the heavenly Jerusalem. Ratzinger underscores the eschatological implications of Christian worship as participation in the sacrifice of the incarnate *Logos*, a sacrifice which "brings heaven into the community assembled on earth, or, rather, it takes that community beyond itself into the communion of saints of all times and places."[18] Communion with the *Logos* in the celebration of the liturgy enables a person to be contemporaneous with the eternal liturgy, in which every member of the communion of the Church and the communion of the saints participates. The common direction which is shared by the people with the priest when the liturgy is offered *ad orientem* is an outward expression of a pilgrim Church united together in its pilgrimage towards the heavenly Jerusalem and accompanied by the entire *communio sanctorum*. This form of prayer follows from the Incarnation, as Ratzinger maintains that "as God assumed a body and entered the time and space of this world, so it is appropriate to prayer—at least to communal liturgical prayer—that our speaking to God should be 'incarnational,' that it should be Christological, turned through the Incarnate Word to the triune God."[19]

If this is the case, then how did it come to pass that many altars have seemingly been arranged for the celebration of the liturgy *versus populum*? Ratzinger accounts for this in part because of the renovations of St. Peter's Basilica in Rome during the papacy of Pope St. Gregory the Great (590–604), when the altar was moved closer to the chair of the bishop in order to be located in closer proximity to the tomb of St. Peter. Ratzinger comments that the purpose of this move was to symbolize "the truth that

---

[17] JRCW11, 42 (JRGS11, 75).
[18] JRCW11, 43 (JRGS11, 75).
[19] JRCW11, 45–46 (JRGS11, 78).

we celebrate the Sacrifice of the Lord in the communion of saints, a communion spanning all times and ages. The custom of erecting an altar above the tombs of the martyrs probably goes back a long way and is an outcome of the same motivation."[20] Ratzinger concludes that the position of the altar at St. Peter's Basilica would be copied by many of the stational churches throughout Rome.[21]

The physical orientation of St. Peter's faced the west because of its unique topography.[22] Based on this archaeological and historical fact, Ratzinger opines: "Thus, if the celebrating priest wanted—as the Christian tradition of prayer demands—to face east, he had to stand behind the people and look—this is the logical conclusion—toward the people."[23] Emphasis was centered upon prayer towards the east, but the people did not always face the priest in churches that faced west like St. Peter's Basilica. French theologian Louis Bouyer maintains, "Even when

---

[20] JRCW11, 46 (JRGS11, 79). On the rearrangement of the altar during the pontificate of Pope St. Gregory, see Lang, *Turning towards the Lord*, 76–77.

[21] See Heid, "Gebetshaltung und Ostung in der frühchristlichen Zeit," 392–97.

[22] JRCW11, 46 (JRGS11, 79). There were churches constructed during this period that had sanctuaries in both the east and west. See John Wilkinson, "Constantinian Churches in Palestine," in *Ancient Churches Revealed*, ed. Yoram Tsafrir (Jerusalem: Israel Exploration Society, 1993), 23–27. Wilkinson affirms the practice of placing sanctuaries in the eastern part of the church beginning with churches that were constructed in Syria. He acknowledges that churches in Bethlehem and Heliopolis were built with a western sanctuary. In an attempt to explain this anomaly, he concludes, "The variety of Constantinian church plans all over the world suggests that local ecclesiastical bodies dictated their architecture. However, the edifices in Palestine and Phoenicia show differences in alignment and proportion that can hardly be the result of some new development taking place during Constantine's reign. They reflect, rather, a long tradition of church planning, which was, I believe, an effort to differentiate between the architecture of churches and that of synagogues" (27). This is an important insight because placing sanctuaries in the western part of the church does not necessarily imply that liturgies were offered *versus populum* in the early Church.

[23] JRCW11, 46 (JRGS11, 79). Concerning other churches, which faced the West like St. Peter's, Gamber comments, "In the basilicas with the apse facing West rather than East, and with the altar situated in the middle of the center nave, the faithful who were standing in the side naves did not have their backs turned towards the altar: because of the holiness of the altar this would have been something unthinkable. With little physical effort, the faithful were able to turn their bodies in the direction of the West, towards the church entrance. Even in the unlikely event that the assembled faithful did not, during the Eucharistic Prayer, face the entrance but the altar, that still would not have resulted in the priest and the people facing one another since, as we have already observed, in the early days of Christianity, the altar was shielded from view by curtains." Gamber, *Reform of the Roman Liturgy*, 159.

orientation of the church enabled the celebrant to pray turned toward the people, when at the altar, we must not forget that it was not the priest alone who, then, turned East: it was the whole congregation, together with him."[24] Consistent with her emphasis on cosmology and eschatology, the Church celebrated the liturgy with her people in unison with the priest oriented together towards the east. The liturgical renewal of the twentieth century, in Ratzinger's estimation, interpreted the situations in which the priest offered the liturgy as he did in St. Peter's Basilica as the norm for Masses celebrated *versus populum*. In the post-conciliar period, this form of celebrating the Mass was deemed by some a necessity for active participation and above all, since it brought with it a "new idea of the essence of the liturgy—the liturgy as communal meal."[25] As was mentioned in chapter two, the essential form (*Grundgestalt*) of the Eucharist is a sacrifice. The essence of the Eucharist cannot be reduced simply to a meal, nor is worship *versus populum* a necessary characteristic of the celebration of liturgy.

The symbolic significance of liturgical worship is one of the central concerns of Ratzinger because external changes can lead to a shift in understanding. This liturgical orientation places an emphasis on the transcendent nature of liturgy. Worship *versus populum* can become anthropocentric, which may reduce the liturgy solely towards what is imminent and immanent. Ratzinger maintains that liturgy celebrated *versus populum* "has turned the community into a self-enclosed circle. In its outward form, it no longer opens out on what lies ahead and above, but is closed in on itself."[26] The liturgy, which is the unified worship of God by the Church, can be characterized as a monologue with this form of worship because the Church visibly fixes her gaze upon herself. By contrast, Ratzinger argues that with the liturgy celebrated *ad orientem*, "[The members of the Church] did not close themselves into a circle; they did not gaze at one another; but as the pilgrim People of God they set off for the *Oriens*, for the Christ who comes to meet us."[27] The eschatological and cosmological symbolism of the liturgy is obscured by worship *versus populum*.

Ratzinger's desire to restore worship *ad orientem* is motivated by his wish to allow the liturgy's true nature to become clearly evident to all participants. Ratzinger opines that worship *ad orientem* "is not a case

---

[24] Bouyer, *Liturgy and Architecture*, 56.
[25] JRCW11, 47 (JRGS11, 80).
[26] JRCW11, 49 (JRGS11, 82).
[27] JRCW11, 49 (JRGS11, 82).

of something accidental; rather, it is a matter of what is essential. Looking at the priest has no importance. What matters is looking together at the Lord."[28] The liturgy, which unfolds in present history, should always be oriented towards the eschaton. The Church's identity as the Body of Christ is best expressed by unity of action and participation within the liturgy. Consequently, the celebrant is never turning his back towards the people when he offers the Mass *ad orientem*. Instead, the celebrant is leading the people in worship towards the Lord. Ratzinger proposes a practical solution which upholds the ancient tradition of worship *ad orientem* that could be easily carried out by any parish.

Consistent with the Christocentric characteristic of his theology and the history of Christian worship, Ratzinger proposes the idea of placing a crucifix on the altar during the celebration of the liturgy as a symbol of the eschatological and cosmological nature of the liturgy.[29] In Ratzinger's estimation, a cross at the center of the altar could symbolize the "interior 'east' of faith."[30] The question of the celebrant's orientation during the

---

[28] JRCW11, 50 (JRGS11, 82).

[29] For a comprehensive treatment of the symbolism of the cross in relation to the Eucharist based on historical, theological, and liturgical sources, see Daniel Cardó, *The Cross and the Eucharist in Early Christianity: A Theological and Liturgical Investigation* (Cambridge: Cambridge University Press, 2020).

[30] JRCW11, 51 (JRGS11, 85). Ratzinger is reechoing a point he has made earlier in his work *The Feast of Faith*: "Traditionally, the 'east' and the image of the cross (that is, the cosmic and soteriological aspects of spirituality) were fused; the cross itself, which may originally have had a purely eschatological significance, called to mind the Lord's suffering, faith in the Resurrection, and the hope of the parousia, that is, it signified the whole tension of the Christian concept of time. It is this tension which has transformed star time into human time and into God's time—for God *is not* time, but he *has* time for us." JRCW11, 391 (JRGS11, 467). In responses to critics of his position, such as Pierre Gy, Ratzinger offers a response that once again reiterates his consistent position: "[T]he great tradition of 'orientation,' the act of turning toward the 'Orient' as the image of the return of Christ, in no way requires that all altars must once again be reversed and that the priest's place be changed as a consequence. . . . [O]ne can satisfy the internal requirements of this apostolic tradition without undertaking great external transformations, by arranging things such that the Cross . . . should be the common focal point of the priest and the faithful—such that it is placed in the middle of the altar, and not to the side. The Christ who was crucified and who returns today is the true *oriens*, the direction of history. He personifies the synthesis of the cosmic and historical orientation of the liturgy, so central in the tradition of prayer towards the Orient." Ratzinger, "*The Spirit of the Liturgy* or Fidelity to the Council: Response to Father Gy," *Antiphon* 11, no. 1 (2007): 98–101. Cf. Michael Kunzler, "Die kosmische Dimension der Eucharistiefeier: Zu Fragen ihrer liturgischen Gestalt bei Joseph Ratzinger," in *Der Logos-gemäße Gottesdienst: Theologie der Liturgie bei Joseph Ratzinger*, ed. Rudolf

liturgy is not superficial. Ratzinger favors liturgy *ad orientem* or the placement of a cross on the altar (which has become known as a "Benedictine arrangement" because this became a standard arrangement for the altar at St. Peter's Basilica with Pope Benedict) as a symbolic *ad orientem* because the essence of the liturgy is made plainly visible to every participant. The Paschal Mystery is at the heart of Christian worship. Consequently, the placement of the cross on the altar symbolizes this centrality within the celebration of the liturgy.[31]

Christ is the true *Oriens*, and it is only fitting that this external symbol be used to manifest this internal reality that is taking place within the sacred liturgy. The placement of the cross at the center of the altar can highlight the place of the Cross and the true meaning of sacrifice that all Christians are called to embrace in imitation of Christ: "Christian sacrifice is nothing other than the exodus of the 'for' that abandons itself, a process perfected in the man who is all exodus, all self-surpassing love. The fundamental principle of Christian worship is consequently this movement of exodus with its two-in-one direction toward God and fellow man."[32] Ratzinger will continue to emphasize that the key to understanding sacrifice, which is at the heart of the exodus that the person is called to, is love and not destruction.[33] The cross serves as a symbol for the fulfillment of the human person's true nature as gift. The Christian is able

---

Voderholzer, (Regensburg: Friedrich Pustet, 2009), 200–203. Kunzler discusses the option of the placement of the cross on the altar symbolizing worship *ad orientem*. He argues that this is only a temporary solution when the ideal should be for the celebrant to face the East with the congregation during the Eucharist. For the larger context of this topic, see his discussion of liturgy *ad orientem* in Kunzler, "Die komische Dimension der Eucharistiefeier," 188–200.

[31] JRCW11, 579 (JRGS11, 701): "The Cross stands in the center of the Christian liturgy, with all of its seriousness. . . . The redemption cost God the suffering and the death of his Son, and its *exercitium*, which is what the liturgy is, according to [*Sacrosanctum Concilium*], cannot take place without the purification and maturation involved in following the way of the Cross."

[32] Joseph Ratzinger, *Introduction to Christianity* [hereafter, *IC*], trans. J. R. Foster (San Francisco: Ignatius Press, 2004), 289; Joseph Ratzinger, *Einführung in das Christentum: Bekenntnis—Taufe—Nachfolge*, Joseph Ratzinger Gesammelte Shriften 4, [hereafter, JRGS4] ed. Gerhard Ludwig Müller (Freiburg: Herder, 2014), 264.

[33] "The fundamental principle of the sacrifice is not destruction but love. And even this principle only belongs to the sacrifice to the extent that love breaks down, opens up, crucifies, tears—as the form that love takes in a world characterized by death and self-seeking." *IC*, 289 (JRGS4, 264). Ratzinger identifies the Christian as having received a call "to the continual exodus of going beyond himself" in imitation of the Pasch of Christ. *IC*, 253 (JRGS4, 233).

to enter into Christ's existence "for" humanity through a life of self-giving love. Not only is the Christian called to worship *ad orientem* (or *ad crucem*), he is called to live his life oriented towards the self-giving love of Christ. Sacrifice is meant to characterize his life, which is why Ratzinger emphasizes the *logikē latreia* as the true nature of Christian liturgy.[34] The sacrificial love of Christ must become a daily reality in the life of a Christian. In this manner, what Christ did "once and for all" (*semel*) is "always" (*semper*) carried out.[35]

The celebration of the liturgy *ad orientem*, or the placement of a crucifix in the center of the altar, serves as a symbol for the entrance of Christ's past sacrifice into the present while at the same time anticipating the future reality of the eschaton. The point of departure for Ratzinger's theology of the liturgy is not the Eucharist offered *ad orientem*, but it is focused on the true nature of the liturgy. In a response to one of his critics, Olivier Bauer, Ratzinger maintains, "My starting point is not the *orientation* of prayer (prayer facing east) but, rather, the question about what 'cult' or 'liturgy' really is—what happens in it and what kind of reality it is. This question must be approached anthropologically and historically."[36] Historically, the Eucharist is *Logos*-centric and has been shaped by worship in the synagogue and the Temple.

The Eucharist enables the human person to participate intimately in the sacrifice of Christ. Ratzinger describes this *logos*-centric anthropology: "It is [the human person], conforming himself to *logos* and becoming *logos* through faith, who is the true sacrifice, the true glory of God in the world."[37] The liturgy assists the human person in actualizing his potency to become a living sacrifice of love like Christ. Ratzinger's insistence on worship *ad orientem* or the use of the Benedictine arrangement on the altar serves the purpose of reinforcing this Christocentric anthropology. Similarly, Ratzinger maintains the central role beauty plays in serving as an outward sign of the mystery of

---

[34] As was noted previously, Ratzinger emphasizes the "[Liturgy] is meant to be indeed a *logikē latreia*, the 'logicizing' [*Logisierung*] of my existence, my interior contemporaneity with the self-giving of Christ. His self-giving is meant to become mine, so that I become contemporary with the Pasch of Christ and assimilated unto God." JRCW11, 34 (JRGS11, 65–66).

[35] See JRCW11, 34–36 (JRGS11, 64–68).

[36] JRCW11, 570 (JRGS11, 685).

[37] JRCW11, 27 (JRGS11, 57). Also see Pope Benedict XVI, *Post-synodal Apostolic Exhortation Sacramentum caritatis* [hereafter, *SCa*] (Vatican City: Libreria Editrice Vaticana, 2007), §§70–71, wherein he reiterates and develops a Eucharistic anthropology or Eucharistic personalism.

Christ and the heavenly Jerusalem present within the sacred liturgy.

The eschatological nature of the liturgy was symbolized clearly when the liturgy was only celebrated *ad orientem*. Despite the critiques and mis-understandings, Ratzinger's main interest in calling for the restoration of worship *ad orientem* or the compromise of placing a cross on the altar has nothing to do with any sort of nostalgia. His desire is for the faithful to understand the cosmic and eschatological nature of the sacred liturgy, which has become displaced by only celebrating the liturgy *versus populum*. The main purpose of his theology of liturgy is to make clear the meaning of the liturgy, which cannot be separated from understanding the Church as the Mystical Body celebrating the liturgy, which joins the celebrant with the congregation in a united focus on Christ as the true *Oriens*. The orientation of the faithful towards Christ the incarnate *Logos* must be reflected in every aspect of life for a people who are made to adore and glorify God.

## Homo adorans

A foundational theme for understanding Ratzinger, which has been established in the previous section, is that his theology of liturgy is characterized by the concept of symbolism. Ratzinger highlights worship *ad orientem* as a clearer symbol of the liturgy's eschatological and cosmological nature. Jesus Christ literally embodies by his nature the type of person that every believer should become by grace. In an address to the Guardini Foundation Congress on October 29, 2010, Pope Benedict XVI explained the symbolic nature of the liturgy highlighted by Guardini, who undoubtedly influenced his own thought:

> The liturgy is symbolic action. The symbol as the quintessence of the oneness of the spiritual and the material is lost when these separate, when the world is split in half, into spirit and flesh, into subject and object. Guardini was profoundly convinced that man is *spirit in flesh and flesh in spirit* and that the liturgy and the symbol therefore [should] lead him to the essence of himself and ultimately, through worship, to the truth.[38]

---

[38] Benedict XVI, *A Reason Open to God: On Universities, Education, and Culture*, ed. J. Stephen Brown (Washington, DC: The Catholic University of America Press, 2013), 204.

The liturgy should be celebrated in such a way that a person can come to know the *Logos,* the incarnation of the Truth, as a living person whom he is called to adore.

The liturgy forms the person into what he was created to be from the beginning, a *homo adorans*, which Schmemann clearly argues is the purpose of human existence:

> All rational, spiritual and other qualities of the person, distinguishing him from other creatures, have their focus and ultimate fulfillment in this capacity to bless God, to know, so to speak, the meaning of the thirst and hunger that constitutes his life. *"Homo sapiens," "homo faber"* . . . yes, but, first of all, *"homo adorans."* The first, the basic definition of the person is that he is *the priest.* He stands in the center of the world and unifies it in his act of blessing God, of both receiving the world from God and offering it to God—and by filling the world with this eucharist, he transforms his life, the one that he receives from the world, into life in God, into communion with Him. The world was created as the "matter," the material of one all-embracing eucharist, and the person was created as the priest of this cosmic sacrament.[39]

The person was created to be a *homo adorans*, but in practice he has become above all else, a *homo faber*. Ratzinger and other theologians of the twentieth and twenty-first centuries have examined the consequence of this loss in the understanding of the human person as a *homo adorans*: the subordination of *logos* to *ethos*, "doing" replacing "being," material progress valued over the pursuit of sanctity, and the individual rights of the autonomous "I" trumping the good of the communal "we."[40] The ability

---

[39] Alexander Schmemann, *For the Life of the World: Sacraments and Orthodoxy* (Crestwood, NY: St. Vladimir's Seminary Press, 1982), 15. On the vocation of the human person to be a *homo adorans*, see David W. Fagerberg, *Theologia Prima: What is Liturgical Theology*, 2nd ed. (Mundelein, IL: Hillenbrand Books, 2004), 19–32. Also see his *Consecrating the World: On Mundane Liturgical Theology* (Kettering, OH: Angelico Press, 2016), 93–113.

[40] One of the thinkers who has played a role in the shift towards the predominance of the human person as a *homo faber* is the Italian philosopher Giambattista Vico (1668–1744). Summarizing Vico's contribution, Ratzinger maintains, "Against the Scholastic equation *verum est ens* (being is truth) he advances his own formula, *verum quia factum*. That is to say, all that we can truly know is what we have made ourselves." *IC*, 59 (JRGS4, 71). As the understanding of truth shifts from being (*ens*) to what is made (*factum*), then worship becomes subject to the whims of human caprice. For further

for the human person to see his sacramental ontology becomes difficult with the predominance of *technē*.

The misunderstanding of human nature and the purpose of the human person, which is a result of understanding the human person apart from his true identity in Jesus Christ, has contributed to the identification of the person as solely a *homo faber*. Commenting on the implications of the materialist ontology, Ratzinger claims "the reduction of the person to *homo faber*, who does not deal with things in themselves but considers them only as functions of work, whose functionary he himself has become" ultimately impedes his ability "to see the eternal fall by the wayside."[41] Consequently, Ratzinger concludes that the person as a *homo faber* "is now imprisoned in his world of work, and his only hope is that later generations will be able to have better working conditions than he did, if he has toiled sufficiently for the creation of such conditions."[42] Although the person was created to be the priest of the cosmos, he has been reduced to a worker, or worse yet, a mere functionary. In order for the person to overcome this trend, he must understand the symbolism and signs employed in worship.

The challenge to engage the human person in liturgy is not without its share of difficult questions. In 1964, Romano Guardini addressed a letter ("Der Kultakt und die gegenwärtige Aufgabe der Liturgie") to a group of bishops, priests, theologians and liturgists gathered for the Third Liturgical Conference in Mainz, where he raised his concerns:

> Is not the liturgical act and, with it, all that goes under the name of "liturgy" so bound up with the historical background—antique or medieval or baroque—that it would be more honest to give it up altogether? Would it not be better to admit that the person in this industrial and scientific age, with its new sociological structure, is no longer capable of a liturgical act?[43]

---

commentary on this shift in the history of ideas, see *IC*, 58–69 (JRGS4, 70–79). Also, see Joseph Ratzinger, *The Nature and Mission of Theology: Approaches to Understanding Its Role in the Light of the Present Controversy* [hereafter, *NMT*], trans. Adrian Walker (San Francisco: Ignatius Press, 1995), 36–37. For an insightful summary of the larger cultural and philosophical ideas that contribute to this triumph of action and technocracy, see Michael Hanby, "*Homo Faber* and/or *Homo Adorans*: On the Place of Human Making in a Sacramental Cosmos," *Communio* 38 (Summer 2011): 198–236.

[41] JRCW11, 166 (JRGS11, 212).

[42] JRCW11, 166 (JRGS11, 212).

[43] Romano Guardini, "Der Kultakt und die gegenwärtige Aufgabe der Liturgie: Ein Brief," in *Liturgisches Jahrbuch* 14 (1964): 101–16. "A Letter from Romano Guardini," *Herder Correspondence* (Special Issue, 1964): 25, quoted in Robert Krieg, ed., *Romano*

A person in the modern (or post-modern) world cannot fully participate in the liturgy without some knowledge and understanding of what the liturgy is and the significance of the various signs, symbols, and gestures.[44] This will help the modern person to recover his existence as a *homo adorans* and to participate and prepare for the eschaton. The visible signs celebrated in the sacraments "have become carriers of [Christ's] historical significance and his spiritual might and thus, in truth, salvific forces and a pledge of the coming glory."[45] One of the fundamental concepts which must be comprehended in order to appreciate the notion of the person as a *homo adorans* is the phrase (which we explained previously) emphasized by the liturgical movement and viewed as a hallmark of the Second Vatican Council's Constitution on the Liturgy: *participatio actuosa*.[46]

Every person is called to participate fully, consciously, and actively in the sacred liturgy, but the controversy surrounds how one defines this participation. In various writings concerning his theology of liturgy, Ratzinger addresses the significance and authentic meaning of *participatio actuosa*.[47] The presupposition for understanding Ratzinger's explication of the meaning of the phrase is to discuss his definition for

---

*Guardini: Proclaiming the Sacred in the Modern World* (Chicago, IL: Liturgical Training Press, 1995), 88.

[44] Pope Emeritus Benedict XVI describes the need for mystagogical catechesis to address this issue: "A mystagogical catechesis must also be concerned with *presenting the meaning of the signs* contained in the rites. This is particularly important in a highly technological age like our own, which risks losing the ability to appreciate signs and symbols. More than simply conveying information, a mystagogical catechesis should be capable of making the faithful more sensitive to the language of signs and gestures which, together with the word, make up the rite." *SCa*, §64.

[45] JRCW11, 164 (JRGS11, 210).

[46] Active participation is a theme emphasized throughout *Sacrosanctum Concilium*. See *Sacrosanctum Concilium*, in Norman P. Tanner, ed., *Decrees of the Ecumenical Councils*, 2 vols. (Washington, DC: Sheed & Ward and Georgetown University Press, 1990), §§11, 14, 27, 30, 41, 48.

[47] See JRCW11, 106–110 (JRGS11, 147–51); JRCW11, 324–29 (JRGS11, 389–95); JRCW11, 440 (JRGS 11, 524); JRCW11, 526–27 (JRGS11, 621–622); JRCW11, 533–34 (JRGS11, 629–30); JRCW11, 585–86 (JRGS11, 707–09). Benedict XVI comments on the common misunderstanding of the authentic meaning of active participation which has occurred following the Second Vatican Council: "[W]e must not overlook the fact that some misunderstanding has occasionally arisen concerning the precise meaning of [active] participation. It should be made clear that the word 'participation' does not refer to mere external activity during the celebration. In fact, the active participation called for by the Council must be understood in more substantial terms, on the basis of a greater awareness of the mystery being celebrated and its relationship to daily life." *SCa*, §52.

the liturgy. In his lecture delivered at Fontgombault, it has been discussed that he uses *Sacrosanctum Concilium* to underscore the meaning of the liturgy as "an action of Christ the Priest and of his Body, which is the Church."[48] Furthermore, Ratzinger emphasizes the Council's insistence on the liturgy as the "work of the redemption that Christ accomplished especially by the Paschal Mystery of His Passion, of his Resurrection from the dead, and his glorious Ascension."[49] Throughout his work, it has become evident that Ratzinger places great emphasis on the liturgy as the celebration of the Pasch in the present. The above texts cited from the Second Vatican Council are ecclesiological and Christological. Although Ratzinger does not use the following definition for liturgy, a Trinitarian definition of the liturgy from Fagerberg certainly demonstrates an affinity between their views:

> *Liturgy is the Trinity's perichoresis kenotically extended to invite our synergistic ascent into deification.* In other words, the Trinity's circulation of love turns itself outward, and in humility the Son and Spirit work the Father's good pleasure for all creation, which is to invite our ascent to participate in the life of God."[50]

What the three definitions share in common is the theme present throughout Ratzinger's theology—namely, that the liturgy is first and foremost an *opus Dei*. What is stressed by the ecclesiological and trinitarian definitions is the cooperation and participation that every believer is called to experience within the sacred liturgy. In light of these definitions of the liturgy, participation is only artificially understood if it is reduced to mere external activity.

Human nature is such that people express themselves externally, but they also have internal dispositions that are a part of their human activity. As a result of the distinction between internal and external activity, a person may externally do something that does not correspond with their internal disposition. A person can simply articulate the responses within the liturgy, merely out of rote habit, without truly thinking or intending what is said. Ratzinger comments, "For community to exist, there must be some common *expression*, but lest this expression be merely external, there

---

[48] *SC*, §7.

[49] JRCW11, 541 (JRGS11, 639). Here Ratzinger alludes to *SC*, §5.

[50] Fagerberg, *On Liturgical Asceticism* (Washington, DC: The Catholic University of America Press, 2013), 9.

must be also a common movement of *internalization*, a shared path inward (and upward)."[51] Simply put, the shared external expression in responses and gestures is not sufficient to have an authentic community celebrating the liturgy together. The key for Ratzinger is the process of interiorizing the outward gestures and responses "by an entering into the liturgical word and the liturgical reality—which is the presence of the Lord—and by enabling [the faithful] inwardly to communicate with him who first communicated himself to us all, in his self-surrender on the Cross."[52] There is no possible way for every person to participate fully if there is an emphasis on external actions or roles in the liturgy to the neglect of the interior aspect of participation. Following the Second Vatican Council, Ratzinger comments, "Where this inner dimension was neglected, the liturgy still seemed 'boring' and 'unintelligible,' with the result that ultimately the Bible was replaced by Marx and the sacrament by a kind of 'party' atmosphere."[53] The stress placed on the external aspect of participation has the risk of overemphasizing the horizontal dimension in worship to the point of absurdity. In an extreme form, the liturgy is reduced merely to the activity or work of the human person.

In a methodical attempt to explain *participatio actuosa*, Ratzinger highlights the significance of *oratio* as the central *action,* in which every believer is called to participate during the liturgy. In light of the liturgical sources, Ratzinger argues, "The real liturgical action, the true liturgical act, is the *oratio*, the great [Eucharistic] prayer that forms the core of the Eucharistic celebration, called *oratio* by the Fathers."[54] In its etymology, *oratio* originally means "solemn public speech," which has great significance as one considers that the Eucharistic prayer is addressed to God "in full awareness that it comes from him and is made possible by him."[55] The liturgy, according to the Second Vatican Council cited previously by Ratzinger, is an action of the entire body of Christ. Hence, the *oratio* is the central act within the liturgy. In the *oratio* of the liturgy expressed by the words "This is my Body" and "This is my Blood," Ratzinger claims this "action of God, which takes place through human speech, is the real 'action' for which all of creation is in expectation. . . . The real 'action' in the liturgy in which we are all supposed to participate is the action of

---

[51] JRCW11, 325 (JRGS11, 390).
[52] JRCW11, 325 (JRGS11, 390).
[53] JRCW11, 526–7 (JRGS11, 622).
[54] JRCW11, 106 (JRGS11, 147).
[55] JRCW11, 107 (JRGS11, 148).

God himself."[56] Such an emphasis seems to preclude human cooperation, but the opposite is true. By the very fact that God himself is acting, the believer is able to participate in the inner life and love of God. One of the distinguishing characteristics of Christian liturgy "lies precisely in the fact that God himself is acting and that we are drawn into that action of God. Everything else is, therefore, secondary."[57] In both liturgy and eschatology, Ratzinger consistently maintains the primacy of God's action without excluding the cooperation of the human person. At this point, Ratzinger is able to address the role of the body in worship.

As discussed in the previous chapter, the believer is able to bring the liturgy to life. Jean Corbon aptly describes the call to live out the liturgy celebrated: "The power of the Spirit has configured us to the crucified body of Jesus [in the liturgy]; it must now manifest in our mortal flesh the power of his Resurrection."[58] The effect of the liturgy must become visible in the "liturgical" life of the Christian: "The true liturgical action is the deed of God, and for that very reason the liturgy of faith always reaches beyond the cultic act into everyday life, which must itself become 'liturgical,' a service for the transformation of the world."[59] The liturgy is meant to be the training or *askēsis* for the body to prepare for the eschaton: "A demand is made on the body in all its involvement in the circumstances of everyday life. The body is required to become 'capable of resurrection' [*auferstehungsfähig*], to orient itself toward the resurrection, toward the Kingdom of God."[60] In the formation of the human person as a *homo adorans*, the understanding of the liturgical gestures and postures is critical. The symbolic actions in the liturgy prepare the person for the eternal

---

[56] JRCW11, 107 (JRGS11, 148).

[57] JRCW11, 108 (JRGS11, 149).

[58] Jean Corbon, *The Wellspring of Worship*, trans. Matthew J. O'Connell, 2nd ed. (San Francisco: Ignatius Press, 2005), 203.

[59] JRCW11, 109 (JRGS11, 150). Corbon comments on the participation of the body as part of the transformation of the person in his entirety: "In order for the celebration [of the liturgy] to effect a transfiguration of the body of Christ, it must involve the whole person, who is a 'body.' If the light of Tabor touches human beings at the level of the 'heart,' that is, the innermost core of the freedom that has been delivered from structures, it is in order that their entire being may be enlightened and divinized. A cerebral celebration inevitably leads by way of compensation to the intellectual or emotional self-satisfaction. In contrast, an integral celebration of the liturgy leads the participant to the center of faith and finds expression in communion, both of the individual and of the community." Corbon, *The Wellspring of Worship*, 123.

[60] JRCW11, 109 (JRGS11, 150). David Fagerberg's work *On Liturgical Asceticism* is devoted to this aspect of the liturgy.

liturgy, but one cannot fully participate in the liturgy when a person lacks a basic knowledge of the symbols.

The symbol used with great frequency in the life of worship and private prayer is the Sign of the Cross. This most basic gesture is "a visible and public Yes to him who suffered for us," which serves as both a "confession of faith" and as a "confession of hope" in Christ whereby "we place ourselves under the protection of the Cross."[61] It is a humble gesture of faith and confidence in Jesus Christ and the power of the Cross. Beyond Christ's Passion and death, the Cross is a sign of the Resurrection, as the Sign of the Cross is connected with faith in the Trinity. Thus, the Sign of the Cross serves as a way to remember one's Baptism.[62]

The sign of the Cross, which is a distinctively Christian symbol, as it is an outward sign of faith in Christ and the Trinity, has older roots in the Old Testament. Citing Ezekiel 9:4–6, Ratzinger describes the use of the Cross as a seal of God's ownership since those who do not participate in the sin of the world are marked according to the prophetic vision by "the last letter of the Hebrew alphabet, the *Tav*, which was written in the form of a cross (T or + or X)."[63] The Fathers of the Church, particularly St. Justin Martyr, discovered in the writings of Plato "the remarkable idea of a cross [the Greek letter *Chi* or X] inscribed upon the cosmos (cf. *Timaeus* 34ab and 36bc)."[64] The Sign of the Cross becomes a truly universal sign that is prophesized by both the Jews and the Greeks. At the end of time, Jesus announced that "the sign of the Son of man" (Matt 24:30) would be manifested for everyone to see.[65] The use of this sign as a blessing would be a profession of faith but also a preparation to see this eschatological sign. Hence, the Sign of the Cross is forever an essential gesture that expresses the great unity between belief (*lex credendi*) and prayer (*lex orandi*).

Throughout the celebration of the liturgy, the faithful engage in a series of postures: kneeling, standing, and sitting. The significance or meaning behind these simple postures is taken for granted. Consequently, people literally go through the motions during the celebration of every liturgy. Kneeling is an expression of faith that did not originate with any particular culture. Its origins as a practice are rooted in Sacred Scripture wherein the Greek word for kneeling, *proskynein*, occurs in several

---

61 JRCW11, 110 (JRGS11, 152).
62 JRCW11, 110–11 (JRGS11, 152–153).
63 JRCW11, 111 (JRGS11, 153).
64 JRCW11, 112–13 (JRGS11, 154–55).
65 JRCW11, 114 (JRGS11, 156).

instances throughout the New Testament. Ratzinger notes that the word is used twenty-four times in the Book of Revelation, "which is presented to the Church as the standard for her own liturgy."[66] Within the New Testament, there are actually three postures, closely related to one another, used by the sacred authors: lying prostrate facedown on the ground before God, kneeling before another, and simply kneeling.[67] Ratzinger describes the straightforward spiritual meaning of kneeling, in its various forms, as an act of worship. Consistent with the authentic meaning of *participatio actuosa*, Ratzinger maintains, "Without the worship, the bodily gesture would be meaningless, while the spiritual act must of its very nature, because of the psychosomatic unity of man, express itself in the bodily gesture. The two aspects are united in one word, because in a very profound way they belong together."[68] The internal act of worship is made visible through the external sign of the body kneeling before the Lord. Within Sacred Scripture, Ratzinger highlights this Pauline text as the most significant passage for the theology of kneeling, as Paul proclaims that Jesus has the "name which is above every name, that at the name of Jesus every knee should bow, in heaven and on earth and under the earth" (Phil 2:9–10).[69] Jesus, crucified and risen from the dead, becomes the one to whom all Christians kneel in worship in unison with the entire cosmos. As a result of God descending to the earth in the Incarnation, kneeling enters the world as an outward sign of adoration. Ratzinger concludes that "the person who learns to believe learns also to kneel, and a faith or a liturgy no longer familiar with kneeling would be sick at the core."[70] As a humble gesture of adoration, kneeling is an essential part of the liturgy.

The outward postures of standing and sitting also reveal certain dispositions that the soul should maintain during the celebration of the liturgy. Patristic scholar Gabriel Bunge describes the general meaning of standing: "For the Christian, standing reverently before God in prayer means that he is aware that in the *Person* of God he has a real *interlocutor* who is most

---

[66] JRCW11, 116 (JRGS11, 158). On the patristic understanding of kneeling, see Gabriel Bunge, O.S.B., *Earthen Vessels: The Practice of Personal Prayer According to the Patristic Tradition*, trans. Michael J. Miller (San Francisco: Ignatius Press, 2002), 163–171.

[67] JRCW11, 116 (JRGS11, 159).

[68] JRCW11, 119 (JRGS11, 162). Elsewhere Ratzinger comments, "When a person kneels, he lowers himself, but his eyes still look forward and upward, as when he stands, toward the One who faces him. To kneel is to be oriented toward the One who looks upon us and toward whom we try to look." JRCW11, 124 (JRGS11, 167).

[69] See JRCW11, 120–21 (JRGS11, 163–64).

[70] JRCW11, 121–22 (JRGS11, 165).

certainly present."[71] Similar to kneeling, the posture of standing is recognition of who God is and what he has done for humanity. Consequently, Ratzinger argues, "[S]tanding was primarily the Easter form of prayer."[72] In light of a canon from the Council of Nicaea that calls for standing during the Eastertide, Easter is "the time of victory of Jesus Christ, the time of joy, in which we show forth the Paschal victory of the Lord, even in the posture of our prayer."[73] The posture of standing is an outward sign of celebration and joy in the Paschal Mystery, in whose victory Christians are called to participate.

Standing is also a sign of readiness in imitation of Christ, who stands at the right hand of God the Father ready to welcome us into the eternal kingdom. Ratzinger describes the readiness symbolized by standing during the liturgy: "When we stand, we know that we are united to the victory of Christ, and when we stand to listen to the Gospel, it is an expression of reverence. When this Word is heard, we cannot remain sitting; it pulls us up."[74] As Jesus is always ready for the faithful to experience the joys of heaven in communion with the saints, Christians must be prepared to give a bold and courageous witness to the love of Christ in the world.[75]

Connected with the posture of standing is the traditional gesture of praying with outstretched hands. It was not unusual to find the portrayal of Christians as *orantes* within early Christian iconography.[76] This particular gesture is eschatological as the *orans* position represents prayer in the glorified state. This gesture of prayer leads Ratzinger to conclude that

---

[71] Bunge, *Earthen Vessels*, 147. For Bunge's summary of the patristic teaching on standing, see Bunge, *Earthen Vessels*, 141–152.

[72] JRCW11, 122 (JRGS11, 165).

[73] JRCW11, 122 (JRGS11, 165–66). The twentieth canon from the First Council of Nicaea declares, "Since there are some who kneel on Sunday and during the season of Pentecost, this holy synod declares that, so that the same observances may be maintained in every diocese, one should offer one's prayers to the Lord standing." "First Council of Nicaea," in Norman P. Tanner, ed., *Decrees of the Ecumenical Councils*, 2 vols. (Washington, DC: Sheed & Ward and Georgetown University Press, 1990), 16.

[74] JRCW11, 123 (JRGS11, 166).

[75] Elsewhere Ratzinger comments on the symbolism of standing as it relates to Corpus Christi processions. See JRCW11, 405–7 (JRGS11, 483–86). There, Ratzinger expresses the solidarity or communion with the other members of the Church represented by standing: "We are standing for the Lord. And the more we stand for the Lord and before the Lord, the more we stand with one another, and our capacity to understand one another grows again, the capacity, to recognize each other as people, as brothers and sisters, and thus, in being together, to build the basis and to open up the possibilities of humanity and of life." JRCW11, 407 (JRGS11, 485–86).

[76] Bunge, *Earthen Vessels*, 149.

"standing prayer is an anticipation of the future, of the glory that is to come; it is meant to orient us toward it. Insofar as liturgical prayer is an anticipation of what has been promised, standing is its proper posture."[77] Standing represents readiness for the eschaton. Finally, sitting is an outward sign of recollection and meditation that listens attentively to the Word of God that is proclaimed and preached. As with the various postures of the body, the gestures used during the liturgy should also reflect outwardly the interior disposition of the soul in order for a person to perfect their actual participation in the liturgy.[78] Every liturgical gesture, if done with proper awareness and understanding, can assist with our preparation for the eschaton.

The centrality of the *Logos* within the liturgy gives the word and the human voice a central role within the liturgy's prayers of *dia-logos*. Ratzinger differentiates between the three different modes in which the human voice is used: (1) the *oratio* of the priest, who on behalf of the community "speaks through Christ, in the Holy Spirit, to the Father," (2) varying kinds of proclamation such as the readings, the Gospel, and the homily, and (3) the response to the word from the congregation.[79] The dynamic between the Word and the response is modelled after the manner in which God reveals himself to his Bride, the Church. Ratzinger outlines this structure of revelation: "God, the Revealer, did not want to stay as *solus Deus, solus Christus* (God alone, Christ alone). No, he wanted to create a Body for himself, to find a Bride—he sought a response. It was really for her that the Word went forth."[80] God himself is dialogical, and, subsequently, his revelation takes on a dialogical form, which calls for the Church to enter into that dynamic of dialogical love. The liturgy is the privileged setting to hear the Word proclaimed and for the Church as one Body to offer her response. Along with the various forms of acclamation

---

[77] JRCW11, 123 (JRGS11, 166).

[78] Bunge summarizes well the relationship between the external action of the body and internal disposition of the soul: "Thus there is a genuine *reciprocity* between one's internal disposition and external posture. This is the 'special property' of the soul, which in the body's posture creates, so to speak, a suitable 'icon' of itself, which therefore always precedes it, as Origen says in this connection. Once such a visible representation exists, though—once a suitable gesture has been formed and has become a 'tradition' in the course of salvation history, then the individual cannot forgo it without harming his 'interior condition.' By making it his own, on the other hand, and 'practicing' it diligently, he forms and strengthens within himself that same interior disposition that once created the gesture, as Joseph Busnaya teaches." Bunge, *Earthen Vessels*, 146.

[79] JRCW11, 131 (JRGS11, 175).

[80] JRCW11, 132 (JRGS11, 176).

are the different responses of "meditative appropriation of the Word" in the form of song: hymnody, psalms, and antiphons.[81]

The Church has consistently taught that silence must have a role in the celebration of the liturgy.[82] After alluding to the need for active participation, the Second Vatican Council teaches "at the proper times all should observe a reverent silence."[83] What are the proper times, and what is reverent silence? Ratzinger offers both theoretical and practical wisdom concerning the role of silence in the liturgy. In describing the type of silence needed, Ratzinger asserts that there must be a "silence with content, not just the absence of speech and action. We should expect the liturgy to give us a positive stillness that will restore us."[84] The faithful need the opportunity to reflect upon the Word of God that has been proclaimed and the sacramental and incarnate Word that we receive at Holy Communion.

In an effort to promote a fruitful reverent silence that is still an "integral part of the liturgical event," Ratzinger emphasizes two periods that can be fruitfully used for silence: the period following Holy Communion and during the presentation of the gifts.[85] Silence after communion is "the moment for an interior conversation with the Lord who has given himself to us, for that essential 'communicating,' that entry into the process of communication, without which the external reception of the Sacrament becomes mere ritual and therefore unfruitful."[86] As a realist, Ratzinger notes that

---

[81] JRCW11, 132 (JRGS11, 176).

[82] On the subject of silence within the liturgy and its inestimable value in the life of individual and society, see Robert Cardinal Sarah (with Nicolas Diat), *The Power of Silence: Against the Dictatorship of Noise*, trans. Michael J. Miller (San Francisco: Ignatius Press, 2017).

[83] *SC*, §30. As Pontiff, Benedict XVI notes the call for more silence from a number of Synod Fathers who gathered in 2008 to discuss *The Word of God in the Life and Mission of the Church*: "The word, in fact, can only be spoken and heard in silence, outward and inward. Ours is not an age which fosters recollection; at times one has the impression that people are afraid of detaching themselves, even for a moment, from the mass media. For this reason, it is necessary nowadays that the People of God be educated in the value of silence. Rediscovering the centrality of God's word in the life of the Church also means rediscovering a sense of recollection and inner repose. The great patristic tradition teaches us that the mysteries of Christ all involve silence. Only in silence can the word of God find a home in us, as it did in Mary, woman of the word and, inseparably, woman of silence. Our liturgies must facilitate this attitude of authentic listening: *Verbo crescent, verba deficiunt*." Benedict XVI, Post-synodal Apostolic Exhortation *Verbum Domini* (Vatican City: Libreria Editrice Vaticana, 2010), §66.

[84] JRCW11, 132 (JRGS11, 176).

[85] JRCW11, 132–33 (JRGS11, 177).

[86] JRCW11, 133 (JRGS11, 177).

there is noise during the distribution of Communion, but nevertheless he affirms the necessity of silence during this period if at all possible.

The purpose of observing silence during the preparation of the gifts is to assist the faithful in realizing that they are "the real gift in the 'Word-centered sacrifice' through [their] sharing in Jesus Christ's act of self-offering to the Father."[87] Communal silence during this period can help the congregation to be prepared to make a sacrifice of themselves with Jesus on the altar and beyond. Both periods of silence will require guidance and catechesis on the value of silence and interior prayer. There are other periods of silence within the liturgy, but the greatest occurs during the consecration.[88] According to Ratzinger, "The Consecration is the moment of God's great *actio* in the world for us. It draws our eyes and hearts on high. For a moment the world is silent, everything is silent, and in that silence we touch the eternal—for one beat of the heart we step out of time into God's being-with-us."[89] Silence has an eschatological quality insofar as it can deepen our communion with God. Reverent silence enables people to pray in a manner that is truly "full, conscious, and active."

Postures, gestures, the use of voice and silence in the liturgy all serve the need of engaging the faithful in the prayer of the liturgy. The key to understanding Ratzinger's remarks on the topics above is to come back to the question of active participation (*participatio actuosa*). In a sermon delivered to the German Bishops' Conference in Fulda, Ratzinger clearly maintains, "No external participation and creativity is of any use unless it is a participation in this inner reality, in the way of the Lord, in God himself. Its aim is to lead us to this breakthrough to God."[90] All of the senses of the body are meant to be engaged in worship, but they are mere external actions if they are not accompanied by an inner awareness, understanding,

---

[87] JRCW11, 133 (JRGS11, 178).

[88] We will not address Ratzinger's theoretical proposal, which has received much criticism, regarding the praying of the Canon in silence. His comments deserve wider attention, but it would exceed our project to address the topic as we attempt to focus on the role of postures, gestures, and silence in the liturgy as means of preparation to participate in the sacrifice of Christ. See Ratzinger's remarks on his thesis regarding a silent Canon in JRCW11, 136–37 (JRGS11, 181–82). On the history of the use of and rationale for the silent recitation of liturgical prayers, see Uwe Michael Lang, *The Voice of the Church at Prayer: Reflections on Liturgy and Language* (San Francisco: Ignatius Press, 2012), 122–135. Also see Matthew S.C. Olver, "A Note on the Silent Canon in the Missal of Paul VI and Cardinal Ratzinger," *Antiphon* 20, no. 1 (2016): 40–51.

[89] JRCW11, 134 (JRGS11, 179).

[90] JRCW11, 533–34 (JRGS11, 630).

and sincerity. In response to Guardini's question cited at the beginning concerning whether a person in our contemporary culture would be capable of engaging in the liturgical act, Ratzinger would most certainly argue that he could, but this presupposes consistent liturgical formation and the support of the Church. In a culture dominated by technocracy, it is difficult for the person to become anything more than a *homo faber*. However, engaging the liturgy soberly with the entire body can assist in recovering the person's identity as a *homo adorans*.

In his discussion of liturgical gestures, Ratzinger underscores their role as a form of *askēsis* for the body. In the discipline and formation that lead the person to become a true *homo adorans*, "The body has a place within the divine worship of the Word made flesh, and it is expressed liturgically in a certain discipline [*askēsis*] of the body, in gestures that have developed out of the liturgy's inner demands and that make the essence of the liturgy, as it were, bodily visible."[91] Both the external movements of the body and the interior disposition of the soul must act with one accord within the celebration of the liturgy. At times, the person bows as a sign of reverence, he kneels as a sign of adoration and humility, he stands as a sign of readiness, or he listens in silence to recollect or prepare himself to meet the Lord. Above all, the person is constantly being invited to train the body and spirit to worship in "spirit and truth."

As discussed above with the Pauline *logikē latreia*, there is both a sacrifice of the body in accordance with *logos* and a renewal of the mind that work together as part of one unified act of worship. Explaining the symbolic meaning of the main gestures used within the liturgy underscores the idea that external actions or movements of the body have significance. At the same time, a person must interiorly kneel in adoration as one physically kneels. The external and internal movements within a person are not mutually exclusive. The discipline of the body and mind within the sacred liturgy is meant to serve as a preparation for and anticipation of the worship of eschatological life. The ultimate goal is for every *homo adorans* to participate fully in *logikē latreia* so that the individual believer can join in the worship not only with the communion of the Body of Christ below but also with the entire cosmos.

---

[91] JRCW11, 109–10 (JRGS11, 151).

# Via Pulchritudinis[92]

In his post-synodal apostolic exhortation *Sacramentum Caritatis*, Pope Benedict XVI maintains that the "liturgy is inherently linked to beauty: it is *veritatis splendor*."[93] The *veritatis splendor* that the liturgy reveals is Jesus Christ himself, who is the glory and personification of the eschaton and the living revelation, an icon, of the Father's love. Beauty is not merely an accidental or ornamental part of the liturgy. Because God himself and the heavenly Jerusalem are unveiled in sacramental form in the celebration of the liturgy, Benedict maintains that beauty is "an essential element of the liturgical action."[94] Through the person's active participation in the liturgy, he is transfigured in the beauty of Christ so that he can transform the culture through a Eucharistic life.

Beauty is a key element in the liturgical and Eucharistic theology of Ratzinger. Tracey Rowland argues that the transcendental of beauty was one of the central themes and concerns of Benedict's pontificate.[95] Ratzinger has the goal of transforming human culture with a theology of beauty that emphasizes cosmology and eschatology.[96] As head of the Congregation of the Doctrine of Faith, then-Cardinal Ratzinger was interviewed by Vittorio Messori. The course of their discussion inevitably led to the topic of the liturgy. In their conversation, Ratzinger states, "The only really effective apologia for Christianity comes down to two arguments, namely, the *saints* the Church has produced and the *art* which has grown in her womb."[97] Holiness and beauty go hand in hand in the

---

[92] Portions of this section were previously published as Roland Millare, "The Sacred is Still Beautiful: The Liturgical and Theological Aesthetics of Pope Benedict XVI," *Logos* 16, no. 1 (Winter 2013): 101–125.

[93] *SCa*, §35.

[94] *SCa*, §35.

[95] See Tracey Rowland, *Ratzinger's Faith: The Theology of Pope Benedict XVI* (Oxford: Oxford University Press, 2008), 8–9; 149–150. Also, see Rowland, *Benedict XVI*, 25–47; George Cardinal Pell, "The Concept of Beauty in the Writings of Joseph Ratzinger," in *Benedict XVI and Beauty in Sacred Art and Architecture: Proceedings of the Second Fota International Liturgical Conference, 2009*, ed. D. Vincent Twomey, SVD and Janet E. Rutherford (Dublin: Four Courts Press, 2011), 24–36; Blanco Sarto, *La Teología de Joseph Ratzinger: Una Introducción* (Madrid: Ediciones Palabra, 2011), 39–57.

[96] With respect to sacred art, Ratzinger posits, "[Sacred] art is always characterized by the unity of creation, Christology, and eschatology: the first day is on its way toward the eighth, which in turn takes up the first. Art is still ordered to the mystery that becomes present in the liturgy. It is still oriented to the heavenly liturgy. . . . In the liturgy the curtain between heaven and earth is torn open, and we are taken up into a liturgy that spans the whole cosmos." JRCW11, 77 (JRGS11, 114).

[97] Joseph Ratzinger, *The Ratzinger Report: An Interview with Vittorio Messori*, trans. Salvator

mind of Ratzinger. This is why the true transfiguration of culture begins with a re-beautification of the liturgy through an authentic "reform of the reform."[98] Ratzinger continues his response in his interview with Vittorio

---

Attanasio and Graham Harrison (San Francisco: Ignatius Press, 1985), 129. Ratzinger offers this position elsewhere, see Joseph Ratzinger, *On the Way to Jesus Christ*, trans. Michael J. Miller (San Francisco: Ignatius Press, 2004), 38: "I have often said that I am convinced that the true apologetics for the Christian message, the most persuasive proof of its truth, offsetting everything that may appear negative, are the saints, on the one hand, and the beauty that the faith has generated, on the other. For faith to grow today, we must lead ourselves and the persons we meet to encounter the saints and to come in contact with the beautiful."

[98] On the "reform of the reform" see Klaus Gamber, *Fragen in der Zeit: Kirche und Liturgie nach dem Vatikanum II* (Regensburg: Pustet, 1972); Gamber, *Reform of the Roman Liturgy: Its Problems and Background* (Fort Collins, CO: Roman Catholic Books, 1993). For a critical analysis of the thought of Klaus Gamber, see John F. Baldovin, S.J., "Klaus Gamber and the Post-Vatican II Reform of the Roman Liturgy," *Studia Liturgica* 33 (2003): 233–239. Cf. Manfred Hauke, "Klaus Gamber: father of the 'new liturgical movement,'" in *Benedict XVI and the Sacred Liturgy: Proceedings of the First Fota International Liturgical Conference*, ed. Janet Elaine Rutherford and Neil Roy (Dublin: Four Courts Press, 2008), 24–69. Also see James Hitchcock, *Recovery of the Sacred: Reforming the Reformed Liturgy* (San Francisco: Ignatius Press, 1995); Aidan Nichols, O.P., *Looking at the Liturgy: A Critical View of Its Contemporary Form* (San Francisco: Ignatius Press, 1996); Klaus Gamber, *The Modern Rite: Collected Essays on the Reform of the Liturgy*, trans. Henry Taylor (Beloit, WI: Dumb Ox Books, 2002); Thomas Kocik, *Reform of the Reform? A Liturgical Debate: Reform or Return* (San Francisco: Ignatius Press, 2003); Laszlo Dobszay, *The Bugnini-Liturgy and the Reform of the Reform* (Front Royal, VA: Catholic Church Music Associates, 2003); Thomas Kocik, "A Reform of the Reform?," in *T & T Clark Companion to Liturgy*, 317–38. Cf. László Dobszay, *The Restoration and Organic Development of the Roman Rite* (New York: T & T Clark International, 2010). Dobszay rejects the notion of a "reform of the reform": "I do not think that the content of the postconciliar reform liturgy can really be reformed. It is enough there to filter out the abuses and extremes, and to shepherd its practices back to that more in keeping with ecclesial tradition—remaining all the while within the sphere of the rite. . . . For those who believe in the higher quality of the classical Roman Rite, the aim of the following years is not the Reform of the Reform, but the Renovation of the Roman Rite and its organic development" (66–67). Also cf. John F. Baldovin, S.J., *Reforming the Liturgy: A Response to the Critics*; Massimo Faggioli, *True Reform: Liturgy and Ecclesiology in 'Sacrosanctum Concilium'* (Collegeville, MN: Liturgical Press, 2012); Paul Post, "Dealing with the Past in the Roman Catholic Liturgical 'Reform of the Reform Movement,'" *Questions Liturgiques* 87 (2006): 264–79. Baldovin offers one of the few nuances of the various critics of the reformed liturgy. He divides the critics into three groups: (1) extreme traditionalists, (2) proponents of "reforming the reform," and, finally, (3) a group comprised of critics who believed the reform was poorly implemented. The first group, which includes the Society of St. Pius X, Alcuin Reid, Didier Bonneterre, and Michael Davies, was very critical of the principles set forth by *Sacrosanctum Concilium*. The second group,

Messori cited above:

> If the Church is to continue to transform and humanize the world, how can she dispense with beauty in her liturgies, that beauty which is so closely linked with love and with the radiance of the Resurrection? No. Christians must not be too easily satisfied. They must make their Church into a place where beauty—and hence truth—is at home. Without this the world will become the first circle of hell.[99]

According to the Russian writer Fyodor Dostoevsky, "Beauty will save the world."[100] From his pre-papal and papal writings, it is clear that Pope Benedict believes beauty will save and reform the liturgy, and subsequently, it will save the world. Yet, it can only be salvific insofar as beauty transcends this world to point towards Christ, who is the form of beauty and sanctity itself. The encounter of Christians with the beautiful face of Jesus Christ is a frequent theme in Pope Benedict's papal addresses and homilies.[101] This

---

which is the major concern of his work, includes critics such as Klaus Gamber, Joseph Ratzinger, James Hitchcock, Kieran Flanagan, and Thomas Kocik. The proponents of "reforming the reform" maintain that the *Consilium ad exsequendam Constitutionem de Sacra Liturgia* went beyond the intention of the Council in their reforms of the liturgy. Finally, the last group, which includes Denis Crouan, Francis Manion, and Baldovin himself, maintain a critique based on the manner in which the liturgical reforms have or have not been implemented. Baldovin, *Reforming the Liturgy*, 134–35. For an overview of Ratzinger's reform of the reform, see Mariusz Biliniewicz, *The Liturgical Vision of Pope Benedict XVI: A Theological Inquiry* (Bern: Peter Lang, 2013), 107–149; Nicola Bux, *Benedict XVI's Reform: The Liturgy between Innovation and Tradition*, trans. Joseph Trabbic (San Francisco: Ignatius Press, 2012).

[99] Ratzinger, *The Ratzinger Report*, 130.

[100] Commenting on this oft-quoted remark from Dostoyevsky, Ratzinger maintains, "Usually people forget to mention, however, that by redeeming beauty Dostoyevsky means Christ. He it is whom we must learn to see. If we cease to know him only through words but are struck by the arrow of his paradoxical beauty, then we will truly come to know him and will no longer merely know about him at secondhand. Then we will have encountered the beauty of truth, of redeeming truth. Nothing can bring us into contact with the beauty of Christ himself more than the world of beauty created by faith and the light that shines upon the faces of the saints, through which his own light becomes visible." Ratzinger, *On the Way to Jesus Christ*, 41.

[101] On the role of Christ's face in the theological aesthetics of Ratzinger, see Joseph Murphy, "The Fairest and the Formless: the Face of Christ as Criterion for Christian Beauty According to Joseph Ratzinger," in *Benedict XVI and Beauty in Sacred Art and Architecture*, 37–53. On the general theme of Christ's face in the writings of Benedict see, Peter J. Casarella, "Searching for the Face of the Lord in Ratzinger's *Jesus of Nazareth*," in *The*

iconic Christology is the source and summit of his theological aesthetics.

In such considerations, he shares and re-echoes the sentiments of the Swiss theologian Hans Urs von Balthasar. Insofar as beauty ultimately reveals the face of Christ, it leads the person to discover the Truth.[102] Often, Pope Benedict makes reference to the *via pulchritudinis*, the path of beauty, which leads to the truth of the Faith. On November 21, 2009, during a meeting with artists in the Sistine Chapel, Pope Benedict notes:

> The theologian Hans Urs von Balthasar begins his great work entitled *The Glory of the Lord—A Theological Aesthetics* with these telling observations: "Beauty is the word with which we shall begin. Beauty is the last word that the thinking intellect dares to speak, because it simply forms a halo, an untouchable crown around the double constellation of the true and the good and their inseparable relation to one another." He then adds: "Beauty is the disinterested one, without which the ancient world refused to understand itself, a word which both imperceptibly and yet unmistakably has bid farewell to our new world, a world of interests, leaving it to its own avarice and sadness. It is no longer loved or fostered even by religion." And he concludes: "We can be sure that whoever sneers at her name as if she were the ornament of a bourgeois past—whether he admits it or not—can no longer pray and soon will no longer be able to love." The way of beauty leads us, then, to grasp the Whole in the fragment, the Infinite in the finite, God in the history of humanity.[103]

---

*Pope and Jesus of Nazareth*, ed. Adrian Pabst and Angus Paddison (London: SCM Press, 2009), 83–93. Also see Ratzinger, *On the Way to Jesus Christ*, 13–31.

[102] This is one of Ratzinger's themes in a message he sent to *Communio e Liberazione* (Communion and Liberation). Joseph Cardinal Ratzinger, "The Feeling of Things, the Contemplation of Beauty," Message to the Communion and Liberation (CL) Meeting, Rimini, August 24–30, 2002, *The Holy See*, accessed July 4, 2010, http://www.vatican.va/roman_curia/congregations/cfaith/documents/rc_con_cfaith_doc_20020824_ratzinger-cl-rimini_en.html.

[103] Benedict XVI, Address of His Holiness Benedict XVI to Artists, November 21, 2009, *The Holy See*, accessed June 23, 2010, https://www.vatican.va/content/benedict-xvi/en/speeches/2009/november/documents/hf_ben-xvi_spe_20091121_artisti.html. Elsewhere, Pope Benedict as Cardinal Ratzinger referred to the work of Hans Urs von Balthasar as his "Opus magnum of Theological Aesthetics." See Ratzinger, "The Feeling of Things, the Contemplation of Beauty." The use of the *via pulchritudinis* in catechesis and evangelization has been emphasized in recent magisterial teaching. See Francis, Post-synodal Apostolic Exhortation *Evangelii Gaudium* (Vatican City:

It is obvious that von Balthasar has had a significant influence on the pope emeritus' understanding of beauty. What differentiates them is that von Balthasar focuses on beauty's unifying role in the unfolding of divine revelation whereas Ratzinger focuses on beauty in the liturgy.[104] Benedict's writings and von Balthasar's theological aesthetics share a mutual foundation in that they are focused on the centrality of Christ. In order to appreciate the role of beauty as a transcendental, it is essential to begin with the development of aesthetics, particularly in the work of Aquinas and von Balthasar.

Oftentimes, Balthasarian scholars ignore the writings of St. Thomas Aquinas while Thomists ignore the work of von Balthasar. A closer reading of von Balthasar reveals that his writings are influenced by Aquinas, particularly through the influence of modern Thomist scholars.[105] Aquinas never developed a systematic theological aesthetics, but certainly one can find a philosophical aesthetics throughout his works.[106] With Dionysius the Areopagite, St. Thomas Aquinas defines the characteristics of beauty: radiance (*claritas*), harmony (*consonantia* or *debita proportio*), and integrity (*integritas*).[107] These characteristics of beauty belong properly to

---

Libreria Editrice Vaticana, 2013), §167.

[104] Rowland, *Ratzinger's Faith*, 8–9.

[105] See Angelo Campodonico's "Hans Urs von Balthasar's Interpretation of the Philosophy of Thomas Aquinas," *Nova et Vetera* 8, no. 1 (2001): 33–53. According to Campodonico, von Balthasar was influenced by "Thomistic scholars of diverse orientations, namely, Przywara, Rahner, de Lubac, Gilson, Pieper, and Siewerth" (34). According to Adrian J. Walker, von Balthasar's work was also influenced by the German Thomist Ferdinand Ulrich. See his "Love Alone: Hans Urs von Balthasar as a Master of Theological Renewal," *Communio* 32 (Fall 2005): 5n12. In a letter addressed to Francesca Aran Murphy, von Balthasar stated that Gilson was his guide to interpreting St. Thomas. Francesca Aran Murphy "Theological Aesthetics after von Balthasar," in *Theological Aesthetics after von Balthasar*, ed. Oleg V. Bychkov and James Fodor (Burlington, VT: Ashgate Publishing Company, 2008), 7.

[106] According to Umberto Eco, "Aquinas did not formulate a clear, specific aesthetic theory in a homogeneous, explicitly body of writings. It is necessary, therefore, to choose an appropriate pathway through his works." *The Aesthetics of Thomas Aquinas*, trans. Hugh Bredin (Cambridge, MA: Harvard University Press, 1988), 19. St. Thomas did not write a separate treatise or work on the transcendental of beauty. There is also some debate among Thomistic scholars as to whether Thomas followed Plato and considered beauty a transcendental indirectly or whether he followed Aristotle and excluded beauty as a transcendental. For a summary of the various positions from the most recent scholarship on this debate, see Daniel B. Gallagher, "What has beauty to do with reason?," in *Benedict XVI and Beauty in Sacred Art and Architecture*, 79–80.

[107] *ST* I, q. 39, a. 8.

God's very essence, but since the person is created in the very image of God, one can recognize beauty within a person. Aquinas believes this recognition of the beautiful in another is to behold a person's participation in the beauty of God himself.[108] Radiance, integrity, and clarity are the proportional form of the beauty of God's creation. These characteristics also serve as the objective criteria of determining the beauty (or lack thereof) of the person's respective artwork, regardless of its medium. The harmonious form "pleases the eye," and subsequently, one apprehends that the person or object in question is beautiful. Beauty is appropriated in a particular way to God the Son. Christ has "integrity" or "wholeness" because he is the Son of the Father. Christ has proportion because he is the perfect image of the Father. Finally, Christ has clarity because he is the Word through which the Father creates.[109] Beauty proper is of the supernatural and does not originate as something "from below."[110]

In accordance with St. Thomas Aquinas, von Balthasar considers beauty a supernatural transcendental "from above." Subsequently, von Balthasar believes that "[t]he beautiful is above all a *form* [Gestalt], and the light does not fall on this form from above and from outside, rather it breaks forth from the form's interior."[111] Beauty is considered a "lost transcendental" for von Balthasar. Since it is bound up with the true and the good, this loss has adverse effects for people embracing the gift of the faith and living a good life. The beautiful is considered the "primordial phenomenon" because it acts as a *praeambula fidei* that is preparatory for receiving the Gospel in its fullness.[112] Scripture is clear that Christ is the living and visible revelation of God the Father (Col 1:15–20). Jesus Christ is the visible icon of the Father's beauty; thus, he is the very form of beauty for von Balthasar. The beauty of this world is an analogy of the fullness of beauty revealed through the Incarnation of Christ.[113] The

---

[108] According to Aquinas, "Something is called beautiful because it is a participant in beauty. Beauty, however, is a participation in the first cause, which makes all things beautiful. So that the beauty of creatures is simply a likeness of the divine beauty in which things participate." Thomas Aquinas, *In librum beati Dionysii De Divinis Nominibus* cap. 4 I, 5, *Corpus Thomisticum*, accessed June 16, 2017, https://www.corpusthomisticum.org/cdn04.html.

[109] *ST* I, q. 39. a. 8.

[110] David Berger, *Thomas Aquinas and the Liturgy* (Naples, FL: Sapientia Press, 2005), 47.

[111] Von Balthasar, *The Glory of the Lord: Seeing the Form, A Theological Aesthetics*, vol. 1, —, trans. Erasmo Leiva-Merikakis (San Francisco: Ignatius Press, 1983), 151.

[112] Nichols, "Von Balthasar's Theological Aesthetics," *Heythrop Journal* 40 (1999): 411.

[113] Hans Urs von Balthasar, *The Glory of the Lord: A Theological Aesthetics*, vol. 2, *Studies in Theological Styles: Clerical Styles*, ed. John Riches, trans. Andrew Louth, Francis

culmination of this revelation is realized fully in the self-giving love of Christ on the Cross.[114]

Von Balthasar's theological aesthetics are informed by a cruciform Christocentrism,[115] in order "to let us see the revelation of God that his lordliness, his sublimity, what Israel calls *kabod* ('glory') and the New Testament *Gloria* can be recognized under all the incognitos of the human nature [of Christ] and [his] Cross."[116] Von Balthasar concludes, "That means God comes not primarily as our teacher or as our purposeful redeemer but *for himself*—to show forth and radiate out what is splendid in his eternal triune love in that disinterestedness which true love has in common with true beauty.[117] The self-emptying (kenosis) of Christ on the Cross fully reveals the beauty of God, which is love. In order for the liturgy truly to be re-formed, it must accentuate the cruciform love of Christ whereby God's glory is truly revealed. This, in turn, will enable the faithful who encounter this true beauty to live the liturgy in a life of sanctity.

As Prefect of the Congregation for the Doctrine of the Faith, Ratzinger captures the source of the faithful's disorientation with regard to the liturgy: "One shudders at the lackluster face of the post-conciliar liturgy as it has become, or one is simply bored with its hankering after banality and its lack of artistic standards."[118] While beauty is the true form of the liturgy, ugliness and banality have triumphed in practice. In an effort to redirect how the liturgy is celebrated through a "reform of the reform," Cardinal Ratzinger has suggested many ways in which we can restore the beauty of the liturgy in all its perfection, integrity, and clarity.

The liturgy realizes its true beauty when it realizes its purpose, which

---

McDonagh, and Brian McNeil, C.R.V. (Edinburgh: T & T Clark, 1985), 11: "If everything in the world that is beautiful and glorious is *epihaneia*, the radiance and splendor which breaks forth in expressive form from a veiled and yet mighty depth of being, then the event of the self-revelation of the hidden, the utterly free and sovereign God in the forms of this world, in word and history, and finally in the human form itself, will itself form an analogy to that world beauty, however far it outstrips it."

[114] See *SCa*, §35. The Paschal Mystery of Christ is described by the pope emeritus as the definitive revelation of beauty.

[115] See Raymond Gawronski S.J., "The Beauty of the Cross: The Theological Aesthetics of Hans Urs von Balthasar," *Logos* 5, no. 3 (Summer 2002): 185–206; and Nathan Lefler, "Cruciform Beauty: Revising the Form in Balthasar's Christological Aesthetic," *Logos* 9, no. 4 (Fall 2006): 33–55.

[116] Von Balthasar, *Mein Werk, Durchblicke* (Einsiedeln-Freiburg: Johannes Verlag, 1990), 62, quoted in Nichols, "Von Balthasar's Theological Aesthetics," 422.

[117] Von Balthasar, *Mein Werk, Durchblicke*, 422.

[118] JRCW11, 423 (JRGS11, 503).

is to glorify and praise God first and foremost. Ultimately, the people of God, as members of the Mystical Body of Christ, are called to participate in the sacrifice of Christ the high priest, the Head of the Church. The constant threat of the anthropocentric culture is that it tends to forget about God.[119] When the faithful obscure the true purpose (*logos*) of the liturgy in order to focus on the person, worship can degenerate into a "festival of self-affirmation." Ratzinger describes this worship as "self-initiated," "self-seeking worship," and "banal self-gratification."[120] This sort of worship is no longer directed towards the transcendent adoration of God but the immanent idolization of oneself. Much of Ratzinger's work focuses on the recovery of the cosmological and eschatological dimension of the liturgy, which has been obscured by the anthropological *eclipse of God*. The liturgy is, first and foremost, an *actio Dei*. Yet the tendency of post-modern liturgy is to focus on the person's work in "creating" *how* he or she worships.

Beauty is an essential characteristic of the liturgy, and it should not be viewed as a matter of subjective preference or taste. In particular, beauty has the purpose of highlighting the true nature of the liturgy, which is eschatological and cosmological. The Second Vatican Council reiterated the call that began with Blessed Pope Pius IX and the early leaders of the liturgical movement to promote the "full, conscious, and active participation" of every member of the faithful during the celebration of the liturgy. The authentic beauty of the *ars celebrandi* (the art of proper celebration) fosters full and active participation.[121] Only an understanding of beauty in Ratzinger's thought will enable people to appreciate his views regarding the *ars celebrandi*, which will be developed in the subsequent section of this chapter.[122]

---

[119] JRCW11, 593 (JRGS11, 718).
[120] JRCW11, 12 (JRGS11, 40).
[121] *SCa*, §38.
[122] On Ratzinger's theology as it relates to the *ars celebrandi*, Baldovin comments, "Cardinal Ratzinger's views on church architecture and liturgical music show how very far he is from the consensus about the nature of active participation that most liturgical scholars support. This is not to say simply that he is wrong and they ("we" if I correctly place myself within this consensus) are right, but only to note that he has a very different vision of postconciliar liturgy." Baldovin, *Reforming the Liturgy*, 86. Ratzinger's comments regarding the manner in which the liturgy has been celebrated and/or the reforms of the Second Vatican Council implemented need to be contextualized in Ratzinger's understanding of beauty and his articulation of the nature of the liturgy as eschatological and cosmic worship. Many of the critics of Ratzinger's theology of liturgy do not adequately address his understanding of beauty. In absence of a treatment of his theological aesthetics, theologians offer a caricature of Ratzinger as simply holding a

## ARS CELEBRANDI

The *ars celebrandi*, which consists of the external aspects of liturgical worship, should be characterized by beauty since they serve as visible signs and symbols of cosmic and eschatological worship. According to Pope Benedict, the "profound connection between beauty and the liturgy should make us attentive to every work of art placed at the service of the celebration."[123] This beauty should be expressed by sacred architecture, sacred art, and sacred music. In the words of the Second Vatican Council: "The Church has been particularly careful to see that sacred furnishings should *worthily* and *beautifully* serve the dignity of worship."[124] Ratzinger consistently argues that Church architecture should serve as a visible manifestation of beauty.[125] In a general audience, Benedict XVI contends that the beauty of the Romanesque and Gothic architecture of the medieval cathedrals reminds the faithful that the "*via pulchritudinis*, the way of beauty, is a privileged and fascinating path on which to approach the Mystery of God."[126] Yet, in practice, many have settled for a utilitarian view in building churches.

The earthly temple was modeled after the heavenly temple, yet most contemporary architecture does not take its cues from any particular paradigm beyond the subjective tastes of the architect.[127] Similarly,

---

negative and pessimistic view of human culture. Baldovin characterizes Ratzinger as having "a very dour view of contemporary Western culture. There is a kind of 'finger wagging' tone to his writing and a somewhat romantic view of the liturgical glories of the past" (89).

[123] *SCa*, §41.

[124] *SC*, §122; emphasis added.

[125] On Benedict's thought on sacred architecture, see "All the great works of art are a manifestation of God: Pope Benedict XVI and the architecture of beauty," in *Benedict XVI and Beauty in Sacred Art and Architecture*, 162–175; Uwe Michael Lang, "Benedict XVI and the theological foundations of church architecture," in *Benedict XVI and Beauty in Sacred Art and Architecture*, 112–121.

[126] Benedict XVI, General Audience, November 18, 2009, *The Holy See*, accessed June 23, 2010, http://www.vatican.va/content/benedict-xvi/en/audiences/2009/documents/hf_ben-xvi_aud_20091118.html.

[127] See the views espoused by modern architects Massimiliano Fuksas and Mario Botta for contemporary examples of this view in Uwe Michael Lang, *Signs of the Holy One: Liturgy, Ritual and Expression of the Sacred* (San Francisco: Ignatius Press, 2015), 71–78. Fuksas denies the existence of sacred architecture, whereas Botta maintains that the sacrality of a building is derived from the human labor that constructs the building. Neither architect adheres to the idea of sacramentality with respect to architecture, yet Fuksas designed the Church of San Paolo in Foligno, Italy, and Botta designed, among many Catholic churches, the Evry Cathedral in France. On the symbolism of church

the place of worship for the New Israel should reflect the beauty of the wedding feast of the Lamb, in which it participates through the celebration of each Eucharist. In other words, church architecture should be a sacramental sign of the eschaton.[128] In light of the Incarnation, the architectural design of churches should prepare the faithful to receive the divine life. As with sacred art and sacred music, Ratzinger underscores the spiritualization that sacred architecture should foster: "To spiritualize means to incarnate in a Christian way, but to incarnate means to spiritualize, to bring the things of the world to the coming Christ, to prepare them for their future form and thus to prepare God's future in the world."[129] The beautiful architecture of churches should incarnate the invisible eschaton. Simultaneously, in the act of incarnating the invisible, sacred architecture should prepare people to enter into the worship with the communion of saints and angels. Closely connected with the discussion above concerning *ad orientem* and relevant to the spiritualization of sacred architecture, Ratzinger emphasizes the orientation of early Christian churches towards Christ, the true *Oriens*.[130] Eastward orientation of churches is an incarnation of the Church's communal pilgrimage towards the Risen Christ.

In view of Ratzinger's emphasis mentioned previously that the theology of liturgy is a "symbolic theology," the signs used by the liturgy in the present should point simultaneously towards the past of salvation history and the future of the eschaton.[131] Ratzinger maintains that the *domus ecclesiae* is both the living assembly of the people gathered for worship and the building where the liturgy was celebrated.[132] The church building symbolically takes its architectural structure and liturgical form from

---

architecture in relation to the heavenly and earthly temple, see John Wilkinson, "Christian Worship in the Byzantine Period," in *Ancient Churches Revealed*, ed. Yoram Tsafrir (Jerusalem: Israel Exploration Society, 1993), 18–22.

[128] Denis McNamara, "Liturgical Architecture and the Classical Tradition," *Communio* 32 (Spring 2005), 142. On the sacramentality of sacred architecture, see Denis McNamara, *Catholic Church Architecture and the Spirit of the Liturgy* (Chicago: Hillenbrand Books, 2009). One of the fundamental theses of McNamara is "architecture can rightly be understood as the *built form of ideas*, with *church architecture as the built form of theology*" (9). Also see Philip Bess, "Sacramental Signs, Neighborhood Center: Thoughts on Catholic Churches in the 21st Century, in Bess, *Till We Have Built Jerusalem: Architecture, Urbanism, and the Sacred* (Wilmington, DE: ISI Books, 2006), 135–150.

[129] JRCW11, 386 (JRGS11, 460).

[130] See JRCW11, 40–43 (JRGS11, 72–75).

[131] See JRCW11, 32–36 (JRGS11, 63–68).

[132] JRCW11, 37 (JRGS11, 68–69).

worship in the Jewish synagogue, which Ratzinger demonstrates is closely connected with the sacrificial worship of the Temple.[133]

A shrine of the Torah was contained in each synagogue, which, according to Ratzinger, "contains a kind of Ark of the Covenant, which means it is the place of a kind of 'real presence.'"[134] This shrine was a symbol for the Holy of Holies within the Temple in Jerusalem, towards which the rabbi along with the people in the synagogue oriented themselves in their synagogal worship. Ratzinger concludes: "This orientation toward the Temple, and thus the connection of the synagogue's liturgy of the Word with the sacrificial liturgy of the Temple, can be seen in its form of prayer."[135] Ratzinger develops the synagogue's close connection to the sacrificial worship of the Temple as he stresses the continuity in the Eucharist with both worship in the synagogue and sacrifice in the Temple.

The close relationship between the synagogue and the Temple also serves as the foundation for Ratzinger to argue for the continuity in worship and the construction of churches *ad orientem* because Christ is the living temple that fulfills the hope left by the absence of the Ark of the Covenant. The altar maintains a prominent position within the church building highlighting the liturgy's primary purpose to re-present the paschal sacrifice of Christ. The emphasis on the altar as the eschatological focal point implies that the sanctuary and the church itself should be

---

[133] In his critique of Ratzinger's assertion of the close relationship between the Christian liturgy and the Temple in *The Spirit of the Liturgy*, Farnés maintains, "I do not believe that Christian liturgy directly evolves from the liturgy of the Jewish Temple. It may be the case that Christian liturgy is not uniquely dependent on the synagogue and has another source of inspiration; but this second source is not the liturgy of the Jewish Temple but the liturgy of the Jewish home and family, and in the New Testament this liturgy passes from the natural family to the family of the ecclesial assembly," 88. Cf. Ratzinger, "Cardinal Joseph Ratzinger's Answer to Pere Farnés," 94–95 (here 95): "In summary: the center of Christian liturgy is the Body of Christ. It is the liturgy of the Body of Christ and, for this reason, the inheritance of the Temple is present, transformed and renewed, and not only from the inheritance of the synagogue or just the inheritance of the 'home' (74). The Apocalypse, the most liturgical book of the New Testament, contains this fundamental insight. It portrays heaven with images of the Temple and teaches us to understand the Church's liturgy as participation in the liturgy of heaven as a cosmic liturgy, and precisely as the liturgy of the true Temple." Ratzinger recommends the following works that provide further insight into his position: Yves Congar, *Le Mystère du Temple* (Parish: Cerf, 1958) and Franz Mussner, "Jesus und 'Das Haus des Vaters.' Jesus als 'Tempel,'" in *Freude am Gottesdienst: Aspekte ursprünglicher Liturgie*, ed. J. Schreiner (Stuttgart: Katholisches Bibelwerk, 1983), 267–275.

[134] JRCW11, 39 (JRGS11, 71).

[135] JRCW11, 40 (JRGS11, 71–72).

constructed to underscore this end. Church architecture must highlight this orientation towards Christ as the true *Oriens* and as the sacrificial Lamb. Beyond these general principles, Ratzinger leaves the applications of these theological foundations undeveloped.[136] Much more development is given to sacred art and sacred music, which can assist with the sacred architecture in highlighting the cosmological and eschatological symbolism of the liturgy.

The teaching of the Second Vatican Council regarding the use of sacred art was that the "practice of placing sacred images in churches so that they may be venerated by the faithful is to be maintained. Nevertheless, their number should be moderate and their relative positions should reflect right order."[137] Tragically, the practice implemented in many churches has reflected a Manichean tendency to strip the walls bare with little or no sacred artwork remaining. This iconoclasm is addressed by Ratzinger in many of his writings concerning sacred images. According to Ratzinger, "The complete absence of images is incompatible with faith in the Incarnation of God. . . . Images of beauty, in which the mystery of the invisible God becomes visible, are an *essential* part of Christian worship."[138] As a result of God becoming man, matter can be sanctified and used to direct the human person to the authentic worship of God.

Icons function in a manner analogous to the celebration of the liturgy *ad orientem* in that they direct the faithful interiorly towards Christ.[139] Ratzinger is emphatic that the resurrected Christ is the "true *Oriens*,"

---

[136] Benedict XVI maintains that sacred architecture "should highlight the unity of the furnishings of the sanctuary, such as the altar, the crucifix, the tabernacle, the ambo, and the celebrant's chair. Here it is important to remember that the purpose of sacred architecture is to offer the Church a fitting space for the celebration of the mysteries of faith, especially the Eucharist. The very nature of a Christian church is defined by the liturgy, which is an assembly of the faithful (*ecclesia*) who are living stones of the Church (cf. 1 Pet 2:5)" (*SCa*, §41). There is similarly no development beyond a very basic statement affirming magisterial teaching. At the same time, the succinct statement reveals the answer that questions revolving around sacred architecture should take their cues from addressing the fundamental question: What is the liturgy?

[137] *SC*, §125.

[138] JRCW11, 81 (JRGS11, 119).

[139] JRCW11, 75 (JRGS11, 111). Throughout his chapter on sacred images, Ratzinger makes constant reference to the work of Eastern Orthodox theologian Paul Evdokimov. For an essay on Ratzinger's theology of sacred images and the influence of Evdokimov in this area, see Aidan Nichols, O.P., *Redeeming Beauty: Soundings in Sacral Aesthetics* (Burlington, VT: Ashgate Publishing Company, 2007), 89-101. For a comprehensive treatment of the relationship between the Incarnation and iconography, see Cardinal Christoph Schönborn, *God's Human Face: The Christ Icon.*

the "object" of worship, even when the faithful look upon Christ on the Cross.[140] Sacred images serve the purpose of drawing the eyes and hearts of the faithful towards the transcendent and eschatological Christ. The importance of icons and sacred artwork is that their beauty enables the faithful to encounter God, who is truly beauty and goodness in himself.[141] The reigning iconoclasm is not Christian because it is a tacit denial of the Incarnation.[142] While the Church has not canonized any particular art form as her own, sacred art should reflect the beauty of the Risen Christ regardless of what the subject depicted might be. In his meeting with artists, Pope Benedict maintains that authentic beauty is "by no means a supplementary or secondary factor in our search for meaning and happiness; the experience of beauty does not remove us from reality, on the contrary, it leads to a direct encounter with the daily reality of our lives, liberating it from darkness, transfiguring it, making it radiant and beautiful."[143] Truly beautiful art can be preparatory for communicants to receive the personification of beauty in the Sacred Host. As a "call to transcendence," it can serve as a witness to the non believer and prepare their heart to receive the *Logos*.[144] Because Christ is beauty itself, then the use of beautiful sacred images can assist people within the liturgy to orient themselves interiorly towards Christ.

Ratzinger's theology of sacred artwork is centered upon Christ the incarnate *Logos*. As Christian worship developed from its synagogal worship, the use of Christian images takes its cues from traditional biblical images found in ancient synagogues. The Christian images found in the catacombs give these images their finality in the sacraments and in Christ himself.[145] Unlike the use of the images in the synagogues, "the point of the images is not to tell a story about something in the past but to incorporate the events of history into the sacrament."[146] What differentiates Christianity from Judaism with respect to worship is the notion of universality in both time and space.

The incarnation and resurrection of Jesus Christ transform the very

---

[140] JRCW11, 77 (JRGS11, 114).

[141] JRCW11, 78 (JRGS11, 115).

[142] JRCW11, 81 (JRGS11, 119).

[143] Benedict XVI, Address of His Holiness Benedict XVI to Artists, November 21, 2009.

[144] John Paul II, "Letter of His Holiness Pope John Paul II to Artists," §10, *The Holy See*, accessed June 27, 2017, https://www.vatican.va/content/john-paul-ii/en/letters/1999/documents/hf_jp-ii_let_23041999_artists.html.

[145] JRCW11, 71 (JRGS11, 107–108).

[146] JRCW11, 71 (JRGS11, 108).

nature of worship: "The centering of all history in Christ is both the liturgical transmission of that history and the expression of a new experience of time, in which past, present, and future make contact, because they have been inserted into the presence of the risen Lord," and thus, "liturgical presence contains eschatological hope within it."[147] This understanding of the liturgy in relation to sacred time leads Ratzinger to maintain, "All sacred images are, without exception, in a certain sense images of the Resurrection, history read in light of the Resurrection, and for that very reason they are images of hope, giving us assurance of the world to come, of the final coming of Christ."[148] Icons do not simply have a pedagogical function to teach or to catechize. Their authentic purpose is to serve as a symbol of both the past in salvation history and to direct the faithful towards the eschaton. The icon directs the person, who looks at the image with eyes of faith, to the resurrected Christ. Ratzinger maintains, "the icon is intended to draw us onto an inner path, the eastward path, toward the Christ who is to return. Its dynamism is identical with the dynamism of the liturgy as a whole. Its Christology is trinitarian."[149]

Sacred artwork truly may reveal aspects of Christ's face and, hence, the image of God the Father in and through the Holy Spirit. The implication of this theology of icons goes beyond the skills of the artist in question. In Ratzinger's theology of sacred artwork, the ability to create sacred icons or sacred art presupposes the gift of faith on the part of the artist. These images serve the liturgy, which means that these images must be the fruit of prayer and contemplation of a person who lives in hopeful expectation of the Risen Christ's return. There can be no sacred artwork divorced from the *logos*, which is the same principle Ratzinger applies to his theology of sacred music.

Given his own interests and experience, Ratzinger's most developed liturgical theology concerning the *ars celebrandi* is in the area of sacred music.[150] When it comes to the celebration of the liturgy, all songs are *not*

---

[147] JRCW11, 72 (JRGS11, 108).

[148] JRCW11, 72 (JRGS11, 108).

[149] JRCW11, 75 (JRGS11, 111).

[150] Early in his childhood years spent in Traunstein, Ratzinger developed a love for music, particularly the work of Mozart. Joseph Ratzinger, *Milestones: Memoirs 1927–1977* [hereafter, *MM*], trans. Erasmo Leiva-Merikakis (San Francisco: Ignatius Press, 1998), 24–25; Georg Ratzinger, *My Brother, the Pope*, trans. Michael J. Miller (San Francisco: Ignatius Press, 2011), 109–111. One of Ratzinger's former students, Vincent Twomey, offers an anecdote that highlights Ratzinger's preoccupation with beauty and music: "While at Tübingen, one student asked another to identify the difference between

created equal.[151] Over and above the other aspects of the *ars celebrandi*, music has a pre-eminent place in the teaching of the Second Vatican Council: "The musical tradition of the universal Church is a treasure of inestimable value, greater even than that of any other art. The main reason for this pre-eminence is that, as a combination of sacred music and words, it forms a necessary or integral part of the solemn liturgy."[152]

In their commentary on *Sacrosanctum Concilium*, Karl Rahner, S.J., and Herbert Vorgrimler promoted the use of utility music within the liturgy, which is chosen not for its beauty (or lack thereof) but for its usefulness and popularity.[153] Similar to the struggles with the visual arts, the reigning approach to music is one that is subjective and individualistic. Despite the clarion call of the Council to preserve the treasure of sacred

---

Professor Ratzinger and another equally famous theologian. The reply was: Ratzinger also finds time to play the piano. He is as open to beauty as he is to truth. He lives outside himself. He is not preoccupied with his own self. Put simply, he does not take himself too seriously." D. Vincent Twomey, S.V.D., *Pope Benedict XVI: The Conscience of Our Age—A Theological Portrait* (San Francisco: Ignatius Press, 2007), 16. On the theology of sacred music in Ratzinger, see Michaela Christine Hastetter, "Liturgie—Brücke zum Mysterium: Grundlinien des Liturgieverständnisses Benedikts XVI," in *Symphonie des Glaubens: Junge Münchener Theologen im Dialog mit Joseph Ratzinger/Benedikt XVI*, ed. Michaela C. Hastetter, Christoph Ohly, and Georgios Vlachonis (St. Ottilien: EOS, 2007), 145–50. Hastetter applies what she identifies as five basic pillars of Ratzinger's theology of liturgy in order to demonstrate the consistency of his theology of church music with his liturgical theology. These five pillars are (1) Semel-Semper-Vita, (2) Innen und Aussen, (3) Logosgemäss—Logikē Latreia, (4) Kosmisch, and (5) Einheit von altem und neuem Testament. Hastetter will briefly analyze the *Magnificat* of J. S. Bach to demonstrate the consistency and wise insight of Ratzinger's theology of liturgy applied to sacred music. For an overview of Ratzinger's writings on sacred music, see Franz Karl Praßl, "Psallite sapienter: Joseph Cardinal Ratzinger und seine Schriften zur Kirchenmusik," in *Der Logos-gemäße Gottesdienst*, ed. Rudolf Voderholzer, 278–300.

[151] *SCa*, §42.

[152] *SC*, §112.

[153] Rowland, *Ratzinger's Faith*, 131. For Ratzinger's response to Rahner and Vorgrimler, see JRCW11, 421–442 (JRGS11, 501–526). Rahner and Vorgrimler's commentary represents what has become known as the fruit of the hermeneutic of discontinuity or rupture, whereas Ratzinger develops a theology of sacred music based upon the hermeneutic of continuity: "Comparing the Council document [*Sacrosanctum Concilium*] itself with the commentary by Rahner and Vorgrimler, we find a contrast that is characteristic of the difference, in general, between what the Council said and how it has been taken up by the postconciliar Church" (at JRCW11, 422 [JRGS, 503]). In the estimation of Benedict XVI, the changes that have taken place within the celebration of the liturgy following the Second Vatican Council "need to be understood within the overall unity of the historical development of the rite itself [hermeneutic of continuity], without the introduction of artificial discontinuities." *SCa*, §3.

music, particularly Gregorian chant and the use of Palestrina,[154] utility music seems to dominate in liturgical practice because of a tendency to subordinate *logos* to *ethos*.

The Incarnation of the *Logos* serves as the foundation for the essence of liturgy and the theology of sacred music. Ratzinger maintains that the *Logos* or the "Word" within the liturgy is "first of all not a text, but a living reality: a God who is self-communicating and who communicates himself by becoming man. This incarnation is the sacred tent, the focal point of all worship that looks at the glory of God and gives him honor."[155] Liturgy allows the *logos* to become incarnate through its various signs and symbols. Among the *ars celebrandi*, sacred music verbalizes the Word for Ratzinger: "The 'musification' [*Musikwerden*] of the faith is a part of the process of the Word becoming flesh. But in a completely unique way this 'musification' is at the same time also ordered to that inner shift of the incarnational event."[156] Music also allows the flesh to become spiritualized as the "wood and brass turn into tone."[157] What is invisible is made visible and simultaneously what is visible becomes invisible. Ratzinger summarizes this incarnational principle: "An embodiment comes into play that is spiritualization, and a spiritualization occurs that is embodiment."[158] The Incarnation enables worship to take on its proper characteristic as a form of praise that allows the human person to become who he truly is, in light of his encounter with God.

In outlining the theological basis for sacred music, Ratzinger enters into dialogue with Aquinas.[159] Ratzinger, towards the latter part of this

---

[154] See *SC*, §116: "The Church acknowledges Gregorian Chant as specially suited to the Roman liturgy: therefore, others things being equal, it should be given pride of place in liturgical services." On the essential role of chant in the celebration of the sacred liturgy, see William Peter Mahrt, "The Propers of the Mass as Integral to the Liturgy," in *Benedict XVI and Beauty in Sacred Music: Proceedings of the Third Fota International Liturgical Conference*, ed. Janet Elaine Rutherford (Dublin: Four Courts Press, 2010), 149–162. For a succinct overview of the history and importance of the use of chants of the *Proprium Missae* in the liturgy, see László Dobszay, "The *Proprium Missae* of the Roman Rite," in *The Genius of the Roman Rite: Historical, Theological, and Pastoral Perspectives on Catholic Liturgy*, ed. Uwe Michael Lang (Mundelein: Hillenbrand Books, 2010), 83–118.

[155] JRCW11, 453 (JRGS11, 539).

[156] JRCW11, 454 (JRGS11, 540).

[157] JRCW11, 455 (JRGS11, 540).

[158] JRCW11, 455 (JRGS11, 540).

[159] JRCW11, 424–439 (JRGS11, 505–22). Here Ratzinger engages with Thomas's thought on the question of music from *ST* II-II, q. 91, aa. 1 and 2. On the liturgy in thought of

excerpt, highlights Aquinas's description of praise of God as an ascent: "Praise itself is a movement, a path; it is more than understanding, knowing, and doing—it is an 'ascent,' a way of reaching him who dwells amid the praises of the angels. Aquinas mentioned another factor: this ascent draws the human person away from what is opposed to God."[160] Sacred music should lift the human person beyond the mere material world towards Christ, who simultaneously transcends this world and pitches his tent among humanity. The earthly liturgy enables the Church on earth to join in the worship of heaven. Sacred music enables the Church to participate in "the liturgy of the heavens that has always been taking place. Earthly liturgy is liturgy because and only because it joins what is already in process, the greater reality."[161] The liturgy is an incarnation of the worship of the heavens.

Sacred music finds its true origins in the *Logos* and leads all of humanity with the created world back to God. Ratzinger develops at length the cosmic origins and characteristics of sacred music:

> [The universe] comes from the Logos, in whom, so to speak, the archetypes of the world's order are contained. The Logos, through the Spirt, fashions the material world according to these archetypes. In virtue of his work in creation, the Logos is, therefore, called the "art of God" (*ars* = *technē*!). The Logos himself is the great artist, in whom all works of art—the beauty of the universe—have their origin. To sing with the universe means, then, to follow the track of the Logos and to come close to him. All true human art is an assimilation to *the* artist, to Christ, to the mind of the Creator. The idea of the music of the cosmos, of singing with the angels, leads again back to the relation of art to *logos*, but now is broadened and deepened in the context of the cosmos. Yes, it is the cosmic context that gives art in the liturgy both its measure and its scope.[162]

Music should be an expression of the *logos* reflected in all of the created order and should affirm the Guardinian primacy of *logos* over *ethos*. Pure subjectivity or music as an expression of pure will (*ethos*) over reason or

---

Thomas, see David Berger, *Thomas Aquinas and the Liturgy.*

[160] JRCW11, 434–435 (JRGS11, 517–18).

[161] JRCW11, 462 (JRGS11, 551).

[162] JRCW11, 96 (JRGS 11, 135–36).

being (*logos*) cannot be the guiding principle for sacred music used in service of the liturgy. Beautiful sacred music mirrors the beauty of the world brought into being through the *logos*: "The beauty of music depends on its conformity to the rhythmic and harmonic laws of the universe. The more that human music adapts to the musical laws of the universe, the more beautiful it will be."[163] The centrality of the *logos* is the underlying foundation for sacred music because God has revealed himself through Jesus Christ as the incarnate *Logos*. The human person has been created through this *Logos*; consequently, every person is a *logoi* or an echo of the very *Logos* of God. Ratzinger is trying to emphasize the connection that the human person has through his art to lead others back to recognize the *Logos* as their origin to the degree that their work is created in harmony with the *logos*.

Contrary to the autonomous individuality and the subjectivity of a secularized world, the liturgy makes visible the communal participation of the Church, as a unified Body of Christ in the Paschal Mystery of Christ. Ratzinger contends, "[F]rom looking at the mystery of a cosmic liturgy that is *Logos*-liturgy there arose the necessity to represent the character of worship as communion, its character as action, and its determination as word in a visible and concrete way."[164] This is the essential context for Ratzinger in understanding the role of music in the celebration of the liturgy. Ratzinger argues, "Church music was no longer supposed to be a performance on the occasion of worship, but was to be liturgy itself, that is, a harmonizing with the choir of the angels and saints."[165] The Church's tradition with respect to sacred music emphasizes the use of Gregorian chant and classical polyphony because it maintains a close relationship with liturgy, which has been characterized as a *Logos*-mystery.[166] Consequently, not all forms of music are appropriate in the context of the sacred liturgy. Ratzinger clearly maintains: "[M]usic that is supposed to serve the Christian liturgy must correspond to the Logos, concretely. It must stand in a meaningful relation to the words in which the Logos has expressed himself."[167] Chant allows the texts of the liturgy to be expressed clearly and soberly. The close relationship of the tone and melody to the text used by chant is the predominant

---

[163] JRCW11, 95 (JRGS11, 135).

[164] JRCW11, 469 (JRGS11, 558).

[165] JRCW11, 469 (JRGS11, 558).

[166] The chants of the *Proprium Missae* are an essential part of the liturgy in the west. See Dobszay, *The Restoration and Organic Development of the Roman Rite*, 159–200.

[167] JRCW11, 471 (JRGS11, 561).

reason why the tradition of the Church gives Gregorian chant an exalted position.[168]

Summarizing the position of the Church with respect to the role and purpose of sacred music, Ratzinger is unequivocal: "[T]he liturgy requires an artistic transposition, originating in the spirit of faith, of the music of the cosmos into human music that glorifies the Word made flesh. Such music obeys a stricter law than everyday music: such music is beholden to the Word and must lead to the Spirit."[169] Beautiful music is not simply the product of the composer's subjective whim. Sacred music reflects the beauty of the incarnate *Logos* and heavenly worship. Although utility music in its various forms may be subjectively more pleasing to a particular group or congregation, it tends to focus on God's descent without a corresponding ascent on the part of the human person.

Gregorian chant is the standard norm and form for sacred music, according to John Paul II: "The more closely a composition for church approaches in its movement, inspiration and savor the Gregorian melodic form, the more sacred and liturgical it becomes; and the more out of harmony it is with that supreme model, the less worthy it is of the temple."[170] Chant is the objective standard for beautiful sacred music because of its close proximity and harmony with the *logos*. Further, chant is sacred, which the musicologist William Mahrt describes as having two complementary characteristics: "[A]n intrinsic suitability or aptness to the sacred purpose, and a process of being received as sacred."[171] Chant incarnates the eschatological beauty of the praise of heaven. Consequently, chant is more sacred than the utility music that has dominated in liturgical practice. Pope

---

[168] See JRCW11, 488–93 (JRGS11, 580–85).

[169] JRCW11, 493 (JRGS11, 585). It would be most accurate to describe the underlying position of Ratzinger on sacred music as *logos*-centric. Cf. Baldovin, *Reforming the Liturgy*, 83: "We need to recognize that there is something we call a Eurocentric bias in Cardinal Ratzinger's thought. Much of what he has to say [regarding sacred music] is very much tied up with a defense of traditional European civilization." The truth of the matter is that Ratzinger is trying to uphold the authentic tradition of sacred music, which conforms to the *Logos* and not a single geographical region.

[170] John Paul II, "Chirograph of the Supreme Pontiff John Paul II the Centenary of the Motu Proprio *Tra le Sollecitudini* on Sacred Music," November 23, 2003, no. 12, *The Holy See*, accessed June 23, 2010, http://www.vatican.va/content/john-paul-ii/en/letters/2003/documents/hf_jp-ii_let_20031203_musica-sacra.html.

[171] William Mahrt, "Music and the Sacrality of the two forms," in *Benedict XVI and the Roman Missal: Proceedings of the Fourth Fota International Liturgical Conference*, 194. For a comprehensive survey on the notion of what is considered sacred based upon anthropology and theology, see Uwe Michael Lang, *Signs of the Holy One*, 17–62.

Benedict has also expressed and reaffirmed the place of chant within the sacred liturgy: "I desire, in accordance with the request advanced by the Synod Fathers, that Gregorian chant be suitably esteemed and employed as the chant proper to the Roman liturgy."[172] The authentic reform and renewal of the sacred liturgy cannot take place without restoring Gregorian chant to its normative place within the liturgy.

The way that the postconciliar liturgy has been celebrated makes Ratzinger shudder at what he describes as its "lackluster face," which bores him because of "its banality and its lack of artistic standards."[173] Focus on utility and function can move the celebration of the liturgy towards ugly boredom and passivity whereas emphasis on the sacred and beautiful can lead the faithful participants towards joyful evangelization. Pope Francis agrees: "Evangelization with joy becomes beauty in the liturgy, as part of our daily concern to spread goodness. The Church evangelizes and is herself evangelized through the beauty of the liturgy, which is both a celebration of the task of evangelization and the source of her renewed self-giving."[174]

The need to renew the liturgy through beauty is a priority that affects the Church's mission of evangelization. Questions about the type of *ars celebrandi* are not superfluous. This need for self-examination with respect to the liturgy was recognized by St. John Paul II, who called for the faithful to "make an examination of conscience so that the beauty of music and hymnody will return once again to the liturgy. They should purify worship from ugliness of style, from distasteful forms of expression, from uninspired musical texts which are not worthy of the great act that is being celebrated."[175]

---

[172] *SCa*, §42. Elsewhere, Benedict notes, "As part of the enhancement of the word of God in the liturgy, attention should also be paid to the use of song at the times called for by the particular rite. Preference should be given to songs which are of clear biblical inspiration and which express, through the harmony of music and words, the beauty of God's word. We would do well to make the most of those songs handed down to us by the Church's tradition which respect this criterion. I think in particular of the importance of Gregorian chant." *Verbum Domini*, §70. For an overview of the insight of Ratzinger/Benedict into Gregorian chant, see Alberto Donini, "Gregorian Chant in the liturgy according to Joseph Ratzinger/Benedict XVI," in *Benedict XVI and Beauty in Sacred Music*, 80–92.

[173] JRCW11, 423 (JRGS11, 503).

[174] Francis, *Evangelii Gaudium*, §24.

[175] John Paul II, "General Audience, Wednesday February 26, 2003," *The Holy See*, accessed June 23, 2010, http://www.vatican.va/content/john-paul-ii/en/audiences/2003/documents/hf_jp-ii_aud_20030226.html.

The foundation for beautiful liturgical music, according to Ratzinger, is that it must conform to the beauty of the *logos* in three ways. First, since sacred music is primarily sung text, it should draw its inspiration from the written word of Sacred Scripture. Second, the music should draw upon the sober and ordered inspiration (inebriation) of the Holy Spirit as opposed to a mere formless intoxication of the senses akin to cultic Dionysian music. Finally, music should be ordered in unison with the harmonious laws of the universe.[176] The tendency is to want to "create" music, while musicians are called to discern the beautiful form of the *logos* as their inspiration for the harmony, order, and transcendence that should resonate within truly sacred music.

Ratzinger is consistent with the preeminence of the eschatological, Christological, and cosmological in the development of his theology of liturgy. The liturgy should always clearly be first and foremost the *actio Dei*, as it emphasizes the primacy of the *logos* in every external expression that is a part of the liturgy. The preference for liturgy *ad orientem* is motivated above all by a concern to ensure that the faithful can understand the symbolism of the liturgy as a participation in the ascent towards the risen Christ. The *ars celebrandi*, in all of its various expressions, can assist the faithful in participating as a unified Body of Christ in heavenly worship, as Benedict XVI posits: "Given the close relationship between the *ars celebrandi* and an *actuosa participatio*, it must first be said that 'the best catechesis on the Eucharist is the Eucharist itself, celebrated well.'"[177] An emphasis and focus on the implementation of beauty in the various forms of the *ars celebrandi* can be a part of this "best catechesis on the Eucharist." The governing norm for the various *ars celebrandi* is beauty, which finds its objective norm in the incarnate *Logos*.

The risen Christ is the true *Gestalt* for beauty in various artistic expressions of the liturgy. The closer a building, icon, or form of sacred music mirrors the radiance, integrity, and clarity of Christ, the more beautiful it becomes. Benedict XVI argues that within salvation history the "epiphany of beauty reaches definitive fulfillment in God's revelation in Jesus Christ: Christ is the full manifestation of the glory of God."[178] The emphasis on the beauty of the *ars celebrandi* will assist the faithful in participating fully in the liturgy because Benedict XVI maintains beauty is "an essential element of the liturgical action, since it is an attribute of God

---

[176] JRCW11, 92–96 (JRGS11, 132–35).

[177] *SCa*, §64.

[178] *SCa*, §35.

himself and his revelation."[179] Further, the beauty manifested within the liturgy should find its way into the lives of Christians, whose full partici-pation in the liturgy should lead them to manifest the reason for their hope through lives of selfless charity. This is the definitive meaning of sacrifice and the essential meaning of worship that Ratzinger wants the faithful to actualize. Beauty is the incarnation of the true nature of the liturgy, and this beauty should take form in the transformed lives of Christians.

## SUMMARY AND CONCLUSION

Romano Guardini maintains that the "liturgy is our teacher. It condenses into prayer the entire body of religious truth. Indeed, it is nothing else but truth expressed in terms of prayer."[180] In this chapter, it has been estab-lished that Ratzinger cares about the symbols of the liturgy because, like Guardini, he recognizes that it is through its symbolism that the liturgy leads us to the truth, the *Logos*. In order to do this, the symbols of the lit-urgy must be rightly presented and understood.

We can only appreciate Ratzinger's arguments favoring the liturgy offered *ad orientem* or his emphasis that beauty is an inherent characteris-tic of the liturgy when we understand that his main interest is to preserve the symbolic *logos* of the liturgy. In Ratzinger's view, the liturgy celebrated *ad orientem* manifests in a visible manner the orientation of the liturgy towards its consummation in the eschaton. The call for the restoration of offering the Mass in this manner universally, or the compromise to place a crucifix on the altar, aims to preserve the eschatological symbolism that is bound up with the liturgy celebrated *ad orientem*.

The liturgy enables the human person to realize his authentic *logos*, which is to love God as a *homo adorans*. Adoration fulfills the nature of the human person. Guardini defines adoration as "the obedience of our being to the being of God. If a being is in truth, then it itself is nothing but truth."[181] The constant subordination of the *logos* to *ethos* has affected the

---

[179] *SCa*, §35.

[180] Romano Guardini, *The Spirit of the Liturgy* [hereafter, GSL], trans. Ada Lane (New York: The Crossroad Publishing Company, 1998), 24.

[181] Romano Guardini, *Auf dem Wege: Versuche* (Mainz: Grünewald, 1923), 21, quoted in Joseph Ratzinger, *Fundamental Speeches from Five Decades*, [hereafter, FSFD], ed. Florian Schuller, trans. Michael J. Miller, J. R. Foster, and Adrian Walker (San Fran-cisco: Ignatius Press, 2012), 247; *Jesus von Nazareth: Beiträge zur Christologie*, Joseph Ratzinger Gesammelte Schriften 6/2 [hereafter, JRGS6/2], ed. Gerhard Ludwig Müller Freiburg: Herder, 2013, 732.

human person's ability to comprehend and appreciate his call to worship. Responding to this call is a safeguard against the predominance of the materialist *logos*, characterized by *technē*, which reduces man to a *homo faber*. The Christian's faithful observance and comprehension of the significance of all the liturgical gestures and postures prepare him for his eschatological vocation of endless adoration. Finally, authentic beauty reveals the true *logos* of the liturgy, which should direct the faithful to participate in the liturgy on earth as a preparation for cosmic worship.

# A Finished Movement within an Unfinished Symphony

THIS BOOK HAS ANALYZED the relationship between the liturgy and eschatology in the symphonic theology of Joseph Ratzinger.[1] Ratzinger's consistent insistence on the primacy of the *logos* and thus the centrality of Christ within his theology unites the various fragments that make up this finished movement within his theology of liturgy eschatology. In the first chapter, I examined the implications of the primacy of the *logos*. When *logos* is subordinated to *ethos* or Christology is not properly prioritized, then both the liturgy and eschatology become subjected to ideological ends driven only by the concerns of *this* world. One of the issues that has arisen in contemporary theology, which Ratzinger has attempted to address, is that it "has been seeking its truth more and more 'in praxis'; not in the apparently unanswerable problem, 'What are we?' [*logos*] but in the more pressing, 'What can we do [*ethos*]?'"[2] In relation to nature, the human person wants "to understand the discovered world only as material for their own creativity."[3] This fundamental shift to the primacy of *ethos* over *logos* consistently leads to an attitude whereby

---

[1]  McGregor uses the symphony metaphor in a similar manner to describe the Christology of Ratzinger: "[O]ne could characterize Ratzinger's spiritual Christology as an unfinished symphony, though not in a Schubertian sense. Rather than missing whole movements, it could be said that the scoring is incomplete. Some sections are more thoroughly scored than others." Peter John McGregor, *Heart to Heart: The Spiritual Christology of Joseph Ratzinger* (Eugene, OR: Pickwick Publications, 2016), 339.

[2]  *ITB*, 80–81.

[3]  Joseph Ratzinger, *In the Beginning: A Catholic Understanding of Creation and the Fall* [hereafter, *ITB*], trans. Boniface Ramsey, O.P. (Huntington, IN: Our Sunday Visitor, 1990), 80–81.

the human person views everything as subject to his "makeability" (*Machbarkeit*).

Building upon Ratzinger's insistence on the primacy of *logos*, I argued in chapter two that the faithful are called to participate in and through this sacrifice of Christ that is re-presented within the celebration of the liturgy, which simultaneously anticipates the eschaton. One of Ratzinger's contributions within his theology of liturgy has been an emphasis on freedom that is achieved as the faithful begin their sacrificial exodus with the *Logos* by entering into communion with him and subordinating their will to his. The human person mystically unites his will with God: "[T]hus the Roman Canon, following the Letter to the Romans [in emphasizing the liturgy as a *logikē latreia*]—has to become, for us ourselves, a process of remolding: bringing us out of our restricted self-will, out into union with the will of God."[4] Entrance into communion with God in Jesus Christ is the beginning of our exodus, which comes to fruition through our participation in the pro-existence of Christ.

Each member of the Church is called upon to subordinate his own "I" to the "Thou" of the divine *Logos* in Christ by participating in the sacrificial exodus of Christ. Ratzinger insists, "In the exodus of Christ's love—that is, in the transition from opposition to community which goes through the cross of obedience—redemption, that is, liberation, truly occurs. This exodus leads from the slavery of *philautia*, the slavery of self-conceit and self-containment, into the love of God."[5] The key to understanding the relationship of Christology and Ratzinger's theology of the liturgy is the primacy of Christ's sacrifice. One can only understand this sacrifice by acknowledging that the union between God and humanity, which began with the Incarnation and was consummated by Christ's exodus via the Cross and Resurrection, comes to fruition in divinization, which is the ultimate end of full participation in the liturgy.

---

[4]  Joseph Ratzinger, *Theology of the Liturgy: The Sacramental Foundation of Christian Existence* [hereafter, JRCW11], ed. Michael J. Miller, trans. John Saward, Kenneth Baker, S.J., Henry Taylor, et al., Collected Works 11 (San Francisco: Ignatius Press, 2014), 351; *Theologie der Liturgie: Die sakramentale Begründung christlicher Existenz* [hereafter, JRGS11], Gesammelte Schriften 11, ed. Gerhard Ludwig Müller (Freiburg im Breisgau: Herder, 2008), 419–20.

[5]  Joseph Ratzinger, *A New Song for the Lord: Faith in Christ and Liturgy Today* [hereafter, *NSL*], trans. Martha M. Matesich (New York: The Crossroad Publishing Company, 1997), 23; *Jesus von Nazareth: Beiträge zur Christologie,* Joseph Ratzinger Gesammelte Schriften 6/2 [hereafter, JRGS6/2], ed. Gerhard Ludwig Müller (Freiburg: Herder, 2013), 81.

In chapter three, I demonstrated that Ratzinger stresses the notion of *communion*, or a Eucharistic ecclesiology, as a central characteristic of the Church, in a manner reminiscent of de Lubac: "She is brought forth by the call of Christ, that is, she is formed out of the sacrament and is therefore herself a sacrament. It is the Eucharist, Christ's presence and sacrament, which builds up the Church."[6] The Church is meant to be a sign of unity, which she herself is as the Body of Christ. Simultaneously, the Church has the mission to draw others into that communion. In a certain sense, *communio* is both the *logos* (as a "sign") and the *ethos* (as part of its mission as an "instrument") of the Church.

The Eucharist defines the *ethos* of the Church as the charity that is foundational for the Church's communion. Ratzinger maintains, "The Eucharist is our participation in the Easter mystery, and hence it is constitutive of the Church, the Body of Christ. This is why the Eucharist is necessary for salvation. The necessity of the Eucharist is identical with the necessity of the Church and vice versa."[7] The Church's mission is to draw all of humanity into that sacramental communion; subsequently, the vertical communion is never mutually exclusive with the horizontal communion. The communion that each believer individually experiences with Jesus Christ should be extended by his or her love of neighbor. Ratzinger emphasizes that every member of the Body of Christ must enter into the "logic" of the Paschal Mystery.

Through the Eucharist, Christians enter into this dynamic of communion and self-giving that should mark their way of life as an *alter Christus*. One of the unique emphases of Ratzinger is the notion that the *Stellvertretung* of Christ, which the faithful encounter in the Eucharist, must become the identity and mission of the Church. In her existence "for" others, the Church is able to draw others into the self-sacrificial love and worship of Christ.[8] Sacrifice finds its fulfillment in commu-

---

[6] Joseph Ratzinger, *The Nature and Mission of Theology: Approaches to Understanding Its Role in the Light of the Present Controversy* [hereafter, *NMT*], trans. Adrian Walker (San Francisco: Ignatius Press, 1995), 85–86.

[7] Joseph Ratzinger, *Behold the Pierced One: An Approach to Spiritual Christology* [hereafter, *BPO*], trans. Graham Harrison (San Francisco: Ignatius Press, 1986), 93; *Zeichen unter den Völkern: Schriften zur Ekklesiologie und Ökumene*, Gesammelte Schriften 8/1 [hereafter, JRGS8/1], ed. Gerhard Ludwig Müller, (Freiburg: Herder, 2010), 326–327.

[8] Joseph Ratzinger, *What It Means to Be a Christian*, trans. Henry Taylor (San Francisco: Ignatius Press, 2006), 55: "Thus, becoming a Christian does not mean grabbing something for oneself alone; on the contrary, it means moving out of that selfishness which only knows about itself and only refers to itself and passing into the new form of existence of someone who lives for others."

nion. Consequently, Ratzinger's ecclesiology offers an alternative form of approaching hope and the polis, in contradistinction with Metz and Moltmann, placing its emphasis upon the primacy of communion with God as the foundation for engaging in charity "for" one's neighbor. Authentic hope leads to the *ethos* of charity, which is preceded by a *logos* of sacramental *communio*.

In light of our development of Ratzinger's Eucharistic ecclesiology and its emphasis on the theme of *communio*, I demonstrated in chapter four that the Church has a mission that is defined above all by charity. The sacrificial offering that is represented in the Eucharist is transformed by Christ, the incarnate *Logos*; subsequently, Ratzinger repeatedly insists upon defining the liturgy as a *logikē latreia*. Ratzinger establishes the significance of the relationship between the *Logos* and self-giving love: "Admittedly, this 'word' that supplants the sacrificial offering is no ordinary word. To begin with, it is no mere human speech, but rather the word of him who is '*the* Word,' and so it draws all human words into God's inner dialogue, into his reason and his love."[9] The very nature of sacrifice is transformed by the Incarnation of Christ, such that our words, in unison with the prayer of the incarnate Word, become part of the *dia-logos* with God. Ratzinger concludes, "The Word is now flesh, and not only that: it is his body offered up, his blood poured out. With the institution of the Eucharist, Jesus transforms his cruel death into 'word,' into the radical expression of his love, his self-giving to the point of death."[10] Sacrifice is definitively transformed into the very *logos* of love that must become incarnate in the life of each believer.

Jesus Christ, whom believers have encountered in sign and symbol, must become a concrete reality impacting every aspect of their lives. Only with this foundation can the faithful begin to comprehend how the Eucharist is "intrinsically fragmented" if it does not result in a concrete practice of charity for one's neighbor.[11] This work has argued that Ratzinger underscores the significance of a new form of worship that extends from the liturgy into everyday life. The "breaking of the bread" is nourishment

---

[9]   Joseph Ratzinger, *Jesus of Nazareth: Holy Week: From the Entrance into Jerusalem to the Resurrection* [hereafter, *JN* II], trans. Vatican Secretariat of State (San Francisco: Ignatius Press, 2011), 80; *Jesus von Nazareth: Beiträge zur Christologie*, Joseph Ratzinger Gesammelte Schriften 6/1 (hereafter, JRGS6/1), ed. Gerhard Ludwig Müller (Freiburg: Herder, 2013), 479–480.

[10]  *JN* II, 80 (JRGS6/1, 480).

[11]  Pope Benedict XVI, *Encyclical Letter Deus Caritas Est* [hereafter, *DCE*] (Vatican City: Liberia Editrice Vaticana, 2005), §14.

for the Church as she offers this transformative eschatological love, which she has received from Christ, to all people through her mission of charity.

In chapter five, I argued that the liturgy should symbolically reflect the reality expressed by the *lex credendi*. Hence, the call to either restore the practice of celebrating the liturgy *ad orientem* or to place a crucifix on the middle of an altar as a practical compromise highlights the reality that the liturgy is inherently eschatological and cosmological. The symbolic meaning that has been overshadowed by abandoning worship *ad orientem* is that the people of God are meant to join the priest in fixing their eyes, hearts, and minds on Christ, the true *Oriens*. This physical orientation of the body towards the incarnate *Oriens* is also a symbol for the essence of the human person as a *homo adorans*. People experience the call to adoration and worship in the very depths of their being, so I have demonstrated in the context of this anthropology the significance of Ratzinger's focus on gestures and postures as a means of disciplining the body as a preparation for the communion and love of the eschaton. The celebration of the liturgy is both an anticipation and realization of the eschaton. The liturgy is the best way to prepare for the Parousia, which presupposes a person's active participation (*participatio actuosa*), which consists of both external actions and internal dispositions.

In order to highlight the *logos* of the liturgy as the heavenly Jerusalem or the manifestation of the new Temple, it has been argued that beauty (the *via pulchritudinis*) is an inherent quality of the liturgy since it helps to symbolize the eschaton proleptically.

The emphasis on the role of beauty within the *ars celebrandi* is not a matter of personal preference or taste for Ratzinger; rather, he desires the truth of what the liturgy is as a participation in heavenly worship to become more explicit. When utility is the governing principle, then the truth of what the liturgy is can become overshadowed, and the emphasis is placed on what is imminent or created by the human person rather than on what is transcendent or sacred.

## EUCHARISTIC PERSONALISM

The manner in which the liturgy is celebrated has been the subject of much critique by Ratzinger because the union between what is human and divine has collapsed, favoring what is simply human. In other words, in practice, the liturgy has become subject to the *ethos* of humanity that has refashioned how the liturgy is celebrated according to a subjective preference or, at its worst, an ideological agenda. Building upon his Christology, Ratzinger weaves together his theology of liturgy, eschatology, ecclesiology, theological anthropology, and moral theology. This method has been described by Ratzinger himself as a Eucharistic personalism.

The personalistic and dialogical nature of the Eucharist can be summarized with Christopher Collins, who maintains that in Ratzinger's theology, "the Christian is drawn into a foretaste of eschatological fulfillment and the inner dynamic of new creation insofar as he or she participates in the paschal mystery of Christ."[12] Collins further explains this dynamic: "Participation in the liturgy is the entrance *par excellence* of the members of the church into the 'I' of Christ. For Ratzinger, to 'enter into the "I" of Christ' is fundamentally to step into the dialogical relationship between divinity and humanity."[13] The dialogical relationship, which God initiates with humanity throughout salvation history, culminates in the Incarnation of Jesus Christ. Christians have the mission to be drawn into that dialogical love and to bring others with them into communion with Jesus and his Church. The experience of this dialogical love in the Eucharist realizes and anticipates the communion of the eschaton. This movement within the symphony of Ratzinger is simultaneously finished and unfinished. The description of the movement that unites the liturgy and eschatology is finished, but the fulfillment of the symphony's finale has yet to come.

Ratzinger places a great deal of emphasis upon the primacy of *logos* over *ethos* as a unifying theme throughout his works. When *logos* is subordinated to *ethos*, the human person becomes subjected to a materialist ontology (a *logos* defined by *technē*) that leads to an *ethos* that is concerned above all by utility and progress, which affects our approach to the liturgy and eschatology. How the liturgy is celebrated becomes subject to the individual whim of one person or a group of people. Eschatology becomes fixated on addressing the temporal needs of a society guided by a narrow conception of hope or political theology. If the human person wants to understand his authentic sacramental *logos* (which is characterized by a *logos* of *communio*), then he must first turn to Christ, the incarnate *Logos*, who reveals to us that we are created for a relationship with God and others. In other words, Ratzinger's *logos*-centric and Christocentric theology underscores the human person's call to a *dia-logos*. The individual "I" enters into a communion of dialogical love with the eternal "Thou," but this can only take place as the individual "I" enters into the identity of the "I" of the Son of God: "The Christian dialogue with God is mediated

---

[12] Christopher S. Collins, *The Word Made Love: The Dialogical Theology of Joseph Ratzinger/Benedict XVI* (Collegeville, MN: Liturgical Press, 2013), 160.

[13] Collins, *The Word Made Love*, 160.

by other human beings in a history where God speaks with men. It is expressed in the 'We' form proper to the children of God."[14] In Ratzinger's estimation, this dialogue within the body of Christ can become a reality "only by becoming a son with the Son, and this must mean in turn by becoming one with all those others who seek the Father."[15] Under the influence of personalism, which he received from Augustine, Buber, and de Lubac, Ratzinger stresses that there is a "we" characteristic of the faith that proceeds from the intimate communion between the human "I" and the "Thou" of God in Jesus Christ. Ratzinger's Christology is strongly connected with his thesis on the primacy of the *Logos*. In his Christology, Ratzinger develops who Jesus is in light of the union of his two natures and the centrality of sacrifice in his mission.

## CHRISTOCENTRIC UNION

The foundation for Ratzinger's spiritual Christology is the Chalcedonian doctrine on Jesus Christ, who was, according to the Third Council of Constantinople, "acknowledged in two natures that undergo no confusion, no change, no separation, no division; at no point was the difference between the natures taken away through the union, but rather the property of both natures is preserved and comes together in a single person and hypostasis."[16] Constantinople clearly builds upon its Chalcedonian Christology by defining that in Christ there are

> two natural volitions or wills and two natural actions, without division, without change, without separation, without confusion. The two natural wills are not—by any means—opposed to each other as the impious heretics assert; but his human will is compliant; it does not resist or oppose but rather submits to his divine and almighty will."[17]

---

[14] Joseph Ratzinger, *Eschatology: Death and Eternal Life*, ed. Aidan Nichols, O.P., trans. Michael Waldstein, 2nd ed. (Washington, DC: The Catholic University of America Press, 2007), 159; *Auferstehung und ewiges Leben: Beiträge zur Eschatologie und zur Theologie der Hoffnung* [hereafter, JRGS10], Gesammelte Schriften 10, ed. Gerhard Ludwig Müller (Freiburg: Herder, 2012), 169.

[15] Ratzinger, *Eschatology*, 159 (JRGS10, 169).

[16] Heinrich Denzinger, *Enchiridion symbolorum definitionum et declarationum de rebus fidei et morum: Compendium of Creeds, Definitions and Declarations on Matters of Faith and Morals* [hereafter, DH], ed., Peter Hünermann, 43rd ed. (San Francisco: Ignatius Press, 2012), 555.

[17] DH, 556.

These excerpts from the Third Council of Constantinople highlight both the unity and distinction between the two natures and two wills of Jesus Christ.

Ratzinger observes in current theological discourse not only a separation of the human and divine natures of Christ but also an emphasis on the human over and above the divine. A study of the relationship between liturgy and eschatology cannot be brought to full fruition without engaging Christology. Ratzinger has warned of a Nestorianism that continues to challenge contemporary theology. The key to maintaining a balanced view of the liturgy and eschatology is to start with a Christology that Aaron Riches argues must begin with the "absolute *unitas* of the human Jesus with the divine Son."[18] When Ratzinger is thought to advocate a "traditionalist" liturgical theology or an eschatology that places too much emphasis on the vertical communion, this criticism misses the mark because the real focus of Ratzinger is the union between humanity and God that begins with the Incarnation of the *Logos* and has been consummated by the Paschal Mystery of Christ. Using the definition of "the two wills in Christ" from the Third Council of Constantinople, we can safely say that Christians are called to "not resist or oppose but rather [submit] to his divine and almighty will."[19]

Emphasizing the Councils of Chalcedon and Constantinople III, Ratzinger stresses the unity of Christ's nature as a remedy against a neo-Nestorianism, which undermines the unity between the human nature of Christ and the divine *Logos*. In view of the unity between Christology and liturgy, if we do not understand Christology correctly, then we will inevitably not celebrate the liturgy properly. In his general audience on St. Cyril of Alexandria (c. 378–444), the major opponent of Nestorius, Pope Benedict highlights this quotation from Cyril as emblematic of Cyril's Christology:

We will profess only one Christ and Lord, not in the sense that we

---

[18] Aaron Riches, *Ecce Homo: On the Divine Unity of Christ* (Grand Rapids, MI: Eerdmans Publishing, 2016), 3–4: "[T]he only tenable starting point for Christology lies in the absolute *unitas* of the human Jesus with the divine Son. This opposes any alternative starting point that would begin from a theoretical or ontological *separatio* of divinity and humanity in Christ in order to proceed discretely 'from below.' To begin 'from below' is to presume that what homo 'is' and it can 'do' in the case of Jesus is something that can be established (with better certitude) apart from the 'one Lord' proclaimed in the *Credo*."

[19] DH, 556.

worship the man together with the *Logos*, in order not to suggest the idea of separation by saying "together," but in the sense that we worship only one and the same, because he is not extraneous to the *Logos*, his body, with which he also sits at his Father's side, not as if "two sons" are sitting beside him but only one, united with his own flesh."[20]

Cyrillian Christology preserves and emphasizes the union between the divine *Logos* and the human nature of the One Person of the Son. As discussed above in chapter two, this insistence upon the unity of the two natures in Christ is a concern of Ratzinger as he perceives that a one-sided emphasis upon the human nature of Jesus seems to prevail in contemporary theology.[21] In response to monophysitism, the Council of Chalcedon brought further clarity, continuity, and development of Cyrillian Christology.[22] The *definitio* of Chalcedon expresses the unity and the distinction between the two natures of Christ:

Following therefore the holy Fathers, we unanimously teach to confess one and the same Son, our Lord Jesus Christ, the same perfect in divinity and perfect in humanity, the same truly God and truly man composed of rational soul and body, the same one in being with the Father as to the divinity and one in being with us as to the humanity, "like unto us in all things but sin" [*cf. Heb* 4:15]. The same was begotten from the Father before the ages as to the divinity and in the latter days for us and our salvation was born as to his humanity from Mary, the Virgin Mother of God. We confess that one and the same Lord Jesus Christ, the only begotten Son, must be acknowledged in two natures, without

---

[20] Cyril, *Second Letter of Cyril of Alexandria to Nestorius*, in PG 77:44–49. Quoted by Benedict XVI, General Audience, October 3, 2007, in *The Fathers*, vol. 1, *Wednesday General Audiences from March 7, 2007–February 27, 2008* (Huntington, IN: Our Sunday Visitor, 2008), 115. On the Christology of Cyril and the Nestorian Controversy, see Aaron Riches, *Ecce Homo*, 21–54; John McGuckin, *Saint Cyril of Alexandria and the Christological Controversy: Its History, Theology and Texts* (Crestwood, NY: St. Vladimir's Seminary Press, 2004); Susan Wessel, *Cyril of Alexandria and the Nestorian Controversy* (Oxford: Oxford University Press, 2004); Thomas G. Weinandy, O.F.M. Cap., "Cyril and the Mystery of the Incarnation," in *The Theology of St. Cyril of Alexandria: A Critical Appreciation*, ed. Thomas G. Weinandy, O.F.M. Cap., and Daniel A. Keating (London: T & T Clark, 2003), 23–54;

[21] See *NSL*, 10.

[22] See Riches, *Ecce Homo*, 55–87.

confusion or change, without division or separation. The distinction between the natures was never abolished by their union but rather the character proper to each of the two natures was preserved as they came together in one Person and one hypostasis. He is not split or divided into two Persons, but he is one and the same only begotten Son, God the Word, the Lord Jesus Christ, as formerly the prophets and later Jesus Christ himself have taught us about him and as has been handed down to us by the creed of the Fathers.[23]

Chalcedon affirms that the union of the two natures of Christ must be recognized "without confusion or change, without division or separation." The Council also stresses their distinction "was never abolished by their union but rather the character proper to each of the two natures was preserved as they came together in one Person and one hypostasis."

The careful review of Ephesus and Chalcedon is critical to validate the significance of the Third Council of Constantinople for Ratzinger's Christology. In view of Chalcedon's teaching, Ratzinger affirms, "the affirmation of the true humanity and the true divinity in Christ can only retain its meaning if the mode of the unity of both is clarified."[24] Chalcedon teaches that the unity of the two natures is preserved by the "one Person" and "one hypostasis," but no further explanation is given.

It is crucial to revisit Ratzinger's brief exploration of the unique insight into the teaching of the Third Council of Constantinople as this aspect of his spiritual Christology will ultimately have implications for his theology of liturgy. The Council of Constantinople, in response to the heresy of Monothelitism, offers the definitive teaching on the two wills of the incarnate *Logos*. Ratzinger summarizes the teaching of Constantinople as he affirms with the Council that "as man, Jesus has a human will which is not absorbed by the divine will. But this human will follows the divine will and thus becomes one will with it, not in a natural manner but along the path of freedom."[25] In the Garden of Gethsemane, Jesus prays to the Father with these words: "Not what I will, but what you will" (Mark 14:36). Acknowledging Maximus the Confessor as the greatest interpreter of this passage of Constantinople, Ratzinger describes the significance of this submission in the Mount of Olives: "[T]he Logos so humbles himself

---

[23] DH, 301–302.
[24] Ratzinger, *BPO*, 38 (JRGS6/2, 712).
[25] Ratzinger, *BPO*, 38–39 (JRGS6/2, 712).

that he adopts a man's will as his own and addresses the Father with the 'I' of this human being; he transfers his own 'I' to this man and thus transforms human speech into the eternal Word, into his blessed 'Yes, Father.'"[26]

In a conference at Fontgombault, Ratzinger offers a definition of the theology of liturgy[27] which is foundational for understanding his thought and emphasizes the primacy and centrality of the incarnate *Logos*:

> Theology of the Liturgy means that God acts through Christ in the Liturgy and that we can [only] act through Him and with Him. We cannot build the way to God on our own accord. This way does not open up unless God Himself becomes the way. And again, the ways of man which do not lead to God are non-ways. Furthermore, Theology of the Liturgy means that the Logos Himself speaks to us in the liturgy; and not only does He speak, He comes in body and soul, flesh and blood, divinity and humanity, in order to unite us to Himself to make of us one "body."

---

[26] Ratzinger, *BPO*, 41 (JRGS6/2, 714).

[27] Ratzinger uses the phrase "theology of liturgy," but his application of it seems to differ from the type of theology critiqued by Schmemann: "[W]e need *liturgical theology*, viewed not as a theology of worship and not as a reduction of theology to liturgy, but as a slow and patient bringing together of that which was for too long a time [fragmented] and because of many factors broken and isolated—liturgy, theology, and piety, their reintegration within one fundamental vision." *Liturgy and Tradition: Theological Reflections of Alexander Schmemann*, ed. Thomas Fisch (Crestwood, NY: St. Vladimir's Seminary Press), 1990, 46. At the same time, there is a distinction between what David Fagerberg differentiates into three approaches: (1) theology *of* worship, (2) theology *from* worship, and (3) liturgical theology. *Theologia Prima: What Is Liturgical Theology*, 2nd ed. (Mundelein, IL: Hillenbrand Books, 2004), 43. For a full development of the nuances characteristic of each of these approaches, see Fagerberg, *Theologia Prima*, 39–72. Arguably, Ratzinger's thought can be characterized as a liturgical theology. The liturgy is the *theologia prima* for Ratzinger, but he never explicitly develops this understanding. At the same time, Ratzinger's theology of liturgy is distinct in its approach from the liturgical theology of Schmemann. For a brief differentiation of Ratzinger's theology of liturgy and the liturgical theology of Schmemann, Aidan Kavanaugh, and Fagerberg, see Helmut Hoping, "Kult und Reflexion: Joseph Ratzinger als Liturgietheologie," in *Der Logos-gemäße Gottesdienst: Theologie der Liturgie bei Joseph Ratzinger*, ed. Rudolf Voderholzer, (Regensburg: Friedrich Pustet, 2009), 13–19. Cf. Philip Caldwell, *Liturgy as Revelation: Re-Sourcing a Theme in Twentieth-Century Catholic Theology* (Minneapolis: Fortress Press, 2014), 497–505. Throughout his conclusion Caldwell's argument is that Ratzinger does not "develop the notion that the liturgy is the form in which the words and gestures of revelation take shape" (500). I am not convinced that this is the case when one addresses the whole of Ratzinger's theology as a unified symphony.

The entirety of salvation history is in the Christian liturgy; even more, the whole history of the human search for God is present, assumed and brought to its goal. The Christian liturgy is cosmic liturgy—it embraces the whole of creation which "awaits the revelation of the sons of God" (Rom 8:19).[28]

A key element in Ratzinger's definition of the liturgy is that the *Logos* becomes incarnate "in order to unite us to Himself to make of us one 'body.'" The liturgy is the worship of God, which is first and foremost an *opus Dei* and not the work or product of the human person.

The faithful are able to participate in the worship of the Body of Christ through the unity of Christ the Priest and with his Body, the Church. The *Catechism of the Catholic Church* notes that the liturgy means the "participation of the People of God 'in the work of God.'"[29] Through our participation in this work of God, worshippers are simultaneously in communion with the past, the present, and the future: creation, history, and the eschaton. According to Ratzinger, what unites time and eternity for the Second Vatican Council is the Pasch of Christ, which "forms the central category of the liturgical theology of the Council."[30]

The unity between the *lex orandi* and the *lex credendi* becomes evident with Ratzinger's consistency in maintaining the view that the key to understanding the liturgy is the Paschal Mystery. In his estimation, the Paschal Mystery, which Ratzinger refers to as simply "the work of Jesus," is "the real content of the liturgy." Continuing this train of thought,

---

[28] JRCW11, 655 (JRGS11, 556).

[29] *CCC* §1069.

[30] JRCW11, 578 (JRGS11, 700). Pope Benedict XVI emphasizes this view as he highlights two passages to define the liturgy from *Sacrosanctum Concilium*: "In [*SC*, §5], it points out, in fact, that the works of God are his actions in history which bring us salvation and which culminated in the death and Resurrection of Jesus Christ; but in [*SC*, §7], the same Constitution defines the celebration of the liturgy as an 'action of Christ.' In fact, these two meanings are inseparably linked. If we ask ourselves who saves the world and man, the only answer is Jesus of Nazareth, Lord and Christ, the Crucified and Risen One. And where does the Mystery of the death and Resurrection of Christ that brings salvation become real for us, for me, today? The answer is: in Christ's action through the Church, in the liturgy, and especially, in the sacrament of the Eucharist, which makes present the sacrificial offering of the Son of God who has redeemed us; in the sacrament of Reconciliation, in which one moves from the death of sin to new life; and in the other sacramental acts that sanctify us (cf. *Presbyterorum Ordinis*, n. 5). Thus the Paschal Mystery of the death and Resurrection of Christ is the center of the liturgical theology of the Council." *Prayer* (Huntington, IN: Our Sunday Visitor, 2013), 263.

Ratzinger concludes, "[T]he present historical moment is transcended [in the liturgy], leading into the permanent divine-human act of redemption. In it, Christ is really the responsible subject: it is the work of Christ; but in it he draws history to himself, into this permanent act which is the locus of our salvation."[31] Through the celebration of the liturgy, the faithful are able to enter into the heart of the faith: the Paschal Mystery. Ratzinger focuses on the sacrificial love of Christ and our participation in this reality in light of the unfolding of salvation history in the present because the faithful have received this gift of Christ's selfless love, so that they might be able to give generously of ourselves in love. Every Christian is called to make the mystery of the Pasch in his or her life through a life of charity that is essential for the Church's mission in the world.

## The *Logos*-centric Theology of Saints

Eschatology must also take its direction from the liturgy properly understood and celebrated. Hope cannot be reduced to the empty promises of progress or politics. The liturgy offers a sacramental ontology that can reorient theologies of hope and political theologies (Moltmann and Metz) back to their proper order, which is first transcendent before it is imminent.[32] The search for the kingdom of God cannot begin with the building up of a perfect and just society here below. On December 12, 2000, in a presentation to catechists and religion teachers on the new evangelization, Ratzinger contended that "[t]heocentrism is fundamental in the message of Jesus and must also be at the heart of the new evangelization. The keyword of the proclamation of Jesus is: the Kingdom of God. But the Kingdom of God is not a thing, a social or political structure, or a utopia. The Kingdom of God is God."[33]

---

[31] JRCW11, 542 (JRGS11, 640).

[32] Commenting upon the theology of liberation developed by Moltmann and Metz, Cardinal Müller maintains, "Ecclesiastic activity is not reconverted by the theology of liberation for the creation of an inner-wordly paradise. On the contrary, it is the participation in the eschatological, the world in history and the transforming and liberation acts of God into eternity." Gerhard Cardinal Müller, *Catholic Dogmatics: For the Study and Practice of Theology*, trans. William Hadfield-Burkardt, vol. 1: Doctrine of Creation—Eschatology (New York: The Crossroad Publishing Company, 2017), 132.

[33] Joseph Ratzinger, "The New Evangelization," Address to Catechists and Religion Teachers, Jubilee of Catechists and Religion Teachers (December 12, 2000), introduction, *EWTN*, accessed July 27, 2016, https://www.cmvic.net/documents/2014/0/address%20to%20catechists%20and%20religion%20teachers.pdf. In this address, Ratzinger also takes note of the major shift in the position of Metz: "In his conference

As with his assertion regarding the liturgy as the *opus Dei*, it can be maintained that Ratzinger stresses that eschatology is also an *opus Dei*. Notably, Ratzinger emphasizes that the fundamental message of Jesus is "theocentrism," which is meant to highlight the contrasting message that reduces the kingdom of God to a form of anthropocentrism. The Gospel introduces us to the reality of the Divine *Logos*, who alone is able to reveal an authentic understanding of our own *logos* to us. In light of his emphasis and understanding of Christ as the incarnate *Logos*, theocentrism, which Ratzinger emphasizes in this address, is synonymous with Christocentrism. In his classical work *Introduction to Christianity*, Ratzinger highlights Augustine's commentary on a passage from John 7:16: *"Mea doctrina non est mea"* ("My teaching is not mine, but his who sent me").[34] In light of this commentary, Ratzinger concludes, "The most individual element in us—the only thing that belongs to us in the last analysis—our own 'I,' is at the same time the least individual element of all, for precisely our 'I' that we have neither from ourselves nor for ourselves."[35] Christ preaches God at the center of his message, and he reveals that the *logos*, which we discover in Christ and not in ourselves, reveals that we are made "for" others. The absence of an authentic or consistent communion with the *Logos* leads to a fixation that subordinates *logos* to *ethos*, which results in the human person subjecting all reality to himself.

One of the greatest interests of Ratzinger has been to emphasize the importance of the saints at the heart of the renewal and reform of the

---

when leaving the University of Münster, the theologian J. B. Metz said some unexpected things for him. In the past, Metz taught us anthropocentrism—the true occurrence of Christianity was the anthropological turning point, the secularization, the discovery of the secularity of the world. Then he taught us political theology—the political characteristics of faith; then the 'dangerous memory'; and finally narrative theology. After this long and difficult path, today he tells us: The true problem of our times is the 'Crisis of God,' the absence of God, disguised by an empty religiosity. Theology must go back to being truly theo-logy, speaking about and with God. Metz is right: the unum necessarium for man is God" Joseph Ratzinger, *Zeichen unter den Völkern: Schriften zur Ekklesiologie und Ökumene*, Gesammelte Schriften 8/2 [hereafter, JRGS8/2], ed. Gerhard Ludwig Müller, (Freiburg: Herder, 2010), 1239.

34 See Joseph Ratzinger, *Introduction to Christianity* [hereafter, *IC*], trans. J. R. Foster (San Francisco: Ignatius Press, 2004), 189–90; *Einführung in das Christentum: Bekenntnis—Taufe—Nachfolge*, Joseph Ratzinger Gesammelte Shriften 4, [hereafter, JRGS4] ed. Gerhard Ludwig Müller (Freiburg: Herder, 2014), 180–81. Ratzinger cites Augustine, *In Ioannis Evangelium tractatus* 29, 3 (on John 7:16), in *Corpus Christianorium* 36:285.

35 *IC*, 190 (JRGS4, 181).

Church: "Saints, in fact, reformed the Church in depth, not by working up plans for new structures, but by reforming themselves. What the Church needs in order to respond to the needs of humanity in every age is holiness, not management."[36] The eschatological renewal that we need is given in every period of history by the saints.

The encounter with Jesus in the Eucharist transforms every aspect of life, so that the saints become living embodiments of the eschaton to come. With the pope emeritus, it is not difficult to maintain that the saints and their encounter with Christ in the Eucharist are the hope for renewal in the Church and the new evangelization. Benedict argues, "If we want the world to move forward a little, the only criterion in terms of which this can happen is God, who enters into our lives as a real presence."[37] The saints in Benedict's estimation have become this "real presence" through the gift of the liturgy: The Eucharist is the place where people can receive the kind of formation from which new things come into being. This is why the great figures who throughout history have really brought about revolutions for the good have been the saints who, touched by Christ, have brought new impulses into the world.[38]

The saints are a prophetic reminder that the "marriage of the lamb has come" (Rev 19:7). Simultaneously, we must realize and anticipate this by affirming that the liturgy is, above all, a *logikē latreia*. The witness and theology of the saints underscores the other Pauline verse, which aptly summarizes the Christocentric theology of the liturgy and eschatology of Ratzinger: "It is no longer I who live, but Christ who lives in me" (Gal 2:20). When we fully participate in the life and worship of Jesus Christ

---

[36] Joseph Ratzinger, *The Ratzinger Report: An Interview with Vittorio Messori*, trans. Salvator Attanasio and Graham Harrison (San Francisco: Ignatius Press, 1985), 53. The saints provide the Church with a lived Christology: "[E]ffective advances in Christology cannot ever derive from purely academic theology, not even from the modern theology which, in critical exegesis, in the history of dogma, in anthropology, pursues human sciences and other disciplines. All this is important, important as academic studies are. But it is not enough. We all need the theology of the saints, the theology which derives from a concrete experience of divine reality. All the effective advances in theological knowledge have their origin in the eye of love, in the strength of its gaze." Joseph Ratzinger, *Journey to Easter: Spiritual Reflections for the Lenten Season*, trans. Dame Mary Groves, O.S.B. (New York: The Crossroad Publishing Company, 1987), 138.

[37] Benedict XVI, *Light of the World: The Pope, the Church, and the Signs of the Times: A Conversation with Peter Seewald*, trans. Michael J. Miller and Adrian J. Walker (San Francisco: Ignatius Press, 2010), 158.

[38] Benedict XVI, *Light of the World*, 158.

and orient our lives towards him as the incarnate *Oriens*, we will become more joyful evangelists, inviting all people to the communion of love with both God and neighbor.

Ratzinger describes his work as having an "incomplete character,"[39] yet I have demonstrated that there is a unity within his "fragmentary" writings that is defined by the primacy and centrality of the *Logos* incarnate. It has been argued throughout this book how the focus on the *logos* consistently unites his eschatology with his theology of liturgy, in whose orbit can also be found his Christology, ecclesiology, theological anthropology, and ethics. In an article on transubstantiation, Ratzinger emphasizes the significance of the Resurrection and the Ascension for the transformation of the human person, as these aspects of the Paschal Mystery represent our "entrance into the new mode of existence of God-given openness toward men."[40] The Paschal Mystery brings the full hominization of the person to its fruition, which requires him to enter into the dynamic of Christ's life and love. Christ's "vicarious representation" (*Stellvertretung*) must become incarnate through our sacrificial love so we can be united as one Body of Christ within the Church, which has the mission of drawing others into a *logos* of communion and an *ethos* of charity.

Ratzinger employs an image that is attributed to St. Basil the Great.[41] Alluding to the prophet Amos and his image of the sycamore tree, Basil maintains that this tree is a symbol for the pagan culture of his time because "it offers a surplus, yet at the same time it is insipid. This comes from living according to pagan customs. When one manages to slit them by the means of the Logos, it [the pagan world] is transformed, becomes tasty and useful."[42] Alone, the sycamore tree and its fruit are incapable of bringing about their own transformation. Ratzinger argues, "The Logos itself must slit our culture and their fruit, so that what is unusable is purified and becomes not only usable but good. . . . Ultimately only the Logos himself

---

[39] Ratzinger has characterized various themes in his theology as "fragmentary," "unfinished," or "incomplete." See Joseph Ratzinger, preface to *Truth and Tolerance* [hereafter, *TT*], trans. Henry Taylor (San Francisco: Ignatius Press, 2004), 10; Ratzinger, preface to *Values in a Time of Upheaval*, trans. Brian McNeil (San Francisco: Ignatius Press, 2006), 8.

[40] JRCW11, 241 (JRGS11, 297).

[41] Ratzinger cites Basil, *In Is* 9, 228 (commentary on Isaiah 9:10), PG 30:516D/517A, cited in Christian Gnilka, *Chrêsis: Die Methode der Kirchenväter im Umgang mit der antiken Kultur*, vol. 2 of *Kultur und Conversion* (Basel, 1993), 84–86. Joseph Ratzinger, *On the Way to Jesus Christ*, trans. Michael J. Miller (San Francisco: Ignatius Press, 2004), 46–47 (JRGS8/2, 1258–59).

[42] Ratzinger, *On the Way to Jesus Christ*, 46 (JRGS8/2, 1258).

can guide our cultures to their true purity and maturity, but the Logos makes us his servants, the 'dresser of sycamore trees.'"[43] The *Logos* can lead the liturgy, eschatology, and ultimately the culture to their authentic end, which is communion with God in Jesus Christ. Ratzinger has consistently demonstrated that the transformation of the person and the culture cannot be realized by humanity's efforts alone. Rather, the incarnate *Logos* has loved us first (1 John 4:10), and we are made for eschatological union with him, anticipated here and now through the Eucharist. Our Lord is here; our Lord, come!

---

[43] Ratzinger, *On the Way to Jesus Christ*, 47 (JRGS8/2, 1258–59).

# Selected Bibliography

## Primary Sources

### Pope Benedict XVI

Benedict XVI [Joseph Ratzinger]. "40 Jahre Konstitution über die Heilige Liturgie: Rückblick und Vorblick." *Liturgisches Jahrbuch* 53 (2003): 209–21.

———. "Address of His Holiness Benedict XVI to Artists." November 21, 2009. *The Holy See.* Accessed June 23, 2010. https://www.vatican.va/content/benedict-xvi/en/speeches/2009/november/documents/hf_ben-xvi_spe_20091121_artisti.html.

———. [Joseph Ratzinger]. "Alcune forme bibliche ed ecclesiali di 'Presenza' dello Spirito nella storia." In *Spirito Santo e storia*, edited by Luigi Sartori, 51–64. Rome: Ave, 1977.

———. *The Apostles and Their Co-Workers.* Wednesday General Audiences from March 15, 2006–February 14, 2007. Huntington, IN: Our Sunday Visitor, 2007.

———. *Apostolic Constitution Anglicanorum Coetibus.* Vatican City: Libreria Editrice Vaticana, 2009.

———. "Apostolic Letter in the Form of '*Motu Proprio' Summorum Pontificum.* July 7, 2007." Appendix I to *The Old Mass and the New: Explaining the Motu Proprio Summorum Pontificum of Pope Benedict XVI*, by Bishop Marc Aillet, 97–103. Translated by Henry Taylor. San Francisco: Ignatius Press, 2010.

———. [Joseph Ratzinger]. *Auferstehung und ewiges Leben: Beiträge zur Eschatologie und zur Theologie der Hoffnung.* Gesammelte Schriften 10, edited by Gerhard Ludwig Müller. Freiburg: Herder, 2012.

———. [Joseph Ratzinger]. *Behold the Pierced One: An Approach to Spiritual Christology.* Translated by Graham Harrison. San Francisco: Ignatius Press, 1986.

———. [Joseph Ratzinger]. *Called to Communion: Understanding the Church Today.* Translated by Adrian Walker. San Francisco: Ignatius Press, 1996.

_____. [Joseph Ratzinger]. "Cardinal Joseph Ratzinger's Answer to Pere Farnés." *Antiphon* 20, no. 2 (2016): 90–95.

_____. [Joseph Ratzinger]. "Christ, Faith and the Challenge of Cultures." March 2–5, 1993 address. Accessed March 8, 2010. https://www.vatican.va/roman_curia/congregations/cfaith/incontri/rc_con_cfaith_19930303_hong-kong-ratzinger_en.html.

_____. [Joseph Ratzinger]. *Christianity and the Crisis of Cultures*. Translated by Brian McNeil. San Francisco: Ignatius Press, 2006.

_____. [Joseph Ratzinger]. *Church, Ecumenism and Politics: New Endeavors in Ecclesiology*. Translated by Michael J. Miller, et al. San Francisco: Ignatius Press, 2008.

_____. [Joseph Ratzinger]. *Co-Workers of the Truth*. Edited by Irene Grassl. Translated by Mary Frances McCarthy and Lothar Krauth. San Francisco: Ignatius Press, 1992.

_____. [Joseph Ratzinger]. *"Der Geist der Liturgie*—Oder: die Treue zum Konzil: Antwort an Pater Gy." *Liturgisches Jahrbuch* 52, no. 2 (2002): 111–15.

_____. [Joseph Ratzinger]. "The Dignity of the Human Person." In *Commentary on the Documents of Vatican II*. vol. 5, edited by Herbert Vorgrimler. New York: Herder and Herder, 1969.

_____. *Doctors of the Church*, Wednesday General Audiences from June 20, 2007–April 6, 2011, Huntington, IN: Our Sunday Visitor, 2011.

_____. [Joseph Ratzinger]. *Dogma and Preaching*: *Applying Christian Doctrine to a Daily Life*. Translated by Michael J. Miller. San Francisco: Ignatius Press, 2011.

_____. [Joseph Ratzinger]. *Einführung in das Christentum: Bekenntnis—Taufe—Nachfolge*. Joseph Ratzinger Gesammelte Shriften 4, edited by Gerhard Ludwig Müller. Freiburg: Herder, 2014.

_____. Encyclical Letter *Caritas in Veritate*. Vatican City: Libreria Editrice Vaticana, 2009.

_____. Encyclical Letter *Deus Caritas Est*. Vatican City: Libreria Editrice Vaticana, 2005.

_____. Encyclical Letter *Spe Salvi*. Vatican City: Libreria Editrice Vaticana, 2007.

_____. [Joseph Ratzinger]. "The End of Time." In *The End of Time? The Provocation of Talking about God*, edited by Tiemo Rainer Peters and Claus Urban, translated by J. Matthew Ashley, 4–25. Mahwah, NJ: Paulist Press, 2004.

_____. [Joseph Ratzinger]. *Eschatology, Death, and Eternal Life*. 2nd ed. Edited by Aidan Nichols, O.P. Translated by Michael Waldstein. Washington, DC: The Catholic University of America Press, 2007.

_____. [Joseph Ratzinger]. *Europe: Today and Tomorrow*. Translated by Michael J. Miller. San Francisco: Ignatius Press, 2007.

_____. [Joseph Ratzinger]. *Faith and the Future*. Translated by Ronald Walls. San Francisco: Ignatius Press, 2009.

_____. *The Fathers*, vol. 1, Wednesday General Audiences from March 7, 2007–February 27, 2008. Huntington, IN: Our Sunday Visitor, 2008.

_____. *The Fathers*, vol. 2, Wednesday General Audiences from March 5, 2008–

October 21, 2009. Huntington, IN: Our Sunday Visitor, 2008.

_____. [Joseph Ratzinger]. *The Feast of Faith: Approaches to a Theology of Liturgy*. Translated by Graham Harrison. San Francisco: Ignatius Press, 1986.

_____. [Joseph Ratzinger]. "The Feeling of Things, the Contemplation of Beauty." Message to the Communion and Liberation (CL) Meeting, Rimini. August 24–30, 2002. *The Holy See*. Accessed July 4, 2010. http://www.vatican.va/roman_curia/congregations/cfaith/documents/rc_con_cfaith_doc_20020824_ratzinger-cl-rimini_en.html.

_____. [Joseph Ratzinger]. "Freedom and Liberation: The Anthropological Vision of the Instruction *Libertatis Conscientia*." *Communio* 14, no. 1 (1987): 55–72.

_____. [Joseph Ratzinger]. *Fundamental Speeches from Five Decades*. Edited by Florian Schuller. Translated by Michael J. Miller, J. R. Foster, and Adrian Walker. San Francisco: Ignatius Press, 2012.

_____. General Audience. November 18, 2009. *The Holy See*. Accessed June 23, 2010. https://www.vatican.va/content/benedict-xvi/en/audiences/2009/documents/hf_ben-xvi_aud_20091118.html.

_____. [Joseph Ratzinger]. *God and the World: A Conversation with Peter Seewald*. Translated by Henry Taylor. San Francisco: Ignatius Press, 2002.

_____. [Joseph Ratzinger]. *God Is Near Us: The Eucharist, the Heart of Life*. Edited by Stephan Otto Horn and Vinzenz Pfnür. Translated by Henry Taylor. San Francisco: Ignatius Press, 2003.

_____. *God's Revolution: World Youth Day and Other Cologne Talks*. San Francisco: Ignatius Press, 2006.

_____. [Joseph Ratzinger]. "Guardini on Christ in our Century." *Crisis* 14 (June 1996): 14–15.

_____. [Joseph Ratzinger] "Handing on the Faith and the Sources of Faith." In *Handing on the Faith in an Age of Disbelief*. Translated by Michael J. Miller, 13–40. San Francisco: Ignatius Press, 2006.

_____. *Heart of the Christian Life: Thoughts on Holy Mass*. San Francisco: Ignatius Press, 2010.

_____. Homily of Benedict XVI. Basilica of St. John Lateran, Holy Thursday, April 9, 2009. *The Holy See*. Accessed January 7, 2017. http://www.vatican.va/content/benedict-xvi/en/homilies/2009/documents/hf_ben-xvi_hom_20090409_coena-domini.html.

_____. *Images of Hope: Meditations on Major Feasts*. Translated by John Rock and Graham Harrison. San Francisco: Ignatius Press, 2006.

_____. [Joseph Ratzinger]. *In the Beginning: A Catholic Understanding of Creation and the Fall*. Translated by Boniface Ramsey, O.P. Huntington, IN: Our Sunday Visitor, 1990.

_____. [Joseph Ratzinger]. *Introduction to Christianity*. Translated by J. R. Foster. San Francisco: Ignatius Press, 2004.

_____. *Jesus of Nazareth: From the Baptism in the Jordan to the Transfiguration.* Translated by Adrian J. Walker. New York: Doubleday, 2007.

_____. *Jesus of Nazareth: The Infancy Narratives.* Translated by Philip J. Whitmore. New York: Image, 2012.

_____. *Jesus of Nazareth, Part Two. Holy Week: From the Entrance into Jerusalem to the Resurrection.* Translated by the Vatican Secretariat of State. San Francisco: Ignatius Press, 2011.

_____. [Joseph Ratzinger]. *Jesus von Nazareth: Beiträge zur Christologie.* Joseph Ratzinger Gesammelte Schriften 6/1 and 6/2, edited by Gerhard Ludwig Müller. Freiburg: Herder, 2013.

_____. [Joseph Ratzinger]. *Joseph Ratzinger in Communio.* Translated by Stephen Wentworth Arndt. Edited by David Schindler and Nicholas J. Healy. 2 vols. Grand Rapids, MI: Eerdmans, 2010–2013.

_____. [Joseph Ratzinger]. *Joseph Ratzinger-Benedict XVI, Der Gott des Glaubens und der Gott der Philosophen. Ein Beitrag zum Problem der theologia naturalis.* Edited by Heino Sonnemans. Leutesdorf: Johannes, 2005.

_____. [Joseph Ratzinger]. *Journey to Easter: Spiritual Reflections for the Lenten Season.* Translated by Dame Mary Groves, O.S.B. New York: The Crossroad Publishing Company, 1987.

_____. [Joseph Ratzinger]. *Kirche—Zeichen unter den Völkern: Schriften zur Ekklesiologie und Ökumene.* Gesammelte Schriften 8/1 and 8/2, edited by Gerhard Ludwig Müller. Freiburg im Breisgau: Herder, 2010.

_____. *Last Testament: In His Own Words.* Translated by Jacob Philips. New York: Bloomsbury, 2016.

_____. [Joseph Ratzinger] *Zur Lehre des Zweiten Vatikanischen Konzils.* Gesammelte Schriften 7/1 and 7/2, edited by Gerhard Ludwig Müller. Freiburg im Bresigau: Herder, 2012.

_____. "Letter of His Holiness Benedict XVI to the Bishops on the Occasion of the Publication of the Apostolic Letter '*Motu Proprio Data*' *Summorum Pontificum on the Use of the Roman Liturgy Prior to the Reform of 1970.*" Appendix II to *The Old Mass and the New: Explaining the Motu Proprio Summorum Pontificum of Pope Benedict XVI*, by Bishop Marc Aillet, 105–11. Translated by Henry Taylor. San Francisco: Ignatius Press, 2010.

_____. *Light of the World: The Pope, the Church, and the Signs of the Times: A Conversation with Peter Seewald.* Translated by Michael J. Miller and Adrian J. Walker. San Francisco: Ignatius Press, 2010.

_____. [Joseph Ratzinger]. *Many Religions, One Covenant: Israel, the Church and the World.* Translated by Graham Harrison. San Francisco: Ignatius Press, 1999.

_____. [Joseph Ratzinger]. *The Meaning of Christian Brotherhood.* 2nd ed. Translated by W. A. Glen-Doeple. San Francisco: Ignatius Press, 1993.

_____. [Joseph Ratzinger]. *Milestones: Memoirs 1927–1977.* Translated by Erasmo Leiva-Merikakis. San Francisco: Ignatius Press, 1998.

_____. [Joseph Ratzinger]. *The Nature and Mission of Theology: Approaches to Understanding Its Role in the Light of the Present Controversy.* Translated by Adrian Walker. San Francisco: Ignatius Press, 1995.

_____. [Joseph Ratzinger]. "The New Evangelization," Address to Catechists and Religion Teachers, Jubilee of Catechists and Religion Teachers. December 12, 2000. Accessed July 27, 2016. https://d2y1pz2y630308.cloudfront.net/5032/documents/2014/0/ADDRESS%20TO%20CATECHISTS%20AND%20RELIGION%20TEACHERS.pdf.

_____. [Joseph Ratzinger]. *A New Song for the Lord: Faith in Christ and Liturgy Today.* Translated by Martha M. Matesich. New York: The Crossroad Publishing Company, 1997.

_____. [Joseph Ratzinger]. *Offenbarungsverständnis und Geschichtstheologie Bonaventuras: Habilitationsschrift und Bonaventura-Studien.* Gesammelte Schriften 2, edited by Gerhard Ludwig Müller. Freiburg im Breisgau: Herder, 2009.

_____. [Joseph Ratzinger]. *On Conscience.* San Francisco: Ignatius Press, 2006.

_____. [Joseph Ratzinger]. *On the Way to Jesus Christ.* Translated by Michael J. Miller. San Francisco: Ignatius Press, 2004.

_____. [Joseph Ratzinger]. "Die organische Entwicklung der Liturgie." *Forum katholische Theologie* 21, no. 1 (2005): 36–39.

_____. [Joseph Ratzinger]. "The Paschal Mystery as Core and Foundation of Devotion to the Sacred Heart," in *Towards a Civilization of Love: A Symposium on the Scriptural and Theological Foundations of Devotion to the Heart of Jesus.* Translated by Erasmo Leiva-Merikakis. San Francisco: Ignatius Press, 1981.

_____. [Joseph Ratzinger]. *Pilgrim Fellowship of Faith: The Church as Communion.* Edited by Stephan Otto Horn and Vinzenz Pfnür. Translated by Henry Taylor. San Francisco: Ignatius Press, 2005.

_____. Post-synodal Apostolic Exhortation *Sacramentum Caritatis.* Vatican City: Libreria Editrice Vaticana, 2007.

_____. Post-synodal Apostolic Exhortation *Verbum Domini.* Vatican City: Libreria Editrice Vaticana, 2010.

_____. *Prayer.* Wednesday General Audiences on Prayer. Huntington, IN: Our Sunday Visitor, 2013.

_____. [Joseph Ratzinger]. *Principles of Catholic Theology: Building Stones for a Fundamental Theology.* Translated by Sister Mary Frances McCarthy, S.N.D. San Francisco: Ignatius Press, 1987.

_____. [Joseph Ratzinger]. *The Ratzinger Report: An Interview with Vittorio Messori.* Translated by Salvator Attanasio and Graham Harrison. San Francisco: Ignatius Press, 1985.

_____. *A Reason Open to God: On Universities, Education, and Culture.* Edited by J. Stephen Brown. Washington, DC: The Catholic University of America Press, 2013.

_____. *Saint Paul.* Translated by *L'Osservatore Romano.* San Francisco: Ignatius Press, 2009.

_____. [Joseph Ratzinger]. *Salt of the Earth: The Church at the End of the Millennium*. Translated by Adrian Walker. San Francisco: Ignatius Press, 1997.

_____. [Joseph Ratzinger]. *The Spirit of the Liturgy*. Translated by John Saward. San Francisco: Ignatius Press, 2000.

_____. [Joseph Ratzinger]. "*The Spirit of the Liturgy* or Fidelity to the Council: Response to Father Gy." *Antiphon* 11, no. 1 (2007): 98–101.

_____. [Joseph Ratzinger]. *Theological Highlights of Vatican II*. Translated by Henry Traub, S.J., Gerard C. Thormann, and Werner Barzel. Rev. ed. Mahwah, NJ: Paulist Press, 2009.

_____. [Joseph Ratzinger]. *Theology of History in St. Bonaventure*. Translated by Zachary Hayes, O.F.M. Chicago: Franciscan Herald Press, 1989.

_____. [Joseph Ratzinger]. *Theology of the Liturgy: The Sacramental Foundation of Christian Existence*. Edited by Michael J. Miller. Translated by John Saward, Kenneth Baker, S.J., Henry Taylor, et al. Collected Works 11. San Francisco: Ignatius Press, 2014. Originally published as *Theologie der Liturgie: Die sakramentale Begründung christlicher Existenz*. Gesammelte Schriften 11, edited by Gerhard Ludwig Müller. Freiburg im Breisgau: Herder, 2008.

_____. *To Look on Christ: Exercises in Faith, Hope, and Love*. Translated by Robert Nowell. New York: The Crossroad Publishing Company, 1991.

_____. [Joseph Ratzinger]. "Truth and Freedom." *Communio* 23, no. 1 (1996): 16–35.

_____. [Joseph Ratzinger]. *Truth and Tolerance*. Translated by Henry Taylor. San Francisco: Ignatius Press, 2004.

_____. [Joseph Ratzinger]. *A Turning Point for Europe?* Translated by Brian McNeil, C.R.V. San Francisco: Ignatius Press, 2010.

_____. [Joseph Ratzinger]. "Um die Erneuerung der Liturgie: Antwort auf Reiner Kaczynski." *Stimmen der Zeit* 219 (2001): 837–43.

_____. [Joseph Ratzinger]. *The Unity of the Nations: A Vision of the Church Fathers*. Translated by Boniface Ramsey. Washington, DC: The Catholic University of America Press, 2015.

_____. [Joseph Ratzinger]. *Values in a Time of Upheaval*. Translated by Brian McNeil. San Francisco: Ignatius Press, 2006.

_____. [Joseph Ratzinger]. "Vicarious Representation." Translated by Jared Wicks, S.J. *Letter & Spirit* 7 (2011): 209–20.

_____. [Joseph Ratzinger]. *Volk und Haus Gottes in Augustins Lehre von der Kirche: Die Dissertation und weitere Studien zu Augustinus und zur Theologie der Kirchenväter*. Gesammelte Schriften 1, edited by Gerhard Ludwig Müller. Freiburg im Breisgau: Herder, 2011.

_____. [Joseph Ratzinger]. *Wege zur Wahrheit: die bleibende Bedeutung von Romano Guardini*. Düsseldorf: Patmos, 1985.

_____. [Joseph Ratzinger]. *What It Means to Be a Christian*. Translated by Henry Taylor. San Francisco: Ignatius Press, 2006.

_____. [Joseph Ratzinger]. *Without Roots: The West, Relativism, Christianity, Islam*. Translated by Michael F. Moore. New York: Basic Books, 2007.

_____. [Joseph Ratzinger]. *Zeichen unter den Völkern: Schriften zur Ekklesiologie und Ökumene.* Gesammelte Schriften 8/1 and 8/2, edited by Gerhard Ludwig Müller. Freiburg im Breisgau: Herder, 2010.

_____. [Joseph Ratzinger]. "Die Zukunft des Heils." In *Das Heil des Menschen. Innerweltlich-Christlich,* edited by Ulrich Hommes and Joseph Ratzinger, 31–63. Munich: Kösel Verlag, 1975.

Ratzinger, Joseph. *See* Benedict XVI.

## MAGISTERIAL SOURCES

Francis. Post-synodal Apostolic Exhortation *Evangelii Gaudium.* Vatican City: Libreria Editrice Vaticana, 2013.

_____. Encyclical Letter *Laudato Sí.* Vatican City: Libreria Editrice Vaticana, 2015.

_____. Encyclical Letter *Lumen Fidei.* Vatican City: Libreria Editrice Vaticana, 2013.

John Paul II. "Chirograph of the Supreme Pontiff John Paul II the Centenary of the Motu Proprio *Tra le Sollecitudini* on Sacred Music." November 23, 2003. *The Holy See.* Accessed June 23, 2010. https://www.vatican.va/content/john-paul-ii/en/letters/2003/documents/hf_jp-ii_let_20031203_musica-sacra.html.

_____. Apostolic Exhortation *Christifidelis Laici.* Vatican City: Libreria Editrice Vaticana, 1988.

_____. Encyclical Letter *Centesimus Annus.* Vatican City: Libreria Editrice Vaticana, 1991.

_____. Encyclical Letter *Ecclesia de Eucharistia.* Vatican City: Libreria Editrice Vaticana, 2003.

_____. Encyclical Letter *Redemptoris Missio.* Vatican City: Libreria Editrice Vaticana, 1990.

_____. *Letter of His Holiness Pope John Paul II to Artists.* Accessed June 27, 2017. https://www.vatican.va/content/john-paul-ii/en/letters/1999/documents/hf_jp-ii_let_23041999_artists.html.

Paul VI. Encyclical Letter *Mysterium Fidei.* Vatican City: Libreria Editrice Vaticana, 1965.

Pius XII. Encyclical Letter *Mediator Dei.* Boston: St. Paul Books & Media, 1947.

## CHURCH DOCUMENTS

*Catechism of the Catholic Church.* 2nd ed. Washington, DC: Libreria Editrice Vaticana-United States Conference of Catholic Bishops, 2000.

Congregation for the Doctrine of Faith. *Libertatis Conscientia* Instruction on Christian Freedom and Liberation. Vatican City: Libreria Editrice Vaticana, 1986.

_____. *Libertatis Nuntius* Instruction on Certain Aspects of the "Theology of Liberation." Vatican City: Libreria Editrice Vaticana, 1984.

Denzinger, Heinrich. *Enchiridion symbolorum definitionum et declarationum de rebus fidei et morum: Compendium of Creeds, Definitions and Declarations on Matters of Faith and Morals.* Edited by Peter Hünermann. 43rd edition. San Francisco: Ignatius Press, 2012.

*Missale romanum ex decreto Sacrosancti oecumenici Concilii vaticani II instauratum, auctoritate Pauli PP. VI promulgatum, Ioannis Pauili PP. II cura recognitum,* typis vaticanis. Città del Vaticano: Libreria Editrice Vaticana, 2002.

Tanner, Norman P., ed. *Decrees of the Ecumenical Councils.* 2 vols. Washington, DC: Sheed & Ward and Georgetown University Press, 1990.

## General

Aillet, Bishop Marc. *The Old Mass and the New: Explaining the Motu Proprio Summorum Pontificum of Pope Benedict XVI.* Translated by Henry Taylor. San Francisco: Ignatius Press, 2010.

Aldazábal, José. "La Liturgia es ante todo obra de Dios." *Phase* 236 (2000): 181–86.

Allen, Jr., John L. *Cardinal Ratzinger: The Vatican's Enforcer of the Faith.* New York: Continuum, 2000.

———. *The Rise of Benedict XVI: The Inside Story of How the Pope Was Elected and Where He Will Take the Catholic Church.* New York: Doubleday, 2005.

Anyama, Vincent, C. *Primacy of Christ: The Patristic Patrimony in Joseph Ratzinger/ Benedict XVI's Analogy in Theology.* Eugene, OR: Pickwick Publications, 2021.

Ashley, James Matthew. *Interruptions: Mysticism, Politics and Theology in the Work of Johann Baptist Metz.* Notre Dame, IN: University of Notre Dame Press, 1998.

Auer, Johann. *The Church: Universal Sacrament of Salvation.* Edited by Hugh M. Riley. Translated by Michael Waldstein. Washington, DC: The Catholic University of America Press, 1993.

Ayres, Lewis, Patricia Kelly, and Thomas Humphries. "Benedict XVI: A *Ressourcement* Theologian?" In *Ressourcement: A Movement for Renewal in Twentieth-Century Catholic Theology.* Edited by Gabriel Glynn and Paul D. Murray, 423–39. Oxford: Oxford University Press, 2012.

Babolin, Albino. *Romano Guardini-Filosofo dell'alterità.* 2 vols. Bologna: Zanichelli, 1968.

Baldovin, John F., S.J. "Cardinal Ratzinger as Liturgical Critic." In *Studia Liturgica Diversa: Essays in Honor of Paul F. Bradshaw,* edited by Maxwell Johnson and Edward Phillips, 211–27. Portland: Pastoral Press, 2004.

———. "The Development of Liturgy: Theological and Historical Roots of *Sacrosanctum Concilium*." *Worship* 87, no. 6 (November 2013): 517–32.

———. "Idols and Icons: Reflections on the Current State of Liturgical Reform." *Worship* 84, no. 5 (September 2010): 386-402.

———. "Klaus Gamber and the Post-Vatican II Reform of the Roman Liturgy." *Studia Liturgica* 33 (2003): 223–39.

_____.*Reforming the Liturgy: A Response to the Critics*. Collegeville, MN: Liturgical Press, 2009.

_____. "Sacrosanctum Concilium and the Reform of the Liturgy: Forty-Five Year Later." *Studia Liturgica* 39 (2009): 145–57.

_____. "The Use of Liturgical History." *Worship* 82, no. 1 (January 2008): 2–18.

Beauduin, Lambert, O.S.B. *Liturgy the Life of the Church*. 3rd ed. Translated by Virgil Michel O.S.B. Farnborough: St. Michael's Abbey Press, 2002.

Belcher, Kimberly Hope. "The Feast of Peace: The Eucharist as a Sacrifice and a Meal in Benedict XVI's Theology." In *Explorations in the Theology of Benedict XVI*, edited by John C. Cavadini, 254–75. Notre Dame, IN: University of Notre Dame Press, 2012.

Benestad, Brian. "Three Themes in Pope Benedict XVI's Caritas in Veritate." *Nova et Vetera* 8, no. 4 (2010): 723–44.

Berro, Alberto. "Pieper y Guardini en Rothenfels: un encuentro fecundo." *La Plata* 59, no. 216 (2004): 339–57.

Biliniewicz, Mariusz. *The Liturgical Vision of Pope Benedict XVI: A Theological Inquiry*. Bern, Switzerland: Peter Lang, 2013.

Blanco Sarto, Pablo. *La Teología de Joseph Ratzinger: Una Introducción*. Madrid: Ediciones Palabra, 2011.

_____. "Liturgia y Eucharistía en la obra de Joseph Ratzinger." *Scripta Theologica* 38, no. 1 (2006): 103–30.

_____. "*Logos*: Joseph Ratzinger y la Historia de una Palabra." *Revista de Filosofía y Psicología* 1, no. 14 (2006): 57–86.

_____. "Los maestros de Joseph Ratzinger." *Humanitas* 54, no. 2 (2009): 289–305.

_____. "The Theology of Joseph Ratzinger: Nuclear Ideas." *Theology Today* 68, no. 2 (2011): 153–73.

Boersma, Hans. *Heavenly Participation: The Weaving of a Sacramental Tapestry*. Grand Rapids, MI: Eerdmans Publishing Company, 2011.

_____. *Nouvelle Théologie and Sacramental Ontology: A Return to Mystery*. Oxford: Oxford University Press, 2009.

Boff, Clodovis. *Theology and Praxis: Epistemelogical Foundations*. Translated by Robert R. Barr. Eugene, OR: Wipf & Stock, 2009.

Boff, Leonardo. *Church: Charism and Power: Liberation Theology and the Institutional Church*. New York: The Crossroad Publishing Company, 1985.

Bonagura, David. "Logos to Son in the Christology of Joseph Ratzinger/Benedict XVI." *New Blackfriars* 93 (August 2011): 475–88.

Bonino, Serge-Thomas, O.P. "'Nature and Grace' in the Encyclical *Deus Caritas Est*." *Nova et Vetera* 5, no. 2 (2007): 231–48.

Borghesi, Massimo. *The Mind of Pope Francis: Jorge Bergoglio's Intellectual Journey*. Translated by Barry Hudock. Collegeville, MN: Liturgical Press Academic, 2017.

Botte, Bernard, O.S.B. *From Silence to Participation: An Insider's View of Liturgical Renewal*. Translated by John Sullivan. Washington, DC: Pastoral Press, 1988.

Bouyer, Louis. *Liturgical Piety*. Notre Dame, IN: University of Notre Dame Press, 1966.

———. *Liturgy and Architecture*. Notre Dame, IN: University of Notre Dame Press, 1967.

Brüske, Gunda. "Spiel oder Anbetung? Romano Guardini und Joseph Ratzinger über den Sinn der Liturgie." In *Der Logos-gemäße Gottesdienst*, edited by Rudolf Voderholzer, 91–110. Regensburg: Friedrich Pustet, 2009

Bunge, Gabriel, O.S.B. *Earthen Vessels: The Practice of Personal Prayer According to the Patristic Tradition*. Translated by Michael J. Miller. San Francisco: Ignatius Press, 2002.

Butler, Sara, M.S.B.T. "Benedict XVI: Apostle of the 'Pierced Heart of Jesus.'" In *The Pontificate of Benedict XVI: Its Premises and Promises*, edited by William G. Rusch, 144–67. Grand Rapids, MI: Wm. B. Eerdmans, 2009.

Bux, Nichola. *Benedict XVI's Reform: The Liturgy between Innovation and Tradition*. Translated by Joseph Trabbic. San Francisco: Ignatius Press, 2012.

Caldwell, Philip. *Liturgy as Revelation: Re-Sourcing a Theme in Twentienth-Century Catholic Theology*. Minneapolis: Fortress Press, 2014.

Cessario, Romanus, O.P. "The Theological Heritage of Pope Benedict XVI." *Nova et Vetera* 5, no. 2 (2007): 267–70.

Collins, Christopher S., S.J. *The Word Made Love: The Dialogical Theology of Joseph Ratzinger/Benedict XVI*. Collegeville, MN: Liturgical Press, 2013.

Conrad, Leo Sven, F.S.S.P. "Liturgie und Eucharistie bei Joseph Ratzinger: Zur Genese seiner Theologie während der Studien und Professorenzeit." PhD diss. Europa-Universität Flensburg, 2016.

Corbon, Jean. *The Wellspring of Worship*. 2nd ed. Translated by Matthew J. O'Connell. San Francisco: Ignatius Press, 2005.

Corkery, James, S.J. *Joseph Ratzinger's Theological Ideas: Wise Cautions and Legitimate Hopes*. Mahwah, NJ: Paulist Press, 2009.

———. "Reflection on the Theology of Joseph Ratzinger (Pope Benedict XVI)." *Acta Theologica* 32, no. 2 (2012): 19–26.

Corkery, Seán. *A Liberation Ecclesiology?: The Quest for Authentic Freedom in Joseph Ratzinger's Theology of the Church*. Bern: Peter Lang, 2015.

Corriveau, Raymond, C.Ss.R. *The Liturgy of Life: A Study of the Ethical Thought of St. Paul in His Letters to the Early Christian Communities*. Bruxelles: Desclée De Brouwer, 1970.

———. "Temple, Holiness and the Liturgy of Life in Corinthians." *Letter and Spirit* 4 (2008):144–66.

Daley, Brian, S.J. "*Logos* as Reason and *Logos* Incarnate: Philosophy, Theology and the Voices of Tradition." In *Theology Needs Philosophy: Acting Against Reason Is Contrary to the Nature of God*, edited by Matthew L. Lamb, 91–115. Washington, DC: The Catholic University of America Press, 2016.

Daly, Robert J., S.J. *Christian Sacrifice: The Judaeo-Christian Background Before Origen*. Washington, DC: The Catholic University of America Press, 1978.

_____. "Robert Bellarmine and Post-Tridentine Eucharistic Theology." *Theological Studies* 61 (2000): 239–60.

De Assunção, Rudy Albino. *La Misa Según Benedicto XVI*. Madrid: Ediciones Cristiandad, 2019.

De Gaál, Emery. *O Lord, I Seek your Countenance: Explorations and Discoveries in Pope Benedict XVI's Theology*. Steubenville, OH: Emmaus Academic, 2018.

_____. *The Theology of Pope Benedict XVI: The Christocentric Shift*. New York: Palgrave Macmillan, 2010.

_____. "Theology as Living Christian Discipleship: Joseph Ratzinger's Contribution to Vatican II's Understanding of the *Loci Theologici*." *Lateranum* LXXIX, no. 2 (2013): 461–63.

De Lubac, Henri, S.J. *Catholicism: A Study of Dogma in Relation to the Corporate Destiny of Mankind*. Translated by Lancelot C. Sheppard. London: Burns, Oates & Washbourne, 1950.

_____. *Corpus Mysticum: The Eucharist and the Church in the Middle Ages*. Translated by Gemma Simmonds with Richard Price and Christopher Stephens. Edited by Laurence Paul Hemming and Susan Frank Parsons. Notre Dame, IN: University of Notre Dame Press, 2006.

_____. *Theological Fragments*. Translated by Rebecca Howell Balinski. San Francisco: Ignatius Press, 1989.

Diederich, S.J., Everett A. "The Unfolding Presence of Christ in the Celebration of the Mass." *Communio* 5 no. 4 (1978): 326–43.

Dobszay, László. *The Bugnini-Liturgy and the Reform of the Reform*. Musica Sacra Meletemata, vol. 5. Front Royal, VA: Catholic Church Music Associates, 2003.

_____. *The Restoration and Organic Development of the Roman Rite*. New York: T & T Clark International, 2010.

Doyle, Dennis M. *Communion Ecclesiology*. Maryknoll, NY: Orbis Books, 2000.

_____. "*Spe Salvi* on Eschatological and Secular Hope: A Thomistic Critique of an Augustinian Encyclical." *Theological Studies* 71, no. 2 (June 2010): 350–79.

Driscoll, Jeremy, O.S.B. "Eucharist: Source and Summit of the Church's Communion." Ecclesia Orans 21 (2004); 203–25.

_____. "Joseph Ratzinger and *The Spirit of the Liturgy*." *PATH* 6, no. 1 (2007): 183–98.

_____. "Romans 12:1–2. Logikē Latreia in Exegesis and in Liturgy." *Ecclesia Orans* 26 (2009): 7–38.

_____. "Worship in the Spirit of Logos: Romans 12:1–2 and the Source and Summit of Christian Life." *Letter and Spirit* 5 (2009): 77–101.

Duffy, Eamon. "Benedict XVI and the Liturgy." In *The Genius of the Roman Rite: Historical, Theological, and Pastoral Perspectives on Catholic Liturgy*, edited by Uwe Michael Lang, 1–21. Chicago: Hillenbrand Books, 2010.

Dulles, Avery, S.J. *Church and Society: The Laurence J. McGinley Lectures 1988–2007*. New York: Fordham University Press, 2008.

_____. "The Eucharist as Sacrifice." In *Rediscovering the Eucharist: Ecumenical Conversations*, edited by Roch Kereszty, 175–87. Mahwah, NJ: Paulist Press, 2003.

_____. "From Ratzinger to Benedict." *First Things* (February 2006): 24–29.

_____. *Models of the Church.* New York: Doubleday Books, 1987.

_____. "Pope Benedict XVI: Interpreter of Vatican II." In Dulles, *Church and Society: The Laurence J. McGinley Lectures 1988–2007*, 468–84. New York: Fordham University Press, 2008.

_____. "Trends in Ecclesiology." In *Called to Holiness and Communion: Vatican II on the Church*, edited by Steven Boguslawski, O.P., and Robert Fastiggi, 1–16. Scranton, PA: University of Scranton Press, 2009.

Dupré, Louis. *The Enlightenment and the Intellectual Foundations of Modern Culture.* New Haven, CT: Yale University Press, 2004.

_____. *Passage to Modernity: An Essay in the Hermeneutics of Nature and Culture.* New Haven, CT: Yale University Press, 1993.

Eco, Umberto. *The Aesthetics of Thomas Aquinas.* Translated by Hugh Bredin. Cambridge, MA: Harvard University Press, 1988.

Evdokimov, Paul. *The Art of the Icon: a Theology of Beauty.* Translated by Steven Bingham. Redondo Beach, CA: Oakwood Publications, 1990.

_____. *In the World, Of the Church: A Paul Evdokimov Reader.* Edited by Michael Plekon and Alexis Vinogradov. Crestwood, NY: St. Vladimir Press, 2002.

Fagerberg, David W. *Consecrating the World: On Mundane Liturgical Theology.* Kettering, OH: Angelico Press, 2016.

_____. *On Liturgical Asceticism.* Washington, DC: The Catholic University of America Press, 2013.

_____. "The Sacraments as Actions of the Mystical Body." *Communio* 39 (Winter 2012): 554–68.

_____. *Theologia Prima: What Is Liturgical Theology?* 2nd edition. Mundelein, IL: Hillenbrand Books, 2004.

Faggioli, Massimo. "Sacrosanctum Concilium and the Meaning of Vatican II." *Theological Studies* 71, no. 2 (2010): 437–52.

_____. *True Reform: Liturgy and Ecclesiology in Sacrosanctum Concilium.* Collegeville, MN: Liturgical Press, 2012.

_____. *Vatican II: The Battle for Meaning.* Mahwah, NJ: Paulist Press, 2012.

_____. "Vatican II: The History and the Narratives." *Theological Studies* 73, no. 4 (2012): 749–67.

Farnés, Pedro. "Una Obra importante sobre la liturgia que debe leerse en su verdadero contexto." *Phase* 247 (2002): 55–76.

Feingold, Lawrence. *The Eucharist: Mystery of Presence, Sacrifice, and Communion.* Steubenville, OH: Emmaus Academic, 2018.

Fidalgo, José Manuel. "El cristocentrismo de Romano Guardini." *Scripta Theologica* 42 (2010): 333–58.

Fletcher, Patrick J. *Resurrection Realism: Ratzinger the Augustinian.* Eugene, OR: Cascade Books, 2014.

Flores, J.J. "Ratzinger y la liturgia." *Communio* 7 (2008): 139–59.

Franco, Philip A. "The Communion Ecclesiology of Joseph Ratzinger: Implications for the Church of the Future." In *Vatican II: Forty Years Later*, edited by William Madges, 3–25. Maryknoll, NY: Orbis Books, 2006.

Gallaher, Brandon F. "Chalice of Eternity: An Orthodox Theology of Time." *St. Vladimir's Theological Quarterly* 57, no. 1 (2013): 5–35.

Gamber, Klaus. *Fragen in der Zeit: Kirche und Liturgie nach dem Vatikanum II.* Regensburg: Pustet, 1972.

———. *The Modern Rite: Collected Essays on the Reform of the Liturgy.* Translated by Henry Taylor. Beloit, WI: Dumb Ox Books, 2002.

———. *The Reform of the Roman Liturgy: Its Problems and Background.* Translated by Klaus D. Grimm. Fort Collins, CO: Roman Catholic Books, 1993.

Gerhards, Albert. *"Versus orientem—versus populum:* Zum gegenwärtigen Diskussionsstand einer alten Streitfrage." *Theologische Revue* 98 (2002): 15–22.

Gerl, Hanna Barbara. *Romano Guardini 1885–1968.* Mainz: Matthias Grünewald, 1985.

Glynn, Gabriel and Paul D. Murray, eds. *Ressourcement: A Movement for Renewal in Twentieth-Century Catholic Theology.* Oxford: Oxford University Press, 2012.

Grace, Madeleine, CVI. "Looking Again at Looking Eastward: *Ad orientem* Worship and Liturgical Renewal." *Antiphon* 14, no. 3 (2010): 285–300.

Granados, José, Carlos Granados, and Luis Sánchez-Navarro, eds. *Opening Up the Scriptures: Joseph Ratzinger and the Foundations of Biblical Interpretation.* Grand Rapids, MI: Eerdmans, 2008.

Gregory, Brad S. *The Unintended Reformation: How a Religious Revolution Secularized Society.* Cambridge, MA: Harvard University Press, 2012.

Gregur, Josip. "Fleischwerdung des Wortes—Wortwerdung des Fleisches: Liturgie als *logikē latreia* bei Joseph Ratzinger." In *Der Logos-gemäße Gottedienst*, edited by Rudolph Voderholzer, 46–76. Regensburg: Friedrich Pustet, 2009.

Gribbin, Anselm J, O. Praem. *Pope Benedict XVI and the Liturgy: Understanding Recent Liturgical Developments.* Herefordshire: Gracewing, 2011.

Guardini, Romano. *Auf dem Wege.* Mainz: Matthias Grünewald, 1923.

———. *Besinnung vor der Feier der heiligen Messe.* 2 vols. Mainz: Matthias Grünewald, 1939.

———. "Der Kultakt und die gegenwärtige Aufgabe der Liturgie: Ein Brief." *Liturgisches Jahrbuch* 14 (1964): 101–16. Quoted in Robert Krieg, *Romano Guardini: A Precursor of Vatican II.* Notre Dame, IN: University of Notre Dame Press, 1997.

———. *The End of the Modern World.* Translated by Joseph Theman and Herbert Burke. Wilmington, DE: ISI Books, 2001.

———. *Letters from Lake Como: Explorations in Technology and the Human Race.* Translated by Geoffrey W. Bromiley. Grand Rapids, MI: Eerdmans, 1994.

———. *No One Could Have Known: An Autobiography: The Early Years, 1904–1945.* Translated by Graham Harrison. San Francisco: Ignatius Press, 1987.

———. *Power and Responsibility: A Course of Action for the New Age.* Translated by

Joseph Theman and Herbert Burke. Wilmington, DE: ISI Books, 2001.

_____. *Sacred Signs*. Translated by Grace Banham. St. Louis, MO: Pio Decimo Press, 1956.

_____. *The Spirit of the Liturgy*. Translated by Ada Lane. New York: The Crossroad Publishing Company, 1998.

_____. *The Word of God: On Faith, Hope and Charity*. Translated by Stella Lange. Chicago: Henry Regnery, 1963.

Guerriero, Elio. *Benedict XVI: His Life and Thought*. Translated by William J. Melcher. San Francisco: Ignatius Press, 2018.

Gutiérrez, Gustavo. *A Theology of Liberation: History, Politics, and Salvation*. Translated by Sister Caridad Inda and John Eagleson. Maryknoll, NY: Orbis Books, 1988.

_____.and Gerhard Cardinal Müller. *On the Side of the Poor: The Theology of Liberation*. Translated by Robert A. Krieg and James B. Nickoloff. New York: Orbis, 2015.

Gy, Pierre-Marie, O.P. "Cardinal Ratzinger's *The Spirit of the Liturgy*: Is It Faithful to the Council or in Reaction to It?" *Antiphon* 11, no. 1 (2007): 90–96.

Hahn, Scott. *Covenant and Communion: The Biblical Theology of Pope Benedict XVI*. New York: Doubleday, 2009.

Hanby, Michael. "Beyond Mechanism: The Cosmological Significance of David L. Schindler's *Communio* Ontology." In *Being Holy in the World*, edited by Nicholas J. Healy, Jr. and D. C. Schindler, 162–189. Grand Rapids, MI: Eerdmans Press, 2011.

_____. "*Homo Faber* and/or *Homo Adorans*: On the Place of Human Making in a Sacramental Cosmos." *Communio* 38 (Summer 2011): 198–236.

Hastetter, Michaela, C., Christoph Ohly, and Georgios, eds. *Symphonie des Glaubens: Junge Münchener Theologen im Dialog mit Joseph Ratzinger/Benedikt XVI*. St. Ottilien: EOS, 2007.

_____. "Einheit Aller Wirklichkeit: Die Bedeutung des symphonischen Denkens des "Mozarts der Theologie" für die Pastoral." In *Symphonie des Glaubens: Junge Münchener Theologen im Dialog mit Joseph Ratzinger/Benedikt XVI*, edited by Michaela C. Hastetter, Christoph Ohly, and Georgios Vlachonis, 15–50. St. Ottilien: EOS, 2007.

_____. "Liturgie—Brücke zum Mysterium: Grundlinien des Liturgieverständnisses Benedikts XVI." In *Symphonie des Glaubens: Junge Münchener Theologen im Dialog mit Joseph Ratzinger/Benedikt XVI*, edited by Michaela C. Hastetter, Christoph Ohly, and Georgios Vlachonis, 131–50. Ottilien: EOS, 2007.

Hauke, Manfred. "The 'Basic Structure' (*Grundgestalt*) of the Eucharistic Celebration according to Joseph Ratzinger." In *Benedict XVI and the Roman Missal: Proceedings of the Fourth Fota International Liturgical Conference*, edited by Janet Elaine Rutherford and James O'Brien, 70–106. Dublin: Four Courts Press, 2013.

Häussling, Alfred. "Der Geist der Liturgie: Zu Joseph Ratzingers gleichnamiger Publikation." *Archiv für Liturgiewissenschaft* 43–44, no. 3 (2001/02): 362–95.

Healy Jr., Nicholas J. "The Eucharist as the Form of Christian Life." *Communio* 39 (Winter 2012): 587–93.

_____. and D. C. Schindler, eds. *Being Holy in the World: Theology and Culture in the Thought of David L. Schindler.* Grand Rapids, MI: Eerdmans Press, 2011.

Heibl, Franz-Xavier. "Theologische Denker als Mitarbeiter der Wahrheit: Romano Guardini und Papst Benedikt XVI." In *Symphonie des Glaubens*, edited by Michaela C. Hastetter, Christoph Ohly, and Georgios Vlachonis, 77–101. St. Ottilien: EOS, 2007.

Heid, Stefan. *Altar und Kirche: Prinzipien christlicher Liturgie.* Regensburg: Schnell & Steiner, 2019.

_____. "Gebetshaltung und Ostung in der frühchristlichen Zeit." *Rivista di Archaeologia Christiana* 72 (2006): 347–404.

Heim, Maximilian Heinrich. *Joseph Ratzinger: Life in the Church and Living Theology.* Translated by Michael J. Miller. San Francisco: Ignatius Press, 2007.

_____. and Justinus C. Pech, eds. *Zur Mitte der Theologie im Werk von Joseph Ratzinger/Benedikt XVI.* Friedrich Pustet, 2013.

Hemming, Lawrence Paul. *Benedict XVI—Fellow Work for the Truth: An Introduction to His Life and Thought.* Harrisburg, PA: Continuum, 2005.

Hernández, Olegario González. "Das neue Selbstverständnis der Kirche und seine geschichtlichen und theologischen Voraussetzungen." In *De Ecclesia: Beiträge zur Konstitution "Über die Kirche" des Zweiten Vatikanischen Konzils*, vol. 1, edited by Guilherme Baraúna, 155–85. Freiburg im Breisgau: Herder, 1966.

Hofmann, Peter, ed. *Joseph Ratzinger: Ein theologisches Profil.* Paderborn: Ferdinand Schöningh, 2008.

Hoping, Helmut. "Christologie und Liturgie bei Joseph Ratzinger/Benedikt XVI." In *Zur Mitte der Theologie im Werk von Joseph Ratzinger/Benedikt XVI*, edited by Maximilian Heim and Justinus C. Pech, 109–21. Regensburg: Friedrich Pustet, 2013.

_____. "Gemeinschaft mit Christus: Christologie und Liturgie bei Joseph Ratzinger," *Internationale katholische Zeitschrift: Communio* 35 (2006): 558–72.

_____. "Kult und Reflexion: Joseph Ratzinger als Liturgietheologie." In *Der Logos-gemäße Gottesdienst*, edited by Rudolf Voderholzer, 12–25. Regensburg: Friedrich Pustet, 2009.

_____. *My Body Given for You: History and Theology of the Eucharist.* Translated by Michael J. Miller. San Francisco: Ignatius Press, 2019.

_____. and Michel Schulz, eds. *Jesus und der Papst: Systematische Reflexionen zum Jesus-Buch des Papstes.* Freiburg: Herder, 2007.

Horn, Stephan Otto. "Zum existentiellen und sakramentalen Grund der Theologie bei Joseph Ratzinger—Papst Benedikt XVI." *Didaskalia* 38, no. 2 (2008): 301–10.

Howsare, Rodney. "Why Being with Love? *Eros, Agape,* and the Problem of Secularism." *Communio* 33, no. 3 (Fall 2006): 423–448.

International Theological Commission. *International Theological Commission: Texts and Documents 1969–1985*. Edited by Michael Sharkey. San Francisco: I gnatius Press, 1989.

Jankunas, Gediminas T. *The Dictatorship of Relativism: Pope Benedict XVI's Response*. New York: Alba House, 2011.

Jungmann, Josef Andreas, S.J. "Abendmahl' als Name der Eucharistie." *Zeitschrift für Katholische Theologie* 93 (1971): 91–94.

_____. *Missarum Sollemnia*. 2 vols. Wien: Herder, 1948.

Kereszty, Roch A., O.Cist., ed. *Rediscovering the Eucharist: Ecumenical Conversations*. Mahwah, NJ: Paulist Press, 2003.

_____. "The Eucharist of the Church as the One Self-Offering to Christ." In *Rediscovering the Eucharist: Ecumenical Conversations*, edited by Roch A. Kereszty, O.Cist., 240–60. Mahwah, NJ: Paulist Press, 2003.

Kerr, Fergus, O.P. *Twentieth-Century Catholic Theologians: From Neoscholasticism to Nuptial Mysticism*. Malden, MA: Blackwell Publishing, 2007.

Koch, Kurt. *Das Geheimnis des Senfkorns: Grundzüge des theologischen Denkens von Papst Benedikt XVI*. Regensburg: Friedrich Pustet, 2010. _____. "A Reform of the Reform?" In *T & T Clark Companion to Liturgy*, edited by Alcuin Reid, 317–38. New York: Bloomsbury, 2016.

Komonchak, Joseph. "The Church in Crisis: Pope Benedict's Theological Vision." *Commonweal* 132 (June 2006): 11–14.

Kreiml, Josef. "Die Enzyklika Papst Benedikt XVI. Über die christliche Hoffnung: 'Spe salvi' als reife Frucht eines langen Denkweges." In *Hoffnung auf Vollendung*, edited by Gerhard Nachtwei, 259–82. Regensburg: Friedrich Pustet, 2015.

Krieg, Robert, C.S.C. "Cardinal Ratzinger, Max Scheler, and Christology." *The Irish Theological Quarterly* 47.1 (1980): 205-19.

_____. *Romano Guardini: A Precursor of Vatican II*. Notre Dame, IN: University of Notre Dame Press, 1997.

_____. ed. *Romano Guardini: Proclaiming the Sacred in a Modern World*. Chicago: Liturgical Training Publications, 1995.

_____. "Romano Guardini's Theology of the Human Person." *Theological Studies* 59 (1998): 457–74.

Kunzler, Michael. "Die kosmische Dimension der Eucharistiefeier: Zu Fragen ihrer liturgischen Gestalt bei Joseph Ratzinger." In *Der Logos-gemäße Gottesdienst*, edited by Rudolf Voderholzer, 172–204. Regensburg: Friedrich Pustet, 2009.

Kupczak, Jaroslaw, O.P. *Gift and Communion: John Paul II's Theology of the Body*. Washington, DC: The Catholic University of America Press, 2014.

La Soujeole, Benoît-Dominique de, O.P. *Introduction to the Mystery of the Church*. Translated by Michael J. Miller. Washington, DC: The Catholic University of America Press, 2014.

Lam, Cong Quy Joseph, C.Ss.R., *Joseph Ratzinger's Theological Retractions*. Bern: Peter Lang, 2013.

_____. "Joseph Ratzinger über Zeit und Eschatologie." In *Hoffnung auf Vollendung*, edited by Gerhard Nachtwei, 40–54. Regensburg: Friedrich Pustet, 2015.

_____. *Theologische Verwandtschaft: Augustinus von Hippo und Joseph Ratzinger/Papst Benedikt XVI*. Würzburg: Echter, 2009.

Lang, Uwe Michael, C.O. "Augustine's Conception of Sacrifice in *City of God*, Book X, and the Eucharistic Sacrifice." *Antiphon* 19, no. 1 (2015): 29–51.

_____. ed. *Ever Directed towards the Lord: The Love of God in the Liturgy of the Eucharist Past, Present, and Hoped For*. Edinburgh: T & T Clark, 2007.

_____. ed. *The Genius of the Roman Rite: Historical, Theological, and Pastoral Perspectives on Catholic Liturgy*. Chicago: Hillenbrand Books, 2010.

_____. *Signs of the Holy One: Liturgy, Ritual and Expression of the Sacred*. San Francisco: Ignatius Press, 2015.

_____. *Turning towards the Lord: Orientation in Liturgical Prayer*. San Francisco: Ignatius Press, 2004.

_____. *The Voice of the Church at Prayer: Reflections on Liturgy and Language*. San Francisco: Ignatius Press, 2012.

Läpple, Alfred. *Benedikt XVI. Und seine Wurzeln: Was den Studenten Joseph Ratzinger prägte*. Augsburg: St. Ulrich Verlag, 2006.

Levering, Matthew. *Betrayal of Charity: The Sins that Sabotage Divine Love*. Waco, TX: Baylor University Press, 2011.

_____. *Christ's Fulfillment of Torah and Temple: Salvation according to Thomas Aquinas*. Notre Dame, IN: University of Notre Dame Press, 2002.

_____. *Engaging the Doctrine of Revelation: The Mediation of the Gospel through Church and Scripture*. Grand Rapids, MI: Baker Academic, 2014.

_____. *Jesus and the Demise of Death: Resurrection, Afterlife, and the Fate of the Christian*. Waco, TX: Baylor University Press, 2012.

_____. *Sacrifice and Community: Jewish Offering and Christian Eucharist*. Malden, MA: Blackwell Publishing, 2005.

López, Antonio, F.S.C.B. "Christian Culture and the Form of Human Existence." *Communio* 40, nos. 2–3 (Summer–Fall 2013): 473–509.

Luciani, Rafael. *Pope Francis and the Theology of the People*. Translated by Phillip Berryman. Maryknoll, NY: Orbis Books, 2017.

Madrigal, Santiago. *Iglesia es caritas: La eclesiología teológica de Joseph Ratzinger—Benedicto XVI*. Santander: Sal Terrae, 2008.

Maher, Daniel P. "Pope Benedict XVI on Faith and Reason." *Nova et Vetera* 7, no. 3 (2009): 625–52.

Marschler, Thomas. "Perspektiven der Eschatologie bei Joseph Ratzinger." In *Joseph Ratzinger: Ein theologisches Profil*, edited by Peter Hofmann, 161–88. Paderborn: Ferdinand Schöningh, 2008.

Marx, Paul, O.S.B. *Virgil Michel and the Liturgical Movement*. Collegeville, MN: Liturgical Press, 1957.

Massa, James, S.J., "The Communion Theme in the Writings of Joseph Ratzinger: Unity in the Church and in the World through Sacramental Encounter." PhD. diss., Fordham University, 1996.

McGovern, Arthur F. S.J., *Liberation Theology and Its Critics: Toward an Assessment*. Eugene, OR: Wipf & Stock, 1989.

McGregor, Peter John. *Heart to Heart: The Spiritual Christology of Joseph Ratzinger.* Eugene, OR: Pickwick Publications, 2016.

McNamara, Denis. *Catholic Church Architecture and the Spirit of the Liturgy.* Chicago: Hillenbrand Books, 2009.

McPartlan, Paul. *The Eucharist Makes the Church: Henri de Lubac and John Zizioulas in Dialogue.* Edinburgh: T & T Clark, 1993.

———. "Liturgy, Church and Society." *Studia Liturgica* 34 (2004): 147–64.

———. "*Ressourcement,* Vatican II, and Eucharistic Ecclesiology." In *Ressourcement: A Movement for Renewal in Twentieth-Century Catholic Theology,* edited by Gabriel Glynn and Paul D. Murray, 392–404. Oxford: Oxford University Press, 2012.

Meeking, Basil. "Celebrating the Liturgy with Pope Benedict XVI." *Logos* 11, no. 1 (Winter 2008): 127–48.

Meier-Hamidi, Frank and Ferdinand Schumacher, eds. *Der Theologe Joseph Ratzinger.* Freiburg: Herder, 2007.

Meiers, Anna Elisabeth. *Eschatos Adam: Zentrale Aspekte der Christologie bei Joseph Ratzinger/Benedikt XVI.* Regensburg: Friedrich Pustet, 2019.

Melina, Livio and Carl A. Anderson, eds. *The Way of Love: Reflections on Pope Benedict XVI's Encyclical Deus Caritas Est.* San Francisco: Ignatius Press, 2006.

Melina, Livio. *The Epiphany of Love: Towards a Theological Understanding of Christian Action.* Translated by Susan Dawson and Stephan Kampowski. Grand Rapids, MI: Eerdmans Publishing Company, 2010.

Menke, Karl-Heinz. *Der Leitgedanke Joseph Ratzingers: Die Verschränkung von vertikaler und horizontaler Inkarnation.* Paderborn: Ferdinand Schöningh: 2008.

——— "Die theologischen Quellen der Enzyklika 'Deus Caritas Est.'" In *Joseph Ratzinger: ein theologisches Profil,* edited by Peter Hofmann, 50–56. Paderborn: Ferdinand Schöningh, 2008.

Merker, Hans and the Katholische Akademie in Bayern, eds. *Bibliographie Romano Guardini (1885–1968).* Paderborn: Ferdinand Schöningh, 1978.

Metz, Johann Baptist. *Faith in History and Society: Toward a Practical Fundamental Theology.* Translated by Matthew Ashley. New York: The Crossroad Publishing Company, 2013.

———. "God: Against the Myth of the Eternity of Time." In *The End of Time? The Provocation of Talking About God,* edited by Tiemo Rainer Peters and Claus Urban, 26–46. Translated by J. Matthew Ashley. Mahwah, NJ: Paulist Press, 2004.

———. *A Passion for God: The Mystical-Political Dimension of Christianity.* Translated by James Matthew Ashley. Mahwah, NJ: Paulist Press, 1998.

———. "Theology in the New Paradigm." In *An Eerdmans Reader in Contemporary Political Theology,* edited by William T. Cavanaugh, Jeffrey W. Bailey, and Craig Hovey, 316–26. Grand Rapids, MI: Eerdmans Publishing, 2012.

———. *Theology of the World.* Translated by William Glen-Doepel. New York: Herder, 1969.

Millare, Roland. "The Hermeneutic of Continuity and Discontinuity between Romano Guardini and Joseph Ratzinger: The Primacy of *Logos*," *Nova et Vetera* 18, no. 2 (Spring 2020): 521–64.

_____. "The Primacy of *Logos* over *Ethos:* The Influence of Romano Guardini on Post-Conciliar Theology." *Heythrop Journal* 57, no. 6 (November 2016): 974–83.

_____. "The Sacred is Still Beautiful: The Liturgical and Theological Aesthetics of Pope Benedict XVI." *Logos* 16, no. 1 (Winter 2013): 101–25.

_____. "The Spirit of the Liturgical Movement: A Benedictine Renewal of Culture." *Logos* 17, no. 4 (Fall 2014): 130–54.

Moltmann, Jürgen. "Christian Hope: Messianic or Transcendent? A Theological Discussion with Joachim of Fiore and Thomas Aquinas." *Horizons* (Villanova) 12, no. 2 (1985): 328–48.

_____. *The Coming of God: Christian Eschatology.* Translated by Margaret Kohl. Minneapolis, MN: Fortress Press, 2004.

_____. *The Future of Creation: Collected Essays.* Minneapolis, MN: Fortress Press, 2007.

_____. "Is There Life After Death?" In *The End of the World and the Ends of God*, edited by John Polkinghorne and Michael Welker, 238–55. Harrisburg, PA: Trinity Press International, 2000.

_____. *Theology of Hope.* Translated by James W. Leitch. London: SCM Press, 2002.

Morrill, Bruce T. S.J. *Anamnesis as Dangerous Memory: Political and Liturgical Theology in Dialogue.* Collegeville, MN: The Liturgical Press, 2000.

Müller, Gerhard Cardinal. *Catholic Dogmatics: For the Study and Practice of Theology.* Translated by William Hadfield-Burkardt. Vol. 1: Doctrine of Creation—Eschatology. New York: The Crossroad Publishing Company, 2017.

Murphy, Joseph. *Christ our Joy: The Theological Vision of Pope Benedict XVI.* San Francisco: Ignatius Press, 2008.

_____. "Joseph Ratzinger and the Liturgy: A Theological Approach." In *Benedict XVI and the Sacred Liturgy*, edited by Neil J. Roy and Janet E. Rutherford, 132–55. Dublin, Ireland: Four Courts Press, 2010.

Nachtwei, Gerhard. *Dialogische Unsterblichkeit: eine Untersuchung zur Joseph Ratzingers Eschatologie und Theologie.* Leipzig: St. Benno-verlag, 1986.

_____, ed., *Hoffnung auf Vollendung: Zur Eschatologie von Joseph Ratzinger.* Regensburg: Verlag Friedrich Pustet, 2015.

Neumann, Veit. "Ideologiekritik und Befreiungstheologie: Der Schutz des Glaubens vor einem totalisierenden System des Geistes, das sich als 'Praxis' versteht." In *Hoffnung auf Vollendung*, edited by Gerhard Nachtwei, 246–58. Regensburg: Friedrich Pustet, 2015.

Nichols, Aidan, O.P. "Benedict XVI on the Holy Images." *Nova et Vetera* 5, no. 2 (2007): 359–74.

_____. *Byzantine Gospel: Maximus the Confessor in Modern Scholarship.* Edinburgh: T & T Clark, 1993.

_____. *Christendom Awake: On Reenergizing the Church in Culture.* Grand Rapids, MI: Eerdmans, 1999.

_____. *Conversation of Faith and Reason: Modern Catholic Thought from Hermes to Benedict XVI*. Chicago: Liturgy Training Publications, 2009.

_____. *Holy Eucharist: From the New Testament to Pope John Paul II*. Dublin: Veritas Publications, 1991.

_____. *Looking at the Liturgy: A Critical View of Its Contemporary Form*. San Francisco: Ignatius Press, 1996.

_____. *Lost in Wonder: Essays on Liturgy and the Arts*. Burlington, VT: Ashgate Publishing Company, 2011.

_____. *Redeeming Beauty: Soundings in Sacral Aesthetics*. Burlington, VT: Ashgate Publishing Company, 2007.

_____. *Rome and the Eastern Churches: A Study in Schism*. Rev. ed. San Francisco: Ignatius Press, 2010.

_____. *Theology in the Russian Diaspora: Church, Fathers, Eucharist in Nikolai Afanas'ev, 1893–1966*. Cambridge: Cambridge University Press, 2008.

_____. *The Thought of Benedict XVI: An Introduction to the Theology of Joseph Ratzinger*. New York: Burn & Oates, 2005.

Nussbaum, Otto. *Der Standort des Liturgen am christlichen Altar vor dem Jahre 1000*. 2 vols. Bonn: Peter Hanstein, 1965.

Oakes, Edward, S.J. "Benedict's Vatican II Hermeneutic." *First Things* (March 2009). Accessed March 2009. https://www.firstthings.com/webexclusives/2009/03/benedicts-vatican-ii hermeneut.

_____. "Resolving the Relativity Paradox: Pope Benedict XVI and the Challenge of Christological Relativism." In *Explorations in the Theology of Benedict XVI*, edited by John C. Cavadini, 87–111. Notre Dame, IN: University of Notre Dame Press, 2012.

O'Callaghan, Paul. *Christ Our Hope: An Introduction to Eschatology*. Washington, DC: The Catholic University of America Press, 2011.

_____. *The Christological Assimilation of the Apocalypse: An Essay on Fundamental Eschatology*. Dublin: Four Courts Press, 2004.

_____. "Hope and Freedom in Gabriel Marcel and Ernst Bloch." *Irish Theological Quarterly* 55 (1989): 213–39.

O'Connor, James T. *Land of the Living: A Theology of the Last Things*. New York: Catholic Books, 1992.

Olver, Matthew, S.C. "A Note on the Silent Canon in the Missal of Paul VI and Cardinal Ratzinger." *Antiphon* 20, no. 1 (2016): 40–51.

O'Meara, Thomas Franklin, O.P. *Church and Catholic: German Catholic Theology, 1860–1914*. Notre Dame, IN: University of Notre Dame, 1991.

_____. "The Origins of the Liturgical Movement and German Romanticism." *Worship* 59, no. 4 (1985): 326–42.

_____. *Romantic Idealism and Roman Catholicism: Schelling and the Theologians*. Notre Dame, IN: University of Notre Dame, 1982.

O'Regan, Cyril. "Benedict the Augustinian." In *Explorations in the Theology of Benedict XVI*, edited by John C. Cavadini, 21–60. Notre Dame, IN: University of Notre Dame Press, 2012.

Pascher, Joseph. *Eucharistia: Gestalt und Vollzug*. Münster und Krailling: Aschendorff und Wewel, 1947.

Pecklers, Keith F. *The Unread Vision: The Liturgical Movement in the United States of America: 1926–1955*. Collegeville, MN: Liturgical Press, 1998.

Pell, George Cardinal. "The Concept of Beauty in the Writings of Joseph Ratzinger." In *Benedict XVI and Beauty in Sacred Art and Architecture*, edited by D. Vincent Twomey, SVD, and Janet E. Rutherford, 24–36. Dublin: Four Courts Press, 2011.

Peterson, Erik. *Frühkirche, Judentum und Gnosis*. Freiburg: Herder, 1959.

————. *Theological Tractates*. Edited and translated by Michal J. Hollerich. Stanford, CA: Stanford University Press, 2011.

Pieper, Josef. *About Love*. Translated by Richard and Clara Winston. Chicago: Franciscan Herald Press, 1974.

————. *Death and Immortality*. Translated by Richard and Clara Winston. South Bend, IN: St. Augustine's Press, 1999.

————. *The End of Time: A Meditation on the Philosophy of History*. Translated by Michael Bullock. San Francisco: Ignatius Press, 1999.

————. *Hope and History*. Translated by David Kipp. San Francisco: Ignatius Press, 1994.

————. *In Tune with the World: A Theory of Festivity*. Translated by Richard and Clara Winston. South Bend, IN: St. Augustine's Press, 1999.

————. *Leisure: The Basis of Culture*. Translated by Alexander Dru. San Francisco: Ignatius Press, 2009.

————. *On Hope*. Translated by Mary F. McCarthy. San Francisco: Ignatius Press, 1986.

Pitre, Brant. *Jesus and the Last Supper*. Grand Rapids, MI: Eerdmans, 2015.

Post, Paul. "Dealing with the Past in the Roman Catholic Liturgical 'Reform of the Reform Movement.'" *Questions Liturgiques* 87 (2006): 264–79.

Power, David N. *The Sacrifice We Offer: The Tridentine Dogma and Its Reinterpretation*. New York: The Crossroad Publishing Company, 1987.

Pozo, Candido, S.J. *Theology of the Beyond*. Translated by Mark A. Pilon. New York: Alba House, 2009.

Ramage, Matthew J. "Benedict XVI, Catholic Doctrine and the Problem of an Imminent *Parousia*." *Josephinum Journal of Theology* 21, no. 1 (2014): 1–25.

————. *Jesus Interpreted: Benedict XVI, Bart Ehrman, and the Historical Truth of the Gospels*. Washington, DC: Catholic University of America Press, 2017.

Ratzinger, Georg. *My Brother, the Pope*. Translated by Michael J. Miller. San Francisco: Ignatius Press, 2011.

Rausch, Thomas P., S.J. *Eschatology, Liturgy, and Christology: Toward Recovering an Eschatological Imagination*. Collegeville, MN: Liturgical Press, 2010.

Rauschen, Gerhard. *Eucharist and Penance: In the First Six Centuries of the Church*. St. Louis, MO: Herder, 1913.

Reid, Alcuin. "The Liturgical Reform of Pope Benedict XVI." In *Proceedings of the First Fota International Liturgical Conference*, edited by Janet Elaine Rutherford and James O'Brien, 156–80. Dublin: Four Courts Press, 2010.

_____. *Looking Again at the Question of the Liturgy with Cardinal Ratzinger*. Farnborough: Saint Michael's Abbey, 2003.

_____. *The Organic Development of the Liturgy*. San Francisco: Ignatius Press, 2005.

_____. ed. *T & T Clark Companion to Liturgy*. New York: Bloomsbury, 2016.

Reyes, Ricardo. *L'Unità nel Pensiero Liturgico di Joseph Ratzinger*. Rome: Edizioni Liturgiche, 2011.

Rhonheimer, Martin. "Benedict XVI's 'Hermeneutic of Reform' and Religious Freedom." *Nova et Vetera* 9, no. 4 (2011): 1029–54.

Riches, Aaron. *Ecce Homo: On the Divine Unity of Christ*. Grand Rapids, MI: Eerdmans Publishing, 2016.

Rollet, Jacques. *Le Cardinal Ratzinger et la Théologie Contemporaine*. Paris: Les Éditions du Cerf, 1987.

Roth, Markus. *Joseph Maria Pascher (1893–1979): Liturgiewissenschaftler in Zeiten des Umbruchs*. Erzabtei St. Ottilien: EOS, 2011.

Rourke, Thomas R. *The Roots of Pope Francis's Social and Political Thought: From Argentina to the Vatican*. Lanham, MD: Rowan & Littlefield, 2016.

Rousseau, Dom Olivier, O.S.B. *The Progress of the Liturgy: An Historical Sketch from the Beginning of the Nineteenth Century to the Pontificate of Pius X*. Westminster, MD: Newman Press, 1951.

Rousselot, Pierre S.J. "Spiritual Love and Apperceptive Synthesis." In *Essays on Love and Knowledge*, edited by Andrew Tallon and Pol Vandevelde, translated by Andrew Tallon Pol Vandevelde and Alan Vingelette, 119–34. Milwaukee, WI: Marquette University Press, 2008.

_____. *Eyes of Faith*. Translated by Joseph Donceel, S.J. New York: Fordham University Press, 1990.

Rowland, Tracey. *Benedict XVI: A Guide for the Perplexed*. New York: T & T Clark, 2010.

_____. *Catholic Theology*. New York: Bloomsbury T & T Clark, 2017.

_____. "Catholic Theology in the Twentieth Century." In *Key Theological Thinkers: From Modern to Postmodern*, edited by Staale Johannes Kristiansen, et. al., 37–53. Burlington, VT: Ashgate Publishing Company, 2013.

_____. *The Culture of the Incarnation*, Tracey Rowland. Steubenville, OH: Emmaus Academic, 2017.

_____. *Culture and the Thomist Tradition: After Vatican II*. London: Routledge, 2003.

_____. "Joseph Ratzinger's Friendship with Augustine, Bonaventure and Aquinas." In *Logos et Musica: In Honorem Summi Romani Pontificis Benedicti XVI*, edited by Elzbieta Szczurko, Tadeusz Guz and Horst Seidl, 163–79. Frankfurt am Main: Peter Lang, 2012.

_____. *Ratzinger's Faith: The Theology of Pope Benedict XVI*. Oxford: Oxford University Press, 2008.

_____. "The World in the Theology of Joseph Ratzinger/Benedict XVI." *Journal of Moral Theology* 2, no. 2 (June 2013): 109–33.

Royal, Robert. *A Deeper Vision: The Catholic Tradition in the Twentieth Century*. San Francisco: Ignatius Press, 2015.

Rusch, William G., ed. *The Pontificate of Benedict XVI: Its Premises and Promises*. Grand Rapids, MI: Eerdmans Publishing, 2009.

Rutsche, Markus. *Die Relationalität Gottes bei Martin Buber und Joseph Ratzinger*. München: Grin, 2007.

Scannone, Juan C. "El papa Francisco y la teología del pueblo." *Razón y Fe* 1395 (2014): 31–50.

Schall S.J., James V. *The Regensburg Lecture*. South Bend, IN: St. Augustine's Press, 2007.

Schenk, Richard. O.P. "The Eucharist and Ecclesial Communion." In *At the Altar of the World: The Pontificate of Pope John Paul II through the Lens of L'Osservatore Romano and the Words of Ecclesia de Eucharistia*, edited by Daniel G. Callahan. Washington, DC: John Paul II Cultural Center, 2003.

Schindler, David, ed. *Catholicism and Secularization in America*. Huntington, IN: Our Sunday Visitor, 1990.

_____. "Christology and the 'Imago Dei': Interpreting *Gaudium et Spes*." *Communio* 23 (Spring 1996): 156–84.

_____. *Heart of the World, Center of the Church: Communio Ecclesiology, Liberalism, and Liberation*. Grand Rapids, MI: Eerdmans, 1996.

_____, ed. *Love Alone Is Credible: Hans Urs von Balthasar as Interpreter of the Catholic Tradition*. Grand Rapids, MI: Eerdmans, 2008.

_____. *Ordering Love: Liberal Societies and the Memory of God*. Grand Rapids, MI: Eerdmans Publishing Company, 2011.

Schindler, D.C. "The Redemption of *Eros*: Philosophical Reflections on Benedict XVI's First Encyclical." *Communio* 33, no. 3 (Fall 2006): 375–399.

Schmemann, Alexander. *For the Life of the World: Sacraments and Orthodoxy*. Crestwood, NY: St. Vladimir's Seminary Press, 1982.

_____. *Liturgy and Tradition: Theological Reflections of Alexander Schmemann*. Edited by Thomas Fisch. Crestwood, NY: St. Vladimir's Seminary Press, 1990.

Schneider, Michael. "Primat des Logos vor dem Ethos—Zum theologischen Diskurs bei Joseph Ratzinger." In *Joseph Ratzinger: Ein theologisches Profil*, edited by Peter Hofmann, 15–45. Paderborn: Ferdinand Schöningh, 2008.

_____. "Zur Erneuerung der Liturgie nach dem II. Vatikanum: Ihre Beurteilung in der Theologie Joseph Ratzingers auf dem Hintergrund seiner Reden in der Abtei Fontgombault." In *Der Logos-gemäße Gottesdienst: Theologie der Liturgie bei Joseph Ratzinger*, edited by Rudolf Voderholzer, 146–52. Regensburg: Friedrich Pustet, 2009.

Scola, Angelo. "The Unity of Love and the Face of Man: An Invitation to Read *Deus Caritas Est*." *Communio* 33 (Fall 2006), 316-45.

Schönborn, Christoph Cardinal. "Zu den Quellen des christologischen Denkens im Werk von Joseph Ratzinger." In *Zur Mitte der Theologie im Werk von Joseph*

*Ratzinger/Benedikt XVI*, edited by Michael Heim and Justinus C. Pech, 104–08. Regensburg: Friedrich Pustet, 2013.

Schumacher, Bernard. *A Philosophy of Hope: Josef Pieper and the Contemporary Debate on Hope*. Translated by D. C. Schindler. New York: Fordham University Press, 2003.

Sciglitano, Anthony, "Pope Benedict XVI's Jesus of Nazareth: Agape and Logos." *Pro Ecclesia* 17, no. 2 (2008): 159–85.

Segundo, Juan Luis, S.J. *Theology and the Church: A Response to Cardinal Ratzinger and a Warning to the Whole Church*. Translated by John W. Diercksmeier. Minneapolis, MN: Winston Press, 1985.

Söding, Thomas. "Die Lebendigkeit des Wortes Gottes." In *Der Theologe Joseph Ratzinger*, edited by Frank Meier-Hamidi and Ferdinand Schumacher, 12–55. Freiburg: Herder, 2007.

Söhngen, Gottlieb. *Das sakramentale Wesen des Meßopfers*. Essen: Augustin Wibbelt, 1946.

———. *Die Einheit in der Theologie*. München: Karl Zink, 1952.

Spezzano, Daria. *The Glory of God's Grace: Deification According to St. Thomas Aquinas*. Ave Maria, FL: Sapientia Press, 2015.

Studer, Basil. "Das Opfer Christi nach Augustins 'De civitate Dei' X, 5–6." *Studia Anselmiana* 79 (1980): 93–108.

Stuflesser, Martin. "*Actuosa Participatio*: Between Hectic Actionism and New Interiority. Reflections on 'Active Participation' in the Worship of the Church as Both Right and Obligation of the Faithful." *Studia Liturgica* (2011): 92–126.

Stuhlmacher, Peter. *Reconciliation, Law, & Righteousness: Essays in Biblical Theology*. Philadelphia, PA: Fortress Press, 1986.

*Synode Extraordinaire: Célébration de Vatican II*. Paris: Cerf, 1986. Quoted in Avery Cardinal Dulles, S.J., "The Reception of Vatican II at the Extraordinary Synod of 1985." In *The Reception of Vatican II*, edited by Giuseppe Alberigo, Jean-Pierre Jossua, and Joseph A. Komonchak. Translated by Matthew J. O'Connell. Washington, DC: The Catholic University of America Press, 1987.

Teifke, Wilko. "Zwischen Vergänglichkeit und Ewigkeit: Die "Memoria-Zeit" als Zeit des Menschen und die Wiederentdeckung der Seelen in der eschatologischen Konzeption Joseph Ratzingers." In *Hoffnung auf Vollendung*, edited by Gerhard Nachtwei, 147–55. Regensburg: Friedrich Pustet, 2015.

Tillard, J. M. R., O.P. *The Eucharist: Pasch of God's People*. Translated by Dennis L. Wienk. New York: Alba House, 1967.

Tremblay, Réal, C.Ss.R. "L 'Exode,' une idée maîtresse de la pensée théologique du Cardinal Joseph Ratzinger." In *Historia, memoria futuri: mélanges Louis Vereecke (70e anniversaire de naissance)*, edited by Réal Tremblay and Dennis Joseph, 435–61. Roma: Editiones Academiae Alphonsianae, 1991.

———. "L'<<Esodo>> tra prologia ed escatologia." In *Ritrovarsi Donadosi: Alcune idee chiave della teologia di Joseph Ratzinger—Benedetto XVI*, edited by Réal Tremblay and Stefano Zamboni, 43–65. Vatican City: Lateran University Press, 2012.

Tura, Robert. "La Teologia di Joseph Ratzinger: Saggio Introduttiva." *Studia Patavina* 21 (1974): 145–82.

Twomey, D. Vincent, S.V.D. *Pope Benedict XVI: The Conscience of Our Age.* San Francisco: Ignatius Press, 2007.

Verweyen, Hansjürgen. *Ein unbekannter Ratzinger: Die Habilitationsschrift von 1955 als Schlüssel zu seiner Theologie.* Regensburg: Friedrich Pustet, 2010.

_____. *Joseph Ratzinger—Benedikt XVI: Die Entwicklung seines Denkens.* Darmstadt: Primus Verlag, 2007.

Voderholzer, Rudolf. "Die biblische Hermeneutik Joseph Ratzingers." *Münchener Theologische Zeitschrift* 56 (2005): 400–14.

_____. "Joseph Ratzinger/Benedikt XVI, und die Exegese." In *Joseph Ratzinger: Ein Theologisches Profil*, edited by Peter Hofmann, 99–121. Paderborn: Ferdinand Schöningh, 2008.

_____, ed. *Der Logos-gemässe Gottesdienst: Theologie der Liturgie bei Joseph Ratzinger.* Regensburg: Friedrich Pustet, 2009.

von Balthasar, Han Urs. *Cosmic Liturgy: The Universe According to Maximus the Confessor.* Translated by Brian F. Daly. San Francisco: Ignatius Press, 2003.

_____. *The Glory of the Lord: A Theological Aesthetics.* vol. 1, *Seeing the Form.* Translated by Erasmo Leiva-Merikakis. San Francisco: Ignatius Press, 1983.

_____. *The Glory of the Lord: A Theological Aesthetics.* vol. 2, *Studies in Theological Styles: Clerical Styles.* Edited by John Riches. Translated by Andrew Louth, Francis McDonagh, and Brian McNeil, C.R.V. Edinburgh: T & T Clark, 1985.

_____. *Romano Guardini: Reform from the Source.* San Francisco: Ignatius Press, 2010.

_____. *Theo-Logic.* vol. 2, *Truth of God.* Translated by Adrian J. Walker. San Francisco: Ignatius Press, 2004.

Wainwright, Geoffrey. *Eucharist and Eschatology.* New York: Oxford University Press, 1981.

_____. "A Remedy for Relativism: The Cosmic, Historical, and Eschatological Dimensions of the Liturgy according to the Theologian Joseph Ratzinger." *Nova et Vetera* 5, no. 2 (2007): 403–30.

_____. "The 'New Worship' in Joseph Ratzinger's *Jesus of Nazareth*." *Nova et Vetera* 10, no. 4 (2012): 993–1013.

Waldstein, Michael. "The Self-Critique of the Historical-Critical Method: Cardinal Ratzinger's Erasmus Lecture," *Modern Theology* 28:4 (October 2012): 732–747.

Washburn, Christian D. "The Theological Priority of *Lumen Gentium and Dei Verbum* for the Interpretation of the Second Vatican Council." *The Thomist* 78 (2014): 107–34.

Weigel, George. *God's Choice: Pope Benedict XVI and the Future of the Catholic Church.* New York: Harper Collins Publishing, 2005.

_____. *Witness to Hope: The Biography of Pope John Paul II.* New York: Harper Collins, 1999.

Weiler, Thomas. *Volk Gottes—Leib Christi: Die Ekklesiologie Joseph Ratzingers und ihr Einfluss auf das Zweite Vatikanische Konzil.* Mainz: Matthias-Grünewald, 1997.

Weimann, Ralph. *Dogma und Fortschritt bei Joseph Ratzinger: Prinzipien der Kontinuität.* Paderborn: Schöningh, 2012.

Weimer, Ludwig. "Die Baugesetze der Geschichtstheologie Joseph Ratzingers." In *Hoffnung auf Vollendung,* edited by Gerhard Nachtwei, 55–74. Regensburg: Friedrich Pustet, 2015.

Weinandy, Thomas G., OFM, CAP, *Jesus Becoming Jesus: A Theological Interpretation of the Synoptic Gospels.* Washington, DC: The Catholic University of America Press, 2018.

White, Thomas Joseph, O.P. *The Incarnate Lord: A Thomistic Study in Christology.* Washington, DC: The Catholic University of America Press, 2015.

Wicks, Jared, S.J. "Six texts by Prof. Joseph Ratzinger as *peritus* before and during Vatican Council II." *Gregorianum* 89, no. 2 (2008): 233–311.

_____. "Vatican II on Revelation from Behind the Scenes." *Theological Studies* 71 (2010): 637–50.

Wiedenhofer, Siegfried. "Politische Utopie und christliche Vollendungshoffnung: Joseph Ratzingers Auseinandersetzung mit Politischer Theologie und Befreiungstheologie." In *Hoffnung auf Vollendung,* edited by Gerhard Nachtwei, 186–245. Regensburg: Friedrich Pustet, 2015.

_____. *Die Theologie Joseph Ratzingers/Benedikts XVI: Ein Blick auf das Ganz.* Ratzinger-Studien 10. Regensburg: Friedrich Pustet, 2016.

Zizioulas, John. *Being as Communion.* Crestwood, NY: St. Vladimir's Seminary Press. 1985.

_____. *Communion and Otherness.* London: T & T Clark, 2006.

_____. *The Eucharistic Communion and the World.* Edited by Luke Ben Tallon. London: T & T Clark, 2011.

# Index of Subjects and Names

## A

Acerbi, Antonio, 131

active participation (*participation actuosa*)
  *ars celebrandi* and, 247
  Beauduin on, 133–34
  Benedict XVI/Ratzinger on, 40n94, 216–17, 218, 221, 225, 227, 234
  in the liturgy, 216–219
  the liturgical movement and, 133, 216
  Pius IX on, 234
  Pius X on, 133
  Vatican II and, 134–35, 216

Acts of the Apostles, The, 53, 122, 170, 171

Afanas'ev, Nikolai, 119n29, 121n33, 122, 127n59

*agape. See* love

Aldazá, José, 3n7

Ambrose, St., 77

Anderson, Carl, 190n105,

Amos, Book of, 80n99

anthropology. *See* theological anthropology

Aquinas, St. Thomas, 37n82, 44n104, 59n6, 100n181,
  on beauty, 231–232; 242–43
  Eucharist and, 163, 183–185
  on praying *ad orientem* 206
  on sacrifice 68–69n52, 74n73

ark of the covenant, 237–38

*ars celebrandi. See* liturgy, celebration of

art. *See* liturgy, celebration of

## B

Augustine of Hippo, St., 23, 43n103, 61, 115n15, 159, 164n4, 165n7, 264
  ecclesiology, 129n 32, 133n78, 175–78
  on sacrifice, 62n19, 64, 79, 175–78

autonomy, 28–29
  in the liturgy, 28
  of the person, 20, 23–24, 28, 50, 52, 61, 67, 83, 105, 114–16, 156–57, 165, 192–93, 214

## B

Baldovin, John, 3n7, 10n22, 204n9, 228n98, 234–35n122, 245n169

Balthasar, Hans Urs von, 19n12, 20n15, 98n177, 110n4, 139, 187n95; on beauty 230–31

Basil the Great, St., 266–67

baptism, 143, 176
  *communio* and, 41, 106, 115, 124, 159
  the cross and, 220
  divine filiation and, 104–5, 106, 115, 143–144, 176
  exodus and, 62–64, 76
  unity and, 106, 159

Barron, Robert, 37n82, 134n82

Bathrellos, Demetrio, 98n177

Bauer, Olivier, 202n6, 212

Bernard of Clairvaux, St., 181

Beauduin, Lambert, 133–34

beauty,
  Aquinas on, 231–32
  Balthasar on, 230–33

Benedict XVI/Ratzinger on, 239
definition of, 231–32
evangelization and, 230–31n103
holiness and, 227–28
Jesus Christ and, 232–33
the liturgy and, 227–40
Bellarmine, St. Robert, 58n2, 132,
  133n78
Benedict XVI/Joseph Ratzinger,
  theology of,
  Augustine, 61n15, 120n32,
    128n62, 264
  Balthasar, 19n12, 187n95, 230–31
  biblical theology, 3n6
  Bonaventure, St., 8, 18n12,
    43n103, 165n7, 181n71
  Buber, Martin, 110, 112–114, 257
  Christocentrism, 2–9, 11, 15–18,
    37, 94–106, 128, 256–57
  christology and, 5–8, 11, 15–16n3,
    44–46, 94–106, 257–63
  culture, 31, 266–67
  de Lubac, Henri, 124–125
  ecclesiology, 3n6; 11–12, 114–118
  eschatology, 4–9, 11–12
  Eucharistic ecclesiology, 11–12,
    83, 106, 118–128, 255–57
  fragmentary character, xiv, 266n39
  Guardini, Romano, 18–19n12,
    31–32
  hope, 135–36, 155–58
  kingdom of God, 137, 140–41,
    143–44, 151–52, 156, 264
  liberation, 5–6n12, 51, 63, 252
  liberation theology and, 6n12, 55,
    63n26, 126–127n59, 140–44,
    150–52
  of liturgy, 2–4n7, 9
  logos-centrism in, 10–11, 32–42
  personalism, 112–14
  Pascher, Josef, 9, 89–90
  Peterson, Erik, 199–200
  Pieper, Josef, 19n12, 135, 153
  politics, 3n6
  primacy of logos, 4–6, 15–20
  sacramental (or liturgical)
    eschatology, 3–9, 10, 140

saints and, 263–67
Schmaus, Michael, 9, 89
Söhngen, Gottlieb, 9, 45n109, 89
symphonic approach in, xv, 32–42
Benedict XVI/Joseph Ratzinger,
  works of
  Behold the Pierced One, 12n23, 44,
    47, 95–99, 101, 109–10n3,
    123, 253, 260–61
  Caritas in Veritate, 155, 186,
    190–92
  Church, Ecumenism, and Politics,
    63, 110n104, 111n7, 118n27,
    121, 122, 127–28n61, 137, 192
  Called to Communion, 12n23,
    54n139, 76, 170n28
  "Communio: A Program," 115n14
  Deus Caritas Est, 61, 135–36n83,
    185–189, 254
  Dissertation on Augustine,
    120n32, 177n54, 177n57
  Dogma and Preaching, 15–16,
    20n14, 36n78, 84, 117n21,
    118n22, 137, 150–51n144
  "Ecclesislogy of Vatican II,
    119n28, 121–22
  Eschatology, 7, 8, 40–41, 42,
    140–43, 151–52, 159n171,
    180–81, 182, 185n83, 257
  Europe: Today and Tomorrow,
    46n112, 48n118
  Faith and the Future, 46n109
  Feast of Faith, 40, 210n30
  God is Near Us, 123
  Fundamental Speeches from Five
    Decades, 33–36, 128, 133n78,
    160
  Habilitationsschrift on
    Bonaventure, 8, 181n71
  "Handing on Faith and the
    Sources of the Faith," 110n4
  In the Beginning, 65, 67n45, 115,
    118, 251
  Introduction to Christianity, 2n5,
    17, 36n78, 43, 44, 46n109, 57,
    96, 101–4, 115n15 214n40,
    264

*Jesus of Nazareth* I, 1n2, 81,
96n119
*Jesus of Nazareth* II, 1n2, 54,
71n61, 74, 77, 81, 84, 92–3,
107n205, 167–69, 181, 254
*Jesus of Nazareth* III, 1n2
*Last Testament*, 45n109, 112–
13n10, 200n2
*Light of the World*, 41, 42, 48n116,
51n127, 100, 265
*Milestones*, 8, 31, 138n95,
151n144, 196n130, 240n150
"The New Evangelization," 263
*Pilgrim Fellowship of Faith*, 16n3,
118, 126n59, 129–31
*Principles of Catholic Theology*,
35nn73–74, 51–2, 84–6,
104–5, 110n4, 116–17, 118,
125–7, 143–44, 195–96n130
*Many Religions, One Covenant*,
68–79, 125
*The Meaning of Christian
Brotherhood*, 116, 117n21,
120n32
*On the Way to Jesus Christ*,
196n130, 266–67
*The Nature and Mission of
Theology*, 35, 215n40, 253
*New Song for the Lord, A*, 7, 63,
64n28, 97, 139, 252, 259n21
*The Ratzinger Report*, 125, 227,
229, 265
"The Regensburg Address," 47–51,
185–187
*Sacramentum Caritatis*, 60, 170,
193–197, 212n37, 216n47,
227, 233n114, 234–35, 241,
247–48
*Saint Paul*, 173–75
*Spe Salvi*, 41, 155–57, 159n181,
195n130
*Theology of Liturgy* (JRCW11):
"Answer to the Open Letter
of Olivier Bauer," 212
"The Artistic Transposition
of the Faith: Theological
Problems of Church
Music," 45n168,
245"Change and
Permanence in Liturgy:
Questions to Joseph
Ratzinger," 216n47, 218
"Eucharist—Communio—
Solidarity," 159n179,
160
"The Eucharist: Heart of the
Church," 75, 85n123,
105–6,
"Eucharist and Mission," 72,
86n124, 101–2, 179,
180, 182
"Is the Eucharist a Sacrifice?,"
71, 73, 75, 80
"Form and Content of
the Eucharistic
Celebration," 90–91, 93
"Fortieth Anniversary of the
Constitution on the
Sacred Liturgy," 86,
211n31, 216n47
"The Image of the World and
of Man in the Liturgy
and Its Expression in
Church Music," 242–44
"On the Meaning of Sunday
for Christian Prayer and
Christian Life," 66
"The Organic Development
of the Liturgy," 234
"'In the Presence of the
Angels I will Sing Your
Praise': The Regensburg
Tradition and the
Reform of the Liturgy,"
67, 199–200n2
"On the Question of
Orientation of the
Celebration," 199,
204–5, 210n30
"The Sacramental Foundation
of Christian Existence,"
38–39, 215–16
"The Spirit of the Liturgy," 8,
16, 18, 39, 52–53, 54, 61,

64, 65, 66–67, 77–78,
80, 82–85, 99n180,
105, 163, 172n36,
178–79, 201, 206–10,
212, 216n47, 218–26,
227n96, 234, 236–41,
243, 247
"On the Structure of the
Liturgical Celebration,"
16, 216n47, 218
"On the Theological Basis of
Church Music," 216n47,
233, 241n153, 246
"The Theology of the
Liturgy," 2, 18, 60, 62,
64, 71n60, 79, 93–94,
130, 179, 217
"Worship in the Parish
Communities Fifteen
Years after the Council,"
216n47, 225
*Truth and Tolerance*, 46, 50n124,
63
*The Unity of the Nations*, 158–59,
172
*Values is a Time of Upheaval*,
46n112, 266n39
*Verbum Domini* 18n11, 49n120,
50n124, 224n83, 246n172
"Vicarious Representation," 73, 79
Berger, David, 232n110, 242–43n159
Berro, Alberto, 19n12
Biliniewicz, Mariusz, 4n7, 4n8, 40n94,
229n98
Blanco Sarto, Pablo, 16n3, 19n12, 37,
164n4, 227n95
Bloch, Ernst, 138n95, 154–55
Boersma, Hans, 37–38
Boff, Clodovis, 141n103
Boff, Leonardo, 117n20, 126–27n59
Bonaventure, St., 8, 18n12, 33, 43n103,
44n104, 165n7, 181n71
Borghesi, Massimo, 141n103
Boersma, Hans, 37, 38nn83–84
Botta, Mario, 235n127
Botte, Bernard, 202n6
Bouyer, Louis, 10n22, 61n17,

204–205n10, 208–9
Brüske, Gunda, 3n7, 64n29
Buber, Martin, 110–11, 112–14
Buffer, Thomas, 131n69
Bultmann, Rudolf, 168
Bunge, Gabriel, 221–22
Burrell, David, 37n82
Butler, Sara, 45n107
Bux, Nicola, 3–4n7, 228n98
Byrne, Brendan, 173–74

## C

Caldwell, Philip, 261n27
Campodonico, Angelo, 231n105
Cardó, Daniel, 210n29
*caritas* (charity). *See* love
Casel, Odo, 35
*Catechism of the Catholic Church*, 33n68,
55n140, 58n3, 122n41, 134n81,
140, 166n10, 166n11, 171n33, 262
*Centesimus Annus* (John Paul II),
191n109
Chalcedon, Council of, 15–16n3,
96–101, 152–53n148, 257–60
Christ. *See* Jesus Christ
christocentric/christocentrism, 5–6,
35n74, 129, 131
christology
of Benedict XVI/Ratzinger, 5–9,
11, 15–16n3, 44–46, 94–106
257–63
chalcedonian, 16n3, 44–45n107,
97–101, 152–153n148,
257–60
Cyrillian, 259–260
eschatology and, 5–8
liturgy and, 5–8, 33–34
spiritual Christology, 10,
44–45n107, 95–97
Chupungco, Anscar, 202n6
church
as anticipation of the eschaton, 170
as *communio*, 12n23, 118–19, 133,
165, 167, 169, 170
the Eucharist and, 118–24, 163,
170–71, 253–54

instrument of *communio*, 167

mission of, 118, 166, 169–71

as body of Christ, 117, 123–24, 131–34, 177, 184–85

as the kingdom of God, 132, 136, 181

as people of God, 125–28

as sacrament, 118, 125–27

representative sacrifice (*Stellvertretung*) and, 166, 175, 253–54

Trinity and, 165–66

*Christifidelis Laici* (John Paul II), 169n26

Chrysologus, St. Peter, 86

Chrysostom, St. John, 164n4, 188

Ciraulo, Jonathan Martin, 182n76

Collins, Christopher, 36n79, 112n9, 113n11, 114n12, 256

*Communio* (journal), 115n14

*communio* (communion)
Ecclesiology and, 111–12, 117–28, 165–70

Eucharist and, 118–24, 170–71

horizontal and vertical, 12, 38n83, 54, 94, 100, 120, 135, 157, 160, 170, 194, 253

mission and, 169–71, 194–95

theological anthropology and, 115–17

Trinitarian, 123

communion of saints, 13, 83, 106, 117, 128, 135, 177, 207–8, 236

Congar, Yves, 80n99, 85, 237n133

Conrad, Leo Sven, 9n20

Constantinople III, Council of, 96–101, 257–260

Corbon, Jean, 219

Corkery, Seán, 3n6

Corkery, James, 4–5, 6n12, 45n109, 154n156, 165

*Corpus Mysticum* (Henri de Lubac), 124

Corbon, Jean, 219

Corriveau, Raymond, 174n44, 176n51

Cosmic, 199–200

covenant, old, 68–71
creation and, 65

the exodus and, 62–63

Jerusalem and, 207

limitation of, 175

Moltmann on, 144–45

on Mount Sinai, 63, 68–70, 121

sacrifice and, 179

Temple and, 205

covenant, new, 72–73
ecclesiology and, 128, 160–61

Eucharist and, 68, 76–77, 121, Jesus and, 64, 125

creation, 16, 26, 37, 65, 115

Cross. *See* Jesus Christ.

culture
beauty and, 227–228

Eucharist and, 227

faith and, 25

formation of, 26–27

German nuances of, 25n35

*logos* and, 46, 191, 266–267

modern, 21–23, 24–26, 38, 50, 52, 156, 193, 226, 234

pre-modern, 22

worship (*cultus*) and, 29, 202n6

Cyril of Alexandria, St., 164n4, 258–60

**D**

Damascene, St. John, 9–10n22

Daley, Brian, 17n8

Daly, Robert, 58n2, 177n60

Daniel, Book of, 174

*De Civitate Dei* (Augustine), 64n31, 79n93, 176–77

Dehellenization, 49–51, 144–46, 187

de Gaál, Emery, 5–6, 18n12, 32n64, 45n109, 112–13n10, 114n12, 152–53, 200n2

de Lubac, Henri, 110–11, 119, 124–25, 142n104, 156, 186n88, 195–96n130

de Margerie, Bertrand, 45n107

Denzinger, Heinrich, 29n52, 58n3

*Dei Verbum* (Vatican II), 129–30, 135, 166–67

*Didache*, 2

Diederich, Everett, 204–205n10

Diekmann, Godfrey, 134n82
divine filiation, 96, 104–5, 115–16,
    134n82, 143–44
Divinization, 13, 61, 64, 76, 134n82,
Dobszay, László, 228n98, 242n154,
    244n166,
Dodd, C.H., 41n99
Donini, Alberto, 246n172
Dostoyevsky, Fyodor, 229
Doyle, Dennis, 117n20,
Driscoll, Jeremy, 176n52
Duffy, Eamon, 3n7
Dulles, Avery, 111, 117n20, 125n53,
    125n55, 127n59, 127–28n61,
    133n78
Dupré, Louis, 37n82

E

Ebner, Ferdinand, 113n10
Ecclesia de Eucharistia (John Paul II),
    49, 197
Ecclesiology
    Benedict XVI/Ratzinger on, 3n6,
        11–12, 83, 106, 114–28,
        212n37; 255–57
    Christology and, 109n3
    Eucharistic, 11–12, 83, 106,
        118–28, 212n37; 255–57
    eschatology and,
    liturgy and, 129–35
    new covenant and, 128, 160–61
Eco, Umberto, 231n106
Emery, Gilles, 124n50
End of the Modern World (Romano
    Guardini), 22–26
Ephesus, Council of, 260
eschatologists, 139–40. See also Pozo
eschatology.
    Christology and, 99–100
    eschaton, 42, 203, 219, 216, 222,
        235–36
    ethics and, 143, 182
    heaven, 41, 67, 82, 207, 243
    immanentization of, 143, 155,
    liturgy and, 1–9, 86, 171, 183–84,
        206, 216, 219–23, 227n96

235–36
    new heaven and new earth, 83,
        171, 182n75
    politics and, 143, 155–56
    remembrance and, 75, 148–50
    resurrection of the body/dead, 51,
        52, 84, 85–86, 105, 123–24,
        219–20.
    See also baptism; communion of
        saints; Jesus Christ; liturgy
eschaton. See eschatology
ethics, 57, 66, 80–81, 82, 138–39, 143.
    Also see ethos; love; and theological
        anthropology
ethos,
    as gratuitousness, 191–92
    primacy of, 16, 137, 148
    of love/charity, 4, 27, 53–55, 68,
        163–65, 184, 253–54,
    of power, 24
    as utility/use, 20–21, 28
Eucharist, celebration of the. See liturgy,
    celebration of.
Eucharist as meal, 60, 209
Eucharist as sacrament
    breaking of the bread and, 122–23
    charity and, 163, 183–96
    of communion, 121–22
    medieval theology of, 124
    Paschal Mystery and, 39, 183
    Trinity and, 193–95
    unity and, 159, 193
Eucharist as sacrifice
    Council of Trent on, 58
    the Cross and, 58–59, 175, 195,
    as the Grundgestalt ("basic
        form"), 57, 87–94, 107–8
    the Last Supper and, 68, 70,
        77–78, 87, 107–8
Evangelii Gaudium (Francis), 246n174
Evangelization, 246
Evdokimov, Paul, 238n139
Exodus, Book of, 57, 62–63, 76, 80, 121
exodus,
    definition of, 62–63
    Eucharist and, 64, 68, 211
    new, 41, 62–64, 68–70, 77–77, 82,

84–85, 92n154
participation in, 71, 85–86, 95, 97,
    103–6, 139, 179, 211, 252
of Jesus Christ, 81–83, 92n154,
    207, 252.
*See also* freedom
Ezekiel, Book of, 11, 39, 57, 65–67,
    68–70, 80, 220

**F**

fall, the, 65, 117–18, 158
Fagerberg, David, 76, 214n39, 217,
    219n60, 261n27
Faggiolio, Massimo, 129–30n66, 131,
    228n98
faith
    beauty and, 230, 232
    culture and, 24–25
    individualistic, 156
    *logos* and, 52, 212
    personal nature of, 36, 186
    reason and, xiii, 23, 45–52
    social, 110–11n4, 115–17,
        196n130, 257
    trinitarian *communio* and, 116
    witness of, 194
    without reason, 23, 47–52, 185
    worship and, 188
*Faith in History and Society* (Johann
    Baptist Metz), 147–50
Farnés, Pere, 3n7, 202n6, 237n133
Feingold, Lawrence, 58n2
Feuillet, André, 71n61
filial adoption. *See* divine filiation.
Fiorenza, Elizabeth Schüssler, 141n103
Fitzmyer, Joseph, 175–176
freedom, 252
    of divinization, 97
    grace and, 143
    of Jesus Christ, 98
    from sin, 65
    exodus and, 65–66
    true, 66–68.
    *See also* exodus
Franco, Philip, 135n83
Francis, Pope, 43n101, 110–111n4,

141n103, 143n108, 246n174
Franklin, R. W., 133n79
Freyer, Hans, 154n156
Fuksas, Massimiliano, 235n127

**G**

Gallagher, Daniel, 231n105
Gamber, Klaus, 203–204n9, 208n23,
    228n98
*Gaudium et Spes* (Vatican II), 135
Gerhards, Albert, 202–203n6
Gese, Harmut, 72
grace, 41, 73, 140, 143, 181
Gray, Timothy, 69n55
Gregory, Brad, 37n82
Gregory the Great, St., 44, 207–8
Gregur, Josip, 3n7, 20n13
Gribbin, Anselm, 3n7
Guardini, Romano, 15, 21–37
    adoration, 34, 248
    Balthasar and, 19n12
    Benedict XVI/Ratzinger and, 9
    Christocentrism in, 36–37,
        186n87
    culture, 25, 26–27, 29
    Eucharist as meal, 89
    history, 22–23
    John Paul II/Wojtyla and, 19n12
    liturgy, 22–30, 33–35
    liturgical act, 215–16
    liturgical movement and, 21–22, 35
    Martin Buber and, 113n10
    medieval culture, 22–24
    modernity, 22–24, 27–28
    nature, 24
    primacy of *logos* in, 18, 22, 31–32,
        34–35
    Pieper and, 19n12
    Power, 24, 25, 30–31
    symbolic nature of the liturgy,
        33–35, 213, 248–49
    *technē*, 18, 24, 27
Guerriero, Elio, 18–19n12, 45n109,
    113n10
Gutiérrez, Gustavo, 6n12, 12n23,
    141n103, 142n104

Gy, Pierre-Marie, 202n6, 210n30

# H

Hamer, Jean Jérôme, 12n23
Hahn, Scott, 3n6
Hanby, Michael, 20–21n15, 215n40
Hastetter, Michaela Christine, 20n13,
    32n64, 241n150
Hauke, Manfred, 4n7, 87n130, 88–89,
    228n98
Heibl, Franz-Xavier, 17n7, 19n12
Heid, Stefan, 10n22, 204n9, 208n21
Heim, Maximillian Heinrich, 3n6,
    16n3, 117n20, 126n56
Hebrews, Letter to the, 58, 71, 81–83
Herwegen, Ildefons, 22
Hildebrand, Dietrich von, 113n10
Hill, Craig, 175n49
Hillary, St., 164n4
Hitchcock, James, 228n98
Hofmann, Peter, 8n17
Hompel, Max Ten, 61n15
Hope
    Benedict XVI/Ratzinger on,
        135–36, 155–58
    Eucharist and, 180,
    imminent, 136–38, 143
    political praxis and, 136
    sacraments and, 143–144, 158–59
    as theological virtue, 138n94, 140,
        153–54
    theologies of, 135–50
Hoping, Helmut, 3n7, 29n52, 45n108,
    58n2, 61n15, 120n29, 261n27
Horn, Stephan Otto, 17n7
Howsare, Rodney, 186n88
Hugh of St. Victor, 44
hypostatic union, 13, 97, 101, 139, 257–
    61. See also Chalcedon, Council of;
    Ephesus, Council of; Incarnation;
    and Jesus Christ

# I

Ignatius of Antioch, St., 121–22, 194
Incarnation, 23, 40, 64, 102–3, 158,

238. See also divine filiation;
    hypostatic union; and Jesus Christ
incarnationists, 139–140. See also Pozo
iconoclasm, 238–239
icons. See liturgy, celebration of
individualism, 157, 191, 192. See also
    autonomy
Israel
    the Exodus and,
    the sabbath and, 65–66
    the Law and, 66, 73
    worship of the golden calf, 16, 39,
        52, 67
Isaiah, Book of, 18n11, 73, 74n71, 80,
    80n99, 266n41

# J

Jaubert, Annie, 92n154
Jenson, Robin, 203n9
Jeremiah, Book of, 72, 80n99
Jesus Christ
    beauty and, 232–33
    Cross, the, 77, 81–83, 233
    day of Atonement and, 71–72, 168
    face of, 229 240
    as God, 15
    Guardini and, 15
    as the last/new Adam, 104, 158,
        159
    last supper and, 72–73, 76–78,
        91–93, 94
    the kingdom of God and, 40, 42,
        92n154, 263, 264
    natures (human and divine) of,
        259–60
    new covenant and, 64, 68, 72–73,
        76–77, 121, 125, 128
    new Passover and, 68, 81–82,
        91–92
    as the new Moses, 70–71
    as the new Temple, 76–77, 81–82,
        84–85,
    as personification of the *Oriens*
        (the East), 206, 209, 211, 236
    as the Paschal Lamb, 80–81, 92
    as priest, 40, 71–72, 167–169, 217

as priest, prophet, and king, 72
pro-existence and, 94–95
redemption, 39, 80, 143–44, 157,
    167, 211n31, 217, 252, 263
Resurrection of, 51–2, 59, 76–7,
    81–82, 85–86, 240, 262n30,
    266,
Sacred Heart of, 44–45n107, 47,
    96
sacred music and, 242–47
suffering servant, 73–74, 75
Temple, 81–81,
Transfiguration of, 63, 81, 95
vicarious representation
    (*Stellvertretung*), 72–75, 169,
    178
washing of the feet and, 167–168
wills (human and divine) of, 257,
    260–61.
*See also* Christology; Hypostatic
    Union; Incarnation; and
    *Logos*
Jewett, Robert, 173
John, The First Letter of, 76, 169,
    187n92, 188–89, 267
John, The Gospel, 49n120, 68–69, 71,
    82, 85, 101, 156, 167–68, 169, 190
John Paul II, Pope, 59–60, 94, 167, 169,
    182n75, 191n109, 197; as Karol
    Wojtyla, 19n12
Jungmann, Josef, 89, 90–91, 202n6
Justin Martyr, 220

**K**

Kant, Immanuel, 50, 113n10, 189
Käsemann, Ernst, 147
Kasper, Walter, 5n10, 12n23
Kilmartin, Edward, 58n2, 64n31
kingdom of God, the, 41, 139–140, 156
    Benedict XVI/Ratzinger on, 137,
        140–41, 143–44, 151–52,
        156, 264
    the Church as, 132, 136, 181
    contrasting views on, 139–40
    eschaton and, 42, 219, 222
    Eucharist and, 42, 164–65

hope and, 140, 156
imminent fulfilment of, 136,
    140–43
Neusner on, 67n44
Jesus and, 40, 42, 92n154, 263,
    264
Moltmann on, 136, 146
Metz on, 137
N.T. Wright on, 92n154
political theology and, 63n26, 135,
    142–43, 151
proclamation of, 263
the world as, 27, 39, 100, 192
Klauser, Theodor, 203n9
Koch, Kurt, 8n17, 43n101
Krieg, Robert, 21n18, 22n19, 22n20,
    113n10
Kunzler, Michael, 3n7, 210–211n30

**L**

La Soujeole, Benoît-Dominique, 125n51
Lam, Cong Quy Joseph, 61n15, 193n119
Lamb, Matthew, 17n8, 52, 55n141
Lang, Uwe Michael, 10n22, 177, 202n6,
    208n20, 225n88, 235n125,
    235–236n127, 242n154, 245n171
Läpple, Alfred, 114n11
*Letters from Lake Como* (Romano
    Guardini), 26–27
Levering, Matthew, 53, 58n2, 59n6,
    78n90, 163n2
Lewis, C.S., 24
liturgy
    body of Christ and, 217
    definition of, 39, 76, 217
    eschatological nature of,
    Jesus Christ as priest and, 217
    as *logikē latreia*, 171–183
    mystagogical catechesis and,
        216n44
    as *opus dei/actio dei*, 1, 29, 40n94,
        67
    paschal mystery and, the, 39, 75,
        78, 130
    symbolism and, 33–34, 201, 210,
        213–14, 219–23, 236–37

theology of, 261
Trinity and, 33, 53n133, 76, 217
analogous to play, 30, 64
liturgy, celebration of,
    active participation (*participation actuosa*) in, 216–19
    *ad orientem* orientation of the celebrant, 201–13
    *ars celebrandi*, 235–49
    *askēsis* for the body in, 219, 226
    beauty and, 227–40
    chant and, Gregorian, 245–46
    cosmic symbolism and, 3–4, 203–5, 227
    cross on the altar ("Benedictine arrangement"), 210–12
    gestures during,
    icons and, 238–39
    placement of the altar, 207–9
    postures in, 220–23
    post conciliar reform of, 233
    reform of the reform of, 228, 233–34
    as preparation for the eschaton, 216, 219–23, 235–36
    responses during the, 223–24
    sacred architecture and, 235–38
    sacred art and, 238–40
    sacred music and, 240–46
    sign of the cross, the, 220
    silence in, 224–225
    symbolism of the altar, 206–207
    synagogue and, 236–37
    the reform of, 130–31, 134
    the Temple and, 235–37
    *versus populum* orientation of the celebrant, 207–10
liberation. *See* freedom
liberation theology (theology of liberation), 137, 141–43
    Benedict XVI, Ratzinger on, 142–43
    de Lubac and, 142n103
    different types of, 142–143n104
    the exodus narrative and, 63n26
    Marxism and, 142n104, 150–51n144

Müller on, 141n103, 142n104
political theology and, 140–141, 141n103, 151
Pope Francis and, 141n103
Rahner and, 141n103
*Libertatis Conscientia* (Congregation for the Doctrine of Faith), 5–6n12
*Libertatis Nuntius* (Congregation for the Doctrine of Faith), 5n12
*logikē latreia*, 17–19, 194–95, 197
    as definition of the liturgy, 17–18, 19–20n13, 49, 75, 171, 212, 252, 254
    love and, 54, 91, 123, 163, 171–179
    *See also logos*; love; and *ethos*
Logos/*logos*
    ancient Greek notion of, 178
    Church Fathers and, 17n8, 18n11
    culture and, 266–67
    definition of, 17n8, 17–18
    eucharistic/sacramental, 27, 31–32, 38, 163–65, 256–57
    as God, 15
    Guardini on, 18, 22
    makeability (*Machbarkeit*) and, 16, 40, 154
    materialistic/secular, 31, 38–39,154, 256
    participation in the, 167, 253
    primacy of, 2–6, 17n7, 22, 46–47
    in relationship to *ethos*, 20–21
    sacred artwork and, 240
    subordinate to *ethos*, 16, 22, 42, 136, 192
    as *communio*, 4, 20, 123–124, 189
    as the Person of Jesus Christ, 18, 36–37, 185–18
    as *technē*, 18, 20, 24, 27
    as truth and love, 43, 46
    Vatican II and, 135
    as word, 178–179
    Worship and, 178–79
Louth, Andrew, 98n177
love
    as *agape*, 186–87
    as *eros*, 186–87
    of God, 187–89

*logikē latreia* and, 54, 91, 123, 163, 171–179

as self-gift, 99n180, 104–6, 122–23, 134, 163–71, 190–94

truth and, 43–45, 189–190, 193

as charity/*caritas*, 54, 184, 186, 188–89

as *logos*, 44

of neighbor, 188–89

Luciani, Rafael, 141n103

Luke, The Gospel of, 68–69, 80, 81, 95, 101, 123

*Lumen Fidei* (Pope Francis), 43n101, 110–11n4

*Lumen Gentium* (Vatican II), 124–26, 129–30, 131–32, 135, 170

Luther, Martin, 60, 87, 90

last supper,

    covenant of Mt. Sinai and, 68–69, 72

    Eucharist (as sacrifice) and, 68, 70, 77–78, 87, 107–8

    Jesus Christ and, 72–73, 76–78, 91–93, 94

    new covenant and, 68, 72–23, 76–77, 121, 125, 128

    new exodus and, 41, 68, 87

    new worship and, 54, 74, 81

    Passover and, 71–72, 81, 88, 91–93

    Suffering Servant and, 73–74

liturgical movement, 21, 22, 133–34

liturgical movement, new, 31


**M**

MacIntyre, 47n115

Madrigal, Santiago, 3n6

Mahrt, William Peter, 242n154, 245

Malevez, Léopold, 139n97, 142–43n104

Marcel, Gabriel, 53, 138n95

Mark, The Gospel of, 68–69, 81–82, 260

Marschler, Thomas, 4n7, 5n11

Massa, James, 3n6

Marx, Karl, 154, 192, 218

Marxism, 126n59, 138n95, 141n144, 150–51n144, 152n156, 192

materialism, 27, 156, 191, 192, 214

Matthew, The Gospel of, 68–69, 80, 81, 206, 220

Maximus the Confessor, 97n176, 98–99, 99n180, 260–61

McGovern, Arthur, 63n26, 126–27n59

McGregor, Peter, 6n12, 44n107, 95, 97n176, 251n1

McGuckian, Michael, 58n2

McNamara, Denis, 236n128

McPartlan, Paul, 134n81

medievalism, 22–23, 25, 49

*Mediator Dei* (Pius XII), 58–59

Meiers, Anna Elisabeth, 95n164, 96n172, 97n173

Meisner, Joachim, 32

Melina, Livio, 164–65

Menke, Karl-Heinz, 6n12, 12n23, 120n31, 187n95

Messori, Vittorio, 227, 228–229

Metz, Johann Baptist, 12n23, 136–43, 147–50

Micah, Book of, 80n99

Milbank, John, 37n82, 151n144

Millare, Roland, 21n17, 32n63, 87n129, 227n92

modernity, 22, 24, 28, 38–39

Möhler, Johann Adam, 132–33

Moltmann, Jurgen, 136–43, 144–46

monophysitism, 99–100, 139

monotheletism, 260–61

Müller, Gerhard, xiii-xvi, 141n103, 142n104, 263–64n32

Murphy, Francesca Aran, 231n105

Murphy, Joseph, 3n7

music. *See* liturgy, celebration of

Mussner, Franz, 237n133

*Mysterium Fidei* (Paul VI), 59


**N**

Nachtwei, 114n11

Negel, Joachim, 61n15

Nestorianism, 99–100, 139

Neumann, Veit, 6n12

Neusner, Jacob, 67n44,

Nichols, Aidan, 7–8, 47n115, 118–19n27, 119n28, 228n98, 238n139

Nicea, Council of, 222
nominalism, 30–31, 38n83, 49
Nussbaum, Otto, 203n9
Nygren, Anders, 186n88

## O

O'Callaghan, Paul, 138n95,
O'Meara, Thomas, 25n35, 133n79
O'Neill, Colman, 176n51
Oakes, Edward, 45n107, 98n177
Olver, Matthew S.C., 224n88
ontology,
    analogy of being, 38n83
    of the Church, 170
    history and, 32n64, 55, 97n174,
        101, 137, 147n128, 150, 152
    incarnation and, 101–2
    materialist, 51–52, 215, 256
    of the person, 83, 144
    sacramental, 51, 38n83, 152, 215,
        263
    univocity of being, 38n83
Origen, 47, 223
Orth, Stefan, 87

## P

Parousia, 7, 9, 139
    *Adventus medius*, 181
    Eucharist and, 7, 9, 180–81, 185,
        204–5, 255
    Metz on the, 150.
    *See also* eschatology
Paschal mystery
    Liturgy and, 217
    participation in, 53, 172, 181–82,
        207, 222, 253, 263
Pascher, Josef, 9, 89, 90
Passover, 80
    Last Supper and, 71–72, 81, 88,
        91–93
Paul, St., 2, 123
    Colossians, Letter to the, 80, 173,
        176, 232
    Corinthians, First Letter to the,
        53, 75, 76, 92, 197

Corinthians, Second Letter to the,
    173n38
Ephesians, Letter to the, 173n38,
    176
Galatians, Letter to the, 264
Philemon, Letter to, 173n38
Philippians, Letter to the, 173,
    173n38, 221
Romans, Letter to the, 18n11, 72,
    172–176 173n38, 188
Timothy, First Letter to, 169,
    173n38
Titus, Letter to, 176
Paul VI, St., 59
Pell, George, 227n95
Perrin, Nicholas, 85, 107n205
person. *See* theological anthropology.
Personalism
    I-Thou ("we") relationship, 41, 43,
        52, 83–84, 105–6, 110–11,
        112–18, 128, 252, 256–57
Peterson, Erik, 173n42, 199–200, 205
Pickstock, Catherine, 37n82
Pieper, Josef, 34n71, 49n121, 138,
    138n95, 153–154, 186n88
Pitre, Brant, 41, 68n51, 69n54, 70,
    92n154
Pius X, St., 133
Pius XII, Pope, 44, 58, 126
Plato, 220
Pneumatology, 115n15
political theology, 136–37, 140–43,
    147–50, 151–52, 200n2
power, 25, 30–31. *See also* progress;
    science; *technē*; and technology
Pozo, Candido, 139, 144–45
Prassl, Franz Karl, 241n150
praxis. *See ethos.*
progress, 26, 155–56. *See also* power;
    science; *technē*; and technology
Prieto, Antonio, 186n88
Proniewski, Andrzej, 113n10, 114n12
Prosper of Aquitaine, 29
Psalms, Book of, 80–81, 174, 205–6
Pseudo-Dionysius the Areopagite, 1,
    43n103, 187n90, 231–32

# R

Rahner, Karl, 99n181, 142–143n104,
    151n144, 241–42
Ramage, Matthew, 181n71
Ratzinger, Georg, 240n150
Rausch, Thomas, 107n204, 200n3
Reali, Nicola, 188n98
Reid, Alcuin, 3n7
reason, 46, 185, 192n115
    faith and, xiii, 23, 45–55,
    Kant and, 50, 189
    as *logos*, 2n5, 4, 17, 112, 187,
        243–44
    love and, 36n78, 43–44, 168, 254
    Marxism and, 192
    without faith, 23, 47, 185
Redemption. *See* Jesus Christ
*Redemptoris Missio* (John Paul II),
    166n9, 166n13, 167n15
Rehak, Marin, 48n116
Revelation, The Book of, 197, 221, 264
Richard of St. Victor, 44
Riches, Aaron, 98n177, 100, 258,
    259n20
Riordan, William, 43n103
Roman Canon, 75, 106, 173, 252
Romans, Letter to the. *See* St. Paul
Rouselot, Pierre, 44n104
Rowland, Tracey, 18n12, 20n15, 25n35,
    32n64, 111n5, 112n10, 114n12,
    119n27, 141n103, 227, 241n153
Royal, Robert, 113n10
Ruddy, Christopher, 79n94, 95n165
Rutsche, Markus, 113n10


# S

sacraments, 143–144, 158–159
sacrifice
    augustinian notion of, 80–81,
        176–78
    of Abraham, 78
    Christian living and, 173
    cultic, 74, 178–78
    divinization and, 64
    as gift, 59–60, 74–75, 82–83
    inadequate, 80, 174

    as love, 61, 103, 211n33, 254
    Passover and, 78
    prayer and, 179
    representative, 72–75, 78–79, 175
    the Temple and, 78–82, 236–37
    worship and, 179–80
*Sacrosanctum Concilium* (Vatican
    II), 129–30, 131–32, 135, 217,
    238n137
Sarah, Robert, 224n82
saints, 227, 263–67
salvation. *See* Jesus Christ
salvation history, 65–68
Samra, James, 176n51
Schall, James, 37n82
Scannone, Juan, 141n103
Schindler, David, 20–21, 33n67, 38
Schindler, D.C., 186n88
Schmaus, Michael, 9, 89
Schmemann, Alexander, 33n67, 119n29,
    214, 261n27
Schmitt, Carl, 200n2
Schmitz, Kenneth, 112n9
Schneider, Michael, 15–16n3, 19n12
Scola, Angelo, 187n89
Schönborn, Christoph, 98, 238n139
Schumacher, Bernard, 138n94
Schürmann, Heinz, 91, 94n163
Schwarz, Hans, 138n95,
science, 26–27, 155, 156–57. *See also*
    power; progress; *technē*; and
    technology
Scotus, Blessed Duns, 37–38, 49
secularism, 156
Segundo, Luis, 6n12, 143
Seewald, Peter, 41
Söhngen, Gottlieb, 9, 89
Sokolowski, Robert, 61n17
solidarity, 150, 189
suffering
    of Christ, 74, 75, 82, 159, 178,
        210n30, 211n31
    of Israel, 178
    human, 147–50
    Metz on, 137, 147, 148n134,
        149–50
    Moltmann on, 137

Spezzano, Daria, 184
*The Spirit of the Liturgy* (Romano Guardini), 28–31
St. Peter's Basilica, 207–9
Steinbüchel, Theodor, 113n10
Stuhlmacher, Peter, 73–74
suffering, 5, 137, 147–50, 178

T

*technē*, 18–20, 24, 27, 249, 256. *See also* power; progress; science; and technology
technology, 156–57. *See also* power; progress; science; and *technē*
Temple, 204, 235–38
Temple, new, 62
Teresa of Calcutta, St., 189
theological anthropology
    autonomy and the person, 20, 23–24, 28, 50, 52, 61, 67, 83, 105, 114–16, 156–57, 165, 192–93, 214
    culture and the person, 24–29
    eucharistic mysticism/personalism, 101–2, 106, 123, 160, 213n37, 255–57
    human development and, 190–91
    participation in the pro-existence of Christ, 103, 123, 171, 252
    person and the heart, 47
    person and nature, 26
    person and work, 27
    person as gift, 172, 190–92, 211–12
    person as *homo adorans*, 12, 213–16, 226
    person as *homo faber*, 214–15, 226
*Theology of Hope* (Jurgen Moltmann), 144–46
theōsis. *See* divinization.
Tillard, J.M.R., 111n6, 117n20, 185
Trent, Council of: *Decree on the Sacrifice of the Mass*, 58–59
Trinity (or Trinitarian), 76, 98, 101, 115, 165–66, 193–95

Truth,
    beauty and, 229, 230,
    being (*ens*) as, 23, 34, 214n40, 248,
    freedom and, 34–36
    goodness and, 20n14
    as Jesus Christ, 36
    loss of, 20n14
    love (charity) and, 43–45, 189–190
    reason and, 44–45
    subordinated to *ethos*, 16n3, 21, 251
    what is made (*factum*) as, 192, 214n40
    worship in spirit and, 73, 82, 84, 226
Twomey, Vincent, 46, 119n27, 158n172, 164n4, 240–41n150

U

Ulrich, Ferdinand, 231n105

V

Vatican II, 1–2, 31, 59, 129–30, 135, 235, 238
Verweyen, Hansjürgen, 8n17, 114n11
violence, 148
    contrary to reason, 48–49, 185–86
Voderholzer, Rudolf, 3n7, 124
Voegelin, Eric, 155
voluntarism, 30, 49–50
von Harnack, Adolf, 49–50
Vorgrimler, Herbert, 242–43

W

Wainwright, Geoffrey, 9–10n22, 199n1
Waldstein, Michael Maria, 17n8
Walker, Adrian, 231n105
Weigel, George, 19n12
Weiler, Thomas, 3n6
Weimann, Ralph, 45–46n109, 154n156
Weimer, Ludwig, 7n15, 181n71
Weinandy, Thomas, 184n82, 205–6n13, 259n20
White, Thomas Joseph, 68n52, 99–100n181

Wiedenhofer, Siegfried, 6n12, 200n2
William of Ockham, 37n82, 49n121
Wilkinson, John, 208n22
Witt, Thomas, 58n2
Worship, new, 54, 62, 193
Wright, N.T., 71n61, 80n100, 92n154
Wright, Tamra, 113n11


# Y

Yannaras, Christos, 17n8


# Z

Zechariah, Book of, 69n55, 70, 80n99,
    206
Zizioulas, John, 119–120n29